T0327542

IT Auditing and Application Controls for Small and Mid-Sized Enterprises

Founded in 1807, John Wiley & Sons is the oldest independent publishing company in the United States. With offices in North America, Europe, Asia, and Australia, Wiley is globally committed to developing and marketing print and electronic products and services for our customers' professional and personal knowledge and understanding.

The Wiley Corporate F&A series provides information, tools, and insights to corporate professionals responsible for issues affecting the profitability of their company, from accounting and finance to internal controls and performance management.

IT Auditing and Application Controls for Small and Mid-Sized Enterprises

Revenue, Expenditure, Inventory, Payroll, and More

JASON WOOD

WILLIAM BROWN

HARRY HOWE

WILEY

Cover Image: © iStockphoto/Andrey Prokhorov
Cover Design: Wiley

Published by John Wiley & Sons, Inc., Hoboken, New Jersey.
Published simultaneously in Canada.

For general information on our other products and services or for technical support, please contact our Customer Care Department within the United States at (800) 762-2974, outside the United States at (317) 572-3993 or fax (317) 572-4002.

Wiley publishes in a variety of print and electronic formats and by print-on-demand. Some material included with standard print versions of this book may not be included in e-books or in print-on-demand. If this book refers to media such as a CD or DVD that is not included in the version you purchased, you may download this material at http://booksupport.wiley.com. For more information about Wiley products, visit www.wiley.com.

Library of Congress Cataloging-in-Publication Data:

Wood, Jason, 1976–
    Information technology auditing and application controls for small and mid-sized businesses : revenue, expenditure, inventory, payroll, and more / Jason Wood, William C. Brown, Harry Howe.
        pages cm. — (Wiley corporate F&A series)
    Includes bibliographical references and index.
    ISBN 978-1-118-07261-5 (cloth) — ISBN 978-1-118-22245-4 (ePDF) —
ISBN 978-1-118-23319-1 (ePub) — ISBN 978-1-118-80102-4 (oBook) 1. Information technology—Auditing. 2. Small business—Information technology. I. Brown, William C. (Business writer) II. Howe, Harry, 1952– III. Title.
    HD30.2.W66 2013
    658.150285—dc23
                                                            2013025396

10 9 8 7 6 5 4 3 2 1

A warm and loving thank you to our respective families, who gave us the time to undergo this effort.

Thank you to my wife, Heather, and children, Stephen, Kaitlyn, and Andrew, for giving me encouragement and support. —Jason Wood

I thank my wife, Bonnie, for being patient and supportive and always wearing a smile. —William Brown

Thank you to my wife, Lauren, and sons, Benjamin and Noah. —Harry Howe

Contents

Preface

RISK IS INEVITABLE. AS AUDITORS, we help our clients manage their risk by performing audits and other assessments. Our work helps the client understand the nature and extent of risks that exist in the control environment. Information technology (IT) controls are a key aspect of that control environment—albeit one that may be less familiar to the auditor than the purely accounting and financial dimensions. The purpose of this book is to illustrate and explain many of the basic IT controls common to the types of reporting systems used by small and mid-sized enterprises (SMEs), and to help financial auditors to provide better services to their clients in the context of application controls.

Historically, IT auditing has not been given the attention it deserves in regard to the financial audit. With an increase in governmental regulations and corporate boards realizing the importance of IT, IT auditing has risen to a level where every company, private or public or nonprofit, regardless of size, needs to understand the risks and controls around their financial applications.

This book is useful for various audiences, including students, academics, practitioners, auditors, and management. It discusses the purpose of information technology auditing, and how it relates to the financial audit. Using QuickBooks (QB) and Microsoft Great Plains Dynamics (also referred to as Microsoft Dynamics GP, GPD, or Great Plains) as illustrative examples of financial applications within SMEs, the book walks through various financial statement cycles to help the reader better understand cycle risks, controls, and illustrative application-level controls. This book is not meant to be exhaustive on the subject matter, but gives executive-level insights into IT auditing and application-level controls for SMEs.

We hope to provide some meaningful insights on the importance of understanding IT risks and controls and how they relate to financial applications.

Acknowledgments

THE AUTHORS ACKNOWLEDGE AND APPRECIATE the many lively conversations and classroom contributions of graduate students at State University of New York–Geneseo and State University of New York–Buffalo, and the assistance of Geneseo accounting majors Alexander G. Rienzie and Stephen Csapo.

Why Is IT Auditing Important to the Financial Auditor and the Financial Statement Audit?

MANY FINANCIAL AUDITORS BELIEVE THAT complex IT environments require a technically trained professional to fully comprehend the technologies employed in the environment. Other financial auditors may decide to rescope the audit (if a non-Sarbanes-Oxley [SOx] engagement) in order to avoid looking at internal controls, or at least the IT controls, while yet others may perform a superficial, high-level review of the IT controls and hope no one notices that it was not very detailed.

Anything that a client provides that is not manually created relies on IT for the accounting process, and you must understand how to test the IT systems and whether to rely on it. By appropriately assessing the IT controls, you may be able to reduce the overall effort of the audit, and bring new observations to your client about the IT environment.

An effective assessment of IT controls may actually increase the amount of time required to perform an audit. However, consistent with Auditing Standards (SASs) Nos. 104–111, if you have an adequate understanding of the entity, its internal control and processes, and its environment and other factors, the cost increase will likely be less because the auditor will have a reduced learning curve. The cost to make audit methodology changes could be significant in the first year, but is likely to increase the efficiency with which you conduct your future audits, minimizing audit fee increases to the less complex clients.

It is common in academic curricula and continuing professional education to describe audits by one of four categories:

1. Internal audits
2. Financial or external audits
3. Fraud audits
4. Information technology audits

Following graduation from an accounting or equivalent program and certification as a Certified Public Accountant (CPA) or in another area (e.g., Certified Internal Auditor [CIA]), the practitioner keeps those definitions in mind. As a practical matter, these "silos" are helpful to delineate the differences between the audits, but they overwhelmingly ignore one common reality: All financial audits require the auditor to understand where the information comes from and what processes ensure its reliability. A second reality is that information technology is becoming increasing pervasive and more sophisticated.

Our philosophy of IT auditing embraces the answer to a question you may have asked: *Where does IT auditing fit into the financial auditing process?* We believe that it should fit in throughout the entire engagement. At any step in the process, when we are retrieving information for any cycle, we need to ask—and to be able to answer— questions about where the information came from and what processes ensure its reliability. In virtually all phases of the audit, the auditor must understand the answers to those questions, including the IT controls that cover a particular system or process and knowing how to test these controls in order to provide evidence that they are working properly.

 ## MANAGEMENT'S ASSERTIONS AND THE IT AUDIT

Auditors are familiar with the concept of *management assertions*, the idea that the financial statements imply a set of claims concerning the reported amounts and balances. Each of these assertions can be associated with potential misstatements and in turn with audit procedures. In the following paragraphs we review the principal assertions and briefly expand the financial-auditing discussion to encompass related IT-auditing issues.

Existence

Many account balances purport to describe quantities that actually exist (e.g., stocks of inventory or amounts owed to the company for past sales). Over- or understatements of these balances may result in material errors, and audit procedures typically rely on a combination of process analysis and physical counts or sampling approaches to evaluate the plausibility of a reported balance. The financial auditor ties information in the system back to transaction (source) documents (which may be paper or another electronic file), and, accordingly, he or she needs to understand the system's overall design, the flow of information, and the nature and location of files.

The IT audit process goes beyond a merely conceptual understanding of these issues in order to focus on specific features of the accounting system. The IT audit must evaluate the likelihood that problems or defects in design or operation could lead to misstatements. Thus there is an IT corollary to the financial statement assertion of existence, namely that the application controls that support processing integrity exist. These include such IT-based items as access controls, proper segregation, and appropriate configurations. For instance, when an IT auditor tests for access control, we would expect the existence of signed forms with management approval that specify the access needed. When an IT auditor tests change management, we would expect to see change control forms with the requested changes that are approved for each change that is captured in the system. In smaller organizations, this type of existence assertion can be challenging to achieve due to lack of supporting documentation.

In later chapters we examine these types of issues in specific detail for each of the major transaction cycles.

Completeness

The completeness assertion refers to the integrity of the recording process and the ability of the company's accounting system to ensure that the effects of all transactions, balances, accounts, estimates, and so on have been included in the financial statements. Traditional audit techniques such as cross-footing and internal validity checks of totals and subtotals can help to ensure that financial information flows correctly (as missing values may cause the statements and supporting schedules not to tie). At the IT level, the auditor is concerned with how the system ensures completeness—for instance, does the report writer pull all the items from the chart of accounts?

There is also an IT corollary to the completeness assertion, namely that all necessary and required controls exist. This completeness assertion differs slightly from the existence assertion: While the latter requires the IT auditor to verify that claimed controls actually exist, the former requires that he critically evaluate the overall system design and perhaps recommend additional controls or procedures. Note also that in smaller organizations it may be challenging to achieve completeness due to lack of understanding of how to determine how the accounting system pulls its data.

Rights and Obligations

This assertion addresses the legal status of a company's assets and liabilities and it can create exposures and areas of interest from an IT perspective. As an example, consider a company that ships merchandise on both a free-on-board (FOB) destination and FOB shipping point basis. The accounting system should be configured so as to properly classify these transactions and support accurate reporting of inventory, receivables, and sales.

There is also an IT corollary to the rights and obligations assertion, namely ownership of and responsibility for information resources controlled within the company's accounting system. Thus, from this perspective, adequate control over segregation of duties becomes an important part of the overall structure of rights and obligations as they affect accounting information. In some organizations, a person may have certain responsibilities that are well-controlled outside the system, but the system itself may not coordinate the necessary data access rights for employees to function effectively. Additionally, the company will usually have an obligation to protect data privacy.

Valuation

The area of valuation can range from the accuracy of original costs to complex and esoteric calculations relating to financial instruments. In order to ensure that account balances, transactions, fair value estimates, and other amounts are reported appropriately, the IT auditor may need to examine things such as links to pricing tables and lookup tables, the design and accuracy of spreadsheet models, and the integrity of proprietary data sources. The widespread use of spreadsheet models for a variety of valuation-related activities creates many exposures related to data transfer and change management.

IT and valuation intersect when the auditor needs to estimate the potential cost exposure from an IT audit issue. For example, if an auditor determines that inappropriate individuals have access to make adjusting journal entries, the auditor should then determine if any unauthorized journal entries were actually made by examining the general ledger entries. If any are identified, then the auditor would need to value the exposure to the financial statements.

Accounting Procedures

The realm of accounting procedures includes classification and aggregation procedures, proper cutoffs at the end of each accounting period, the preparation and posting of adjusting entries, the preparation of disclosure and supporting schedules, and the final presentation of the financial statements. It also presumes the fundamental accuracy of arithmetic processes and conformity with appropriate accounting standards.

At the general financial level, the auditor may review personnel records in order to evaluate the suitability of individuals who perform these various tasks. The IT analog would include an analysis of access rights and log-on records. For instance, the IT auditor might run all the adjusting entries, check to see who posted them, and evaluate the list according to a chart of responsibilities.

In addition, the auditor should examine the configuration settings in the computer system to ensure that proper cutoff is achieved. For example, does the computer system configuration close the accounting period, or does the accounting period remain open indefinitely? Does the system have the correct days set for each month? When the financial statements are being produced, the IT auditor needs to ensure that all data within the accounting system are being pulled to the financial statements, confirming, for example, accurate tie-backs between subledgers, the general ledger, and the financial statements.

A Note on Sarbanes-Oxley

The discussion in this text does not focus on the Sarbanes-Oxley Act (SOx), in part because most SMEs do not have to comply with these provisions, and in part because there is already a significant quantity of published guidance in this area. It's worth noting, however, that many items of SOx guidance could be useful for a variety of general controls and as part of a program that addresses other company-specific control issues.

OBJECTIVES OF DATA PROCESSING FOR SMALL AND MEDIUM-SIZED ENTERPRISES (SMEs)

There are several paradigms and methodologies for conducting IT audits. As discussed in the sidebar titled "Committee of Sponsoring Organizations," many of these focus on high-level concepts and principles that should guide the IT audit process. These paradigms share three pervasive IT objectives: the *confidentiality*, *integrity*, and *availability* (CIA) of data. From the Guide to the Assessment of IT Risk (GAIT) methodology we focus on three crucial IT domains: (1) change management, (2) operations, and (3) security.

In this section we briefly discuss CIA and then identify some crucial intersections.

1. **Confidentiality:** The confidentiality of data refers to both internal and external users. Internally, the system of rights and permissions to access and modify data is an essential building block in the design of properly segregated duties (or a key feature to analyze when insufficient personnel make it impossible to achieve an ideal level of segregation). Externally, the confidentiality of data rests on such IT constructs as firewalls, encryption, and access protocols.
2. **Integrity:** In an accounting context, data integrity relates directly to the management assertions discussed in the preceding section, and to the Conceptual Framework's notion of *representational faithfulness*. Thus, accounting information should represent what it purports to represent—quantities that actually exist, calculated from complete records, with due consideration to appropriate legal rights and obligations, and correctly valued in accordance with acceptable accounting procedures.
3. **Availability:** Data that is not available to users is by definition useless to them. Relevant IT concerns include server reliability, access controls, protocols for distributing data, and concurrency issues.

As Figure 1.1 suggests, there are crucial interconnections between these objectives. Confidentiality and integrity intersect in the design of a company's internal control system, as inadequate attention to confidentiality issues may create exposures that either

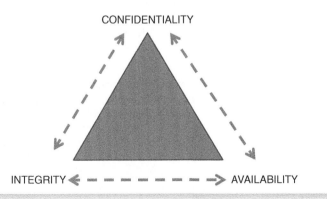

FIGURE 1.1   CIA

Committee of Sponsoring Organizations

The Committee of Sponsoring Organizations (COSO) was organized in 1985 to sponsor the National Commission on Fraudulent Financial Reporting, an independent private-sector initiative that studied the causal factors that lead to fraudulent financial reporting (COSO 2013a). COSO is comprised of five organizations, including the Institute of Management Accountants, the American Accounting Association, the American Institute of Certified Public Accountants, the Institute of Internal Auditors, and Financial Executives International. The stated goal of COSO is to provide thought leadership on governance, enterprise risk management (ERM), internal controls, and fraud deterrence. The 1992 COSO report is recognized as an authoritative source on internal controls and provides a framework against which internal control systems may be assessed. In 2006, COSO issued guidance on how to apply the COSO framework to smaller public companies. Chapter 9 includes an extensive discussion of COSO's guidance for smaller public companies as many of the concepts apply to SMEs regardless of whether they are public or private.

COSO released an updated *Internal Control—Integrated Framework* in 2013 (COSO 2013b). The most current release formalizes many of the fundamental concepts introduced in the original COSO framework. The five principles of internal controls in 2013 were the five concepts of internal controls in the previous COSO release. Consistent with earlier frameworks, the 2013 principles provide the user with assistance in the design and implementation of internal controls and a framework against which internal control systems may be assessed.

Sarbanes-Oxley

In response to the series of business failures and corporate scandals that began with Enron in 2001, the U.S. Congress enacted the Sarbanes-Oxley Act of 2002 (SOx). The stated purpose of SOx is to protect investors by improving the accuracy and reliability of corporate disclosures made pursuant to the securities laws (Public Law 107–204 2002). There are 11 sections of SOx-defining auditor and corporate responsibilities, including expectations for financial disclosures, strong penalties for white-collar crimes, and protection for whistleblowers. Like many legislative acts, the U.S. Congress did not provide the necessary specificity for implementation. Practitioners from public accounting and companies that had to comply reached back to the 1992 COSO report as an authoritative source to produce the necessary specificity to implement SOx.

SOx also created the Public Company Accounting Oversight Board (PCAOB) to oversee the audits of public companies to protect the interests of investors and to further public interest by the preparation of accurate and independent audit reports. The PCAOB issued guidance for IT controls and thus falls within the broader topic of IT audit concerns.

COBIT

While COSO provides thought leadership on governance, ERM, internal controls, and fraud deterrence, COBIT 4.1 provides thought leadership and guidance within the IT function to address risk management, internal controls, and other relevant best practices. Chapter 10 provides an extensive discussion of COBIT 4.1 and its intersection with COSO. Chapter 10 also includes a discussion of previous PCAOB guidance and its intersection with COBIT. The intersection of COBIT with COSO is extremely important to the financial or IT auditor, given COSO's significance to risk and internal control guidelines regardless of whether the enterprise is small, large, public, or private. COBIT 5, an update of COBIT 4.1, remains very relevant to COSO as this framework shifts from an IT-centric view to an enterprise view and considers IT and its collective contribution (e.g., enterprise data) within the larger risk framework.

TABLE 1.1   IT Objectives and Domains Mapped to CIA

IT Objectives/ IT Domains	Confidentiality	Integrity	Availability
Change Management	Segregation, authorization	Accuracy and reliability of changes	Rollback procedures
Operations	Safety of backups, access to backups, access control	System restorability	Server capacity, licenses, personnel backups
Security	Permissions, log-on histories	Nature and reliability of controls	Security roles exist, passwords exist

corrupt the integrity of data or, at a minimum, raise concerns about the potential for this to happen. Confidentiality intersects with availability where the scheme of permissions and access rights is defined. Availability and integrity intersect at the point where information is required to process transactions (e.g., data from a customer's subledger account must be available when a payment is received), make estimates (e.g., receivables and collection data should be available in order to estimate credits to the valuation allowance), or prepare statements and schedules.

Table 1.1 illustrates some of the important intersections between CIA objectives and the three IT domains of change management, operations, and security. The change management process should minimize the exposures created by transition from one state to another, and ensure that the change results in a stable endpoint. Operations need to occur in a stable and secure fashion. Security is a pervasive concern.

Confidentiality

- **Change management:** Segregation refers to the well-established principle that programmers should not have access to data, and that those entrusted with data should not have programming rights. As examined in detail in later chapters, we define *programming* broadly so as to encompass the many methods of altering how software functions and the results it produces. When an IT auditor tests change management, we would expect to see change control forms with the requested changes that are approved for each change that is captured in the system.
- **Operations:** Confidentiality concerns in the operations domain include issues such as the storage location of backup tapes. There's a difference between a sock drawer and a fireproof safe! It's important to remember that the data on the backup tape is confidential and may be readily converted to useful information without someone having access to the system. With respect to access control, IT auditor tests should expect the existence of signed forms with management approval, specifying the access needed.
- **Security:** This intersection includes topics such as passwords, permissions, log-on histories (detective control), and penetration testing. The auditor should determine whether company personnel have access only to the data they need—or to more. It is important to understand and *document* the business reason for data access protocols.

> ## Hard and Soft Controls
>
> At the organizational level, the terms *hard control* and *soft control* refer to the dichotomy between formal and restrictive policies that represent externally imposed discipline, and the sorts of informal, shared values that promote high levels of cohesion and commitment to the unit's objectives. In the IT domain these terms have an analogous relationship to each other, but generally refer to the specific features of the software that either prevent a user from doing certain things (hard control) or warn her about specific consequences or problems (soft control).
>
> As an example, consider an Excel template that is used for pricing. A soft control would be an error flag that produced a warning message if input values fell outside of a specified range. A hard control would be a protected sheet with pricing inputs restricted to input from a dropdown menu or a lookup table. Data entry to unprotected cells can be restricted in various ways.

Integrity
- **Change management**: The IT audit should ensure that appropriate end-user testing has occurred and that changes are working as intended and in a manner that can be relied upon.
- **Operations:** Concerns in this area include testing of backup tapes for system restorability. If data cannot be restored, the company may have incomplete records.
- **Security:** The auditor should understand whether she can rely on the system's security. Are there ways in which it could be bypassed or compromised? What are the overriding security controls? Are they soft or hard?

Availability
- **Change management:** Is the source code in a location where it can be restored? Are there rollback procedures in case of a failed change? Is the backup tape available in case management needs to access data that is not currently in the system?
- **Operations:** The IT auditor should consider the ability of the server system to handle the day-to-day load. Does management have all the needed licenses and are they current? Are there any concerns about the computer system's availability? The location and availability of backup tapes is important. How, if it were necessary, would an employee access prior-year information that is no longer kept in the system?
- **Security:** Whereas the primary security concern is unauthorized access, it's also important that the system not lock out users who have innocently lost or forgotten a password. The IT auditor should understand procedures that ensure, as well as restrict, availability.

 ## SPECIAL CHALLENGES FACING SMEs

How a Small Business Evolves

Almost everyone has heard the story of how Steve Jobs and Steve Wozniak developed a business from a single concept that preceded the Lisa and the Macintosh and led to a series of steps that eventually evolved into Apple Computer (Apple 1 2013). The characteristics of the first business created by Jobs and Wozniak are emblematic of many SMEs: a high concentration of ownership, a high emphasis on revenue generation and cash, a niche product, and a handful of valued employees. The working relationships were very close as familiarity bred longtime friendships and real or perceived trust. Wozniak was among the first to be interviewed following Jobs' death and described the passing of Steve Jobs as a significant loss (Metz 2011). Jobs and Wozniak sold their first "Apple 1s" to the Byte Shop in Mountain View, California, for $666 each. Apple 1s were the first single-board computers with onboard read-only memory and included a video interface—a niche product with a narrow geographical reach.

Although little documentation exists about the early stages of Apple 1, it's reasonable to speculate that bookkeeping and the associated controls were low priorities. It's unlikely a full-time, seasoned Certified Public Accountant was on the payroll to supervise and prepare the financial statements, let alone was an internal audit function established to review compliance to internal controls and assess enterprise risk. A positive cash flow versus compliance to generally accepted accounting principles (GAAP) was more likely the first priority as Steve Jobs sold a Volkswagen minibus for investment infusion into a newly found passion. The bookkeeping was probably very simple, e.g. a checkbook, and did not include Excel spreadsheets, QuickBooks, or Microsoft Dynamics as those products were not yet invented. No one was concerned whether program changes to the bookkeeping software were unauthorized or whether anyone using the software was qualified because the software didn't exist. With data captured in a checkbook, daily data backups in the office and another with more time periods in another offsite location are not required. Beyond the bookkeeping and financial reporting, what else is relevant to the internal controls for this small business?

The opportunities for management override of internal controls (assuming some controls existed) by either Steve Jobs or Steve Wozniak was a significant risk as either could have taken the proceeds of a product delivery and "disappeared." But each partner knew the operations, including product deliveries, revenue proceeds, and a sense of reasonableness. Unusual transactions would have been noticed immediately. Developing an environment in a smaller business with reduced risk requires clear objectives with an organization qualified and trained for the responsibilities. The tone at the top or at the senior management level emphasizes integrity and value systems consistent with a sound control environment. It is very likely that technical skills related to the Apple 1 were highly revered by Jobs and Wozniak with administrative and internal control skills as a distant second or even a remote priority. Competent personnel at all levels of the enterprise were something for the future, but not when they were selling personal assets to finance the business. The concepts of *IT governance* or the Committee of Sponsoring Organizations (COSO) did not exist in Steve Jobs' or many Fortune 1000 board members' vocabulary or list of priorities. Steve Jobs never lamented the role of a weak or nonexistent board of directors for the Apple 1 business. The previous three paragraphs describing Apple 1 and Steve Jobs during its early years, albeit hypothetical, are very different from the SME environment that exists today.

Although there was no evidence of fraud in the early business ventures by Jobs and Wozniak (nor are we in any way implying that fraud existed), research by the

Association of Certified Fraud Examiners (ACFE) suggests that small companies are among the most vulnerable to fraud and loss. According to a report from ACFE, *The 2012 Report to the Nation on Occupational Fraud and Abuse* (ACFE 2012), small businesses, defined as those with less than 100 employees, suffered both a greater percentage of frauds (32 percent) and a higher median loss ($147,000) than their larger counterparts. These findings accentuate the problems associated with SMEs. They are limited in the amount of financial and human resources, including trained IT personnel, to deter fraud and abuse. According to ACFE research, billing schemes, skimming, cash larceny, and payroll fraud were noticeably more common in businesses with less than 100 employees. Across all sizes of organizations and government entities, tips were the most common detection method, followed by internal controls and internal audits. Pragmatically, few if any SMEs employ internal audits and must rely on other vehicles, if any, for fraud detection. Publicly traded companies cited the smallest percentage of fraud detected by external audits even though they are the only type of organization that is required to have an external audit.

The 2012 ACFE report is reinforced with more recent experience from the U.S. Secret Service and Verizon Communications Inc.'s forensic analysis unit, which investigates hacking attacks (Fowler and Worthen 2011). The forensic units responded to a combined 761 data breaches, up from 141 in 2009. Of those, 482, or 63 percent, were at companies with 100 employees or fewer. Visa Inc. estimates about 95 percent of the credit-card data breaches it discovers are on its smallest business customers. Hackers would rather spend time on SMEs and make a quick harvest than break into a Fortune 500 with substantially more effort. According to Symantec, the credit cards and bank accounts offered in the underground economy are worth more than US$7 billion.

The Control Environment for SMEs

Since Apple 1, software applications and the Internet have emerged to be significant control topics for the SME. Today, an SME would likely use Excel spreadsheets, Quick-Books, or Microsoft Dynamics with the potential of cloud applications such as Google Apps for Business. QuickBooks has an active user base of 4.5 million companies and is the world's most popular accounting software (Collins 2011). While much has changed since Apple 1 with the evolution of new software products such as QuickBooks and Microsoft Dynamics, much remains unchanged. Adequate staffing, segregation of duties, competent personnel, qualified board members, the tone at the top, and general controls are among the topics for SMEs that remain constant before and after the emergence of Excel spreadsheets, QuickBooks, or Microsoft Dynamics. While these controls remain constant, they must be adjusted for the new reality of software applications that did not exist in the previous generation of SMEs. For example, the definition of competent personnel must now include an employee who understands QuickBooks at a minimum level of proficiency. A new genre of internal controls described as *IT controls* has emerged with a reliance on the new software technology.

Adequate staffing to support segregation of duties is an ongoing concern with SMEs. The person who opens the mail and logs payments should not be the same person who makes deposits and maintains the bookkeeping records. Additional segregations of duties should be in place: Receipts should be offered to all customers with the requirement that subsequent transactions be accompanied by a receipt; excessive voided sales should be investigated; all credit memos and write-offs should require management approval; and management should investigate customer complaints about unusual balances (Raimondi 2011). Segregation of duties is also important for cash disbursements: A review of the original invoice should be made prior to payment; purchase orders should be used for all significant purchases; the purchase orders should use an approved vendors' list (management approves the list of approved vendors); the check signor should not be the bookkeeper; all online payments are approved by a second person; and one person controls payments while a second person controls blank checks and monitors check numbers. Additional areas that should require segregation of duties include payroll reviews, fixed asset inventories and reviews, and bank credit card activities. Has anything else changed as a result of QuickBooks, Microsoft Dynamics, and Excel in the SME? Management and auditors alike need to reflect on this question in order to ensure that all risks and controls have been considered.

The need for general, often physical, controls outside of the IT environment, including locked doors, cash registers, offices, file cabinets, and control of blank checks, has changed little with the emergence of QuickBooks, Microsoft Dynamics, and Excel. Within the IT environment, the emergence of server cabinets and backup files has increased the need for greater security for servers (and backup servers) and offsite storage of files. Wireless access to the SME network should include the appropriate encryption (e.g., WiFi-protected access [WPA2] or a more recent product). With software on servers and Internet availability, restricted access through passwords and the appropriate implementation of firewalls and ongoing file backups should be normal protocol. Background checks and security cameras should be implemented wherever appropriate and particularly where high-value inventory exists. A broader discussion of general controls for SMEs occurs later in this book.

Significant application controls for Excel, Microsoft Dynamics, and QuickBooks include access controls, closing dates, a variety of reports validating the data, budgetary controls, customer credit card protection, and user preferences. In this chapter, we introduce application topics for further review in more detail in later chapters. In QuickBooks, user names and passwords can be administered for sales and accounts receivable, purchases and accounts payable, checking and credit cards, inventory, time tracking, payroll and employees, sensitive accounting activities, sensitive financial reports, changing or deleting transactions, and changing closed transactions. In the QuickBooks Enterprise Solution, customization to enable application control fine tuning includes predefined roles, individual reports, bank accounts, lists, and activities with the ability to customize each user's access to view-only, create, modify, delete, and print. Controlling transactions in closed periods is particularly important to the integrity of financial reporting. In QuickBooks, the closing date password can be established with the ability to restrict access to prior periods. A closing date exception report is available for management review. Additional application controls include reports for the audit trail, voided/deleted transactions, previous reconciliation, discrepancy, closing date, and exception report. Additional application controls will be reviewed in later chapters.

The Board's and Management's Roles in the SME Control Environment

According to the SEC's Office of Economic Analysis, insiders own on average approximately 30 percent of the company's shares (GAO 2006) for those public companies with a market capitalization of $125 million or less. With the high concentration of ownership in smaller public companies, the same need for significant investor SEC protection in a Fortune 1000 company with broad stock ownership does not exist. However, while there is some benefit in concentrated management and ownership, there are also extensive and numerous risks, including management override of internal controls.

While the risk of management override exists with a concentration of management and ownership, greater oversight, exposure, and transparency of the business can also evolve from a smaller company, provided senior management creates the leadership for those characteristics to evolve. Steve Jobs and Steve Wozniak were hands-on during the evolution of Apple 1 and were very aware of product movement, product costs, and administrative expenses. Achieving and evaluating effective internal controls over financial reporting can be simplified if management maintains hands-on involvement and awareness of sales, costs, and administrative expenses.

SME shareholders, the board, managers, and audit committees (if an audit committee exists) should actively (and periodically) evaluate their organizational maturity for all software implementations, including Excel, QuickBooks, and Microsoft Great Plains Dynamics. The assessments should be based on the premises that:

- All organizations are at risk due to a lack of resources or ineffective leadership, but SMEs are particularly at risk given the evidence from Sarbanes-Oxley implementations and research from the Association of Certified Fraud Examiners.
- A minimum of internal controls should be attained for any software implementation.
- Successful IT implementations are inextricably linked to qualified staff and effective project management. A priority for the audit committee, the board, corporate officers, and the external auditor is to understand the impact of IT requirements on internal controls, as IT domain weaknesses spill over to other IT and non-IT internal control effectiveness in other COSO domains.

Recruiting a qualified board for SMEs can be very challenging as qualified board members are in high demand and those who do qualify may want to avoid the board member liabilities associated with higher-risk SMEs. Recruiting qualified board and audit committee members for SMEs creates the potential for board members to add perspective, value, and oversight for financial reporting in a longer-term relationship. However, many prospective recruits to the board or audit committee may perceive excessive risk in a smaller company given the potential for shareholder litigation for a variety of reasons, including fraudulent financial reporting. Meaningful internal controls can facilitate board member recruiting.

Internal controls can be strengthened by active and visible participation by management in the internal controls for SMEs. For example, managers can review system reports of detailed transactions; select transactions for review of supporting documents;

oversee periodic counts of physical inventory, sign off on system access or program changes, and compare equipment or other assets with accounting records; and review reconciliations of account balances or perform them independently. In many SMEs, managers already are performing internal control procedures, but documentation is less than complete. Credit should be taken for their contribution to effective internal control through written job descriptions and logs that document the periodic steps taken to support their written job descriptions.

The authors believe that a critical success factor lies in an organization's capability to implement and maintain financial software while sustaining or improving internal controls. Most SMEs have the advantage of simpler operating requirements, which should translate into the acquisition of software packages to meet operating requirements and avoid risks associated with in-house developed systems. Maintenance and development are borne by the vendor, which is a much better choice than the IT staff of an SME who typically lack technical expertise in that particular software. Commercially available software can offer features for controlling data access, performing checks on data processing completeness and accuracy, completing system and data backup, and maintaining related documentation. Over the last decade, additional application controls have been added in Excel, QuickBooks, and Microsoft Dynamics as those products have evolved. Although management may be able to take the leadership in training operating staff on general and application controls, it is more likely that outside resources such as CPAs with sufficient depth in internal controls would be required for periodic consulting engagements. With appropriate training, application controls can help improve operational consistency, facilitate log reviews, automate reconciliations, provide meaningful exception reporting, and support proper segregation of duties.

RESEARCH CONFIRMING THE RISKS ASSOCIATED WITH SMEs

The awareness of control challenges associated with SMEs has increased significantly since the first pronouncement by the Committee of Sponsoring Organizations of the Treadway Commission (CSOTC) in 1992. It's reasonable to assume that controls that we associate with CSOTC were rarely in place for many SMEs up to and including the implementation of SOx. The events that followed the implementation SOx in 2002 include independent research from academia, congressional hearings, reports from the General Accounting Office (GAO), and eventually a new pronouncement by COSO in 2006 that shed light on the state of controls in SMEs. The report from the ACFE, *The 2012 Report to the Nation on Occupational Fraud and Abuse* (ACFE 2012), confirmed the vulnerability of businesses with fewer than 100 employees to fraud and higher average losses.

The original 1992 CSOTC report defined *internal control* as a process, affected by an entity's board of directors, management, and other personnel, designed to provide reasonable assurance regarding the achievement of effectiveness and efficiency of operations, reliability of financial reporting, and compliance with applicable laws and regulations. Five concepts were emphasized by the 1992 CSOTC: (1) a sound control environment defined by a qualified board, the tone at the top, and competent personnel throughout the organizational structure; (2) ongoing risk assessment of financial reporting including the potential of fraud; (3) both procedural and information technology controls that respond to a broader risk assessment of the enterprise and the environment; (4) effective financial and internal control reporting; and (5) ongoing evaluations of the internal control environment to enable management to respond. COSO remains tethered to *Enterprise Risk Management—Integrated Framework* (ERM) whether it's an SME or a large public company. Following the 1992 pronouncement by CSOTC, numerous events, including the failure of Enron, the initial implementation of SOx in 2004, and subsequent assessments by the GAO, Congress, and COSO (2007), led to a reemphasis on the five components of COSO for SMEs whether they are public or private.

Independent research on firms that reported at least one material weakness for those companies in the initial SOx implementations from 2002 to 2005 found that these firms were more likely smaller, younger, riskier, more complex, and financially weaker, with poorer accrual earnings quality. In their independent research, Klamm and Watson (2009) examined 490 firms reporting material weakness in the first year of SOx compliance to evaluate the interrelatedness of weak COSO components and IT controls. Their research identified relationships between the reported material weakness and the five components of COSO, including:

▪ A weak control environment has a positive association with the remaining four weak COSO components; that is, COSO components are likely to affect one another.
▪ IT-related weak COSO components frequently spill over to create more non-IT-related material weakness and misstatements.
▪ IT-related weak COSO components negatively affect reporting reliability and add to the number of non-IT material weaknesses reported.

Moreover, the conclusion from Klamm and Watson's research is that the IT domain appears to affect overall control effectiveness.

Cumulative evidence from IT projects in the past 15 years and SOx suggest several risk drivers for internal controls, including:

▪ Complexity of the enterprise, including the number of subsidiaries and the nature of assets and liabilities
▪ Smaller, younger, riskier, more complex, and financially weaker organizations that lack either adequate resources or the leadership to execute an effective or controlled change management

The General Accounting Office (GAO 2006) in its *Report to the Committee on Small Business and Entrepreneurship*, U.S. Senate, in 2006, identified the resource limitations that make it more difficult for smaller public companies to achieve economies of scale, segregate duties and responsibilities, and hire qualified accounting personnel to prepare and report financial information. Segregation of transactions and the associated division of responsibilities in a smaller company absorb a larger percentage of the company's revenues or assets than in a larger company. About 60 percent of the smaller public companies that responded to the GAO survey reported that it was difficult to implement effective segregation of duties. Several executives reported difficulty in segregating duties due to limited resources. Other executives in the GAO survey commented that it was difficult to achieve effective internal control over financial reporting because they lacked expertise within their internal accounting staff to complete the accounting for such complex topics as stock option valuations. So while it's more difficult to implement internal controls, the AICPA noted that smaller public companies often do not have the internal audit functions referred to in COSO's internal framework guidance and therefore cannot provide oversight (GAO 2006). The nature of SMEs creates difficulties with internal controls and oversight, leading to modified expectations for shareholder protection.

In connection with SOx compliance, the SEC requires the implementation of *Enterprise Risk Management—Integrated Framework* (ERM), authored by the Treadway Commission's Committee of Sponsoring Organizations (COSO 1992). The report, *Internal Control for Financial Reporting: Guidance for Smaller Public Companies*, issued in 2007 by COSO following the GAO report, reemphasizes the five concepts originally identified in 1992. The five concepts are:

1. A sound control environment defined by a qualified board, the tone at the top, and competent personnel throughout the organizational structure.
2. Ongoing risk assessment of financial reporting, including the potential of fraud.
3. Both procedural and information technology controls that respond to the risk environment.
4. Effective financial and internal control reporting.
5. Ongoing evaluations of the internal control environment to enable management to respond. COSO remains tethered to *Enterprise Risk Management—Integrated Framework* (ERM), whether it's an SME or a Fortune 100 enterprise, after the original pronouncement 14 years earlier.

In the *Internal Control for Financial Reporting: Guidance for Smaller Public Companies*, COSO reemphasized the need for management to weigh costs against benefits particularly for those companies that have focused considerable attention on the costs associated with Section 404 compliance. While the costs of internal control are apparent, the benefits of capital market access to provide funds for innovation and market expansion may not be as obvious. Additional benefits include more reliable financial reporting; consistent mechanisms for processing transactions across an organization; enhancing speed and reliability; and the ability to accurately communicate business performance to partners and customers. Private companies that do not rely on public financing still require bank financing and, potentially, external investors from time to time.

A FRAMEWORK FOR EVALUATING RISKS AND CONTROLS, COMPENSATORY CONTROLS, AND REPORTING DEFICIENCIES

A review of the Apple 1 business identified numerous internal control challenges that are associated with small businesses. Small staffs with the inability to segregate the transaction cycle, the potential for management override because of management's dominance of day-to-day activities, qualified accounting personnel with adequate training in Excel, QuickBooks, or Microsoft Dynamics, and maintaining current updates for software applications are among the control challenges for SMEs. All of these examples deliver threats to the ability of the enterprise to provide reliable financial transactions, accounting records, and financial statements. So when does a threat become a *material weakness* and which framework is applicable to making an assessment about the appropriateness of various controls?

In 2007, in the context of a Section 404 discussion within SOx (SEC 2007a), the SEC delivered clarification on the term *material weakness* as "a deficiency, or combination of deficiencies, in internal control over financial reporting, such that there is a reasonable possibility that a material misstatement of the company's annual or interim financial statements will not be prevented or detected on a timely basis." A *significant deficiency* exists if one or more control deficiencies exist that create a financial reporting misstatement that rises to a level that is less than a material weakness. "Our guidance enables companies of all sizes to focus on what truly matters to the integrity of the financial statements—risk and materiality," said Securities and Exchange Commission chief accountant Conrad Hewitt. While the following discussion applies to publicly traded SMEs, the principles provide a framework for risks and controls for financial reporting for all SMEs irrespective of the capital structure and the ultimate regulatory framework.

The SEC delivered its interpretive guidance in 2007 for public companies of all sizes, including publicly listed SMEs, around two key principles:

1. Management should evaluate whether it has implemented controls that adequately address the risk that a material misstatement of the financial statements would not be prevented or detected in a timely manner using a top-down, risk-based approach including the role of entity-level controls (including general controls).
2. The evaluation procedures should be aligned with those areas of financial reporting that pose the highest risks to reliable financial reporting with more extensive testing in high-risk areas.

For principle 2, the evaluation procedures include a five-step process that requires management:

1. To identify those risks of misstatement that could, individually or in combination with others, result in a material misstatement of the financial statements
2. To evaluate whether it has controls placed in operation to adequately address the company's financial reporting risks

3. To consider the nature of the entity-level controls and how those controls relate to the financial reporting element
4. To consider the adequacy of both general controls and application controls for IT processing underlying the integrity of financial statement reporting
5. To maintain reasonable support for its assessment, including documentation of the design of the controls management has placed in operation to adequately address the financial reporting risks

Management should be able to assess the financial reporting risks underlying their internal controls. (See Figure 1.2.) Higher risks associated with financial reporting risks require more evidence; lower risks associated with financial reporting require less evidence.

In the SEC's interpretive guidance in 2007 of how to assess Section 404 of SOx, an example of how management should evaluate the likelihood of the possibility of a control failure included an assessment of eight attributes of controls, all of which are applicable to SMEs (SEC 2007b). Management's assessment of financial reporting misstatements includes both the materiality of the financial reporting element and the susceptibility of the underlying account balances, transactions, or other supporting information to a misstatement that could be material to the financial statements. The attributes that would be evaluated are:

1. The type of control (i.e., manual or automated) and the frequency with which it operates
2. The complexity of the control
3. The risk of management override

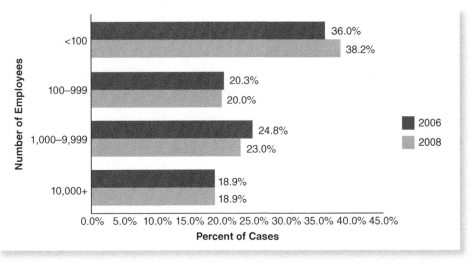

FIGURE 1.2 Determining the Sufficiency of Evidence Based on Internal Control over Financial Reporting (ICFR) Risk

Source: Commission Guidance Regarding Management's Report on Internal Control Over Financial Reporting Under Section 13(a) or 15(d) of the Securities Exchange Act of 1934 (SEC 2007b), www.sec.gov/rules/interp/2007/33-8810.pdf.

4. The judgment required to operate the control
5. The competence of the personnel who perform the control or monitor its performance
6. Whether there have been changes in key personnel who either perform the control or monitor its performance
7. The nature and materiality of misstatements that the control is intended to prevent or detect
8. The degree to which the control relies on the effectiveness of other controls (e.g., IT general controls), and evidence of the operation of the control from prior year(s)

Evaluation of these eight attributes could be applied to the Apple 1 business described earlier and to any SME that employed Excel, QuickBooks, or Microsoft Dynamics.

A *risk-based audit approach* (Romney and Steinbart 2011):

1. Determines the threats.
2. Identifies the control procedures to prevent, detect, or correct the threats.
3. Evaluates that the controls that are purported to exist actually exist.
4. Makes a final determination as to whether the purported controls are adequate or effective and whether additional audit procedures should occur.

After determining the threats in Step 1, Step 2 in the risk-based audit approach, the identification phase, includes all controls that management has put into place. Step 3, the evaluation step, includes a system review to determine whether control procedures are in place and tests to determine whether the controls are working as intended. If the controls are inadequate or ineffective in Step 4, compensating controls should be considered as a replacement for the primary controls. The SEC defines *compensating controls* as controls that serve to accomplish the objective of another control that did not function properly, helping to reduce risk to an acceptable level. To have a mitigating effect, the compensating control should replace the original control to prevent or detect a material misstatement to the financial statements.

A sample framework for the audit of QuickBooks processing controls integrating a risk-based audit approach would include the following assessment in four categories.

Types of Errors and Fraud

The types of errors and fraud determinants in the framework include:

- Failure to detect incorrect, incomplete, or unauthorized input data (e.g., override by management)
- Failure to properly correct errors flagged by data editing procedures
- Introduction of errors into files or databases during updating (e.g., updates from add-in inventory system that were not reviewed using reasonableness tests, or management override)
- Improper distribution or disclosure of QuickBooks output (e.g., password controls with strong passwords)

▪ Intentional or unintentional inaccuracies in reporting (e.g., a monthly review of reports on missing inventory, excessive credit memos, or adjustments to accounts receivable)

Control Procedures

The control procedures in the framework include:

▪ Data editing routines of source data
▪ Reconciliation of batch totals
▪ Effective error correction procedures (e.g., management approval for voiding or deleting transactions in QuickBooks)
▪ Competent supervision of QuickBooks with trained personnel
▪ Effective handling of data input and output by data control personnel (e.g., predefined user roles are available in the Enterprise edition of QuickBooks, which limit a user's role in extreme detail)
▪ Maintenance of proper environmental conditions in the computer facility (e.g., locked server cabinets, background checks on key personnel, etc.)

Audit Procedures

The audit procedures in the framework that follow fall into two categories: system review and tests of controls.

System Review

▪ Review administrative documentation for processing control standards (e.g., a review of the logs of management approval for voided or deleted transactions).
▪ Review systems documentation for data editing and other processing controls (e.g., a review of logs of data backup and testing of files).
▪ Document operations for completeness and clarity.
▪ Observe computer operations and data control functions.

Tests of Controls

▪ Evaluate adequacy of processing control standards and procedures.
▪ Evaluate adequacy and completeness of data editing controls.
▪ Verify adherence to processing control procedures by observing computer and data.
▪ Verify that application system output is properly distributed.
▪ Reconcile a sample of batch totals; follow up on discrepancies.
▪ Trace a sample of data edit routines errors to ensure proper handling.
▪ Verify processing accuracy of sensitive transactions (e.g., management approval for accounts receivable write-offs).
▪ Verify processing accuracy of computer-generated transactions (e.g., test credit card transactions).
▪ Check accuracy and completeness of processing controls by using test data (e.g., the transaction list by vendor should be reviewed for check detail, purchases by vendor detail, purchases by item detail, open purchase orders, and budget vs. actual).

Compensating Controls

Finally, the Audit Trail Report in QuickBooks is an example of a compensating control to use to answer three essential questions:

1. Who added/edited/deleted the transaction?
2. When was the transaction added/edited/deleted?
3. What were the relevant details of the transaction (i.e., date, amount, accounts, names)?

 ## SUMMARY: THE ROAD AHEAD

A robust implementation of COSO's *Internal Control—Integrated Framework*, and an implementation of the Control Objectives for Information and related Technology (COBIT) framework, are effective responses to the risk drivers for the SME. The authors believe that the board, management, IT, business operations, and accounting organization must be able to support COSO on a *systematic and repeatable level*—and that the controls are integral to the operation of the enterprise. The authors also believe that even with commercially available financial applications, organizational maturity may be a major risk factor for SMEs as evidenced by the conclusions of reports of SOx compliance, GAO, ACFE, the U.S. Secret Service, Verizon, and others. Given the high level of risk exposure to fraud and abuse in SMEs and low levels of success attributable to external audit and the near-absence of internal audits in smaller businesses, effective internal controls and COSO compliance are critical success factors in the financial health of the SME.

CHAPTER TWO

General Controls for the SME

T HIS CHAPTER REVIEWS THE CONCEPTS of *fair presentation* of financial statements and internal controls, and general controls, and the relevancy of those controls to the *fair presentation* of financial statements. The chapter also addresses internal controls and IT general controls relevant to QuickBooks, Microsoft Dynamics, and Microsoft Excel. While QuickBooks, Microsoft Dynamics, and Microsoft Excel are applications and require application controls, they must operate in a secure IT environment. *So why are general controls for the IT environment important?*

An insecure or mismanaged IT environment will create a wall of worry for the IT auditor for any financial applications or any of the systems or subsystems that feed material financial information to the financial statements. For the very small enterprise, a handyman or a person with limited IT experience may be in charge of the company's networks, servers, and databases. For the auditor, the first challenges are to get comfortable with IT governance and to gain some assurance that IT general controls (ITGCs) are in place, effective, and operating as described on a consistent basis. Without assurances that ITGCs are in place and operating effectively and consistently, the auditor may have a very steep wall of worry to climb. That wall of worry may ultimately be insurmountable.

An integrated view of general controls (Palmas 2011) shows general controls encapsulating the IT environment that holds all business processes, business units, and application controls (Figure 2.1). Application controls are specific to a business process and each business process supports a business unit. A particular business process may support several business units. For public and other Sarbanes-Oxley-compliant companies, tests are appropriate for both business processes and the IT environment. Consistent with the IT environment and the business processes (the larger box and everything that's in the box), the objectives of financial reporting, the assertions of existence, completeness, rights and obligations, accuracy, cutoff, and classifications, must meet the financial statement reporting objectives of the enterprise.

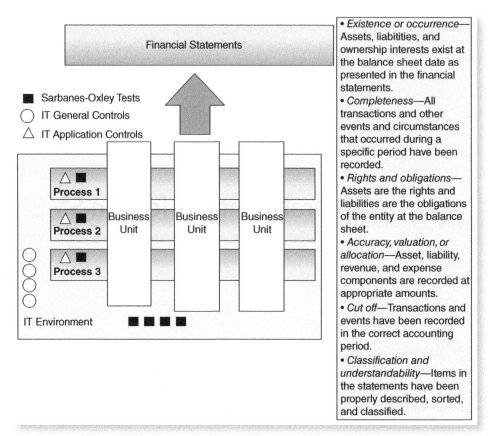

FIGURE 2.1 IT General and Application Controls

Source: Adapted from Palmas 2011.

This chapter discusses what (or who) is responsible for IT general controls and what types of general controls support the financial assertion objectives. Later in this chapter, we will step through the *COSO process*, a best practice, to include an integrated view of the financial statements, assertions, risks, control objectives, and eventually application controls. The application controls for any particular account (e.g., Revenue) will be residing in a business process within the IT environment as shown in Figure 2.1. The IT environment and ITGCs have a significant role in the COSO process, where we will examine the financial statements and specific IT controls and whether they are in place and working to support the financial assertions.

 GENERAL CONTROLS: SCOPE AND OUTCOMES

The term *general controls* offers little insight into what it encapsulates in the context of controls for an SME. The definitions used by COSO, ISACA, and other authoritative bodies in the field typically define general controls in terms of *what the controls do or their intended outcomes within their scope of activity.*

COSO was among the first to create a framework and to create definitions that divide IT controls into two types: (1) general computer or IT controls and (2) application-specific controls. Outcomes and their scope define general controls:

▪ Data center operations (e.g., job scheduling, backup, and recovery)
▪ Systems software controls and access security
▪ Application system development and maintenance controls

Application controls:

▪ Control data processing of a particular application.
▪ Ensure the integrity of transactions, authorization, and validity.
▪ Encompass how different applications interface and exchange data.

Figure 2.1 includes general controls in the IT environment, while application controls are included in specific business processes.

ISACA's IT Assurance Framework (ITAF) (ISACA 2013) ranks at or near the top as the most comprehensive framework for an audit of general controls and according to ISACA provides a single point of reference to host standards, guidelines, tools, and techniques to conduct IT assessments. Section 3000 of the ITAF identifies IT processes or IT audit processes and includes a narrative description of the guideline item, presents information about the subject area and the assurance issues, and provides direction to IT audit and assurance professionals. More specifically, Section 3630 of the ITAF, Auditing ITGCs (ISACA 2013), includes definitions of general controls and the corresponding IT assessments.

▪ An introduction to ITGCs, the components of ITGC, and the difference between ITGCs versus IT application controls
▪ Information resource planning, IT planning processes, and the alignment of enterprise initiatives, budgets, and planning
▪ IT services delivery, standards of delivery, and existence of service-level agreements
▪ Information systems operations, end-user computing, education and support, networks and network management, and human resources (HR) issues, including staffing, training, and career management
▪ HR issues unique to IT, skill identification, management challenges, and governance
▪ Outsourced and third-party activities, insourcing, offshoring, facilities management, and the issues concerning each
▪ Information security management within IT and end-user IT controls over security management
▪ Systems development life cycle (SDLC) over traditional internal development, customizing packages, acquiring enterprise resource planning (ERP) systems, and nontraditional development models that include outsourcing and offshoring
▪ Business continuity planning (BCP) and disaster recovery planning (DRP), impact assessments, scenarios, responses, and communications

- Database management and controls to ensure up-to-date and readily available information
- Network management and controls, the protection of the networks, internal and external risks, and encryption
- Systems software support, migration issues for new software and hardware changes, version management, maintenance, release control, and patch management
- Hardware support, acquisition, maintenance, and deprovisioning
- Operating system management and controls, implementation, version and patch management
- Physical and environmental control, security, network switches, wiring closets, end-user computing, and notebooks in use while away from the usual place of business
- Enterprise portals, e-business, open and closed user groups, and various means to protect the organization from disruptions in the enterprise portals

Particularly noteworthy in the ITAF discussion is the scope within the organization. While many general controls can be isolated to the IT organization (e.g., network security), and strategic alignment of the IT function to the enterprise, many topics, including budgeting, ERP systems, and IT human resources, are among the significant IT issues that reach into the executive office and ultimately corporate governance. The chairman, president, and CEO are involved with general control and governance issues for the IT organization.

Types of Controls

For either general controls or application controls, three types of controls generally coexist: (1) preventive controls, (2) detective controls, and (3) corrective controls.

Preventive controls avoid errors, fraud, or events not authorized by management. Preventive controls are designed to stop undesirable acts before they occur. A discussion of preventive controls for security and access includes such topics as locked doors or intrusion alarms. A retinal eye scan or other biometric preventive controls prevent unwelcomed intruders into a protected space; a lock prevents access to a car, house, or other protected space. However, a creative burglar can circumvent a lock with either brute force or creative problem solving; retinal eye scans are more difficult to override. Ultimately, a cost benefit analysis drives the design of the preventive controls.

Because preventive controls can fail, *detective controls* may be required. A fire alarm detects smoke, makes a shrill noise, and is a detective control, but it cannot prevent a fire nor can it extinguish a fire. The role of a detective control is to communicate a warning or a failed condition.

Finally, *corrective controls* are those steps undertaken to correct an error or problem uncovered via detective controls. A recovery of a file, a building, or a business is a corrective control and restores a situation back to its original state before an event occurred. A corrective control cannot prevent a catastrophe but it plays a very significant role in risk management. Concepts such as preventive, detective, or corrective controls begin to emerge and are part of the overall fabric of general controls. Preventive, detective, or corrective controls for financial recordkeeping would appear as an application control in Process 1, 2, or 3 in Figure 2.1.

It is typical that 60 to 70 percent or more of the controls in an environment are preventive, another 20 to 30 percent are detective, and the remaining 10 to 20 percent are corrective. As such, the controls should be used in combination to reinforce one another with selective redundancy, much like a portfolio manager would structure various investments to manage risk. As one control fails, another control will compensate for the first control's failure. A log (frequently used as a detective control) can identify intruders if the intruder overrides a preventive control. The objective is to create an outcome greater than what any single control can deliver by itself. It is unlikely that any one preventive or detective control can survive a determined individual whose objective is to override the system.

Perhaps the most significant corrective control is a business or disaster recovery plan, which requires active support and sponsorship from the chief executive officer (CEO) and the board. Without an effective business recovery plan, the survival of an enterprise is vulnerable to catastrophic events. This corrective control restores an enterprise back to its original operating mode. While the initial introduction to preventive, detective, or corrective controls discusses locks, fire alarms, retinal eye scans, and the like, the most significant controls require support from the CEO and the board, where the lack of a control can have a devastating impact on an organization.

Examples of General Controls

For purposes of illustration, sample preventive, detective, or corrective controls for authentication of users and limiting unauthorized access, hacking and other network break-ins, and the physical environment and physical security of the system and business continuity are included in Tables 2.1, 2.2, and 2.3.

IT Governance and General Controls

Preventive, detective, or corrective controls apply to all levels of the organization, including the board, senior management, corporate governance, and IT governance, as well as the accounting clerk who opens the accounts receivable submissions at his or her desk. A frequently referenced preventive control is to hire qualified staff at all levels, including the CEO, the controller, and even the mailroom clerk. The most significant driver for general controls is IT governance as it defines the hiring process and ultimately the employed personnel, the internal processes, the leadership, and the organizational structures. The authors concur with the definition of IT governance that Shimamoto suggests (2011): "IT governance is the leadership, structures, and processes that business owners put in place to ensure that their business's IT sustains and extends their business strategy and objectives."

TABLE 2.1 Authentication of Users and Limiting Unauthorized Access

User IDs	**Preventive:** Must be unique for each user.
Authentication of Users	**Preventive:** A process or procedure in an IT system to ensure that the person accessing the IT system is a valid and authorized user.
Passwords	**Preventive:** A secret set of characters that identify the user as the authentic owner of that associated user ID. Significant attributes include (but are not limited to): ▪ Passwords should be at least eight characters in length and contain at least one nonalphanumeric character. ▪ Passwords should be case sensitive and changed at least every 90 days.
Two-factor Authentication: Smart Card	**Preventive:** The smart card authenticates a valid user. ▪ The smart card is a credit-card-size device with an integrated circuit that displays a constantly changing ID code. ▪ The user enters her password, and then the smart card displays an ID that she uses to log in the system. ▪ The smart card changes the user ID systematically every few minutes or so.
Two-factor Authentication: Security Token	**Preventive:** A security token plugs into the USB port and thereby eliminates the need for a card reader. The purpose and use of the security token are equivalent to the smart card.
Computer Log	**Detective:** All accesses should be logged with a complete record of all dates, times, and uses, for two purposes. ▪ Abnormalities in login or use can be examined to determine any weaknesses in login procedures. ▪ The login procedures and logs establish nonrepudiation of users.
Limit Login Attempts	**Preventive:** The login procedure should be established so that the session is terminated after three unsuccessful attempts and that these terminated sessions are also logged. The purpose of the log is to allow proper follow-up if there are patterns of abnormal login or terminated logins. To maintain a record of login attempts, the system should keep an automated log to detect suspicious or unusual login attempts.
User Profile	**Preventive:** Should be established for every authorized user. ▪ Determines each user's access levels to hardware, software, and data according to the individual's job responsibilities. ▪ The level of access should be established within the authority tables.
Authority Table	**Preventive:** A list of valid, authorized users and the access level granted to each one. One user within the payroll area may need to both read and write data, while another may need only read access. These user profiles are defined in the authority tables.
Configuration Tables	**Preventive:** Configuration tables for hardware, software, and application programs that contain the appropriate set-up and security settings. It is important to limit user access to these configuration tables so that security settings are not changed by unauthorized users. The hardware and operating system configuration table contains security and operating settings for hardware and the operating system.

Source: Adapted from Turner and Weickgenannt 2008.

TABLE 2.2 Hacking and Other Network Break-Ins

Firewall	Hardware, software, or a combination of both that is designed to block unauthorized access. All data traveling between the internal network and the Internet should pass through a firewall.
Encrypted	Plain text data converted into encrypted code is referred to as *cipher text*.
Symmetric and Public Key Encryption	Symmetric encryption uses a single encryption key that must be used to encrypt data and also to decode the encrypted data. The sender of the data and the receiver must have the same encryption key. Public key encryption uses both a public key and a private key.
Wired Equivalency Privacy, or WEP	An encryption method for wireless network equipment, wired equivalency privacy (WEP) employs 64, 128, or 256 encryption methods.
Wireless Protected Access, or WPA	WPA offers improved encryption and user authentication. With the improved encryption method, WPA can check to determine whether encryption keys have been tampered with.
Service Set Identifier (SSID)	The SSID is a password that is passed between the sending and receiving nodes of a wireless network. Most wireless network equipment sets a default SSID of "any" so that any wireless equipment can connect to it.
Virtual Private Network	Authorized employees should connect to the IT system by using a virtual private network, or VPN, which utilizes tunnels, authentication, and encryption within the Internet network to isolate Internet communications so that unauthorized users cannot access or use certain data.
SSL	In addition, network traffic between the organization and all authorized users that is sent via the Internet should limit access by the use of web-based technology called secure sockets layer, or SSL.
Viruses	A virus attaches itself to other programs and data and performs malicious actions such as deleting files or shutting down the computer.
Worm	A worm is a small piece of program code that attaches to the computer's unused memory space and replicates itself until the system becomes overloaded and shuts down.
Vulnerability Assessment	To monitor exposure long range, the organization should engage in vulnerability assessment, intrusion detection, and penetration testing.
Intrusion Detection Systems	Intrusion detection systems are specific software tools that monitor data flow within a network and alert the IT staff to hacking attempts or other unauthorized access attempts.

Source: Adapted from Turner and Weickgenannt 2008.

TABLE 2.3 Physical Environment Table and Business Continuity Planning

Controlled Environment	**Preventive:** A large-scale IT system must be located in a building that properly controls dust, temperature, and humidity. The fire prevention systems should use gas such as Halen that eliminates oxygen in the room, since a fire cannot burn without oxygen.
Uninterruptible Power Supply	**Preventive and Corrective:** The computer system should also have both an uninterruptible power supply (UPS) and an emergency power supply (EPS). ■ A UPS includes a battery to maintain power in the event of a power outage in order to keep the computer running for several minutes after a power outage. ■ An EPS is an alternative power supply that provides electrical power in the event that a main source is lost.
Access Control	**Preventive and Detective:** The hardware and data in an IT system are also vulnerable to damage, destruction, disruption, or theft if an unauthorized person can physically access them. Large-scale IT systems should be protected by physical access controls. Such controls may include: 1. Limited access to computer rooms through employee ID badges or card keys 2. Video surveillance equipment 3. Logs of persons entering and exiting the computer rooms 4. Locked storage of backup data and offsite backup data
Business Continuity Planning (BCP)	**Preventive and Corrective:** Business continuity planning (BCP) is a proactive program for considering risks to the continuation of business and developing plans and procedures to reduce those risks. BCP focuses on key personnel, resources, and activities critical to business continuation. A strategy should be in place for backup and restoration of IT systems, to include redundant servers, redundant data storage, daily incremental backups, a backup of weekly changes, and offsite storage of daily and weekly backups.
Backup Systems for Hardware, Software, and Data	**Preventive and Corrective:** If IT systems are to continue without interruption, it is important to have backups for hardware, software, and data. ■ One approach to a backup processing system is called redundant servers—two or more computer networks or data servers that can run identical processes or maintain the same data. If one of the servers fails, a redundant server functions in its place. ■ In many IT systems, redundant data storage is accomplished by the use of redundant arrays of independent disks (RAIDs), often set up such that two or more disks are exact mirror images. If one disk drive fails, the mirror image on a second drive can serve in its place. ■ This backup protection is improved by off-site backup, an additional copy of the backup files stored in an offsite location. In some cases, on-site backups may be destroyed and the offsite backup files would be necessary. ■ The plan for the continuance of IT systems after a disaster is called a disaster recovery plan (DRP). Whereas BCP is proactive planning, DRP is a more reactive plan to restore business operations to normal after a disaster occurs.

Source: Adapted from Turner and Weickgenannt 2008.

Weill and Ross (2004) describe IT governance as "specifying the decision rights and accountability framework to encourage desirable behavior in the use of IT." Hall (2011) describes IT governance as "a broad concept relating to the decision rights and accountability for encouraging desirable behavior in the use of IT." For very small organizations, the outside auditor may be the first party to ask any questions about how IT governance supports the organization's strategies and objectives.

IT Governance for the SME

Those responsible for IT governance usually address large enterprises, including the examples in the preceding paragraph. The IT governance discussion typically assumes that the enterprise has a chief information officer (CIO), vice president (VP) of operations, VP of sales and marketing, and so on. Therefore, many of the corporate officers are members of a strategy council that is involved with strategy planning, program management, and project management, and is outward-facing from IT to the enterprise (Shimamoto 2011). Typical issues for the large enterprise include whether (1) the business units and IT operate in separate silos, and (2) IT function is centralized or decentralized. The environment can be very different for an SME.

Although statistics are limited, it is more likely that many SMEs have CEOs who play multiple roles in the enterprise. The CEO may assume the role of day-to-day marketing, operations, human resources, customer service, and logistics. The chief financial officer (CFO) may assume the role of the CIO, who manages the day-to-day IT operations of the enterprise. With major IT projects, the SME is required to outsource IT to external providers. The question is whether the CFO, the IT manager, and the outside contractor have the IT and business acumen for a larger set of questions. It is more common to have technically qualified individuals who lack business acumen. The issues for the SME are:

- Clear and open communication between the enterprise and IT operations
- Lack of understanding from SME owners of IT to perform alignment to business needs and opportunities
- Potentially a large portion of IT capabilities being outsourced and IT service providers servicing multiple customers

While the risk of a complete IT failure is lower with an external service provider, failure can be due to materially reduced benefits in the form of lower throughput, service delays, inaccurate processing, and so on.

The most fundamental problem for the SME is the enterprise operating on a day-to-day basis without IT expertise. *Without an understanding of the day-to-day operations, how can IT leadership provide the necessary preventive, detective, and corrective controls?* Without clear responsibilities and accountabilities within the IT organization, it is very possible an SME faces less-than-optimal use of its IT operations while simultaneously creating an insecure IT environment. Common complaints from IT in the SME environment include (Shimamoto 2011):

- "Nobody told us it was changing!"
- "We didn't receive any training for the new technology."

- ▪ "The data is organized differently from the old system."
- ▪ "The computations are performed differently from the old system."

The outside auditor should verify that IT responsibility and accountability is established for:

- ▪ **Availability:** It is available for use *when* needed.
- ▪ **Accessibility:** It is usable *where* needed.
- ▪ **Functionality:** It provides the functionality needed.
- ▪ **Accuracy:** Computations are correct.
- ▪ **Integrity:** The integrity of data/files is complete.
- ▪ **Usability:** It is easy to use and intuitive.
- ▪ **Responsiveness:** Actions are responsive within a reasonable time or expected time.
- ▪ **Security:** Data/files are secure (including addressing confidentiality and privacy).

Change management is a very significant consideration given the possibility of low communications between IT and the enterprise on a day-to-day basis. These changes sometimes mean that compromises in availability, accessibility, functionality, and security occur.

Frequently, strong personalities drive SMEs and, as such, their confidence pervades all communications ranging from employee relations to financial reporting. Competency and effective governance at all levels of the enterprise, including financial reporting, IT, the board, and the CEO, are essential for ongoing success. While the primary purpose of this chapter is to discuss financial statements, general controls and corporate and IT governance have very important roles in the ongoing ability of an enterprise to successfully conduct business.

IT will continue to expand its role in the SME and the respective business processes. The external auditor must come to grips with significant trends within his or her SME client base, and the major variables that drive risk factors and that ultimately affect audit reports. IT governance (or lack thereof) is a major contributor to the risk environment. In addition to IT governance, this chapter reviews internal control objectives, a fair presentation of the financial statements and COSO, and preventive, detective, and corrective controls within the context of general controls for the IT environment. IT governance is a particularly significant preventive control for the SME and rates as critical to the well-being of internal controls.

 ## THE "COSO PROCESS"—PUTTING IT ALL TOGETHER: FINANCIAL STATEMENTS, ASSERTIONS, RISKS, CONTROL OBJECTIVES, AND CONTROLS

This chapter introduces COSO in reference to general controls, with a more complete discussion in Chapters 9 and 10 as it relates to COBIT, financial reporting, and application controls.

In December 2006, the Auditing Standards Board issued SAS Nos. 104 through 111, including eight standards with new guidance for auditors assessing risks and controls in financial statement audits:

1. SAS No. 104, Amendment to Statement on Auditing Standards No. 1, Codification of Auditing
2. SAS No. 105, Amendment to Statement on Auditing Standards No. 95, Generally Accepted Auditing Standards
3. SAS No. 106, Audit Evidence
4. SAS No. 107, Audit Risk and Materiality in Conducting an Audit
5. SAS No. 108, Planning and Supervision
6. SAS No. 109, Understanding the Entity and Its Environment, and Assessing the Risks of Material Misstatement
7. SAS No. 110, Performing Audit Procedures in Response to Assessed Risks and Evaluating the Audit Evidence Obtained
8. SAS No. 111, Amendment to Statement on Auditing Standards No. 39, Audit Sampling

Given the IT environment described in Figure 2.1, the financial statements, the assertions, the risks, the control objectives, and the applications controls, how does it all fit together into an integrated framework? Moreover, what roles do general controls have in this evaluation process? In addition, given the release of SAS Nos. 104 through 111, what additional requirements should those responsible for IT meet within the COSO process?

Following the implementation of the eight audit standards in 2006, Charles Landes, AICPA Vice President–Professional Standards and Services, recommended an implementation of the COSO process as a best practice as auditors evaluate the internal controls related to the financial statements (Ramos 2009). To implement the COSO process, the auditor starts at the highest level of aggregation of the financial statements. (See Figure 2.2.) The auditor then proceeds through a sequence of analyses that become increasingly granular until he or she ultimately assesses the application control activities related to the financial statements (see Controls below Control Objectives in Figure 2.2).

It is important to note that the controls at the lowest level in Figure 2.2 are *application controls*. It is also important to note that the balance sheet accounts (the highest level of aggregation) are contained within the general ledger, and related financial recordkeeping. The general ledger and the respective accounts are a part of the *IT general controls* and reside on a server within the IT environment that supports the accounting department. For the SME, it's not unusual to have sales and marketing, operations, human resources, and other applications reside on the same server and thus the general controls have a larger role to fulfill beyond the financial reporting. Beyond an examination of an individual account (e.g., the revenue as in the case in the previous paragraph), Auditing Standards Board pronouncements in 2006 (Fogarty, Graham, and Schubert 2007) carry a larger set of implications and responsibilities for the financial auditor:

▪ Auditors must consider risk and determine a materiality level for the financial statements *taken as a whole.*

Financial Statements:

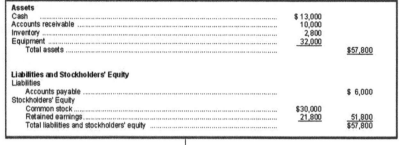

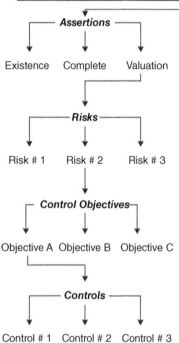

Assertions
Existence   Complete   Valuation

Risks
Risk # 1   Risk # 2   Risk # 3

Control Objectives
Objective A   Objective B   Objective C

Controls
Control # 1   Control # 2   Control # 3

- Auditors are required to obtain a sufficient understanding of the entity and its environment, including its assertions, risks, control objectives, and controls to assess the risk of material misstatement in the financial statements.
- Auditors must consider risk and determine a materiality level for the financial statements *taken as a whole.*
- Using that criteria, the auditor should concentrate on particular material assertions, e.g. accounts receivable.
- An examination of accounts receivable may determine that valuation is a significant issue.
- SMEs potentially have more risks in general and application controls than mature enterprises, e.g. the SME has a high percentage of aged receivables that are not systematically reviewed.
- The auditor must assess the effectiveness of the controls and ultimately whether they are working as intended as the auditor evaluates accounts receivables.

FIGURE 2.2   The COSO Process

Source: Adapted from Ramos 2009.

- The auditor must assess the effectiveness of the internal controls and ultimately whether they are working as intended as the auditor evaluates the financial statements.
- At the end of an audit, the auditor must evaluate whether the financial statements taken as a whole are free of material misstatements.
- Auditors are required to obtain a sufficient understanding of the entity and its environment, including its internal controls, to assess the risk of material misstatement in the financial statements.

The auditors must develop audit plans to reduce the audit risks to acceptably low levels. To rely on the effectiveness of company internal controls, the auditor must test both general and application controls, but only after assessing that the design is effective. *The auditors must understand whether a control design is effective before testing the controls.* If the design is effective, the auditor may rely on control tests and other evidence from prior audits when the audit evidence and related subject matter have not changed.

The *Vasa*: Governance and General Control Failures

The legacy of the *Vasa* illustrates the lack of general controls in a shipbuilding effort using new technology in the 1620s, almost 400 years ago. Governance, whether it is the king of Sweden or the CEO of an SME, whether in shipbuilding or state-of-the-art IT systems to achieve an aggressive organizational strategy, has similar characteristics. The purpose of this story is to illustrate general controls for the SME.

The *Vasa* legacy describes an entrepreneurial effort with seemingly skilled staff that created a disastrous outcome. The Swedish warship *Vasa*, built in the 1620s, characterizes a case study of strategy, requirements, and an architectural solution that created demands for new organizational capabilities similar to many SMEs. While IT and related technologies did not exist 400 years ago, this story is about the application of new shipbuilding technologies that were evolving rapidly. Financial constraints did not exist and the Swedish government underwrote the development of the newest shipbuilding technologies. A new shipbuilding technology could create an edge in geopolitical armed conflicts during that era. In 1625, the Swedish king, Gustavus Adolphus, ordered the construction of the *Vasa* at the Stockholm shipyards (*Vasa* Museum 2012). Henrik Hybertsson, an experienced and well-respected Dutch shipbuilder, was to lead the shipbuilding.

Henrik Hybertsson's experience was much needed as the *Vasa* was to be the most formidable warship in the world, armed with 64 cannon on two decks. Two gun decks were a significant departure from traditional shipbuilding in the 1620s—a configuration that significantly changed the weight distribution of a ship built in that era. On August 10, 1628, the *Vasa* sailed on her maiden voyage. Spectators filled the beaches around Stockholm. The maiden voyage was to be an act of propaganda for the ambitious King Gustavus Adolphus. The *Vasa* set sail and fired a salute. Shortly after the gun salute to commemorate her sailing, the ship began to heel over. The *Vasa* righted herself slightly—and then heeled over again. Water gushed in through the open gun ports and to everyone's disbelief, the *Vasa* suddenly sank!

What factors contributed to the disaster? King Gustavus Adolphus was anxious to acquire a ship with as many heavy cannon as possible. The king had personally approved the dimensions, the cannon configuration, and the timetable; he was anxious to have the *Vasa* in service as soon as possible. With heavy cannon on two decks and the capacity to carry a large number of armed troops, the *Vasa* and a fleet of comparable ships could alter the balance of power in Europe.

Hybertsson was a skilled shipbuilder with an excellent reputation and many previous successes. He developed the requirements with the king, and succumbed to the demands of the king despite the fact that current ship technology had not yet attempted what the king was requesting. Most analysts now believe the ship was disproportionately narrow for a second tier of heavy cannon. Hybertsson extended the standards typically used for smaller warships of that day but did not factor the weight distribution appropriately. His unexpected death a year prior to *Vasa*'s completion complicated the final stage of product delivery.

Admiral Klas Fleming could have stopped the shipbuilding for further engineering review after the *Vasa* failed a stability test just prior to the maiden voyage. Thirty men ran back and forth across the *Vasa*'s deck just prior to sailing. The men had to stop after three runs, well before the test was complete; otherwise, the ship would have capsized. Fleming, one of the most influential men in the navy, monitored the tests. He acquiesced to the king's pressure to have the *Vasa* sail as soon as possible and agreed to let her sail her maiden voyage.

Captain Söfring Hansson sailed a new ship with new shipbuilding technology with no precautions (open gun ports) or a backup plan. The *Vasa* sank when water gushed in through the lower gun ports after the ship leaned heavily to one side after the cannon fired a salute in the harbor. After the *Vasa*, many successful ships included two, three, and even four gun decks. What are the lessons learned?

The Vasa Was an Architectural Failure

Even with access to government resources and some of the best shipbuilders of the day, the *Vasa* was an architectural failure.

- One of the most successful project leaders built the *Vasa*, but past successes do not assure future success when deploying new technology.
- Senior management (the king) signed off on the final requirements at key decision points in the project, but true alignment did not exist between risk and value, as the shipbuilder could not deliver the requirements.
- The king ignored risk management and should not have, as signs during the ship-building process would have foretold the fate of the *Vasa*.
- The *Vasa* was an entirely new concept, using an extension of existing technology. The new concept did not use an effective weight distribution, creating a fundamental design flaw.
- The project leader appeared unwilling to confront the king in his quest for new technology and an aggressive timetable to complete the new design that leapfrogged earlier shipbuilding technology.

Vasa Governance Was a Failure

The belief systems espoused by King Gustavus Adolphus communicated urgency, large numbers of cannon, and a willingness to do whatever is necessary to meet the objectives. The king's boundaries were apparently undefined and unlimited provided the deadline remained. The king was unwilling to share the responsibility of seeking the best solution and signed off on the design, but ultimately had no idea what he was signing. He neither had a grasp of the risks and threats nor did he or could he develop responses and action plans to proactively deal with high-level issues, including the replacement of the original shipbuilder/designer.

General Controls Were Weak or Nonexistent

The *Vasa* legacy and its failure reach well beyond a singular preventive, detective, or corrective control. The *Vasa* legacy includes one preventive control: 30 men ran back and forth across the deck. Moreover, when the ship began to lean heavily, the captain ordered those men to cease their activities. The captain chose to ignore the warning when the ship leaned to one side. What other observations are available from *Vasa's* general controls?

The scope of preventive controls reaches into the competency of personnel and governance. The qualifications of the personnel and the governance of the *Vasa* project were flawed at several levels. Although it appears the king hired the most competent shipbuilder available, a less-than-competent designer replaced the shipbuilder. Auditors frequently overlook governance as a critical part of designing effective general controls.

A top-down risk assessment did not occur or, if it did, the king ignored it. An effective risk assessment evaluates the linkage between functions. The *Vasa* had to operate upright (a normal operating mode) while simultaneously shooting a cannon. Ultimately, the *Vasa* could not operate in an upright fashion while shooting its cannon.

It appears that the king and his lead designer also ignored other controls, including detective and corrective controls. The king chose not to establish an advisory panel around him that would provide him better insight into shipbuilding and mixing new technologies of the day. In today's environment, that advisory panel would be the board of directors and it would be labeled *corporate governance* and *IT governance* (which is part of corporate governance).

 SUMMARY

As part of the final review in an IT audit, one or more reviewers (the team leader, audit manager, partner, or some combination) will assess the general controls in the context of risks and the related control objectives (Singleton 2013). Particularly in the context of financial reporting, the reviewer(s) will want to examine the relevant IT general and application controls for financial reporting to gain a proper understanding of applications, transactions, and infrastructure that affect the financials. Risk remains a significant driver as to the scope and nature of the IT audit and the nature of documentation. A publicly traded company, a company with a significant reliance on IT, or a company with significant weaknesses in general controls may be considered a higher-risk environment and, as such, all aspects of the audit that are relevant to those risks must be addressed accordingly. As the risk increases or as the audit environment grows in complexity, more reviews may be appropriate and the reviewer credentials may have to be elevated (e.g., subject matter expert) to match the circumstances of the audit.

An IT audit should have identified existing general and application controls and provided an assessment of the design effectiveness. The audit work papers should include documented IT process maps and existing controls. Tests to evaluate controls and an assessment of operating effectiveness are integral to the design process itself. The work papers support the assessments through identified control deficiencies and analysis of whether the deficiency elevates to a significant or material weakness. Any follow-up on the control deficiencies with management through subsequent periods is integral to the work papers and their design. Deficiencies remediated during the audit year and additional testing procedures require documentation in the work papers. The audit work papers should be prepared in sufficient detail to provide a clear understanding of nature, timing, extent, and results of procedures performed, evidence obtained, and conclusions reached.

CHAPTER THREE

3

Application-Level Security

A PPLICATION-LEVEL SECURITY IS A CRITICAL component in ensuring the integrity of data within a financial application, the supporting financial cycles, and associated sub-processes. Application-level security can be defined as the collection of preventive and detective controls that support the confidentiality, integrity, and availability of data. Within small and mid-sized organizations, management must ensure the protection of the data within the accounting information system. This is imperative in order for internal and external users to rely on the financial information. The protection of the information is achieved by ensuring various security controls are designed into the system, either inherently or via configured attributes; security is also achieved through the manual intervention of management in reviewing information within the system to make intelligent security decisions.

 KEY CONSIDERATIONS

There are several key considerations for application-level security:

- **Administrator ID and passwords:** This is the *super-user* account that has full access to the system and the full functionality of the system. While this access is typically reserved for information technology (IT) personnel, some end users in the finance or accounting organization are given this type of access. Management must secure and restrict who has the keys to the kingdom. In addition, the passwords for administrator accounts should be more robust than typical end-user accounts, resulting in longer, more complex passwords that are changed more frequently.

▪ **End-user IDs and passwords:** This is the setup and configuration of user IDs and password settings for end users. This is where management should have a common naming convention for the issuance of user IDs, and the passwords should meet appropriate complexity requirements and other password configuration settings to ensure that access to the account is not compromised. This is synonymous with having a key to the front door of the application and the key has to be protected (i.e., protect the password).

▪ **Access rights:** Access is assigned to end users based on the assignment of roles, menus, or tasks. This is synonymous with opening the front door, but once the user is in, the user is restricted to only those rooms that can be visited according to the access rights assigned. Management needs to ensure that the access rights assigned are commensurate with the user's job responsibilities and do not violate segregation-of-duties concepts.

▪ **User management:** This includes the management of how new users get access to the system, how existing users have access modified in the system (e.g., change in job roles, transfer), and how users are removed/disabled from the system (e.g., termination). Management needs to ensure robust user management practices are implemented so that security remains a defensible fortress.

▪ **Security logs and audit trails:** This includes the capture of security information that can be reviewed by management (e.g., failed login attempts). Some systems will enable management to capture data on security events that can be reviewed either in real time or at a later date for forensics purposes.

These key considerations can be addressed by examining the risk exposures within application-level security. Application-level security contains several risk exposures. These include:

▪ **Initial security setup:** Are system users assigned user IDs that align with a naming convention? Are employees provided with an initial password to access the system? Are employees required to change their initial password? Do management and appropriate data owners sign off on and authorize the access rights given to a user during initial setup? Are the access rights assigned specific to the user or is it simply a "give access like Jane has" assignment?

▪ **Security role design:** Are the security roles defined in a manner that is consistent with segregation of duties? Does the naming convention of roles align with the actual tasks assigned to that role? Does management have a process in place for the addition and modification of security roles and the respective design of the security role? Does management perform a periodic review of the security role design to ensure that unauthorized changes to the design have not occurred?

▪ **Password configuration:** Are passwords required? Do passwords have to consist of a combination of alphabetic, numeric, and special characters with at least one uppercase character and one lowercase character? Are passwords required to be a certain length? Can passwords be repeated or is password history enforced? Do passwords have to be changed within a certain interval? How many failed login attempts are allowed? Are administrator password configuration requirements more stringent than end-user password configuration requirements?

- **Segregation of duties:** Are users assigned access rights based on their job responsibilities? Are access rights within and across systems analyzed to determine if segregation-of-duties conflicts exist? What prevents incompatible duties from being assigned to a user? How does management minimize the risk if segregation of duties cannot be enforced?

- **Access reviews:** Does management review the access rights assigned to individuals to ensure that appropriate access is granted? How often are the access reviews performed? Does management accept the risk of segregation of duties conflicts and review reports to ensure that inappropriate activity has not occurred with the conflicted access?

- **Accumulation of access rights:** Are employees' access rights revoked and/or reviewed when job responsibilities change? Are access rights from previous roles removed or disabled if the employee no longer needs that functionality in the new job role? How does management ensure that access rights assigned to users across disparate systems do not create an accumulation-of-access-rights concern?

- **Removal of access rights:** Are access rights removed or disabled when an employee is terminated? Is the removal or disablement done in a timely manner? Are logs reviewed to determine if terminated individuals have inappropriately accessed the system after the termination date? Are logs reviewed to determine if other individuals have used terminated individuals' login credentials after the termination date?

- **Reports:** Does management review security logs, audit trails, and reports to determine if inappropriate or unauthorized activity has occurred? Is activity monitoring turned on in the system, or does management not have reports available?

- **Human error:** Do employees know how to protect the security of the system? Do employees write down passwords? Do employees use screensavers or lock their computer screen when leaving their computer area? Are employees adequately trained in security awareness? Do employees share passwords?

These risk exposures can be further analyzed to illustrate what management could do to prevent, detect, or minimize the risk associated with the risk exposure. For any risk within an organization, management has to decide if the cost associated with preventing, detecting, or minimizing the risk is in line with the financial wherewithal of the organization or the risk is within its risk tolerance levels. Management needs to remember that, with application-level security, adequate financial and personnel resources should be dedicated to the protection of the financial information. Financial information that cannot be secured runs the risk of being unusable to internal or external users without costly auditing and supporting evidence to validate that the data has integrity/reliability. Some organizations could have spent less money implementing preventive or detective security controls instead of retroactively evidencing the integrity of the financial data.

INITIAL SECURITY SETUP

When an organization first sets up its financial system, initial security configuration settings are established. These settings can impact how the data is processed within the system on a go-forward basis. One of the initial security configuration settings is how user IDs and passwords are set up in the system.

Users are assigned a unique user ID and password. The user ID should follow a standard naming convention such as last_name_first_initial (e.g., "smithj"). The standard naming convention will help management keep track of who has an account and can help facilitate management reviews and revocation of access.

When the users are set up, management will have the option to indicate if the user will be forced to comply with the password policy or if alternative password configuration settings are needed.

Figures 3.1 and 3.2 illustrate the requirement to have a user ID and password to access the Microsoft Great Plains Dynamics (GPD) system.

Figure 3.3 shows the password setup screen for the system administrator (SA) for QB where users granted these privileges would be configured with ID and password. Note that the password has to be confirmed by reentering it. An important application control configuration setting is the "enforce password policy" option that enforces password expiration and required change of the initial password immediately after the first login. Figure 3.4 shows the setup for a user in QB that requires a password.

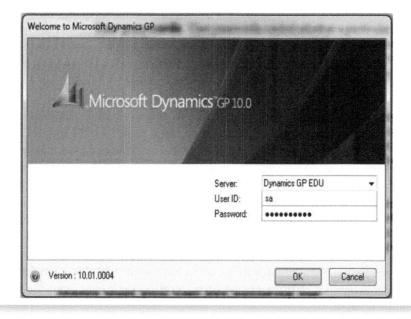

FIGURE 3.1   Login Screen for GPD

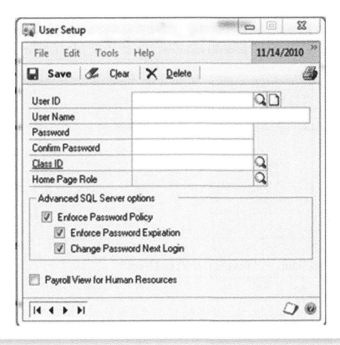

FIGURE 3.2   User Setup for GPD

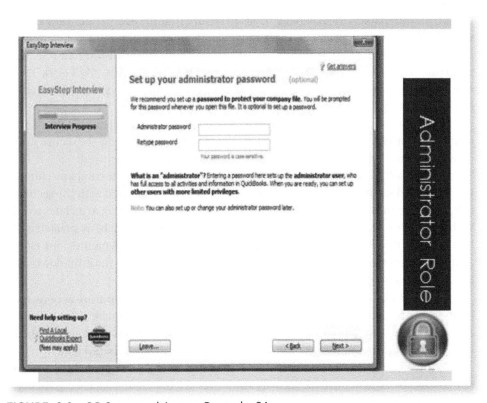

FIGURE 3.3   QB Setup and Access Control—SA

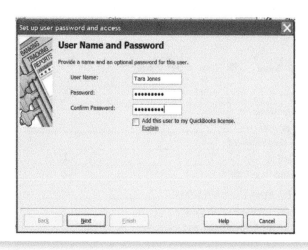

FIGURE 3.4 QB Setup and Access Control—User

 SECURITY ROLE DESIGN

The design of the security role is a critical component of ensuring a strong security environment. When companies use preconfigured roles that come with a system or build customized roles, the company needs to ensure that the access rights associated with that role are appropriate for the company. In addition, the naming convention of the role needs to be descriptive to reflect the access rights given within that role. It is unfortunately common that some companies give a generic title (e.g., "A/R clerk") to a role, but the role in fact has privileges beyond what is typically expected of an A/R clerk (e.g., A/P posting).

Companies should put in place a robust process to protect the creation and modification of security roles. On an annual basis, a company should review the security role design to ensure that no unauthorized changes to the role have occurred.

In Microsoft Dynamics, security roles can be set up whereby the company can use the predefined security role or add/remove security tasks associated with the security role, as shown in Figure 3.5. Checking a task, as shown in Figure 3.6, associates a task with a security role. If the task is unchecked, then the task would not be associated with that security role. To access the security role setup in Microsoft Dynamics, one clicks Administration>Security Role Setup and chooses the role ID from the drop-down list. The system shows the tasks assigned to a role.

Microsoft Dynamics allows A/R clerks to process only certain transactions and limits access to data that is not related to their job. A/R clerks are unable to input transactions that they are not authorized to perform. This security control prevents unauthorized modification as well as facilitates segregation of duties in the system.

Within QuickBooks, users are assigned roles, but the roles are predefined and are not changeable. Having default security roles that are not changeable is a good control; however, it reduces the ability for a company to specifically design its own optimal access roles.

FIGURE 3.5 GPD Security Role Setup

Source: Brunsdon, Romney, and Steinbart. 2009. This image was taken using the dataset provided from this book. Note that the screenshot says "S&S Incorporated," which is the dataset of these authors.

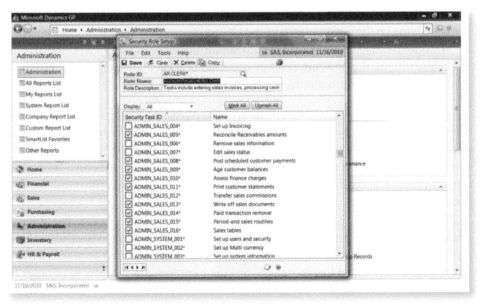

FIGURE 3.6 GPD Security Role Setup—Task Selection

Source: Brunsdon, Romney, and Steinbart. 2009. This image was taken using the dataset provided from this book. Note that the screenshot says "S&S Incorporated," which is the dataset of these authors.

PASSWORD CONFIGURATION

Password configurations represent the keys to the front door of a computer system. Unfortunately, end users sometimes get password fatigue and become lazy in the creation and protection of passwords. Passwords need to be kept secure and be of a certain caliber to prevent unauthorized access to the system.

In general, passwords should have the following characteristics:

- **Alphanumeric/special characters:** Passwords should require at least one uppercase alphabetic character, one lowercase alphabetic character, one numeric character, and one special character.
- **Password length:** Passwords should be at least eight characters in length. It is common for administrator passwords to be longer.
- **Password change intervals:** Passwords should generally be changed every 30, 60, or 90 days, depending on the sensitivity of the data that the password grants access to. It is common for administrator passwords to change more frequently and, in some organizations, tokens are used where passwords change every 60 seconds to prevent unauthorized access.
- **Password history and reuse:** A password history should be maintained and users should be prevented from repeating previous passwords. Some organizations use 5, 10, or higher history settings to prevent the reuse of a password. In addition to password history, organizations should limit how often passwords can be changed so an end user does not simply reset the password x times to get back to his or her original password (usually performed in a matter of minutes).
- **Failed login attempts:** Systems should be configured so that the account is locked after a certain number of failed login attempts. Typically, password failures should be set to a minimum of three, but the limit could be higher or lower depending on the sensitivity of the data being accessed. When an account reaches the maximum login tries, the account should either be locked for a period of time before automatically being reset or released, or locked for manual intervention by the system administrator.

Figure 3.7 demonstrates configuration of the password settings in GPD. In order to change the user password, which is especially important if there have been signs of a breach in security, click on User Preferences, which will open the "User Preferences" window. Click on Passwords to open a new window, "User Password Setup," where the company must first confirm the old password before entering and confirming the new password.

Figure 3.8 shows three activities within GPD that can be tracked: failed login attempts, successful login attempts, and successful logout attempts. Also, the tracking can be set to follow a specific user or many users, and elections can be made to track specific databases. Failed login attempts are the most important to track, in order to determine if an unauthorized person has tried to gain access to the system. Tracking the successful logins is also of importance. This allows the administrator to determine if only authorized users actually gain access to the system and detect any persons who should no longer have access capabilities.

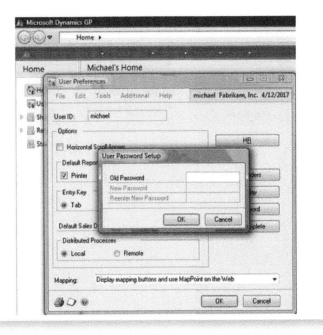

FIGURE 3.7 GPD Password Settings Configuration

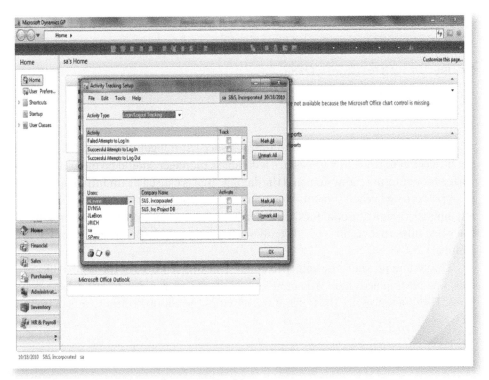

FIGURE 3.8 GPD Password Activity Tracking

Source: Brunsdon, Romney, and Steinbart. 2009. This image was taken using the dataset provided from this book. Note that the screenshot says "S&S Incorporated," which is the dataset of these authors.

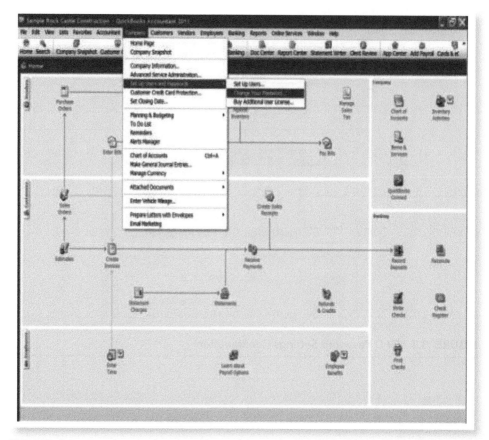

FIGURE 3.9   QB Password—Menu

Source: Intuit, Rock Castle data file.

Although GPD offers the ability to track successful logout attempts, they would not be as vital to track as logins since a database manager should be more concerned with who is entering the system and the damage that is caused by unauthorized access, as opposed to whether someone logs out. Additionally, tracking login and logout attempts requires additional hard drive space, so for efficiency purposes it is best not to track activities that do not provide truly useful information (Brunsden, Romney, and Steinbart 2009).

The system provides the ability to enable tracking features of the access, file, process, and posting activities. All activities include the user and database selection features. The differences are the types of subactivities the administrator wants to track.

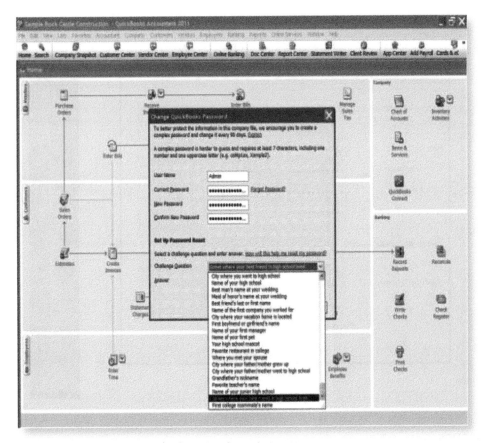

FIGURE 3.10   QB Password—Security Questions

Source: Intuit, Rock Castle.

Figures 3.9, 3.10, and 3.11 outline the QuickBooks (QB) security process. A user's password can be changed by going to Company>Setup Users and Password>Change Your Password. When the user changes the password, the old password has to be entered before the new password can be entered. In addition, the new password has to be confirmed to continue. Users also have the ability to set up a security-challenge question that further protects the account. Users have various security questions that could be chosen to answer.

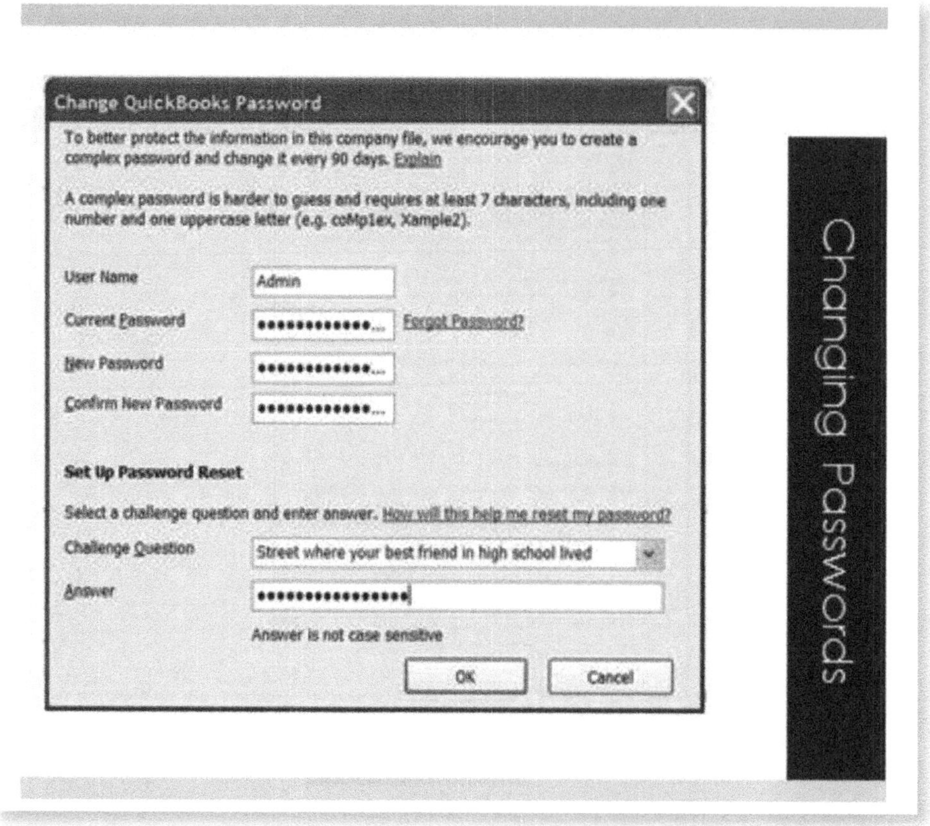

FIGURE 3.11   QB Password—Changes

SEGREGATION OF DUTIES

Segregation of duties (SOD) is one of the most critical controls within a system. Unfortunately, this area is where small and mid-sized companies typically struggle due to a lack of resources. Within the system, each user ID is assigned a role or collection of roles in order to perform tasks within the system. Depending on the system, the user ID may be relegated to a single role or may have the ability to be assigned multiple roles. Each role shall be defined such that the segregation of duties is preserved and, accordingly, each role shall be input into the system. Each role shall be defined in the system so that when an employee signs into the system, her defined role has already been assigned and the system will only allow this employee access to the documents suitable for that role. Access to individual documents shall also be restricted to one person at a time, so that if a second person wished to open the document she would only be able to access a read-only version of the file. The reason that the segregation of duties is so important is that it hinders theft and fraud within an organization. For example, if someone has access to the inventory item and can also record transactions related to that time, then he can steal it and falsify the records to show a sale, whereas a thief wouldn't be able to cover up his theft if he couldn't record the transaction needed to account for the drop in inventory. Companies need to ensure that only authorized personnel have access to the information they need in the system.

Security of an application system takes different forms:

- Administrator account setup with a password that meets certain criteria.
- Each user needs to be set up in the system. The individual user will be assigned roles and tasks associated with the rights and responsibilities that that person will need to do his or her job. Also, each individual needs to have a password set up and it needs to meet certain criteria.

If we look ahead, many companies are challenged with too few people to do too many jobs. The result is typically poor or inadequate security and the possibility that financial data is at risk for errors or inaccuracies. Preventive controls in the system such as strong passwords, good security roles design, careful user-role assignment to ensure appropriate SOD, or good detective controls for unavoidable SOD conflicts can mitigate the security risks. The detective controls may be in the form of management reviewing reports to determine if something bad has happened. For example, in the general ledger, what happens if someone has access to the general ledger and she needs that for her job role? Management can typically review who has posted entries into the general ledger and trace back to source data.

 ## PERSONNEL, ROLES, AND TASKS

Personnel, roles, and tasks can be divided into general authorization and specific authorization. For general authorization management can authorize employees or the system to handle routine transactions. However, for specific authorization, certain activities or certain transactions require management to authorize that transaction. How this is often done is that thresholds are set within the system; purchases, for example, can have levels set so that if they are small purchases an employee can approve the transaction, but if they go over a preset amount, then the transactions will not go through without specific authorization from a manager.

The recording roles are where source documents are created and the journals are maintained, but they cannot specifically authorize the transactions they are dealing with, nor will they have access to the assets within the transactions that they are recording. The ability to record transactions should be restricted to authorized personnel.

The custody roles are where the person has physical access to the asset. For example, the person counts and stores the inventory. Segregation in this case is achieved not only by preventing this person access to the accounts controlling these calculations, but also by not having people in the other two roles. For the accounting information system (AIS) this is also the person who receives the checks or money from the client but would not be able to apply them to the client's accounts (Romney and Steinbart 2009).

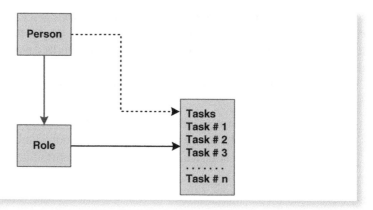

FIGURE 3.12 Personnel, Roles, and Tasks

Figure 3.12 illustrates the desired (bold, solid lines) and potentially problematic relationships between personnel, software-designed roles, and tasks associated with roles. Access to various system tasks is assigned to roles, which can be either generic default roles defined by the software vendor or custom roles designed by the system administrator. By selecting tasks that are consistent with an overall segregation of duties, the system administrator can help to ensure that, when these roles are assigned to specific individuals, a reasonable level of internal control is supported and maintained.

Problems may arise when the system allows someone to redefine the scope of a role by adding additional tasks to it, or to assign additional task rights directly to a specific user.

The IT auditor should check to ensure that roles are properly designed (as previously discussed) to ensure that segregation of duties is not inappropriately designed into the system's roles. However, most SOD conflicts arise when user IDs are associated with multiple roles. The roles on a stand-alone basis provide adequate segregation of duties; however, the collection of multiple roles may present SOD conflicts. Management should review reports of access given to users to ensure that the access associated with the roles assigned to the users does not cause a segregation-of-duties conflict. If a conflict exists, the auditor needs to ensure that management has alternative controls in place to monitor the user's activities to ensure that inappropriate activities have not occurred.

As a specific instance of potentially incompatible duties, consider the list of functions traditionally associated with some part of the accounts receivable (A/R) process. Figure 3.13 sets these out in roughly chronological order: A new customer is entered into the system; the credit department determines suitability and appropriate limits; pricing information enters the system; sometimes this pricing information is modified by the terms of a special promotion; order information is entered into the system (frequently by an accounting clerk, who receives this data from someone in the sales department); invoices are generated (automatically in many cases), reviewed, and dispatched to customers; information concerning returned goods must be used to adjust customer account balances; and transactions are posted to customer accounts (with a control posting to the general ledger).

X marks indicate incompatible duties that should ideally be assigned to different personnel. X* marks indicate tasks that might be assigned to the same person, given

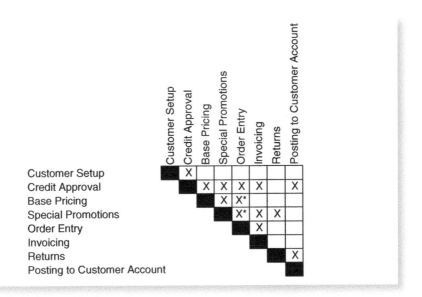

FIGURE 3.13 Tasks, Roles, and Incompatible Duties—Accounts Receivable

controls such as tolerance levels or preapproved guidelines. An empty cell indicates the absence of a strong incompatibility. Here is the reasoning behind our marks:

- Ideally, credit approval serves as an independent check on the validity of a customer's assertion regarding its promise to provide valuable consideration entity assets obtained via sales transactions. Combining setup and credit approval violates the independence and provides the risk exposure that fraudulent or financially suspect entities will gain undesirable access to the company's goods and/or services.

- Credit approval is so potent a trigger to the departure of entity assets that very few other A/R functions are truly compatible with it. The potential abuse of authority in the case where one individual had responsibility for both credit status and sales terms justifies the common practice of maintaining a separate credit department (or function) within an organization. The clerical duties of processing customer returns relate to sales processes that originated and were processed independently, and so might be a function that, in a very small enterprise, could be assigned to a credit specialist without creating a definable risk exposure.

- Pricing policy affects the sales–A/R cycle right from its start, and the potential for manipulation of pricing terms and sales initiation suggests the desirability of maintaining these functions independently. In the case where a company follows a standard policy of marking up merchandise a fixed percentage over cost, the IT auditor should control who has access to override company policy within the system.

- It would be desirable to isolate order entry from invoice processing in order to provide independent review of sales terms for conformity with company policies. The IT auditor should verify which tasks provide access to this functionality to ensure that the functionality is appropriately restricted to authorized personnel.

- Returns and posting to accounts involve the classic conflict of physical custody and recordkeeping, the two inherently incompatible roles.

1 Credit Approval

2 Customer Setup

2 Base pricing

3 Special Promotions

3 Posting to customer account

4 Order entry

5 Invoicing

6 Returns

FIGURE 3.14 Role Design in an Ideal System—AR

Given this, an ideal configuration of responsibilities might include half a dozen individuals, as illustrated in Figure 3.14. The paired numbers (2 and 3) indicate functions that one individual might perform, while the single numbers (1, 4–6) indicate functions that ideally should be performed by different individuals. Needless to say, a very significant percentage of SMEs would find this staffing requirement impractical or prohibitive. Thus, IT controls that compensate for inherent SOD exposures are an important aspect of secure and reliable processing of financial information.

Even with the best SOD setup, it is difficult for management to prevent collusion. Frauds have occurred in many organizations where appropriate segregation of duties was set up within the system, but two or more users colluded to perform actions within the system to bypass controls.

The IT auditor should understand the organization and the number of employees available to perform duties. In some instances, cross-functional support and backups between personnel may be acceptable without creating additional SOD risks; however, when SOD conflicts are created due to the lack of personnel, then management needs to implement alternative detective controls to minimize the risks. The detective controls typically include a review of reports to determine what transactions have occurred to ensure unauthorized activity has not taken place.

With Microsoft Dynamics, once a user has been created within the system, management would open the User Security Setup window by clicking on Microsoft Dynamics Button >Tools> Setup> System> User Security Setup. The ideal situation for this is that each employee has only one role. For smaller companies this may not be possible. In that case you want to assign each employee to one type of role.

Figure 3.15 shows the GPD window accessed in order to set up user security.

FIGURE 3.15 GPD User Security Setup

Within QuickBooks, a user is assigned specific roles during various screens of the setup process. The user can be granted no access, limited access, or full access to the functionality/process. When management assigns these accesses, it needs to ensure that segregation of duties is maintained. If full access is granted to a specific area, a pop-up box may ask if this is correct before proceeding. This is an important application control to ensure that full access is appropriate. If a user tries to access functionality that has not specifically been granted, then a pop-up box typically warns the user that the access has not been granted.

When initially setting up a user in QB, the system administrator needs to make decisions regarding the scope of access to be provided. Figure 3.16 illustrates how the user can be assigned to some areas of QB, all areas, or provided the role of external accountant, with the limitations on this last role noted in Figure 3.16.

Figure 3.17 illustrates a soft control that prompts the system administrator for confirmation when assigning sensitive access such as the external accountant role.

If the user was set up for selective access, the system administrator would have gone through additional screens to identify specific types of access within various modules, as, for example, illustrated in the case of Sales and A/R (Figure 3.18) or Checking and Credit Cards (Figure 3.19).

Figure 3.20 illustrates attempted access to unauthorized functions prevented by a hard control.

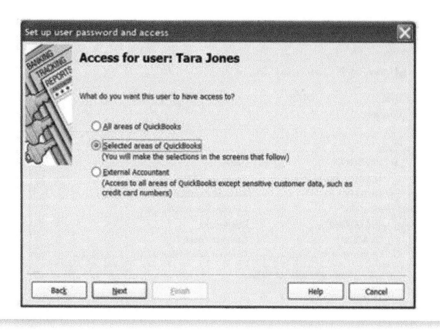

FIGURE 3.16 QB User Security Setup

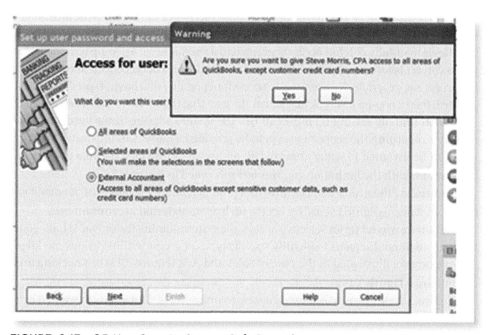

FIGURE 3.17 QB User Security Setup—Soft Control

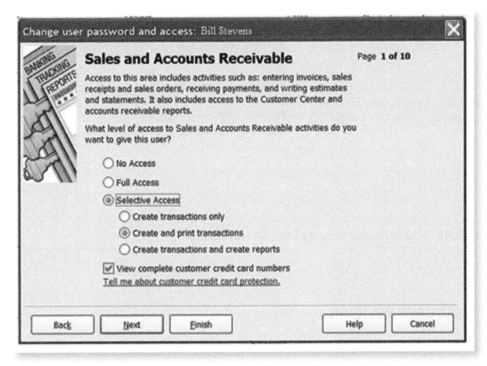

FIGURE 3.18   QB User Security Setup—Sales and A/R Access

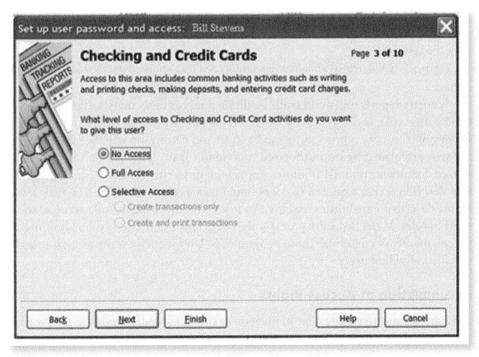

FIGURE 3.19   QB User Security Setup—Checking and Credit Cards

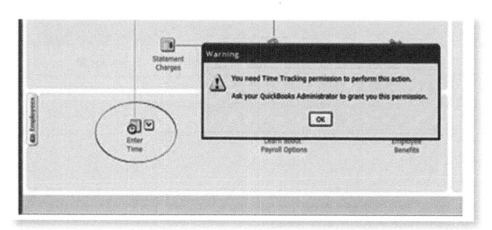

FIGURE 3.20 QB User Security Setup—Hard Control

 ACCESS REVIEWS

On a periodic basis, management should verify the access of the users within the system. Ideally, access was initially designed and issued to users while maintaining segregation of duties. However, it is not uncommon for good processes to inadvertently not be followed, which could result in inappropriate access. In addition, new, transferred, or terminated users may have affected the users within the system. For example, access reviews are a great way to determine if all terminated users have been properly removed from the system.

Figure 3.21 illustrates an access review screen that shows a user's assigned access rights.

Security reports and audit trails facilitate analysis of security setups in the system by user, role, task, or activity. Such a report allows management to review the history of transaction processing (audit trail) and determine whether the processing was performed by an authorized individual. It is also possible to tie back to source documentation. GPD allows management to run various security reports that describe access assigned to users, and tasks assigned to roles. The task setup report describes capabilities assigned to tasks and the security role setup assigns tasks to roles. Many tasks are preassigned to specific roles. The system administrator can modify or customize these assignments. User security setup assigns roles to specific individual users.

Accumulation of Access Rights

Companies want to ensure that management has given individuals the access they need to do their jobs; however, the access should not accumulate to create segregation-of-duties conflicts. However, small and mid-sized organizations may not be able to

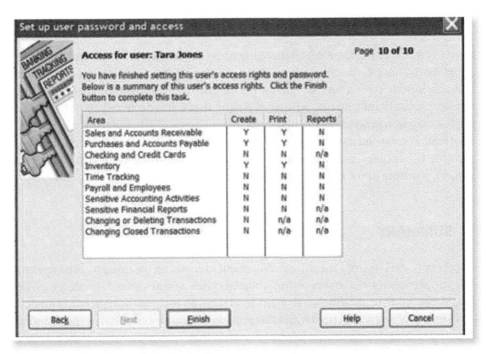

FIGURE 3.21 QB User Security Review

avoid certain SOD conflicts. Given this, management should ensure that good detective controls are in place if someone has to wear multiple hats and have multiple accesses in the system that would traditionally be considered SOD conflicts. In QB and GPD, there are different reports in the various cycles so management can see what activities have happened and can determine if the conflicted access was inappropriately taken advantage of.

Removal of Access Rights

When a user no longer needs access due to changing roles within the organization, or termination, retirement, or death, management needs to permanently disable or remove the access right for that user ID. This enables the account to go into an inactive status, if disabled, or to be removed entirely. Depending on the application, removal of a user ID could disrupt transactions associated with that ID, so some organizations have the practice of disabling the ID until the historical transactions can be assessed.

Many times, organizations rely on either HR or department managers to notify IT when a user needs to be removed from the system. However, this communication does not always occur in a timely manner. Ultimately, a user account should be removed immediately or within a short period of time after the notification date depending on the severity of the removal (hostile termination) or the access level that the terminated user had (super-user).

HUMAN ERROR

Human error is one of the most challenging areas in security. When security breaches occur, many times it is due not to poor design of the security within the system but rather to simple human error. Users may inadvertently give out login information and/or other sensitive security information without realizing that it has occurred. Social engineering is a common practice where nefarious individuals will attempt to extract security information from end users by posing as legitimate users that need access to address a problem. Other times, users may write down security information in a visible location, thereby resulting in someone being able to log in as that user.

 ## SUMMARY

Application-level security is a critical component in ensuring the integrity of data within a financial application, the supporting financial cycles, and associated subprocesses. Key considerations in evaluating application-level security include the review and analysis of permissions and access rights, and this process necessarily entails that the IT auditor obtain a wide understanding of job design within the organization. Given the relatively limited resources available to most SMEs, achieving appropriate segregation of duties—or compensating for its absence—remains a key challenge.

The concepts shared in this chapter highlight the importance of logical security within the financial application. Without robust application-level security and segregation of duties, the financial application is at risk of endangering the integrity of its confidential information.

CHAPTER FOUR

General Ledger and the IT Audit

THE *CHART OF ACCOUNTS* IS a list of all *general ledger* accounts an entity uses for financial reporting in connection with compliance, regulatory, and bank loan requirements and management reporting for internal management and control.

The structure of the chart allows transaction data classification, coding, and entry into the proper accounts. The chart of accounts structure is a critical dimension of financial reporting within the general ledger system (see Table 4.1) because it directly affects the preparation of financial statements and reports. The chart of accounts and the general ledger system:

- Are at the heart of the system; all financial modules and interfaces flow into them.
- Define ease of use, flexibility, and competency of execution of financial and management reporting.
- Provide a foundation for expansion as well as storage of current and historical information.
- Provide the basis for compliance and bank reporting, including footnote disclosure.
- Provide the basis of granularity or adequate account detail to enable an organization to manage its operations effectively.

This chapter reviews the concepts associated with the chart of accounts and IT audit issues for SME environments and then identifies those characteristics associated with QuickBooks (QB) (see Figures 4.2 through 4.5) and Microsoft Dynamics implementations for SMEs.

THE GENERAL LEDGER: A CLEARINGHOUSE OF FINANCIAL INFORMATION

The general ledger system (see Figure 4.1) is a clearinghouse that collects financial information from other subsystems such as payroll, billing, and accounts receivable. Applications outside the general ledger record events in separate subsystems using special journals and subsidiary accounts. Summaries of these transactions flow into the general ledger and become sources of input for the management reporting system and financial reporting system. The bulk of what flows into the general ledger system comes from the transaction processing subsystems. Also, note that information from the financial reporting system and management reporting system flows back into the general ledger system.

Table 4.1 shows the chart of accounts for Luther Sound Exploration Inc. (LSE), a company that produces imaging equipment used in the extractive industries. Each account code is four digits long. Typical of most charts of accounts, the LSE uses the first 2999 account numbers for the balance sheet, with the remainder (3000 through 9999)

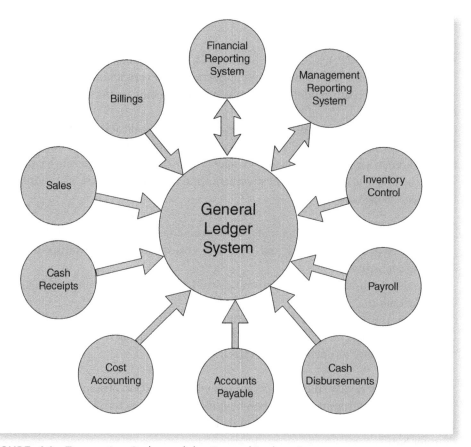

FIGURE 4.1 Transaction Cycles and the General Ledger System

TABLE 4.1   Chart of Accounts for Luther Sound Exploration, Inc.

Account Code	Account Name	Account Code	Account Name
	Current Assets		**Equity Accounts**
1010	Checking Account	4000	Common Stock
1040	Savings Account	4100	Retained Earnings
1050	Petty Cash		**Revenues**
1200	Accounts Receivable	5010	Cash Sales
1260	Allowance for Doubtful Accounts	5020	Credit Sales
1300	Notes Receivable	5100	Sales Returns & Allowances
1360	Allowance for Notes Receivable		
1500	Inventory—Raw Materials	5110	Sales Discounts
1520	Inventory—Work in Progress	5200	Interest Revenue
1550	Inventory—Finished Goods	5300	Miscellaneous Revenue
1600	Supplies		**Expenses**
1700	Prepaid Rent	6000	Cost of Goods Sold
1800	Prepaid Insurance	6110	Wages Expense
	Noncurrent Assets	6120	Commissions Expense
2000	Land	6130	Payroll Tax Expense
2100	Buildings	6200	Rent Expense
2150	Accumulated Depreciation—Buildings	6300	Travel Expense
		6400	Supplies Expense
2300	Equipment	6500	Bad Debt Expense
2350	Accumulated Depreciation—Equipment	7010	Depreciation Expense—Buildings
2400	Furniture & Fixtures	7020	Depreciation Expense—Equipment
2450	Accumulated Depreciation—Furniture & Fixtures		
		7030	Fixtures
2500	Other Assets	7100	Income Tax Expense
	Liabilities		**Summary Accounts**
3000	Accounts Payable	9100	Income Summary
3100	Wages Payable		
3210	Employee Income Tax Payable		
3220	FICA Tax Payable		
3230	Federal Unemployment Tax Payable		
3240	State Unemployment Tax Payable		
3300	Accrued Interest Payable		
3600	Other Liabilities		

of the code numbers utilized for the income statement and summary accounts. Accounts in the general ledger appear in the same order of their appearance in financial statements accounts and use assigned numbers to match the order of their appearance in financial statements accounts. Thus, account 1200 represents accounts receivable and 1300 represents notes receivable.

A chart of accounts reflects the nature and purpose of an organization. For example, the chart of accounts for LSE indicates that the company is a corporation. A partnership would include separate capital and drawing accounts for each partner, instead of common stock and retained earnings. Likewise, because LSE is a manufacturing organization, it has only three types of general ledger inventory accounts. In a simple retail company, management may elect to use one inventory account.

Subsidiary ledger accounts often have longer account codes than general ledger accounts. At LSE, each account receivable will have a six-digit code.

- The first four digits are 1200, the code for accounts receivable.
- The next two identify up to 99 individual customers' journals. A journal collects transaction data before entry into the ledger (for simplicity, the customer codes omitted in Table 4.1).
- A journal entry shows the accounts and amounts debited and credited.
- A *general journal* records infrequent or nonroutine transactions, such as loan payments and end-of-period adjusting and closing entries.
- A *specialized journal* records large numbers of repetitive transactions such as sales, cash receipts, and cash disbursements.

 ## CHART OF ACCOUNTS FOR QUICKBOOKS

A chart of accounts in QB can originate from a generic chart of accounts offered with the software or it can originate from another source. Using the Easy Step Interview within QB allows a user to select the appropriate legal form and industry chart of accounts as shown in Figures 4.2 through 4.5.

If a user is unable to find his or her precise industry, importing a chart of accounts into QB is an option. To view a chart of accounts in the QB Home page's Company panel, click "Chart of Accounts" (or press Ctrl+A).

Subaccount Tracking in QuickBooks

Subaccounts can track details such as airfare, lodging, and limousine services. When users post transactions to subaccounts only, a grand total for a report shows subtotals for the subaccounts and a grand total for the parent account, such as a travel account and its subaccounts, airfare, lodging, and limousine. Subaccounts are useful for assigning similar expenses to different lines on a tax form. For example, the IRS does not treat all travel expenses the same, so only 50 percent of the

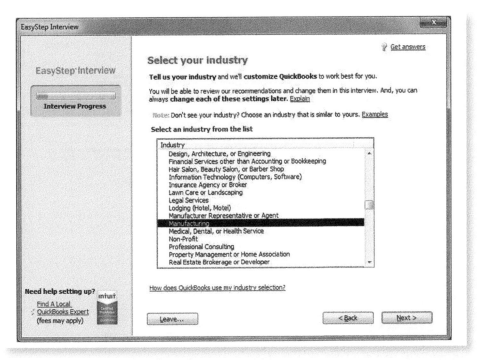

FIGURE 4.2 QB Choosing the Industry

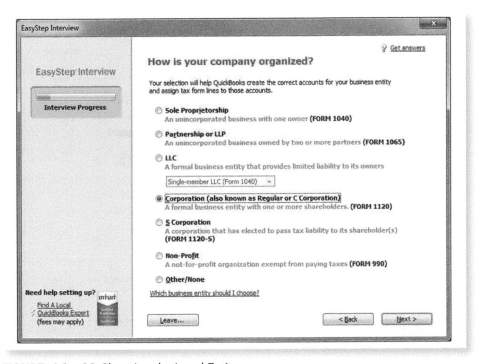

FIGURE 4.3 QB Choosing the Legal Entity

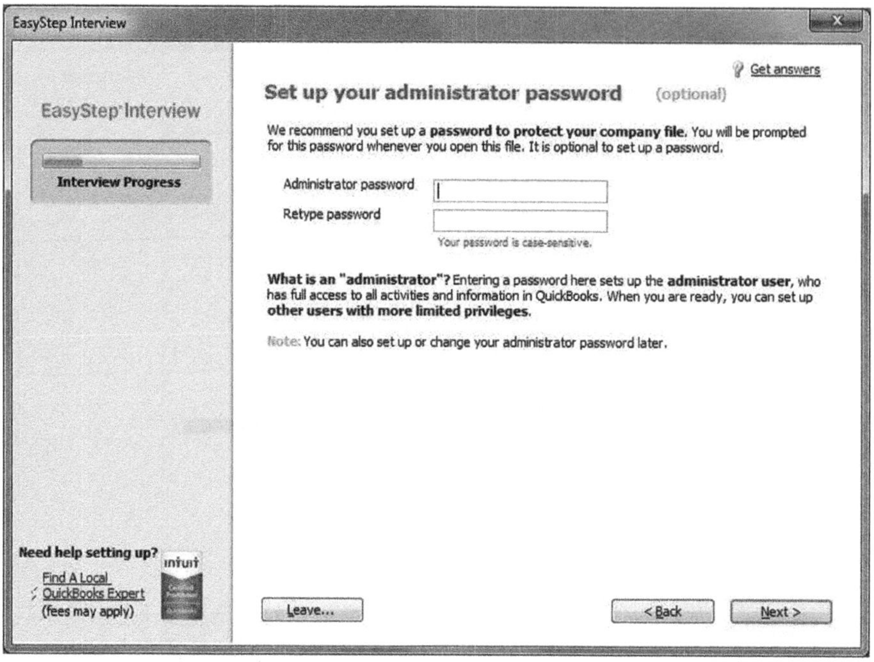

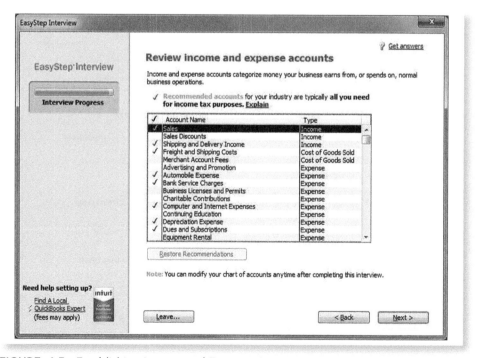

FIGURE 4.4 QB Establishing the Administrator Password

FIGURE 4.5 Establishing Income and Expense Accounts

meal and entertainment expenses are deductible while other travel expenses are fully deductible.

Changing Account Types in QuickBooks

QuickBooks has several restrictions regarding changing account types. Account types cannot change if the account's type has:

- Subaccounts
- An accounts receivable or accounts payable account

To modify an account, in the Chart of Accounts window, select the account you want to edit and then press Ctrl+E.

Account Deletion in QuickBooks

Users have the option of hiding accounts not used in QB. The records of past transactions are important, whether a compliance or tax report is for a bank or the IRS. Deleting accounts is a far more serious undertaking. For example, LSE should not delete an Exploration Service income account because of termination of the service. The income earned from that service is taxable and retained in the records. Hiding accounts does not mean withholding key financial investigative queries. Hidden accounts in QB continue to hold historical transactions even though the account does not appear in account lists.

SME RISKS SPECIFIC TO THE GENERAL LEDGER AND THE CHART OF ACCOUNTS

Risks *specific* to the chart of accounts and general ledger activities can arise or change because:

- A new account number may go into the system without approval or review in contrast to a previous time when the company was much smaller. Changes in the operating environment can result in changes in competitive pressures and significantly enhance risks as an enterprise faces financial pressure resulting in reduced staff levels or new personnel taking on new and unfamiliar tasks. Management that once dominated a smaller enterprise may not have the capacity or the time to manage a growing and fast-changing environment.
- New personnel may have unfettered access to password controls, and may not fully understand system permissions or understand the consequences of account changes, misclassifications, or omissions. New personnel may have inadequate understanding of internal control as training typically falls into second priority with SMEs. Particularly challenging for SMEs is hiring qualified personnel.
- New or revamped information systems as significant and rapid changes occur in information systems can change the risk relating to internal control. Upgrades and

changes in information systems require a transition of old account numbers to new account numbers with numerous opportunities for the integrity of the data to be compromised.

▪ New business models, products, or technology are common in the technology sector and other parts of the U.S. economy, creating new business areas or transactions (and new accounts). An entity that has little experience may introduce new risks associated with internal control.

▪ Corporate restructuring may be accompanied by staff reductions and changes in supervision and controls; for example, the segregation of duties may significantly change the risk associated with internal control.

▪ Expanded foreign operations create all new dimensions of risk, including all aspects of when to recognize revenue and currency changes. New and often unique risks that may affect internal control can also be created, such as additional or changed risks from foreign currency transactions.

 ASSERTIONS UNDERLYING THE FINANCIAL STATEMENTS AND GENERAL LEDGER CONTROLS

Financial statement assertions are affected by factors that include the IT controls underlying the chart of accounts, the monthly closing process, the creation of new accounts, the closure of old accounts, the misclassification of accounts, and the omissions of journal entries. Financial statement assertions are management's implicit or explicit representations regarding the recognition, presentation, and disclosure of information in the financial statements and related disclosures. Assertions underlying the financial statements fall into three categories (Ratcliffe and Landes 2009):

1. Appropriate classification of transactions
2. Accurate account balances
3. Presentation and disclosure

A complete discussion of all the assertions underlying the financial statements and a more comprehensive discussion of IT controls in connection with financial statement reporting occurs later in this book.

 IT CONTROLS, THE TRANSACTION LEVEL, AND THE GENERAL LEDGER

At the *entity level*, the IT planning committee should oversee the development of the IT internal control strategic plan and assess other risks, such as IT management, data security, program change, and development. At the *activity level* there should be risk assessments throughout the systems development methodology, the infrastructure operation and change process, and the program application change process. Common design errors for the chart of accounts that strongly suggest ineffective systems development methodology, infrastructure operation, and change process include:

- Adopting a chart of accounts from a previous general ledger system and migrating that system to a new release without a conscious design of current or anticipated needs.
- Creating a chart of accounts without discussion and feedback from management or the outside auditors. As such, the accounting system may be very short-lived before major changes are likely to be required in the accounting structure.
- Country, industry, compliance, and organizational factors on reporting requirements and chart of accounts structure are ignored in the design of the chart of accounts.
- Inadequate reporting and summarization of data in the general ledger.
- Replication of data between subledgers or modules, leading to inaccurate financial reporting.

Whether the enterprise is extremely small or has 500 employees, senior management has a role in identifying all aspects of internal control associated with financial reporting. Self-assessments measure the effectiveness of an internal control linked to a specific type of financial reporting risk. Corporate governance experts should review risk and control matrixes to ensure an appropriate level of control is in place to fit the risk profile (completeness, cutoff, presentation, recording, safeguarding assets, validity, valuation, and fraud). Risk and control monitoring should include company, department, and secondary controls appropriate for the type of business models in place.

Within an SME, internal controls surrounding the financial closing process are essential, particularly with lean staffs, undertrained personnel, or middle or senior management that may not always be available to monitor activity or to sign off on journal entries. Without structure, timetables, and adequate documentation, the assertions of the financial statements are potentially at risk (Kelso 2011). A complex entity will require more communication, more documentation, and potentially more flexibility. As the complexity of an entity increases, the potential for surprises also increases as the variability of the quality and timeliness of the information are more at risk for decline. With more complexity, more structure may be required to offset the risk of an incomplete or flawed financial close.

There are eight essential controls for the financial closing process (Kelso 2011):

1. A secure password environment to prevent unauthorized access to the chart of accounts and financial reporting systems [a preventive control]
2. A closing calendar [a preventive control]
3. Specific procedures identified on the calendar [a preventive control]
4. A month-end journal entry checklist [a detective control]
5. Templates for journal entries [a preventive control]
6. Standard analytical review processes [a detective control]
7. Report generation and analyses [both preventive and detective]
8. Communication and risk management [both preventive and detective]

An SME should, at a minimum, use some variation of the eight controls the previous paragraph identifies. A more expansive list of controls is available by integrating

COBIT 4.1 application controls (ISACA 2007) into steps 1 through 8. Specific to the chart of accounts and associated activities, COBIT 4.1 ensures six application controls:

1. Accurate and authorized source data
2. Data input is performed in a timely manner by authorized personnel
3. Transactions are accurate, complete, and authentic
4. Transactions are processed with integrity and validity
5. There is adequate output review, reconciliation, and error handling
6. Authentication and integrity exist for processing between applications

For each of the six items just addressed, an illustrative set of application controls for a general ledger application is enumerated using COBIT 4.1 in the following discussion. This discussion identifies controls in the context of the SME adapted from COBIT 4.1 and other sources. It is reasonable to assume that Microsoft Excel will play a significant role in application controls in most SMEs. An end-user computing policy should be in place to ensure that every worksheet is protected, version control and release dates are adhered to, and a supervisor has reviewed all worksheets for accuracy and risk before implementation. The reader is encouraged to review the chapter on Microsoft Excel controls.

COBIT 4.1 Application Control 1: Source Data Preparation and Authorization

The first of six COBIT 4.1 application controls ensure that source data is accurately prepared and authorized:

> Ensure that source documents are prepared by authorized and qualified personnel following established procedures, taking into account adequate segregation of duties regarding the origination and approval of these documents. Minimize errors and omissions through good input form design. Detect errors and irregularities so they can be reported and corrected.*

Illustrative controls for the SME supporting source data preparation and authorization include (adapted from COBIT 4.1 and other sources):

▪ Each area of responsibility creates journal entries using a standard template. For most SMEs, journal entries should originate through Microsoft Excel spreadsheets and as such are the basis of templates for month-to-month entries. The templates have as many attributes prefilled as possible to ensure accuracy (legal entity or corporation number, account, or center); contain hidden help (acceptable date formats); and detect errors (e.g., debits and credits are not equal and offsetting).

▪ An online library retains templates and has a specific journal identifier and a narrative describing the nature of the transaction posting. In addition to the mini-

---

mum attributes required by the local general ledger posting system, an effective spreadsheet organization requires contact information identifying the area, owner, or creator in the details available for subsequent querying of posted transactions.

- Source documents support accuracy, control the workflow, and facilitate subsequent reference checking.
- Unauthorized documents are returned to the submitting originators for correction. Logs track incoming journal entries and returns of entries to originators.
- A person with supervisory authority periodically reviews logs to verify that corrected documents return for ultimate disposition.
- Pattern analysis and root cause review are part of the accounting supervisor's responsibilities. With the appropriate design, Microsoft Excel spreadsheets can support pattern analysis and root cause review.

COBIT 4.1 Application Control 2: Source Data Collection and Entry

The second of six COBIT 4.1 application controls ensure that source data is accurately prepared and authorized.

> Ensure that data input is performed in a timely manner by authorized and qualified staff. Correction and resubmission of data that were erroneously input should be performed without compromising original transaction authorization levels. Where appropriate for reconstruction, retain original source documents for the appropriate amount of time.*

Illustrative controls for the SME supporting the second COBIT application control include (adopted from COBIT 4.1 and other sources):

- Resubmit corrected data that was erroneously inputted without compromising original transaction authorization levels.
- Define and communicate criteria for timeliness, completeness, and accuracy of source documents. Microsoft Excel templates reflect the criteria used for timeliness, completeness, and accuracy.
- Use only prenumbered source documents for critical transactions. If proper sequence is a transaction requirement, identify and correct out-of-sequence source documents. If completeness is an application requirement, identify and account for missing source documents.
- Define and communicate who can input, edit, authorize, accept, and reject transactions, and override errors. In the SME, it is likely that only one or two people on the accounting staff will have this authority. Implement access controls and record supporting evidence to establish accountability in line with role and responsibility definitions.

---

* COBIT 4.1 ©2007 IT Governance Institute. All rights reserved. Used by permission.

- Define procedures to correct errors, override errors, and handle out-of-balance conditions, as well as to follow up, correct, approve, and resubmit source documents and transactions in a timely manner. These procedures should consider things such as error message descriptions, override mechanisms, and escalation levels.
- Generate error messages in a timely manner as close to the point of origin as possible. Microsoft Excel templates for journal entries can include multiple real-time messages to the journal entry originator with the appropriate design. Processing stops unless errors are corrected or appropriately overridden or bypassed. Errors not corrected immediately are logged in an automated suspense log, and valid transaction processing continues. A person with accounting supervisory authority should review error logs in a reasonable period. In practical terms, the small accounting staff of the SME with management being in close proximity should facilitate close communications and timely error reconciliation.
- Review errors and out-of-balance reports within a reasonable period and, where necessary, senior managers review exceptions. Automated monitoring tools identify, monitor, and manage errors.
- Ensure that source documents are safe-stored (either by accounting or by IT) for a sufficient period in line with legal, regulatory, or business requirements.

COBIT 4.1 Application Control 3: Accuracy, Completeness, and Authenticity Checks

The third of six COBIT 4.1 application controls ensure that transactions are accurate, complete, and authentic:

> Ensure that transactions are accurate, complete and valid. Validate data that were input, and edit or send back for correction as close to the point of origination as possible.*

Illustrative controls for the SME to support accurate, complete, and valid transactions for general ledger transactions include (adapted from COBIT 4.1 and other sources) the following:

- Implement a comprehensive financial close calendar for the entire fiscal year, including the year-end. The financial close calendar considers holidays, vacations, major business events, and the external audit or review schedule. All parties to the financial close, including the IT support organization, vendors, senior management, and outside partners, should be aware of all critical dates in the financial closing calendar. System upgrades, maintenance, company picnics, annual meetings, training events, fire drills, office moves, or facility

---

changes and upgrades avoid conflicts with the financial close calendar. Vendors and other third-party service providers outside the enterprise are aware of the financial close calendar.

▪ Implement a month-end journal entry checklist that includes details about the journal entry originator, type (revenue, expense, asset, liability, etc.), brief description, date executed, effective date, amount, legal entity number, general ledger account number, cost or profit center number(s), account name, journal number identifier, currency, and other local system ledger information.

▪ Verify that all journal entries are posted as expected by viewing the financial system accounts and reporting and updating the checklist accordingly. Review and exceptions during the close process and make corrections before the final system cutoff. This checklist is an essential component of the organization's corporate governance compliance process.

▪ Itemize subsystems that require closure before the general ledger is closed by using a monthly close schedule. Each financial close participant should identify specific procedures that detail required deliverables such as journal-entry posting (accruals, recurring-entry setup), financial system querying, financial system report processing, consolidation rules, allocation processing, financial system maintenance, and tax rate processing. For example, payroll systems should be closed one or two days before the payroll information is posted to the general ledger. This would allow a review and sign-off of all payroll entries moving into financial reporting. Materiality thresholds and methods for approval of post-close adjustments for financial corrections are documented and posted.

▪ Ensure that transaction data are verified as close to the data entry point as possible and interactively during online sessions. Ensure that transaction data, whether people-generated, system-generated, or interfaced inputs, are subject to a variety of controls to check for accuracy, completeness, and validity. Provide understandable error messages immediately such that efficient remediation occurs.

▪ Implement controls to ensure accuracy, completeness, validity, and compliancy to regulatory requirements of data input. Controls may include sequence, limit, range, validity, reasonableness, table lookups, existence, key verification, check digit, completeness (e.g., total monetary amount, total items, total documents, hash totals), duplicate and logical relationship checks, and time edits. Validation criteria and parameters should be subject to periodic reviews and confirmation.

▪ Establish access control and role and responsibility mechanisms so that only authorized persons input, modify, and authorize data.

▪ Define requirements for segregation of duties for entry, modification, and authorization of transaction data, as well as for validation rules. Implement automated controls and role and responsibility requirements.

▪ Report transactions failing validation and post them to a suspense file. Report all errors in a timely fashion, and do not delay processing of valid transactions.

▪ Ensure that transactions failing edit and validation routines are subject to appropriate follow-up until errors are remediated. Ensure that information on processing failures allows for root cause analysis to help adjust procedures and automated controls.

COBIT 4.1 Application Control 4: Processing Integrity and Validity

The fourth of six COBIT 4.1 application controls ensure processing integrity and validity:

> Maintain the integrity and validity of data throughout the processing cycle. Ensure that detection of erroneous transactions does not disrupt processing of valid transactions.*

Illustrative controls for the SME supporting the fourth COBIT application control include (adapted from COBIT 4.1 and other sources) the following:

- Maintain the integrity and validity of data throughout the processing cycle. Ensure that detection of erroneous transactions does not disrupt processing of valid transactions. IT should be able to support recovery throughout the data processing cycle.
- Establish and implement mechanisms to authorize the initiation of transaction processing and to enforce that only appropriate and authorized applications and tools are used.
- Verify that automated tools completely and accurately identify and correct errors, where appropriate. Controls may include checking for sequence and duplication errors, transaction/record counts, referential integrity checks, control and hash totals, range checks, and buffer overflow.
- Post and report failed validation routines to a suspense file. Where a file contains valid and invalid transactions, ensure that the processing of valid transactions avoids delays. Identification of errors is timely and available for review. Ensure that information on processing failures allows for root cause analysis and helps adjust procedures and automated controls, to ensure early detection or to prevent errors.
- Ensure that transactions failing validation routines are subject to appropriate follow-up. Remediation of errors occurs or the transaction terminates.
- Ensure production jobs do not acquire extraneous data or delete data during processing.
- Verify the unique and sequential identifier to every transaction (e.g., index, date, and time).
- Maintain the audit trail of transactions processed. Include date and time of input and user identification for each online or batch transaction. For sensitive data, before and after images ensure that accuracy and appropriate authorization exist.
- Maintain the integrity of data during unexpected interruptions in data processing with system and database utilities. Ensure that controls are in place to confirm data integrity after processing failures or after use of system or database utilities to resolve operational problems. A business owner reviews changes before processing.
- Review all adjustments, overrides, and high-value transactions in detail for appropriateness with an appropriate level of supervision.
- Reconcile file totals. For example, a parallel control file that records transaction counts or monetary value as data should be processed and then compared to master file data once transactions post. Identify, report, and act on out-of-balance conditions.

COBIT 4.1 Application Control 5: Output Review, Reconciliation, and Error Handling

The fifth of six COBIT 4.1 application controls ensures output review, reconciliation, and error handling:

> Establish procedures and associated responsibilities to ensure that output is handled in an authorized manner, delivered to the appropriate recipient and protected during transmission; that verification, detection and correction of the accuracy of output occur; and that information provided in the output is used.*

Illustrative controls for the SME supporting the fifth COBIT application control include (adopted from COBIT 4.1 and other sources) the following:

- Use a standard checklist within each area of the SME that creates or runs financial reports (for internal or external users) to verify report attributes. Parameters of accuracy exist for key report elements to indicate a level of comfort from historical reporting and the experience of senior-level report creators. Report reviewers should scan the reporting for accuracy indicators and sign off on checklist items. The review process should use comparative periods (prior month, prior quarter, and prior year). Investigate and document large-dollar, large-percentage, and other anomalies in variances. Document all exceptions for supervisory review, which is performed before the report is issued, with particular attention paid to all exceptions (variances) noted. The SME management and potentially the owners of the enterprise should be actively reviewing reports.
- Follow defined procedures and consider privacy and security requirements for handling and retaining output from IT applications. Define, communicate, and follow procedures for the distribution of output.
- Inventory all sensitive output, such as negotiable instruments, and compare it with inventory records. Create procedures with audit trails to account for all exceptions and rejections of sensitive output documents.
- Match control totals in the header and/or trailer records of the output at data entry to ensure completeness and accuracy of processing. If out-of-balance control totals exist, the differences should be reported to an appropriate level of management.
- Validate the completeness and accuracy of processing before other operations using the same data begin. If electronic output is used as input into a subsequent operation, ensure that validation has occurred prior to subsequent uses.
- Review by the SME's middle and senior management of final output for reasonableness, accuracy, and completeness. Supervisory authority in the accounting department and business owners report potential errors, log the errors in an automated centralized logging facility, and resolve errors in a timely manner.

Implement distribution controls for sensitive output, including who can receive it, using labels that are recognizable by people and machines, and implement the controls accordingly.

---

* COBIT 4.1 ©2007 IT Governance Institute. All rights reserved. Used by permission.

COBIT 4.1 Application Control: Transaction Authentication and Integrity

The sixth and final COBIT 4.1 application controls ensure transaction authentication and integrity:

> Before passing transaction data between internal applications and business operational functions (in or outside the enterprise), check it for proper addressing, authenticity of origin and integrity of content. Maintain authenticity and integrity during transmission or transport.*

Illustrative controls for the SME supporting the sixth COBIT application control include (adopted from COBIT 4.1) the following:

- Implement agreed-on standards of communication and mechanisms for authentication, error handling, and log reconciliation. The standards should include the responsibilities of all parties and how exceptions are handled. This control is particularly important for SMEs with transaction processing at multiple locations.
- Maintain adherence to industry standards to facilitate counterparty authentication, provide evidence of nonrepudiation, and allow for content integrity verification upon receipt by the downstream application.

Analytical Reviews Using the General and Subsidiary Ledger Data

A basic premise underlying the application of analytical procedures is that relationships may exist among the chart of the accounts, the subsidiary ledger, and the general ledger data. Items such as unusual journal entry dates, missing entries, new account numbers, unusual patterns of activity, and payments made after the close of the general ledger exemplify conditions that require follow-up. Analytical procedures from AU Section 329 do the following (PCAOB 2013b; AICPA 2013):

- Assist the auditor in planning the nature, timing, and extent of other auditing procedures.
- Act as a substantive test to obtain audit evidence about particular assertions related to account balances or classes of transaction.
- Serve as an overall review of the financial information in the final stage of the audit.

Analytical procedures range from a simple review of journal entry dates (e.g., identification of weekend journal entries or the identification of missing journal entries that should exist in a prenumbered sequence) to the use of sophisticated statistical

---

* COBIT 4.1 ©2007 IT Governance Institute. All rights reserved. Used by permission.

techniques such as Benford's Law with the implementation of tools known as computer-assisted audit techniques (CAATs).

Forensic analytics, a closely related discipline to financial analytical reviews, can detect accounting errors such as under-billing, overpayments, fraud, and unusual transactions. The main steps in forensic analytics are:

1. Data collection
2. Data preparation
3. The use of forensic analytics
4. Evaluation, investigation, and reporting (Nigrini 2011)

These analytic methods can be directed at determining the likelihood or magnitude of fraud occurring. They would be a part of a fraud deterrence cycle that would include other steps such as employment screening procedures, including background checks. Given the high rate of fraud in the SME, these methods are particularly relevant. In particular, cash and cash-related accounts, including accounts payable and accounts receivable, are the most common areas of fraud in the SME. The techniques outlined in the following discussion (Shein and Lanza 2009; Nigrini 2011) use account data in the general ledger, usually transactional data, but at times other data such as statistical data or aggregated data. What is important in this discussion is to recognize that the general ledger or subsidiary ledgers (depending on the structure of the system installation) by themselves offer fertile ground for investigation.

Excel, Access, and CAATs

The availability of computing power in Excel and Access and the relatively easy access to audit tools such as ACL (ACL 2013), IDEA (CaseWare 2013), and ActiveData for Excel (InformationActive 2013), known as CAAT, have accelerated the analytical review process. Within the normal course of an engagement, external auditors, internal auditors, data analysts, and forensic analysts should have access to the electronic records supporting the general ledger. With access to the accounting server and related applications to the general ledger (e.g., inventory), CAATs are very powerful companions. A demonstration of how to use Excel and Access or any of the audit tools referenced using these investigative techniques is beyond the scope of this text.

Descriptive Statistics

Descriptive statistics provide simple summaries about the sample and about the observations available through further analysis. Such summaries may be either quantitative (e.g., summary statistics using ratios or percentages), or visual (e.g., simple-to-understand graphs). These summaries may form the basis of the initial description of the data as part of a more extensive statistical analysis, or they may be sufficient in and of themselves for a particular investigation. The objective of using descriptive statistics is to isolate unusual patterns in comparative general ledger data to enable the auditor to make specific queries and meaningful drill-downs.

Vendor Summary Analysis for the Evaluation of Period-to-Period Comparison

The purpose of the vendor evaluation is to identify trends in vendor purchase history. A trend analysis can identify key vendors that have increased or decreased substantially in purchase volume. Based on the changes in the business environment and/or new company projects, a reasonableness assessment identifies major changes in vendor activity. A common fraud is an employee(s) submitting invoices for a fraudulent legal entity that does not exist. That legal entity should appear in a vendor review and analysis with a significant increase in purchasing activity.

Benford's Law

Benford's Law originates from the late Dr. Frank Benford, a physicist at the General Electric Company. Benford's Law theorizes the expected frequencies of the digits in tabulated data (Benford 1938). Benford found that contrary to intuition, the digits in tabulated data are not all equally likely and skew in favor of the lower digits (Nigrini 2011; Huxley 2013). Benford showed that on average 30.6 percent of numbers had a first digit "1," and 18.5 percent of the numbers had a first digit "2." This means that 49.1 percent of his large data samples had a first digit that was either a 1 or a 2. At the other end of the digit-scale, only 4.7 percent of his samples had a first digit "9." The actual proportion for the first digit 1 was almost equal to the common logarithm of 2 (or 2/1), and the actual proportion for the first digit 2 was almost equal to the common logarithm of 3/2. This logarithmic pattern continues through to the "9" with the proportion for the first digit 9 approximating the common logarithm of 10/9.

Why is this important? Fraudsters are more likely to use fraudulent invoice numbers using either an equal distribution assuming that the first digit 1 will appear 10 percent of the time or another invoice number pattern that does not resemble the predicted distribution using Benford's Law. Most contemporary CAATs support Benford's Law.

Above-Average Payments to a Vendor

Unusually large payments to a vendor in relation to the average are signs of error (i.e., key error) or fraud (i.e., kickback scheme where vendors pay kickbacks to an employee). For vendors with unusual payments above the average, a sample of the "average" payment invoices as well as the unusual payment invoice is part of the review. The documentation determines the reasonableness of the purchase. The auditor should be aware of unusual payments and/or the possibility of the vendor deliberately overcharging the organization.

Duplicate Payment Testing

Duplicate payments to vendors may represent errors that the QB or another general ledger system was unable to detect. In most systems, a check confirms whether the vendor number, invoice number, and amount are the same. This test ensures this basic control is operational and tests for other permutations of duplication. Any results from this test should indicate trends with a visual inspection. For example, rent payments that occur on a monthly basis may appear to duplicate payments when in fact they are simply regularly occurring payments.

Payments Made after Period-End for Valid Liabilities at Period-End

This analysis identifies unrecorded liabilities. A common scheme is for an organization to hold an invoice by not entering the payable into the system. Then, after period-end, the invoice enters into the system, thereby evading the expense charge in the year under review. The invoices identified in this test are reasonable and material using visual inspection. If not material, further test work is not necessary. If material, trends or patterns can identify types of invoices, vendors, or the supervisor or manager who approved the invoice.

Journal Entry Gap Test

Gaps may signal incomplete data processing or, in the situation of journal entries, possible hidden entries. Usually, a method to identify these occurrences, along with a review by an independent party, is sufficient to ensure the completeness and accuracy of processing. Gaps in the journal entry sequence raise questions and require the accounting department to answer simple queries. The test work should answer:

- What procedures exist to document and approve all gaps in the respective sequences?
- How is management made aware of the gaps?

Identify Standard and Nonstandard Journal Entries Made after Year-End

Nonstandard journal entries generally are those posted manually. Such entries are more prone to error and fraud due mainly to human error, judgment normally applied in the support for the entry, and the possibility for management override in authorizing the entry. This is especially true for entries made just after year-end (related to the prior year, as these entries are more prone to be adjustments for the fiscal year's annual reporting). Given all these possibilities, the test of these entries should include a review of the journal entry and associated supporting documentation, ensuring the approvals are appropriate for the size and nature of the journal entry, and assessing whether generally accepted accounting principles (GAAP) are being applied.

Summarize Activity by User Account

This test looks for:

- Standard password names such as "DEFAULT" or "TEST." Replacements for these generic passwords should be strong passwords (e.g., wBROWN6633#) or passphrases associated with that person.
- Unrecognized or terminated employees. This test focuses more on the IT function to ensure that at any point only authorized employees are on the list.
- Users who have access beyond their level of responsibility. This access may highlight a lack of segregation of duties where a person has an opportunity to commit fraud by being able to initiate, authorize, and/or record a transaction.

  Recommendations include:

- Replacing weak passwords with specific IDs using strong password design.
- Deleting employees not on the active employee roster.
- Reviewing users that are posting high activity or may have access to other nonsegregated functions to assess whether other controls are needed to mitigate the access level being afforded to the individual.
- Reviewing all procedures and permissions that allow access to the passwords.

Identify Weekend Journal Entries

This analysis evaluates entries made during the weekend. Except for a year-end close or a close delayed for uncontrollable circumstances, a company does not typically close the general ledger over the weekend. Therefore, it is useful to extract all of these entries to determine if there are any patterns in their processing. For example, a particular user may be constantly processing a certain set of entries over a weekend to reduce the processing load during the week. If the test finds weekend entries, the auditor should review these entries to determine whether there are any unusual patterns or entries posted during these unexpected times to escape detection and approval.

 SUMMARY

Whether the system is manual or computerized, access to the general ledger should occur only when proper authorization exists. In a manual general ledger system, segregation of duties would not allow general ledger employees simultaneously to do the following three tasks:

1. Authorize journal vouchers.
2. Have custody of assets.
3. Have recording responsibility for any special journals or subsidiary ledgers.

Microsoft Dynamics and QB achieve segregation by allowing different levels of access to different employees. Only certain employees have access to the general ledger functions, including account creation, postings, and other activities. Segregation of duties is maintained in Excel spreadsheets by requiring a second party to review complex spreadsheet designs, analytical reviews of month-to-month journal entries, and journal entry creation. The second party of the Excel review would not have access to assets or have conflicting responsibilities for journal entries or ledgers.

An organization must have a well-defined chart of accounts to maintain internal control. The chart of accounts must have adequate granularity (i.e., adequate breakdown of accounts) to facilitate the accurate classification and control of transactions. Adequate breakdown of revenue and expense categories should occur to enable a meaningful management review. Coarse-grained charts of accounts are typical for an SME, but as the SME grows in revenue and complexity of operations increases, finer granularity (i.e., more accounts) should be sought to maintain an understanding of the operations.

All transactions should have an audit trail to enable transaction tracing from their initial source documents through the general ledger. The audit trail should also enable general ledger account tracing to the original source documents. It is likely the audit trail will include electronic and manual documents as well as transaction logs, transaction files, and master files.

The ultimate output of the general ledger includes the balance sheet, income statement, statement of cash flows, and statement of owners' equity. Internal reporting should enable analytical reviews such as an aging analysis of accounts receivable or an analysis of production hours and labor costs if the organization is a manufacturer. A retail organization may focus on an inventory analysis of fast- or slow-moving inventory items as well as stockouts of high-demand inventory. A treasurer or CFO may focus on cash management and future financing requirements. The chart of accounts is the source of internal reporting and is a critical source of information for the financial health of the organization. For the auditor, the activity related to the general ledger itself (e.g., Sunday closing entries or above-average payments to a vendor) provides information about unusual activity related to the financial closing and reporting process for the general ledger and subsidiary ledgers.

CHAPTER FIVE

The Revenue Cycle

T HE REVENUE CYCLE ENCOMPASSES ALL processes, personnel, and activities that relate to the receipt of purchase orders from customers, credit approval, delivery of goods and/or services, and receipt of payment. Process descriptions of the revenue cycle are relatively universal, with differences generally reflective of processing technology (e.g., batch or continuous), specific company policies (e.g., credit-related, exception routines for backorders, etc.), and goods-based versus services-based business models.

 RISK EXPOSURES AND SUBPROCESSES

The revenue cycle contains several risk exposures. These include:

- **Sales:** Is the order from a valid customer? Does the system contain correct and up-to-date information about the customer? Are there holds or credit limits on the customer's account? Has the transaction been properly authorized? Are recorded transactions valid? Have all valid transactions been recorded accurately?
- **Credit approval:** Does the credit approval process protect the organization against excessive credit losses?
- **Warehouse:** How are assets protected against loss or theft? Does the accounting system provide good detective controls that would bring shrinkage to the attention of management? How often are inventory counts reconciled to accounting records? Are ordered goods available in sufficient quantity to satisfy customer demand? Are backorder processes in place to protect against customer dissatisfaction from stockouts?

- **Shipping:** What controls are in place to ensure the accuracy and timeliness of shipped orders? Are processes in place to manage multiple ship-to addresses?
- **Billing:** What controls are in place to ensure the accuracy and timeliness of billings? Are backorders, partial fills, returns, and other nonroutine transactions processed in such a way as to ensure accurate and complete records?
- **Cash receipts:** Does the organization use lockboxes? Do cash receipt processes provide independent audit trails? What segregation of duties (SOD) controls are there to prevent one person from exercising incompatible functions?

There are several subprocesses within the revenue cycle. These include:

- **Customer setup:** Preparation or modification of the customer records includes such vital information as credit limits, ship-to addresses and, if applicable, class attributes (i.e., customers that share a specific set of attributes such as access to special promotional pricing, shipping instructions, or payment terms).
- **Pricing and promotions:** Input and modification of pricing-related information requires special attention to access controls.
- **Order entry:** This subprocess also requires careful attention to role-based security, in order to ensure that only authorized personnel can input orders. The data fields require application controls such as dropdown boxes for customers and pricing overrides.
- **Invoicing:** This originates in the billing and accounts receivable (A/R) department and must reflect both the original sales order and actual shipping quantities. In the case of a service company, invoicing must tie back to evidence of service delivery. The invoice amount needs to tie to the sales order, and controls should be in place to limit overrides.
- **Accounts receivable:** This subprocess combines cash receipts and record updating. Companies need sound controls to ensure accurate posting of cash receipts to a customer's account.
- **Product shipment:** Controls need to ensure accurate fulfillment of customer orders and tracking of shortages, back orders, and other exceptions.
- **Returns:** This *reverse logistics* subprocess must ensure appropriate crediting of the customer account and inventory record management. Decisions regarding the resale value of returned items should have appropriate authorization, including pre-approval forms and accurate matching of quantities returned and related records.

These risk exposures can affect the financial audit in a number of different ways, and each risk exposure relates to one or more cycle subprocesses. (See Table 5.3, later in the chapter, which illustrates these links at a high level, showing, for each of several illustrative risks, the potential impact on one or more of the assertions underlying the financial statements.* Table 5.3 also ties these risks to specific revenue cycle subprocesses.)

Application controls can mitigate these exposures, and it is thus important for the auditor to have a working knowledge of what these controls are, how they should function, and points of vulnerability. The numbered references in Figures 5.1 and 5.2 identify

---

* These assertions are discussed from both a financial and IT audit perspective in Chapter 1.

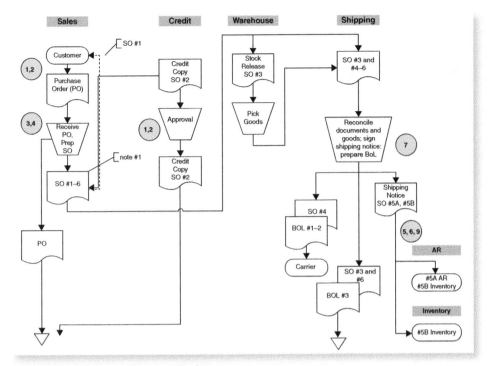

FIGURE 5.1 Generic Revenue Cycle

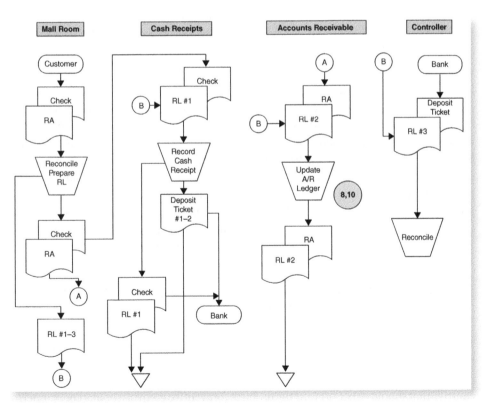

FIGURE 5.2 Generic Cash Receipts Cycle

TABLE 5.1 Note 1—Sales Order Distribution

Copy No.	Name	Remarks
1	Customer Copy	Returning a customer copy of the sales order allows the customer to follow its own internal processes for reconciling the original purchase order to anticipated fulfillment. Note the operational importance of providing the customer with reasonable assurance that the company will be able to fill the order.
2	Credit Copy	The credit process should ensure that new orders are consistent with the terms of a customer's account.
3	Stock Release	The stock release (sometimes referred to as a *pick list*) authorizes warehouse employees to assemble inventory for shipment to a customer.
4	Packing Slip	The packing slip accompanies the bill of lading (BOL) and describes the contents of the order.
5	Shipping Notice	The shipping notice provides essential information for the A/R-billing function, including detail on the actual shipment, freight charges, and shipping date. Figure 5.1 shows copies of the sales order (#5A) going to the A/R department for billing and to the inventory department (#5B) for updating stock records.
6	File Copy	The shipping department retains file copies of the sales order (adjusted for actual shipment) and the bill of lading in order to process information requests relating to the shipment.

locations of specific risks discussed in the next section. These figures (adapted from material found in Hall 2011) illustrate typical revenue and cash receipts cycles for a small goods-based business. The drawings in Figures 5.1 and 5.2 are not intended to be comprehensive or applicable to all business models; rather, the intent is to highlight the broad relationships between common processes and frequently occurring risks. The use of document output in the flowcharts reflects the fact that, although the accounting process is computerized, paper output is frequently generated (e.g., packing slips, customer invoices). Figures 5.1 and 5.2 should be read in terms of information flows and with the tacit understanding that some of these occur with physical paper output and others via screen reading only. Table 5.1 provides detail on the information flows for the sales order (SO) distribution.

APPLICATION CONTROLS, REVENUE CYCLE RISKS, AND RELATED AUDIT PROCEDURES

This section begins with a general introduction to application controls. We then consider an illustrative set of risks that arise in the revenue cycle. These include operational risks (i.e., what could go wrong) and financial statement risks. We examine these risks and the controls that should either prevent the problem (preventive controls) or alert personnel to the problem so that it can be remediated (detective controls). Within the context of each risk exposure and related controls we also discuss appropriate IT audit procedures.

Application Controls

Application controls are system-enabled controls within standard business processes. They are designed to enforce specific work requirements and, traditionally, are preventive in nature. Examples of application controls include:

- Logical access controls (i.e., application security)
- Date entry/field validations (e.g., validation of entered credit card numbers)
- Workflow rules (e.g., electronic routing and signoff of purchase requests)
- Field entries being enforced based on predefined values (e.g., pricing information)

In discussing application controls, it is useful to observe the distinction between inherent and configurable controls. The former are programmed to perform the control through either custom coding or packaged delivery, while the latter can be modified by the end user.

Table 5.2 provides brief definitions for major control types. All of these general types of control are designed to limit the risk of inappropriate input, processing, or output of data.

The level of automation associated with a control provides another set of fundamental distinctions. In general, controls can be manual, automated, or IT-dependent manual. This last category refers to controls performed by a person who relies on automated output. Most are detective controls that rely on computer-generated information or computer functionality. For example, management reviews a monthly variance report and follows up on significant variances. Because management relies on the computer-produced report to identify and generate the variances, the IT auditor needs to determine that there are controls in place to ensure that the variance report is complete and accurate.

Risks, Processes, and Application Controls

Table 5.3 provides an illustrative set of risk exposures and the ways in which these both impair the validity of management assertions about the financial statements and involve

TABLE 5.2 Major Application Control Types

Edit Checks	These controls relate to field format. For example, dollar amounts should be entered in numeric format.
Validations	Validation controls depend on the confirmation of a test. Examination of verified customer, appropriate credit limit, and/or correct pricing list would be examples of validation controls relating to the revenue cycle.
Calculations	Calculations can be used to ensure that a computation is occurring accurately. Extensions and footings can be cross-checked with one another in order to address the risk that portions of a customer statement may not be included in the totals.
Interfaces	Interfaces can be designed to address risks posed by data transfers from one system to another (e.g., counts that verify the number of records uploaded from the sales subledger to the general ledger).
Authorizations	Authorizations that limit access to data are a fundamental building block of control. Roles should be defined within the system and used to restrict the ability to modify records. For example, only the purchasing manager should have the ability to add vendors to the vendor master.

TABLE 5.3 Revenue Cycle Risks

	Illustrative Risks	Assertions					Cycle Subprocess						
		Existence/Occurrence	Completeness	Rights and Obligations	Valuation/Allocation	Accounting Procedures	Customer Setup	Pricing/Promotions	Order Entry	Invoicing	Accounts Receivable	Product Shipment	Returns
1	Sales made to customers with bad credit	X	X				X						
2	Unauthorized changes to customer accounts	X					X						
3	Incorrect prices entered into the system				X	X		X	X	X	X		
4	Duplicate sales invoice numbers	X	X							X	X		
5	Incorrect sales posting		X		X	X				X	X		
6	Erroneous invoices		X		X	X		X		X	X		
7	Shipping errors	X		X							X	X	
8	No authorization for issuance of credit memos	X	X	X						X	X		X
9	Revenue not recognized in proper period			X		X				X	X	X	
10	Incorrect posting of cash receipts	X	X		X						X		

specific subprocesses. While accounting scholars and practitioners could debate which assertions and subcycle processes are affected by each illustrative risk, this book focuses on a limited set of the most prominent intersections.

Sales Made to Customers with Bad Credit

As previously noted, the completeness assertion refers to the integrity of the recording process and the ability of the company's accounting system to ensure that the effects of all transactions, balances, accounts, and estimates have been included in the financial statements. A process that permits a sales process that runs contrary to credit process fails this test.

Credit sales to customers with poor credit pose the operational risk of uncollectable receivables and the audit risk of overstated revenues. The applicable controls include the setting of credit limits for customers, limit checks that ensure that a customer's preapproved credit limit is not exceeded, and credit approval by a credit manager who is independent of the sales function. In Microsoft Great Plains Dynamics (GPD), the credit limits for customers can be configured as shown in Figure 5.3.

In GPD, once the total order amount exceeds the customer's credit limit, a window opens and prompts for a password in order to override the credit limit. This hard control prevents an order from being processed without proper approval. The auditor should review the password configuration setup and related business processes in order to understand how overrides occur in practice, as shown in Figure 5.4.

Figure 5.5 illustrates a contrasting soft control approach for sales terms found in QuickBooks (QB). The figure shows initial configuration, and then a sales order that exceeds the credit limit. In order to verify appropriate credit limits the auditor should examine a sample of customer setup records. QB can be configured to run such a report to evaluate compliance with company credit policy. In QB the credit limit configuration setting resides under the payment information tab. If used, QB has

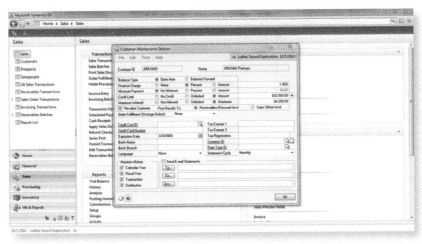

FIGURE 5.3   GPD Configuration Control for Customer Credit Limit

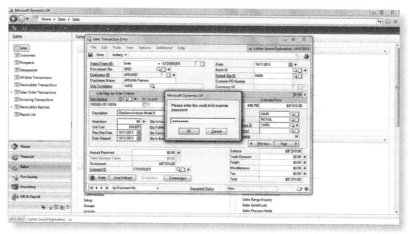

FIGURE 5.4 GPD Hard Control for Customer Credit Limit

established soft control warnings for the user to help manage a customer's current credit balance.

If an invoice is created that would cause the customer's balance to exceed its credit limit, a warning box appears, as shown in Figure 5.6. This is a soft control and does not prevent an order from being processed. The auditor should review credit limit balances configured in the system to the accounts receivable ledger

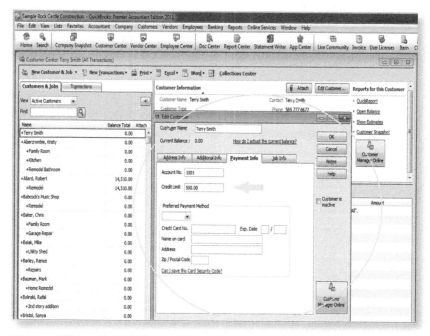

FIGURE 5.5 QB Credit Limit Setup

Source: Intuit, Rock Castle.

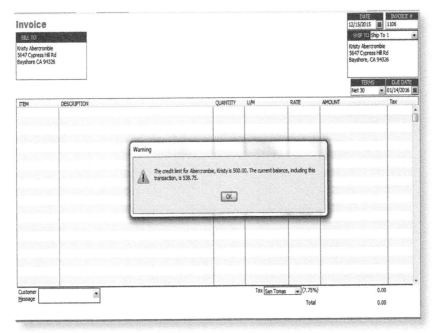

FIGURE 5.6 QB Soft Control for Customer Credit Limit—1

to determine if there is exposure for bad debt that has not been addressed in the allowance accounts.

The user receives an additional soft control popup box in QB prior to recording the transaction. Once again, this is a soft control that does not prevent the transaction from being processed, as shown in Figure 5.7.

In QB, the auditor could run a report with all customers with credit limits and then run a report that compares the A/R aging summary against customer credit limits, as shown in Figures 5.8 and 5.9

Unauthorized Changes to Customer Accounts (Including Prices and Credit Limits)

Unauthorized changes to customer accounts could include resetting of sales discounts, credit limits, ship-to addresses, and pricing (e.g., bulk discounts, preferred customer pricing, etc.) As previously noted, the IT corollary to the financial statement assertion of existence implies that the application controls that support processing integrity exist.

Software packages that permit soft controls can, as illustrated in Figure 5.10, allow potential unauthorized overrides. The auditor needs to reconcile actual terms provided to customers to the terms on customer records in order to determine whether changes have been made, and, if so, how they were authorized.

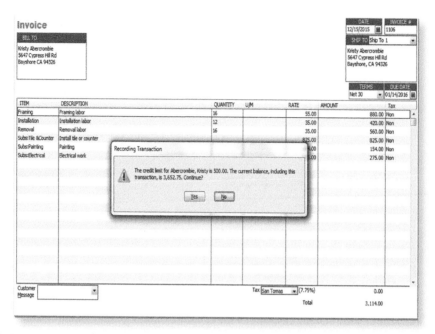

FIGURE 5.7 QB Soft Control for Customer Credit Limit—2

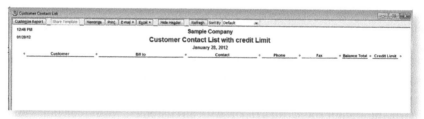

FIGURE 5.8 QB Customer Contact List with Credit Limit

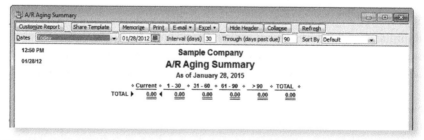

FIGURE 5.9 QB Aging Summary

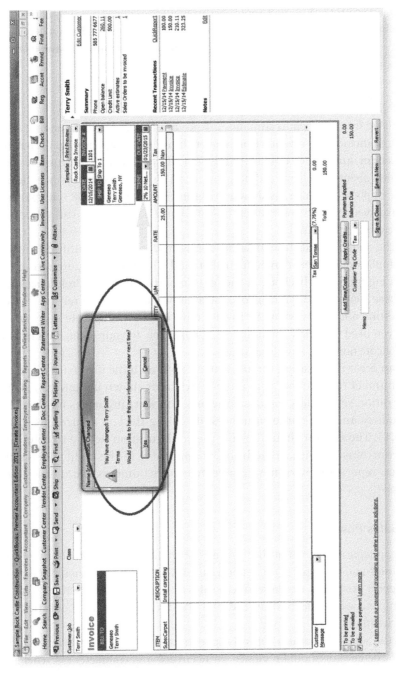

FIGURE 5.10 QB Controls for Customer Account Details

Source: Intuit, Rock Castle.

Incorrect Prices Entered into the System

The risk exposures in this category include erroneous price cards, incorrect matching of price series with customers when more than one pricing or rate schedule exists, and incorrect sales discounts. While data entry errors would be caused by human input, the system may have price lists where only certain prices can be chosen from a dropdown box or only certain discounts or price tolerances can be accepted without having further workflow approvals.

Duplicate Sales Invoice Numbers

The risks arising from duplicate estimates, invoice numbers, or credit memos entered into the system include lost revenue from one or the other, misapplication of cash to a customer account, and related financial statement effects. In QB, a dialogue box opens with a warning about a duplicate estimate number. This is a soft control since the user can keep the duplicate number, as shown in Figure 5.11. Although QB automatically numbers estimates and sales orders after the last completed, the user is still able to keep the duplicate number if desired.

In QB, the auditor needs to review the configuration setting within QB. Warnings about duplicate numbers can be turned on and off via the configuration screen, as shown in Figure 5.12 (checkbox at the bottom of the Company Preferences tab). Although these controls are soft controls, the auditor may be able to rely on the configuration setting and then review the invoice reports for any duplicate numbers. As an auditor, you need to review the numbers, if applicable to your audit, to determine whether duplicate numbers have been used.

In QB, an error notification (input control) pops up if the user tries to change an invoice number to a number that already exists, as shown in Figure 5.13. The QB configuration screen lets the user uncheck the warning boxes for duplicate invoice numbers and sales order numbers, disabling the soft control, as shown in Figure 5.14. The auditor should review the configuration setting to determine if the soft control is in place. In addition, if applicable to the audit, the auditor should review reports to determine if duplicate invoice numbers and/or sales order numbers exist.

Incorrect Sales Posting

Incorrect sales posting refers to unauthorized, misattributed, missing, or otherwise erroneous sales information posted to the general ledger (GL). The auditor should determine whether a report exists that would reconcile sales activity to the GL posting. To determine the completeness of sales posting, the total from the sales journal should tie to one or more entries in the GL.

In GPD the sales edit list is a control report over posting to the GL, as shown in Figure 5.15. The auditor should review it for accuracy and completeness. This is an example of an IT-dependent manual control.

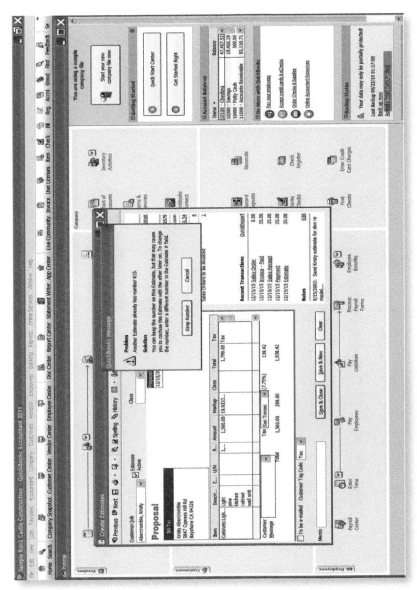

FIGURE 5.11 QB Error Notification

Source: Intuit, Rock Castle.

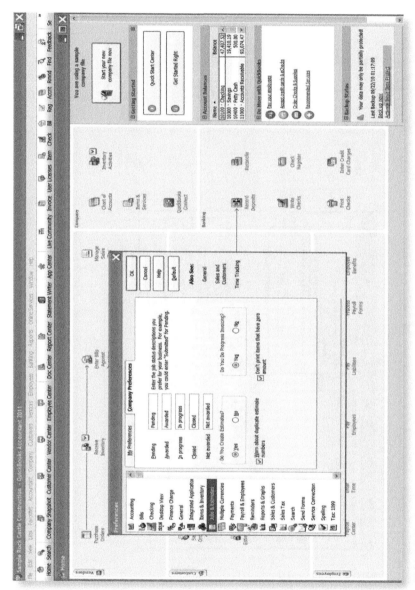

FIGURE 5.12 QB Error Notification

Source: Intuit, Rock Castle.

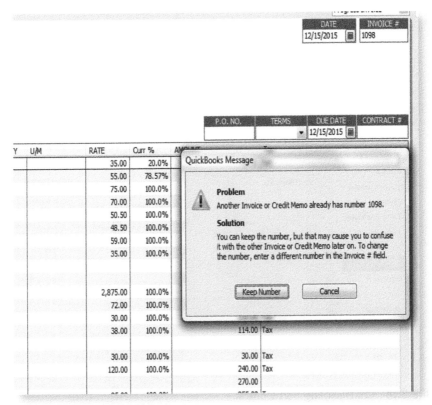

FIGURE 5.13 QB Input Control

Erroneous Invoices

Invoice copies were not illustrated in Figure 5.2 for the sound reason that quantities sold may vary from quantities shipped. This creates the risk, however, that when generated the invoices may be incomplete or otherwise erroneous, or that they may fail to be generated by the A/R-billing department. Figure 5.16 illustrates a control in QB that requires an invoice to be generated before the sales order is processed. A window double-checks the quantity of goods to be shipped to those invoiced, as shown in Figure 5.17.

In GPD, when creating an invoice, the system automatically retrieves the information from the inventory master file, as shown in Figure 5.18. This can help prevent possible pricing mistakes.

Shipping Errors

When filling in the sales transaction entry form, if a customer shipping address is missing, a message box prompts the user for a shipping address, as shown in Figure 5.19. This is an example of a hard control in GPD relating to a completeness check.

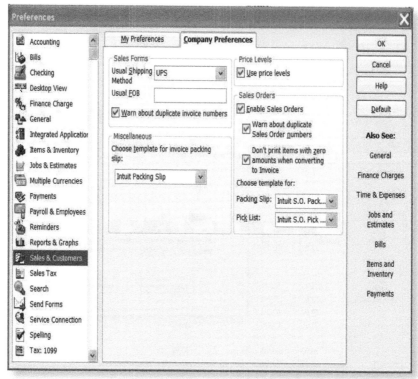

FIGURE 5.14 QB Disabling Soft Control

No Authorization for Issue of Credit Memos

A credit memo enables the company to reduce the accounts receivable that a customer owes due to an authorized reason. Credit memos should not be processed within the system without proper authorization. While many small and medium-sized enterprises may use manual credit memo processes to approve the accounts receivable reduction, the system may have authorization workflows set up that require approvals before the credit memo can be processed. Initially, security should be set up in the system to ensure that only authorized individuals can create credit memos, and then security should be set up for the approval process.

Revenue Not Recognized in the Proper Period

This exposure arises when invoiced products are in transit, loaded on trucks but not shipped to customers. Companies need to ensure that proper cutoff occurs at the end of the accounting period and only authorized revenue is recorded in the proper accounting period. Unfortunately, the system may process transactions that would trigger the recognition of revenue, even though the inventory does not leave the shipping docks. This is where the auditor could review revenue recorded near the end of

```
System:     12/4/2010    7:29:02 PM            S&S, Incorporated                                Page:      1
User Date:  12/4/2010                          SALES EDIT LIST                                  User ID:  sa
                                               Sales Order Processing

Batch ID:        SO031707                                            Audit Trail Code:
Batch Comment:   SO March 17 2007

Approved:                         Batch Total Actual:    $122,445.00       Batch Total Control:      $0.00
Approved By:                      Trx Total Actual:                2       Trx Total Control:            0
Approval Date:   0/0/0000


Type  Document Number  Doc Date   Post Date   Customer ID   Name                      Salesperson
         Subtotal     Trade Discount  Freight Amount  Misc Amount    Tax Amount   Document Total  Discount Avail

INV   INV00000212      12/4/2010  3/17/2007   TUBESTUR001   Tubes & Turners, Inc.     MTN3987
         $94,500.00               $0.00            $0.00        $0.00         $0.00   $94,500.00         $0.00

Item Number                       Description                                        Markdown
                                  U of M    Site            Quantity                 Unit Price        Extended Price

HESB51DVD                         SEBO 38 DVD 5.1 Home Entertainment                     $0.00
                                  Unit      MAIN                   50               $1,890.00           $94,500.00
                                                                                                       $94,500.00

Account Number                    Account Description              Account Type       Debit Amount     Credit Amount

1200-00                           Accounts Receivable              RECV               $94,500.00             $0.00
4100-03                           Sales - West                     SALES                   $0.00        $94,500.00
5200-00                           Commission Expense               COMMEXP               $283.50             $0.00
```

FIGURE 5.15   GDP Sales Edit List

Source: Adapted from T. Brunsdon, M. Romney, and P. Steinbart (2009).

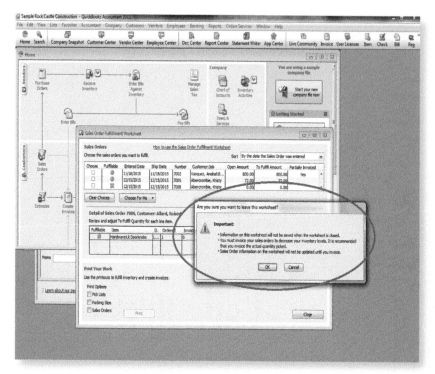

FIGURE 5.16 QB Sales Order Processing

Source: Intuit, Rock Castle.

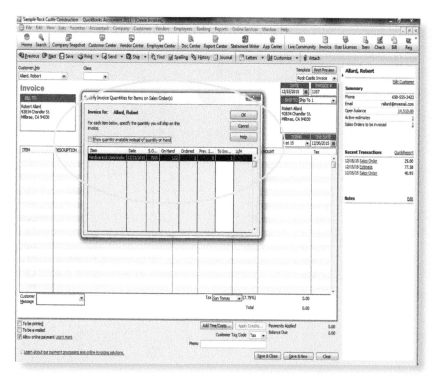

FIGURE 5.17 QB Error Checking

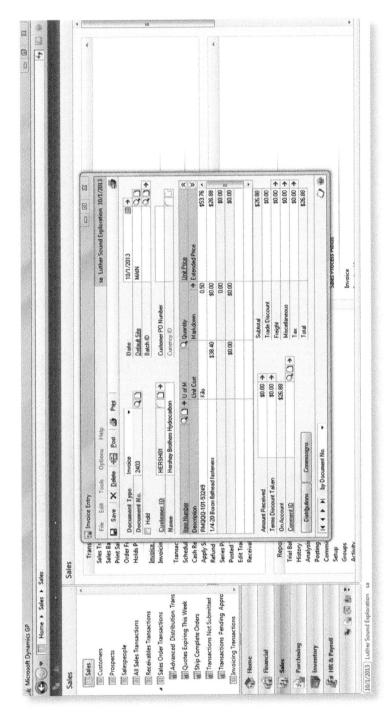

FIGURE 5.18 GPD Pricing Data from Inventory Master File

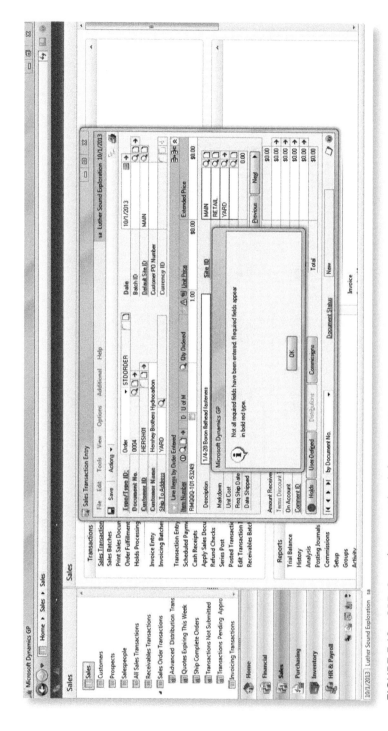

FIGURE 5.19 GPD Completeness Check for Sales Transaction

the accounting period to determine if the goods were actually shipped and/or if an actual purchase order was received. It is difficult for the system to prevent the revenue from being recognized in the wrong period when you have the other human factors that could prevent the shipment of the goods, for example, but management can use reports generated from the system to understand what revenue has been recognized for further scrutiny.

Incorrect Posting of Cash Receipts

When cash is received, the system needs to be updated to the customer's records. When cash receipts are misapplied to customer accounts, companies will affect customer accounts and potentially the relationship with that customer. Purposeful misapplication of cash receipts could also be indicative of potential fraudulent activity (e.g., covering up of a lapping scheme).

In QB, invoices are marked *paid* after payment is received, as shown in Figure 5.20. This will help prevent the invoice from having multiple cash receipts applied toward it, helping to prevent duplicate payments from customers.

In QB, a hard control strictly limits the accounts to which deposit can be attributed, as shown in Figure 5.21. This helps ensure that cash receipts are properly recorded in the correct deposit account.

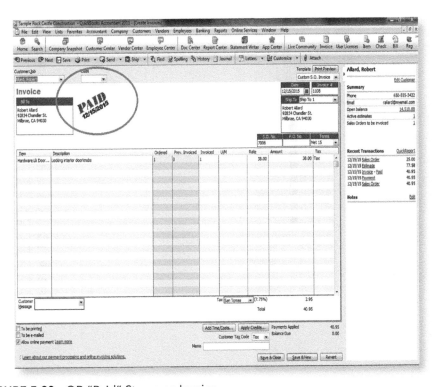

FIGURE 5.20 QB "Paid" Stamp on Invoice

Source: Intuit, Rock Castle.

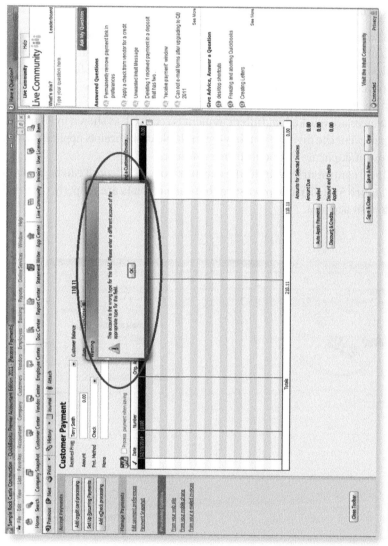

FIGURE 5.21 QB Hard Control on Cash Receipts Application

Source: Intuit, Rock Castle.

Interestingly, though, in QB, there are limited controls for credit card payment. As Figure 5.22 demonstrates, the credit card payments can be processed against the account even though there is no card number or expiration date entered. This is probably due to the ability to receive the payments through third-party processors, but this does indicate a limitation of the software in allowing payments to be credited without verification. Management needs to ensure that credit card payments posted against customer accounts are reconciled against the credit card processor's records.

In GPD, the cash receipt cannot be less than the amount applied to the invoice, as shown in Figure 5.23. After the A/R clerk has posted the receipt and applies it to an invoice, he or she can post the transaction to the proper customer account to complete the revenue cycle.

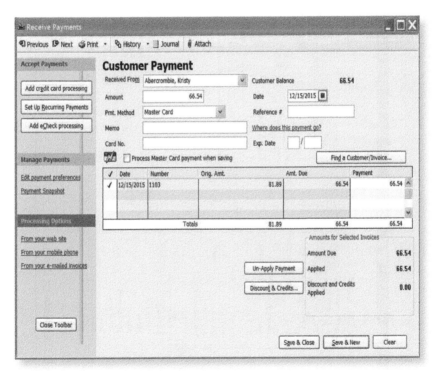

FIGURE 5.22 QB Credit Card Processing

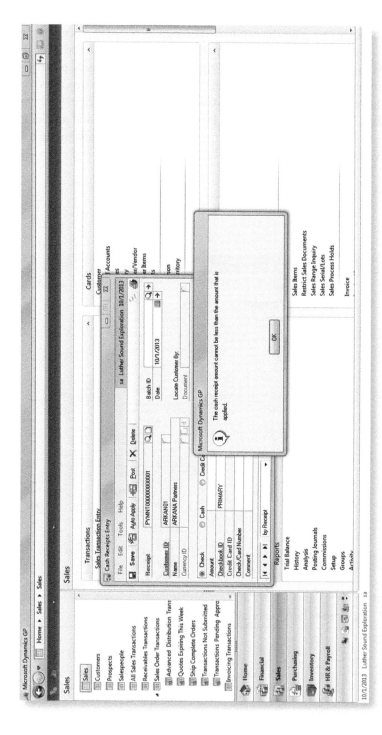

FIGURE 5.23 GPD Cash Receipt Posting

SUMMARY

Now that we've reviewed the revenue cycle you should have a better understanding of the IT application and configuration controls that can affect the accounting for sales and collections, and a keener sense of how to ensure that the appropriate controls are in place. The specific requirements of an IT audit will vary by company and by the particular accounting software used by the company, but the broad principles discussed in this chapter should be applicable to most SME environments.

CHAPTER SIX

The Expenditure Cycle

THE EXPENDITURE CYCLE ENCOMPASSES ALL processes, personnel, and activities that relate to the ordering and receipt of goods and services, and the related accounting for payables and payments. These processes include the creation and management of purchase orders (POs); the matching of goods and services received against invoices and POs; and the subsequent cash disbursements.

RISK EXPOSURES AND SUBPROCESSES

The expenditure cycle contains several risk exposures. These include:

- **Purchases:** Is the order made to a valid vendor? Does the system contain correct and up-to-date information about that vendor?
- **Credit limit issues:** Do credit limit issues occur at both the purchasing agent level (does the agent have authorization to initiate the PO) and the vendor level (does the contemplated purchase exceed the available credit on the account)?
- **Receiving:** Risks include receipt (does the entity receive the goods that it ordered?), variances of type and/or quantity, and pricing.
- **Invoicing:** Risks include the possibility of invoices for goods and services that were not received, and the possibility that invoiced prices exceed previously quoted prices beyond some specified tolerance level.
- **Cash disbursements:** Risk exposures include all possible concerns relating to unauthorized or inappropriate distribution of corporate cash.

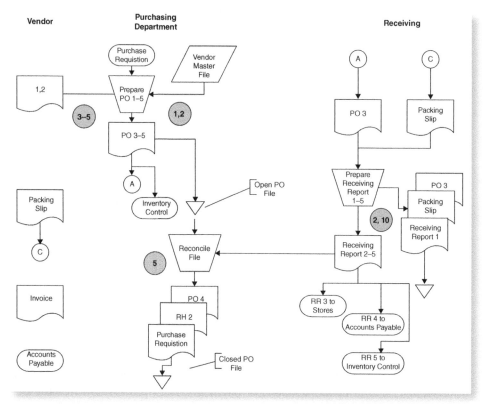

FIGURE 6.1 Generic Purchasing Cycle

There are a few principal subprocesses within the expenditure cycle as follows:

- **Purchasing:** Purchasing refers to all activities and procedures necessary for the entity to procure goods or services. Typical activities include selection and/or identification of a vendor, setup or modification of a vendor account, price scrutiny, approval of a new PO, and so on.
- **Receiving:** Receiving includes both the physical receipt of goods and services and all of the information work required to ensure appropriate accounting.
- **Cash disbursements:** Cash disbursements are only authorized disbursements made for goods and services actually received (within reasonable tolerance levels). Payment approval policies should ensure all disbursements fall within authorized limits.*

These risk exposures can affect the financial audit in a number of ways, and each risk exposure relates to one or more cycle subprocess. Table 6.4 in the next section illustrates these links at a high level, showing, for each of several illustrative risks, the potential impact on one or more of the assertions underlying the financial statements.† Table 6.4 also ties these risks to specific expenditure cycle subprocesses.

Application controls can mitigate these exposures, and it is thus important for the auditor to have a working knowledge of what these controls are, how they should function, and points of vulnerability. The numbered references on Figures 6.1 and 6.2

---

*Some organizations require dual signatures for checks exceeding a prespecified limit.
†These assertions are also discussed from both a financial and an IT audit perspective.

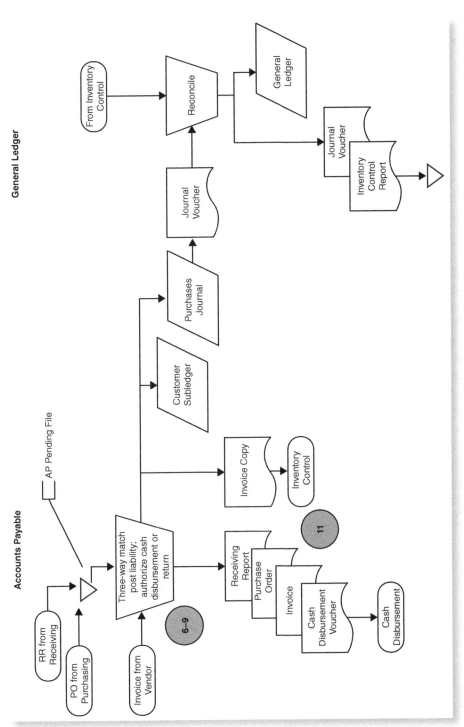

FIGURE 6.2 Generic Cash Disbursements Cycle

109

TABLE 6.1   Note 1—PO Distribution

Copy No.	To	REM
1, 2	Vendor	Figure 6.1 shows two copies of the PO going to the vendor.
3	Receiving	PO blind copy may be filed for some period of time between its creation and use as reconciling document when goods are received (filing not shown). *Blind copy* refers to the fact that quantity and pricing information are not provided. This control procedure is designed to ensure that receiving personnel perform counts instead of relying on information provided by the vendor.
4	Purchasing	The purchasing department traditionally retains a copy for review in the Open PO file. Copies of the receiving report forwarded to purchasing are matched against open POs and then filed.
5	Inventory Control	Data flow to inventory department supports updating of key inventory records.

identify locations of specific risks discussed in the next section. They illustrate typical expenditure and cash disbursement cycles for a small goods-based business. The drawings in Figures 6.1 and 6.2 are not intended to be comprehensive or applicable to all business models; rather, the intent is to highlight the broad relationships between common processes and frequently occurring risks. The use of document output in the flowcharts reflects the fact that, although the accounting process is computerized, paper output is frequently generated (e.g., billing notices). The drawing should be read in terms of information flows and with the tacit understanding that some of these occur with physical paper output and others via screen reading only. Table 6.1 provides detail on the information flows for the PO distribution. Table 6.2 provides detail on the information flows of the receiving report distribution.

TABLE 6.2   Note 2—Receiving Report Distribution

Copy No.	To	REM
1	Receiving	Copy #1 of the receiving report remains in the Receiving department for matching with a copy of the PO (shown as copy #3) and the packing slip.
2	Purchasing	Matched with purchase requisition and PO #4 for permanent filing in Closed PO file.*
3	Stores (shop-floor recordkeeping)	Records in the Stores department support timely reordering of low-stock items.
4	Accounts Payable	Backup for authorization to issued cash disbursements voucher.
5	Inventory Control	Data flow to Inventory department supports updating of key inventory records.

---

*Utilities are available in some general ledger packages and/or through third-party vendors to manage the deletion of old records. Design, implementation, and management of a records retention policy have clear implications for the completeness of accounting records.

APPLICATION CONTROLS, EXPENDITURE CYCLE RISKS, AND RELATED AUDIT PROCEDURES

This section begins with a general introduction to application controls. We then consider an illustrative set of risks that arise in the expenditure cycle. These include operational risks (i.e., what could go wrong) and financial statement risks. We examine these risks and the controls that should either prevent the problem (preventive controls) or alert personnel to the problem so that it can be remediated (detective controls). Within the context of each risk exposure and related controls we also discuss appropriate IT audit procedures.

Application Controls

Application controls are system-enabled controls within standard business processes. They are designed to enforce specific work requirements and, traditionally, are preventive in nature. Examples of application controls include:

- Logical access controls (i.e., application security)
- Date entry/field validations (e.g., validation of vendor prices)
- Workflow rules (e.g., electronic routing and signoff of expenditure requests)
- Field entries being enforced based on predefined values (e.g., vendor selection)

In discussing application controls, it is useful to observe the distinction between inherent and configurable controls. The former are programmed to perform the control through either custom coding or packaged delivery, while the latter can be modified by the end user.

Table 6.3 provides brief definitions for major control types. All of these general types of control are designed to limit the risk of inappropriate input, processing, or output of data.

TABLE 6.3 Major Application Control Types

Edit Checks	These controls relate to field format. For example, dollar amounts should be entered in numeric format.
Validations	Validation controls depend on the confirmation of a test. The well-known *three-way match* in which a check to a vendor cannot be generated without a matched PO, receiving report, and invoice can be automated at the application level. In the expenditure cycle, the PO and invoice could be matched.
Calculations	Calculations can be used to ensure that a computation is occurring accurately. Extensions and footings can be cross-checked with one another in order to address the risk that portions of an invoice may not be included in the totals.
Interfaces	Interfaces can be designed to address risks posed by data transfers from one system to another (e.g., counts that verify the number of records uploaded from the expenditure subledger to the general ledger).
Authorizations	Authorizations that limit access to data are a fundamental building block of control. Roles should be defined within the system and used to restrict the ability to modify records. For example, only the purchasing manager should have the ability to add vendors to the vendor master.

The level of automation associated with a control provides another set of fundamental distinctions. In general, controls can be manual, automated, or IT-dependent manual. This last category refers to controls performed by a person who relies on automated output. Most are detect controls that rely on computer-generated information or computer functionality. For example, management reviews a monthly variance report and follows up on significant variances. Because management relies on the computer-produced report to identify and generate the variances, the IT auditor needs to determine that there are controls in place to ensure that the variance report is complete and accurate.

Risks, Processes, and Application Controls

Table 6.4 provides an illustrative set of risk exposures and the ways in which these both impair the validity of management assertions about the financial statements and involve specific subprocesses.

Table 6.4 highlights major intersections between certain identified risks, the assertions, and principal subprocesses. There are many interpretations of these interrelationships, and the absence of an *x* doesn't mean that the control doesn't exist.

Access to Vendor Master File Is Not Restricted

Within the expenditure cycle, logical security access within the computer system is important to maintain appropriate segregation of duties. For example, access to the vendor master needs to be restricted to appropriate individuals to ensure that only appropriate individuals can add/change/delete vendors. The company may have additional controls outside of the system to ensure adequate vendor management, including an appropriate vendor selection process.

By having access to the vendor master file, the company could be exposed to potential fraudulent activity, including:

- A user could create a fictitious vendor and have goods delivered to an erroneous address, whereby the company may lose inventory and not get paid.
- A user could create a fictitious vendor and send a fake invoice to the company for payment (depending on the access levels within the system, the user that created the fictitious vendor could approve the payment for processing, which could circumvent other controls implemented within the company).
- A user could modify an existing, real vendor and change the address where the goods and/or invoice would be sent (this could cause loss of inventory that goes unpaid).

There are other potential risks with having inappropriate access to the master vendor file; these examples are illustrative in nature and do not cover every possible scenario. These risks may also be mitigated or minimized by other controls implemented at the company outside of the computer system.

TABLE 6.4 Risks, Assertions, and Subprocesses in the Expenditure Cycle

	Illustrative Risks	Existence/Occurrence	Completeness	Rights and Obligations	Valuation/Allocation	Accounting Procedures	Purchasing	Receiving	Cash Disbursements
		Assertions					**Cycle Subprocess**		
1	Access to vendor master file is not restricted	X	X	X			X	X	X
2	System roles not segregated for incompatible duties	X	X	X			X	X	X
3	PO not approved	X	X	X			X		
4	PO altered after being issued to vendor		X	X	X		X	X	X
5	Duplicate POs generated				X	X	X	X	X
6	Discounts differ from authorized amounts		X		X	X			X
7	Duplicate or overpayment for goods or services		X		X				X
8	Inaccurate processing of purchase credits for returns	X	X		X			X	X
9	Check numbers (not generated, not accurate)		X						X
10	Goods received do not agree to quantity ordered or authorized		X	X	X		X	X	
11	Invoices do not match PO and/or receiving reports	X	X					X	X

113

Within the computer system, the auditor can inspect access setups and vendor setups to determine if access to master vendor files is appropriate. Depending on the scope of the audit, the auditor can review the access and vendor setups at different levels of detail. Typically, access is reviewed either at a 100 percent sample for completeness or on a sample basis if a large number of users have access to the vendor master file.

Within QuickBooks (QB), as an example, a user can be assigned access to the vendor master file. In order to test who has access, the auditor needs to review appropriate access listings. After the auditor has determined who has access to the vendor master setup, then the auditor can determine if the access is appropriate based on review of that person's role and responsibilities and discussions with management. Note that many organizations, large and small, may grant users access to the vendor master file and to other access rights that may pose an overall segregation-of-duties concern, even if access to the vendor master file is appropriate and needed for that person's role and responsibility. Given this, the auditor and the company need to ensure that appropriate other controls are in place to mitigate or minimize the risk of inappropriate activity. (See Figure 6.3.)

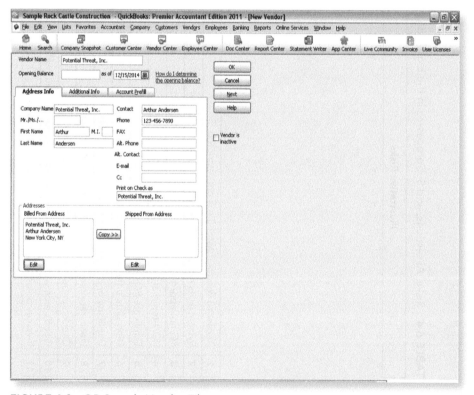

FIGURE 6.3   QB Sample Vendor File

Source: Intuit, Rock Castle.

In addition, within QB, access to the vendor master needs to be secured to ensure that only authorized vendors are set up within the system. The screenshot in Figure 6.3 shows the various inputs for vendor information within QB. Ensuring appropriate access to the vendor master can reduce the risk of fictitious vendors. If fictitious vendors were created, this could potentially lead to fraudulent transactions.

Within Microsoft Great Plains Dynamics (GPD), access to the vendor master file is set up using tasks and roles that are assigned to users. These tasks may vary depending on how the system was implemented. The auditor can review the specific tasks within the computer system and then identify the tasks that appear to be relevant to the scope of the audit being performed as it relates to vendor master file. After the tasks have been identified, the auditor should run a report that identifies the roles that have the associated tasks. This will enable the auditor to understand the roles that may grant access to the vendor master file. Note that the naming of the roles may not be intuitive and the auditor is cautioned not to rely only on the naming of the roles without truly understanding the tasks associated with that role. For example, there could be a role called "Vendor Read Only," but in fact that role may have add/change/delete rights to the vendor master file due to the assignment of a task. During setup, the company has the ability to modify which tasks are associated with which roles, and name the roles however the company desires for their purposes. Granted, not every company will change the vanilla setup that is delivered within the system, but the auditor needs to assume that some customization of the role setups has occurred in order to ensure that appropriate segregation of duties exists.

After the auditor has identified the roles associated with the tasks deemed to be of audit interest, then the auditor needs to identify the users associated with these roles. After the auditor has identified the users associated with these roles, then the auditor, as in the previous example, needs to ensure that the access is appropriate based on roles and responsibilities and discussion with management.

System Roles Not Segregated for Incompatible Duties

As discussed within the access to the vendor master file, ensuring segregation of duties is a primary control within and outside the computer system. This risk expands the discussion where the auditor and the company need to be concerned with all financially significant access within the system. Many organizations fail in this area because although management may have implemented good processes outside the system that ensure appropriate segregation of duties, the company does not ensure that the access rights granted within the system are commensurate with the roles and responsibilities of the users. This means that the auditor needs to ensure that system rights assigned to users are appropriate based on the users' job responsibilities within the system. Some auditors forget to look inside the system to verify the actual capabilities of the user and simply rely on an organizational chart. This is not enough testing and the auditor should not gain reliance on segregation of duties without analyzing the access rights within the system. In addition, the auditor needs to ensure that the system rights granted do not create a segregation-of-duties (SOD) conflict. Typical SOD conflicts within the expenditure cycle include any roles that combine recordkeeping authority with physical custody of assets.

Within QB, system rights are configured based on activities. For purchases and accounts payable, system rights that could be granted include entering and paying bills, entering credit card charges, and entering POs. They also include access to the Vendor Center and accounts payable reports.

When granting these system rights to a user, the administrator will select no access, full access, or selective access. Full access will give the user access to all activities within the purchases and accounts payable area. Selective access can be specific to creating transactions only, creating and printing transactions, or creating transactions and creating reports. (See Figure 6.4.)

For checking and credit cards, the activities within this area would include writing and printing checks, making deposits, and entering credit card charges. Once again, the user can be assigned to no access, full access, or selective access. When the auditor reviews the configuration of access for a sample of users, the auditor needs to not only review the individual system rights granted for each area, but take a holistic view of all areas to ensure that SOD conflicts do not occur. (See Figure 6.5.)

In order to do a full analysis of access rights within QB, the auditor should review the specific access rights granted to the user within the system. After the auditor has this information, the auditor can compare the system rights with the roles and responsibilities of the user and discuss with management the appropriateness of such access. In addition, the auditor should ensure that the system access rights within QB and possibly other information systems, whether manual or automated, do not create an SOD concern for any particular user. In most organizations, an SOD conflict will arise. This does

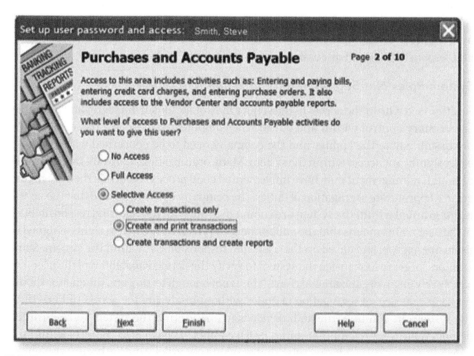

FIGURE 6.4 QB Limiting Access to Accounts Payable

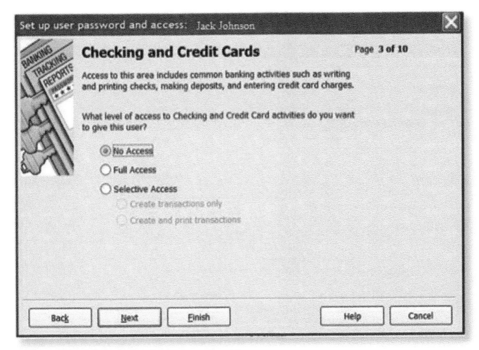

FIGURE 6.5   QB Limiting Access to Checking

not mean that the auditor cannot rely on the system or overall control environment. The auditor needs to understand, based on the specific situation, what other controls exist within the computer system or outside the computer system that may mitigate or minimize the associated risks.

Within GPD, user security is more granular and specific tasks can be assigned to users. Within the expenditure cycle, the following tasks could be assigned to a user.

In order to review what access has been assigned within GPD, the auditor could identify potential SOD conflicts, and, as described in the access to vendor master file section, go through a process to identify each financially significant task of audit interest and associate the task with the roles and the users in order to have a comprehensive analysis of what access rights the users have within the system. These should be evaluated in order to determine if the access is appropriate. (See Figures 6.6 and 6.7.)

Purchase Order Not Approved

During a financial and/or operational audit, an auditor may be concerned with the PO approval process. POs should not be executed unless appropriately approved. Ensuring that a PO is approved prior to execution is a good internal control. This approval could occur within or outside of the system depending on the overall control environment.

Within GPD, the PO approval occurs within the system. There are controls around printing the PO prior to approval and ensuring that approval limits are configured for buyers to reduce the risk of excessive buying beyond predetermined levels. (See Figure 6.8.)

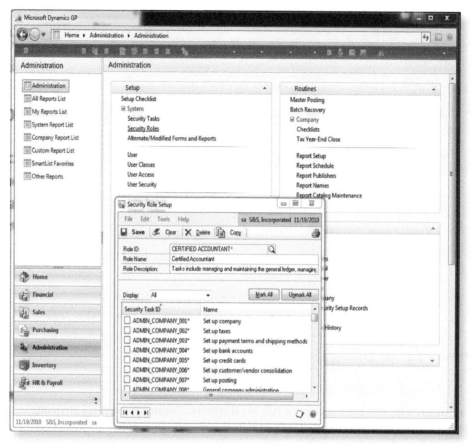

FIGURE 6.6 GPD System Rights Access

Source: Brunsdon, Romney, and Steinbart. 2009. This image was taken using the dataset provided from this book. Note that the screenshot says "S&S Incorporated," which is the dataset of these authors.

Within GPD, the approval status needs to be set to "Approved" before the PO can be printed. Some threats involved with this include purchasing goods from unauthorized suppliers, ordering unnecessary items, and purchasing goods at inflated prices or at inferior quality. Suppliers included in the master list need to be authorized. If they are not and a fake supplier is included on a PO, the approval requirement can still act to prevent the PO from being sent out. This process of approving the PO will also prevent unnecessary items from being ordered, perhaps because the warehouse manager will realize she has more inventories on hand than previously assumed and the PO can be canceled instead of approved. Finally, if there are applicable discounts that can be taken advantage of, but not provided in the PO, the manager can prevent the PO from being approved and modify the PO before it is sent out. (See Figure 6.9.)

In this situation within GPD, the buyer is not authorized to issue a PO for the amount listed. The buyer's approval authorization requirements may need to be changed.

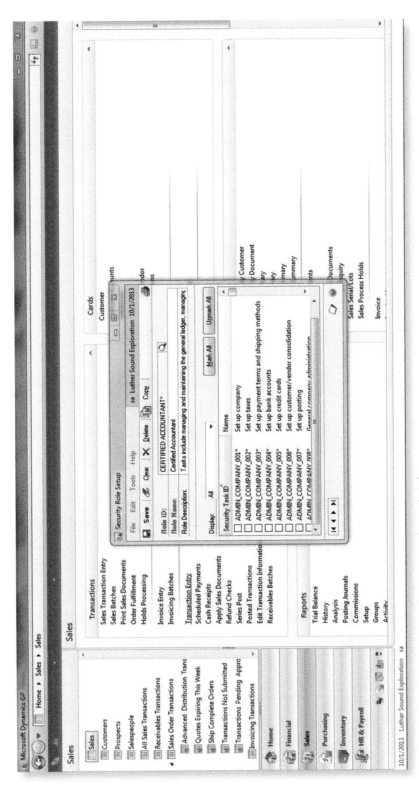

FIGURE 6.7 GPD System Rights Access, through Sales

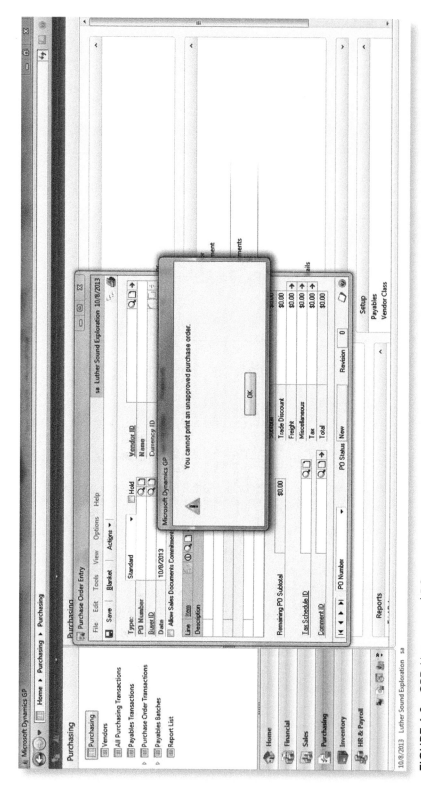

FIGURE 6.8 GPD Unapproved PO

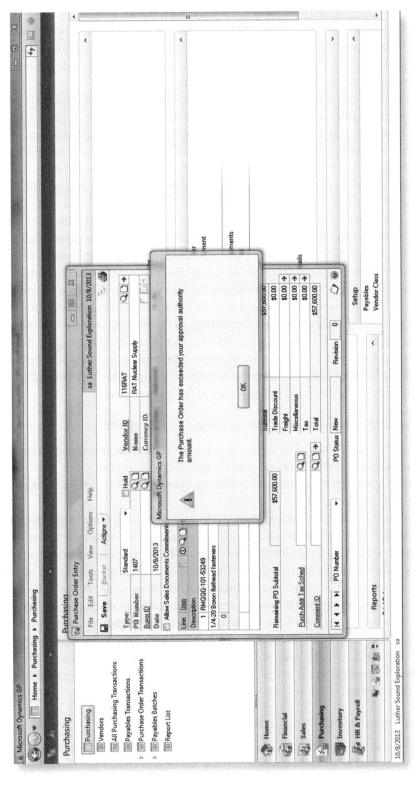

FIGURE 6.9 GPD Exceeding Purchasing Amount

The administrator of the system sets the buyer's limit for amounts that can be issued on a PO. Only the administrator has the authority to change these limitations. This avoids threats such as employees ordering items for their own personal use or over-ordering goods, and inflated prices that were entered in error.

There is a risk that buyers could purchase goods or services beyond their preapproved limits and thus cause excess obligations to the business. (See Figure 6.10.)

The buyer ID on the PO links to a user ID. In order to have the PO approved, the administrator needs to be given unlimited approval authority. Buyers cannot set the limits for themselves or anyone else. Only the administrator has the authority to do so, and administrators need to be given unlimited authority to process any modifications. (See Figure 6.11.)

This screen output indicates that the PO has been approved. It is important to note that a PO has been approved before it is sent to the vendor in order to ensure that a correct PO is sent. If a PO is not approved and is sent out, the company could risk buying unnecessary items, buying goods at inflated costs, buying from false vendors that were not in the master list, or not taking advantage of purchase discounts. (See Figure 6.12.)

As indicated on the PO, there is a signature line that requires authorization of the PO prior to its being mailed to the vendor. Although the system has approved the PO, it must then be authorized by the purchasing manager. Through this example it can be seen that the activity of recording a PO is segregated from authorizing or printing the PO. Great Plains bases the print approval activity on the user ID that is logged into the system and not on the buyer ID that is linked to the transaction.

Purchase Order Altered After Being Issued to the Vendor

The alteration of a PO after issuance could potentially affect items ordered and pricing. When an alteration of the PO occurs, the PO should be reapproved.

Within Dynamics, the system will inform the user when a PO has been altered after issuance. (See Figure 6.13.)

After printing, or authorizing, the PO, the status at the bottom of the document changes to "Released." Per internal control reasons, Great Plains has restrictions on the modification of POs that have already been released. If this restriction were not in place, employees could easily go into the PO and modify it by changing the quantity or prices listed in the PO. After making these changes, the PO status would still say "Released" and it would be close to impossible to detect what changes were made. (See Figure 6.14.)

If any modifications have been made to the released PO, the PO status changes to "Change Order," indicating that modifications have been performed and that the PO needs to be reprinted. In the example shown in the screenshot, we increased the quantity ordered as a modification to the original PO. This action of changing the PO status is a detective control.

Duplicate Purchase Orders Generated

Duplicate PO numbers could potentially cause issues within the expenditure cycle. When goods are received or invoices are received, the incorrect PO may be used to apply the goods and invoice. Some threats involved with the numbering of POs include paying the

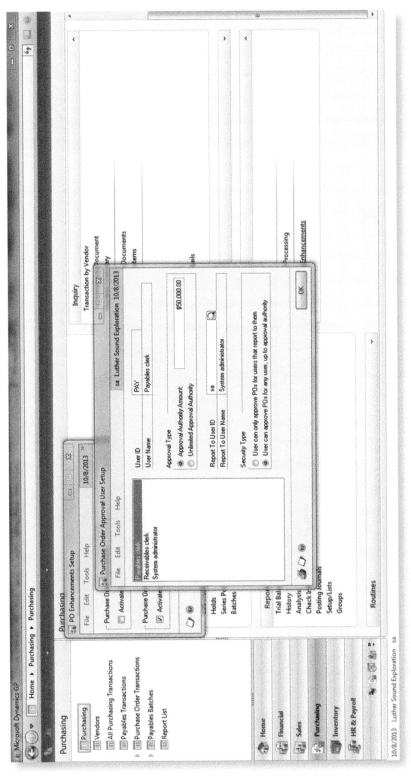

FIGURE 6.10 GPD PO Approval

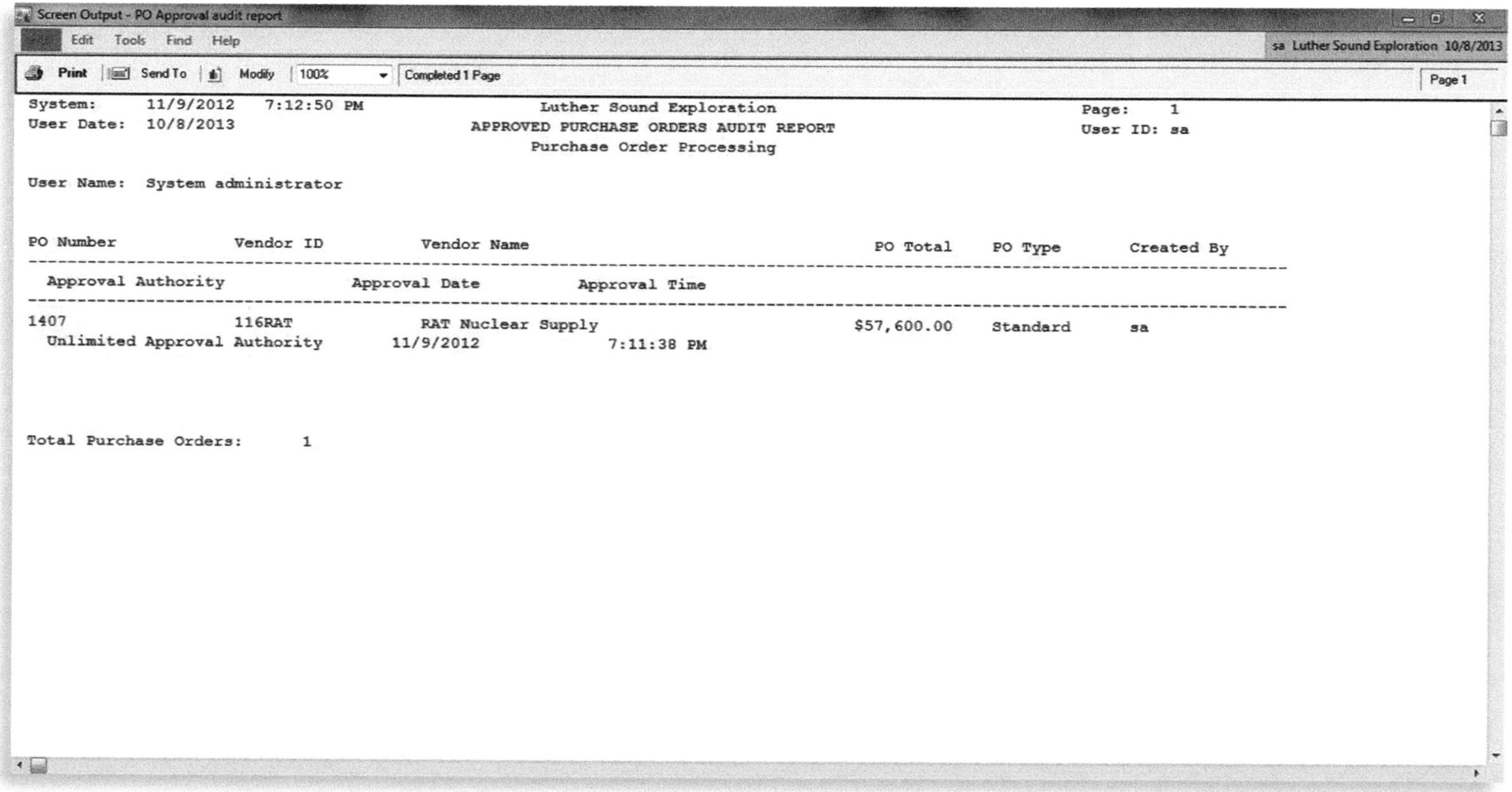

FIGURE 6.11 GPD PO Approval Audit Report

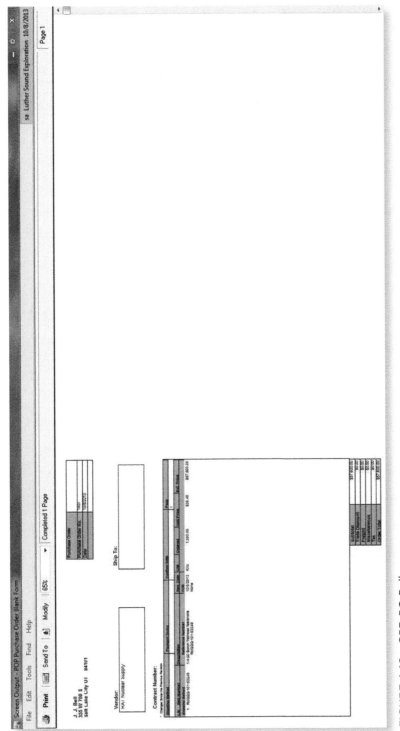

FIGURE 6.12 GPD PO Rollup

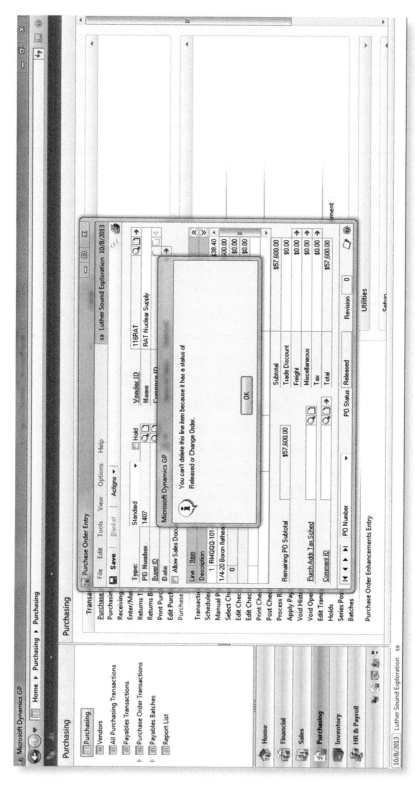

FIGURE 6.13 GPD Altering POs

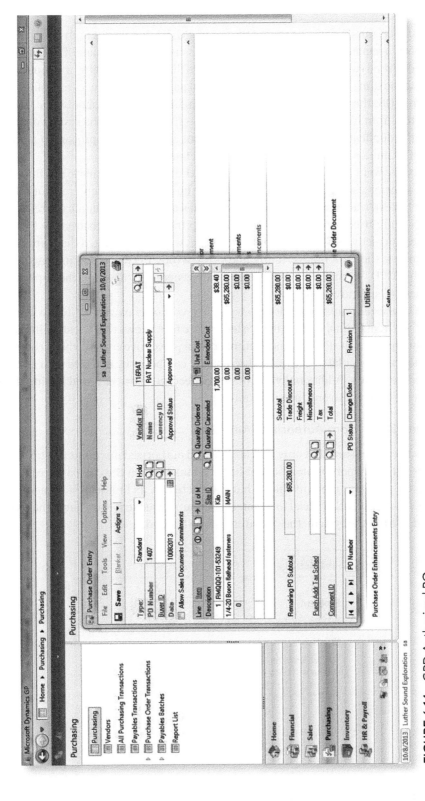

FIGURE 6.14 GPD Authorized PO

same PO twice, missing POs, or paying the wrong PO. It is important to ensure that POs are numbered sequentially so as to catch any errors. In certain instances, if a PO number is skipped or used twice, the company could believe that a PO is missing or it could wind up issuing the same PO twice, which may result in paying that PO twice as well.

Within QB, the system warns the user that a duplicate PO is about to be used to prevent this from happening. However, this is a soft control and the system does not prevent the duplicate PO. Therefore, management should have a process in place to review PO numbers to minimize duplicates. (See Figure 6.15.)

When we went to save the PO, QB prompted the first soft control we ran into. The window informs users that another PO already has the number entered but allows the user to keep the number anyway. This creates an issue with duplicate reference numbers being used. Auditors will need to be extra careful to ensure that POs are numbered correctly. This is a soft control. The risk would exist that, if there are duplicate numbers, the clerk inadvertently marks the wrong PO when making payment.

Within GPD, PO numbers are automatically generated to prevent the duplication of numbers. (See Figure 6.16.)

A PO is a legal commitment from a buyer to a vendor to pay for an item when it is received. In Great Plains, POs are not posted. Figure 6.16 shows that Great Plains automatically populates the PO document number. As a preventive control, the PO number is automatically calculated because a discrepancy can be easily detected if an error in the sequence occurs. Additionally, PO numbers need to be tracked, and having them sequenced is a sign of strong internal controls.

Discounts Differ from Authorized Amounts

Auditors need to ensure that only appropriate and authorized discounts are taken for purchases. If an inappropriate discount has been taken, then the company could still be liable for a greater amount than what is reflected on its financial statements. As such, this could potentially lead to a material amount owed to a third party that is not captured. Within the system, the discounts can be tracked.

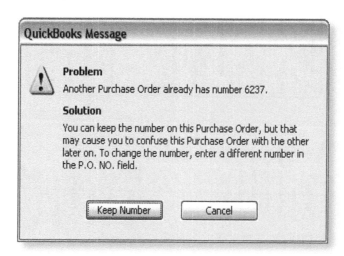

FIGURE 6.15   QB Duplicate POs

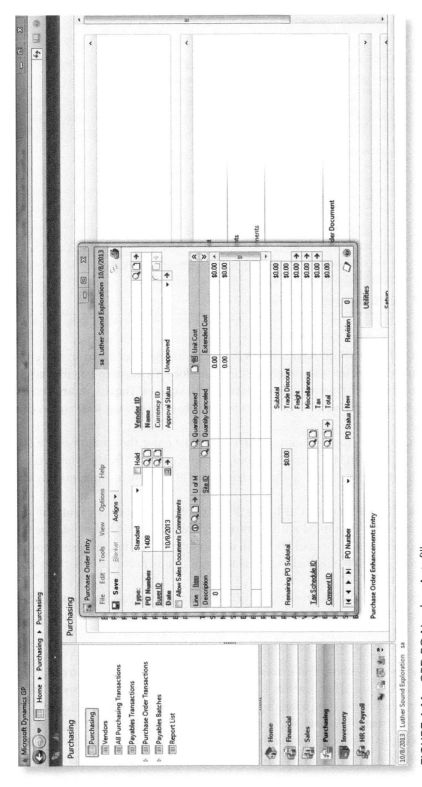

FIGURE 6.16 GPD PO Number Autofill

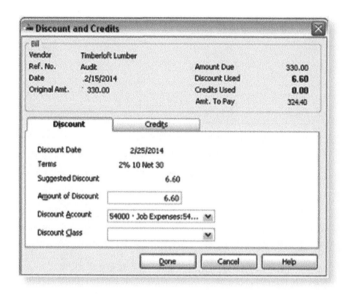

FIGURE 6.17 QB Suggested Discounts

Within QB, the discounts screen shows the suggested discount based on the terms with the vendor. However, the suggested discount does not have to be adhered to. Instead, the user could input a higher or lower discount amount. The risk we are focused on is the input of the higher discount, thus potentially short-paying the vendor. (See Figure 6.17.)

Figure 6.18 shows the Discounts screen. You must enter the amount of the discount you wish to use and the account to charge the discount to. You can change these preferences located under "Edit" at the top left of the QB window to automatically use discounts.

To see how far QB would let us take a discount, we entered the full value of the invoice but were not prompted with a warning. We found this to be a deficiency because simple human error could result in underpaying a vendor and losing potential discounts. QB also lets you charge the discount to any account under the sun. This is unacceptable.

A benefit of this Discount screen is that QB calculates the suggested discount for the user. This reduces user error when determining discounts.

Duplicate or Overpayment for Goods or Services

Management needs to ensure that invoices are paid once, and not more than once. The IT auditor should ensure that controls exist that would prevent duplicate payments or payments that vary more than a small predetermined amount from that determined by the three-way match. As part of this review, the auditor should determine whether the system prevents or at least reports on duplicate versions of an invoice. This situation could arise when a clerk inadvertently enters a second (dunning) notice as a distinct invoice.

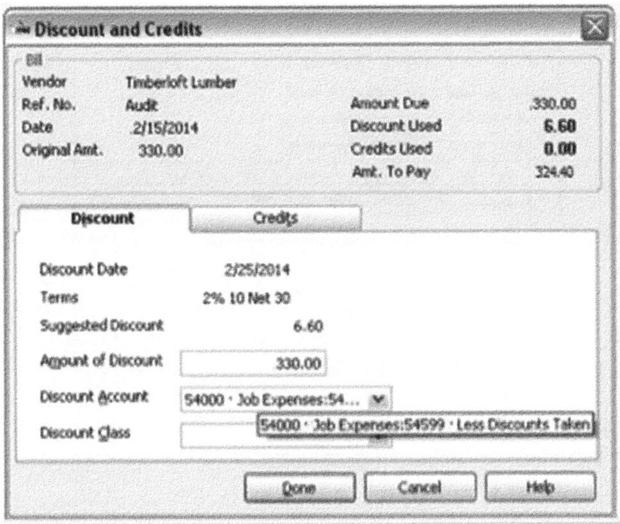

FIGURE 6.18 QB Assigning Discounts to an Account

Inaccurate Processing of Purchase Credits for Returns

When purchased items are returned to the vendor for credit, the auditor needs to ensure that the appropriate credits are applied to the financial statements. Within the computer system, there may or may not be controls that will prevent the appropriate application of the credit.

Within QB, you cannot create a credit that receives against a PO. If you try to receive the credit against a PO, QB stops you with no other option but to continue without a PO. (See Figure 6.19.)

Check Numbers (Not Generated, Not Accurate)

The preassignment of check numbers within the system could be a good control to help prevent duplicate check numbers. (See Figure 6.20.)

The last step in the Bill Pay process is assigning the check number. QB can automatically assign check numbers to maintain a sequential line of checks. Note, however, that users may enter any check number they care to, even if this is a duplicate check number.

FIGURE 6.19 QB Error of Credit Receiving against a PO

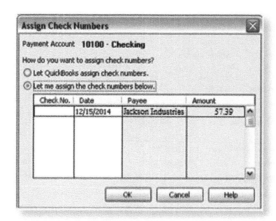

FIGURE 6.20 QB Preassignment of Check Numbers

Goods Received, but Do Not Agree to Quantity Ordered or Authorized

The auditor needs to ensure that only goods ordered and authorized are received. In some companies, a vendor may inadvertently send the company a shipment of goods when it was not previously ordered. The receiving department may in fact receive these goods into the system. The auditor can compare the POs report with the goods received report in order to find any discrepancies. Depending on the system, the system may have a reconciliation report that identifies goods received, but not ordered or authorized.

In both GPD and QB, the auditor can print the POs report and compare it to the goods received report. This will enable the auditor to identify these transactions. The company needs to ensure that it does not pay the invoice associated with the receipt of these goods. In many instances, this process happens outside of the system and the goods are not entered into the system. Leading practices would be to return the goods to the vendor and not enter into the system, and/or contact the vendor to identify the issue prior to entering into the system.

Invoices Do Not Match Purchase Order and/or Receiving Reports

One of the most well-known controls in the expenditure cycle is the three-way match. In the three-way match, the auditor wants to ensure that the PO matches the goods received and the invoice within a reasonable tolerance level.

Within many systems, the three-way match can be configured to automatically process invoices if the quantity billed at a given price is within the tolerance level. The tolerance level is also configured within the system.

If invoices are received that do not match the PO or goods received, then the company is at risk of being erroneously billed. The payment of invoices for goods not received or at the wrong price could adversely affect the profit of the company.

Within GPD, one example of a soft control is where the user gets a warning if the invoice cost is different from the PO cost. (See Figure 6.21.)

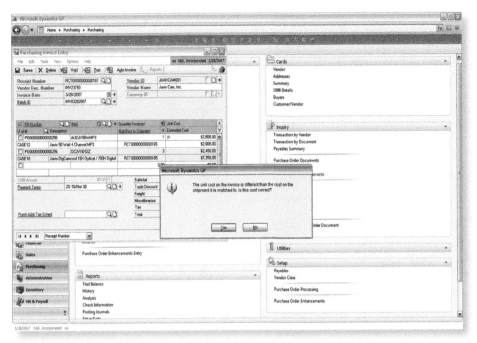

FIGURE 6.21 GPD Matching PO Costs to Invoice Costs

Source: Brunsdon, Romney, and Steinbart. 2009. This image was taken using the dataset provided from this book. Note that the screenshot says "S&S Incorporated," which is the dataset of these authors.

The PO displays $1,800 as the cost for the first item. Javix's invoice shows a different cost. The unit cost on Javix's invoice states $2,000. As a detective control, GPD issues a warning to indicate a cost variance from the receipt. The threat that is prevented by this control is failing to catch errors in vendor invoices. Vendor invoices may contain errors such as discrepancies between quoted and actual prices charged or miscalculations of the total amount due. Consequently, the prices and quantities listed must be verified with those indicated on the PO and receiving report.

SUMMARY

Because the expenditure cycle encompasses all processes, personnel, and activities that relate to the ordering and receipt of goods and services, the key risk exposures lie in the possibility that erroneous or inappropriate transaction processes will result in the undesired outflow of corporate cash or the undesired inflow of goods or services. Application controls are a key tool in the mitigation of this exposure.

The Inventory Cycle

THE INVENTORY CYCLE ENCOMPASSES ALL processes, personnel, and activities that occur between initial receipt of goods and shipment of finished goods to the customer. This chapter commences at the point where the purchasing cycle finishes. The primary focus of this chapter is on manufacturing-type companies that add value by transforming raw materials into finished goods. Due to the potentially unlimited complexity and variety of manufacturing processes, we confine most of our discussion to a generalized illustration of basic functionality, and omit extended detail on features found in specialized manufacturing modules.

Third-Party Inventory and Supply Chain Management Software

The complexity of inventory tracking and costing that is briefly described in this chapter indicates the need for highly adaptable and specialized software to process allocation calculations that can occur in high volume, vary significantly across items, and/or require frequent adjustment. While some of these activities might be accomplished within the general ledger (GL) package, in many instances the number of required exceptions, adjustments, and workarounds would make this approach cumbersome if not completely unworkable. One obvious approach to this circumstance involves the use of customized Excel worksheets, one of the topics that receive extended consideration at other points in this book.

(continued)

Several alternatives to this approach have been developed in the last few years for both the internal inventory cycle addressed in this chapter and the broader area of supply chain management (SCM). Broad areas and desired functionalities within SCM include distribution, picking, stock levels on an available-to-promise basis, and forecasting of demand on both the purchasing and revenue sides.

Interfaces between these applications and the accounting software present several IT audit risk exposures. The auditor should determine whether the application was made specifically for the GL package, or a specialized interface had to be created. In the latter circumstance, tests should be designed and conducted in order to assure the auditor that data passes accurately and reliably between the systems. Hash and control totals can help to ensure that correct dollar amounts and numbers of accounts have been transferred. The auditor should also evaluate when and under what circumstances the data transfer occurs: Is it manual or automated? Do transactions cause transfers on a real-time basis, or are they handled in batches?

RISK EXPOSURES AND SUBPROCESSES

The inventory cycle contains several areas of risk exposure. These include:

- **Warehouse:** Are item cards set up appropriately? Are processes in place to ensure that the company can accurately process orders for replacement inventory? Are logical access controls to inventory records set up appropriately? Are the inventory records appropriately updated when raw material is received? Do the perpetual inventory records represent the actual amount on hand? Will the system support possible expansion in the number of types of inventory items? Does the shipping information from the inventory cycle accurately transfer to the revenue cycle for revenue recognition purposes?
- **Manufacturing:** If there are multiple stages of manufacturing processes, are items of work in process correctly classified, insofar as this information is needed for accounting and operational purposes? Are all costs required for external reporting processes captured (e.g., in addition to direct material, other full-absorption costs such as direct labor and overhead)?
- **Repair:** Does the system require return authorization prior to acceptance of an item for return, repair, or replacement? Are items transferred to a repair process accurately classified and tracked? Does the system alert administrators to potential business exposures such as fraudulent or defalcatory misclassification of inventory items? Are the inventory records appropriately updated to reflect the goods received as part of the return, repair, or replacement process?

These risk exposures can affect the financial audit in a number ways, and each risk exposure relates to one or more cycle subprocess. Table 7.4 (later in the chapter) illustrates these links at a high level, showing, for each of several illustrative risks, the potential impact on one or more of the assertions underlying the financial statements.* The table also ties these risks to specific inventory cycle subprocesses.

Subprocesses in the inventory cycle include the warehouse storage of goods (raw material, finished goods), movement of goods between manufacturing stages, and the shipment of finished goods to the customer. There are potentially many variations and iterations of basic manufacturing processes, and no set of illustrations could capture all of these. Process descriptions of the inventory cycle are widely available from various sources. Allowing for differences in processing technology (e.g., batch or continuous), specific company policies (e.g., credit-related, exception routines for backorders, etc.), and goods-based versus services-based business models, the essential features of the inventory cycle are generally similar across businesses.

Some of the key subprocesses within the inventory cycle examined or discussed in this chapter include:

- **Material item setup:** Before the inventory cycle processes can track the flow of goods, it is necessary to define the material items set up in the system. Preparation or modification of these item records include such vital information as item description, unit(s) of measurement, amounts and methods of costing and pricing, tolerances for variances, and vendor(s).
- **Receipt of goods and initial entry into the system:** This includes the physical receipt of goods, the verification of goods that were ordered, and the entry of related financial information into the system. This is part of the typical three-way match that links the purchasing, cash disbursement, and inventory cycles. Initial entry should reflect the full landed cost of items (e.g., freight and related costs).
- **Initial storage of goods:** This stage in the inventory cycle represents the temporary storage of raw materials while waiting for manufacturing processes. It is important that the system track physical location (referred to in GPD as "sites," e.g., "Boston facility") and processing stage (referred to in GPD as "bins," e.g., "material available for issue," "Work in process [WIP] at stage one of three-part manufacturing process," etc.). The design of a company's manufacturing processes will affect the length of time that an item remains in initial storage—from weeks or months in some cases to virtually instantaneous movement for a just-in-time (JIT) system.
- **Goods issued to the manufacturing process and work-in-process management:** Depending on the complexity of the manufacturing process, this stage may represent a single transaction wherein raw materials are issued to the manufacturing process and transformed into WIP, or an iterated sequence of such transactions, as raw materials go through an initial process, the resultant WIP is stored for a period of time and then modified in a subsequent process, is again stored for a period of time prior to entering another subsequent process, and so on. (See Figure 7.3 later in the chapter.)
- **Finished goods received from the manufacturing process and stored in the warehouse awaiting final shipment to customer:** Inventory recognized as finished goods (FG) generally connotes an exit stage in the manufacturing process.

---

* These assertions are discussed from both a financial and an IT audit perspective in Chapter 1.

Within the broad FG category it may be important to distinguish between goods manufactured for sales fulfillment and buffer stock manufactured for anticipated sales. Note also that accounting standards typically require that the account balance of FG include full-absorption costing of direct labor (DL) and allocated overhead.

▪ **Shipment to customers**: The terms of shipment link this stage to revenue recognition issues. This is an important part of the system controls for appropriate revenue recognition.

▪ **Reverse logistics—vendor:** Counts and costs need to be adjusted when goods are returned to a vendor. The return process may represent the simple cancellation of a sale, or the simultaneous return of goods and ordering of new replacement goods.

▪ **Reverse logistics—customer:** Customer-based reverse logistics will generally present more issues for a company than vendor-based returns. These include processing of the customer's requisition request, receipt of the goods, disposition of returned items (returned to inventory, sent to repairs, or scrapped) and the related effects on customer receivables and enterprise sales.

▪ **Repairs:** FG sent to a repairs department may reflect external (customer warranty claim) or internal (quality control inspection) processes.

▪ **Scrap and obsolescence:** Maintaining records of inventory that has been damaged, determined to be obsolete, or scrapped for some other reason allows the company to calculate net loss after any recovery, update counts, perform efficiency analysis, and so on.

Figures 7.1 and 7.2 illustrate a typical inventory cycle for a small goods-based business. The drawings are not intended to be comprehensive or applicable to all business models; rather, the intent is to highlight the broad relationships between common processes and frequently occurring risks. The use of document output in the flowcharts reflects the fact that, although the accounting process is computerized, paper output is frequently generated (e.g., receiving records, cycle count reports, shipping records). Figures 7.1 and 7.2 should be read in terms of information flows and with the tacit understanding that some of these occur with physical paper output and others via screen reading only. Table 7.1 provides detail on the physical flow of goods in a generic manufacturing system. Table 7.2 provides detail on the information flows in a generic manufacturing system.

Application controls can mitigate these exposures, and it is thus important for the auditor to have a working knowledge of what these controls are, how they should function, and points of vulnerability. The numbered references in Figure 7.2 identify locations of specific risks discussed in the following pages.

Figure 7.1 also identifies some key accounting processes that accompany the physical flow of goods through the manufacturing process. Heavily weighted lines indicate transactions and physical flows that involve external parties: vendors and customers. Dashed lines indicate FGs that have been repaired or remanufactured.

On receipt, goods can be assigned to a physical location and logged in as raw materials (RM). Issuing RM to the manufacturing process requires accounting reassignment

TABLE 7.1 Note 1—Physical Flow of Goods in a Generic Manufacturing System

n 1	Inventory cards setup is required before purchase orders can be issued. Note that aspects of this process reflect external concerns (choice of vendors) and other aspects are rooted in the physical description of inventory items (units of measure and other important descriptors).
n 2	Costs of repair are entered into the system and assigned to inventory. For mass production these costs may be an item of overhead, and for specific identification systems they may attach to particular items of inventory (e.g., a job shop utilizing construction-type accounting). Irregular or unusual (and generally immaterial) repair costs may be expensed for the period.
n 3	Disposition of scrap quantities will generally result in some recovery amounts; the net difference between WIP entering repair and related recoveries is recorded as a loss for financial reporting purposes.
n 4	Repaired warranty goods returned to customer.

from RM to WIP. The drawing omits detail on the many specific features of manufacturing processes that involve repetitive or elaborate movement of WIP through different processes and between various geographic locations. During the manufacturing process, costs are accumulated in the system in order to fully absorb the direct labor and overhead costs in addition to the direct material costs that result in the cost of goods manufactured (i.e., one wants to ensure that the system shows all the actual and allocated costs in FG so the appropriate amounts will be released to the cost of goods sold when revenue is recognized). For many companies, this process may be done offline via spreadsheets or other third-party software. While the transaction-based direct labor (DL) and various types of overhead (OH) costs can be readily accumulated within the GL package, spreadsheet software is widely used to perform the allocations. Very few general ledger packages have the robust flexibility to handle the numerous and somewhat unpredictable variety of calculations required by full-absorption costing

TABLE 7.2 Note 2—Accounting Information Flows in a Generic Manufacturing System

n 11	Initial costing of raw materials (RM) may be at standard or actual pricing.
n 12	Issuance of RM may involve transportation, allocated storage, or other additional costs.
n 13	Full-absorption costing requires accounting information relating to payroll and general overhead costs. There may be additional loops of information flows between the General Ledger department (GL) and various manufacturing departments.
n 14	Cost of good manufactured (COGM) information is added to other accumulated costs.
n 15	Shipping terms analysis and consideration of multiple elements issues tie into revenue cycle.
n 16	Accounting treatment of scrap recoveries may result in reduction of COGM, complete write-off, or separate source of revenue.
n 17	Potential recoveries from vendors for warranty costs.
n 4	Repaired warranty goods returned to customer.

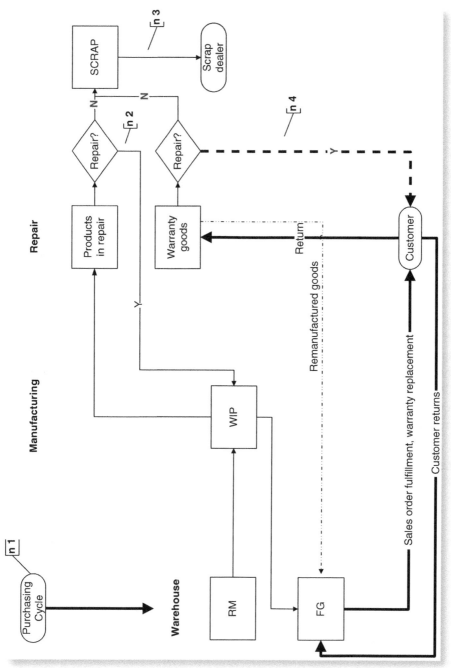

FIGURE 7.1 Physical Flows of Inventory in a Generic Manufacturing Setting

Source: See Table 7.1 for notes.

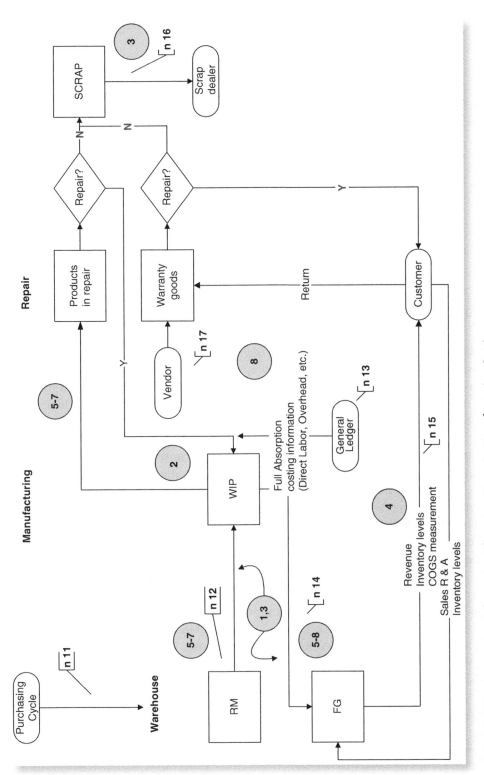

FIGURE 7.2 Accounting Information Flows in a Generic Manufacturing Setting

Source: See Table 7.2 for notes and Table 7.4 for risks, assertions, and subprocesses.

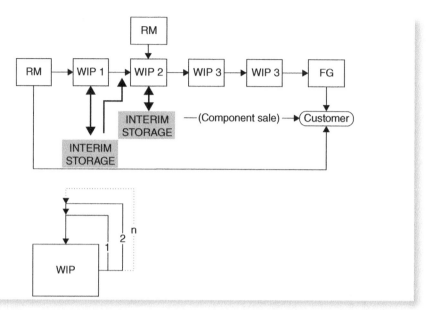

FIGURE 7.3 Inventory Flows

without becoming so cumbersome as to be virtually unusable. Other chapters address some of the common Excel-based IT exposures. The inherent complexities of costing inventory provide a prime instance of why so many businesses find the awkward process of rekeying data between applications less objectionable than attempting to house all accounting processes within one massive system.

At the conclusion of the manufacturing process WIP becomes FG and moves to a warehouse location, which for simplicity we show as the same location where raw materials were received. The accounting classification of this stock must be updated to FG.

Not all WIP emerges from the manufacturing process as merchantable FG. Figure 7.1 stylizes the repair process with an initial assignment to products-in-repair status, from which the goods are either scrapped or returned to manufacturing. In the first case, the accounting process needs to record the loss, net of any recoveries. In the second case, the additional costs need to be recognized in inventory or as a period expense, as appropriate.

Customer returns of defective goods for warranty repair go through a similar process. In some cases the goods are repairable and shipped back to the customer (heavy dashed line in Figure 7.1). For internal accounting purposes the costs and liabilities for parts and labor need to be recorded, even though an estimate of these may have been recognized at an earlier point in time for external reporting purposes. Assuming the passage of time between receipt of returned goods and determination of whether the item was repairable, placing the returned goods under accounting control allows the company to accumulate a dollar balance for these goods, an amount necessary for the determination of realized losses on scrapping unrepairable goods. Customers may also return goods for sales credit.

Figure 7.3 is intended to suggest the variety of accounting issues raised by various iterations of the manufacturing process. A relatively straightforward situation exists when raw materials enter a process that transforms them into work in process and the FG that are then sold to the customer. Depending upon the nature of the process, however, it may be necessary to identify discrete stages along the way and to prepare reports or record account balances for each of them. This would be important for both internal (costing) and external reporting.

As examples of alternative paths that materials might take through the production cycle, consider:

- WIP may be produced in excess of current processing requirements and stored offline for a period of time before reentering the production flow (as shown with WIP 1 and an interim storage location). The production accounting system would need to maintain accurate counts for planning purposes.
- An entity's value chain (see Figure 7.4) may be physically dispersed across multiple geographic locations. In addition to production accounting system requirements, the external reporting may need to report segment or line of business (LOB) disclosure (e.g., WIP 1, WIP 2).
- RM may enter the value chain at various stages of production. The production accounting system needs to support cost tracing and related reporting.
- Some WIP may be sold as a component. The production accounting system needs to support any required adjustments to the allocation process that result from a dual-use model for items of WIP.

The lower panel in the drawing in Figure 7.3 describes WIP that goes through an iterative succession of processes that are separated by distinct intervals of time. When the accumulation of items for batch processing occurs quickly there is seldom a requirement for any elaborate accounting treatment, but should this accumulation span two or more accounting periods there may well be a need to identify WIP by the stage of a completion. A classic example of this process is the aging of whiskey and the identification of five-year stock, six-year stock, seven-year stock, and so on.

APPLICATION CONTROLS, INVENTORY CYCLE RISKS, AND RELATED AUDIT PROCEDURES

This section begins with a general introduction to application controls. We then consider an illustrative set of risks that arise in the inventory cycle. These include operational risks (what could go wrong) and financial statement risks. We examine these risks and the controls that should either prevent the problem (preventive controls) or alert personnel to the problem so that it can be remediated (detective controls). Within the context of each risk exposure and related controls we also discuss appropriate IT audit procedures.

Application Controls

Application controls are system-enabled controls within standard business processes. They are designed to enforce specific work requirements and, traditionally, are preventive in nature. Examples of application controls include:

- Logical access controls (i.e., application security)
- Date entry/field validations (e.g., validation of entered raw materials received or FG shipped)

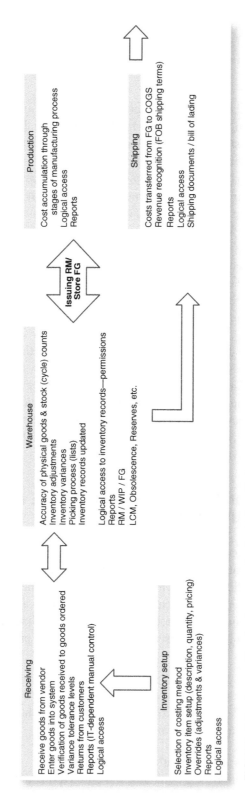

FIGURE 7.4 Accounting for Inventory in the Value Chain

- Workflow rules (e.g., electronic routing and signoff of write-offs and repairs)
- Field entries being enforced based on predefined values (e.g., item card information)

In discussing application controls, it is useful to observe the distinction between inherent and configurable controls. The former are programmed to perform the control through either custom coding or packaged delivery, while the latter can be modified by the end user.

Table 7.3 provides brief definitions for major control types. All of these general types of control are designed to limit the risk of inappropriate input, processing, or output of data.

The level of automation associated with a control provides another set of fundamental distinctions. In general, controls can be manual, automated, or IT-dependent manual. This last category refers to controls performed by a person who relies on automated output. Most are detective controls that rely on computer-generated information or computer functionality. For example, management reviews a monthly variance report and follows up on significant variances. Because management relies on the computer-produced report to identify and generate the variances, the IT auditor needs to determine that there are controls in place to ensure that the variance report is complete and accurate.

Risks, Processes, and Application Controls

Table 7.4 provides an illustrative set of risk exposures and the ways in which these both impair the validity of management assertions about the financial statements and involve specific subprocesses.

Inappropriate System Access to Inventory Master File and Item Setups

Logical security of the inventory master files and associated records is one of the most important IT controls within the inventory cycle. From a logical security perspective,

TABLE 7.3 Major Application Control Types

Edit Checks	These controls relate to field format. For example, inventory amounts should be entered in numeric format.
Validations	Validation controls depend on the confirmation of a test. The well-known *three-way match* in which a check to a vendor cannot be generated without a matched purchase order, receiving report, and invoice can be automated at the application level. In the inventory cycle, we generate the receiving report based on the items received.
Calculations	Calculations can be used to ensure that a computation is occurring accurately. Extensions and footings can be cross-checked with one another in order to address the risk that portions of an invoice may not be included in the totals.
Interfaces	Interfaces can be designed to address risks posed by data transfers from one system to another (e.g., counts that verify the number of records uploaded from the inventory subledger to the general ledger).
Authorizations	Authorizations that limit access to data are a fundamental building block of control. Roles should be defined within the system and used to restrict the ability to modify records. For example, only the inventory manager should have the ability to add items to the inventory records.

TABLE 7.4 Risks, Assertions, and Subprocesses in the Inventory Cycle

#	Illustrative Risks	Existence/Occurrence	Completeness	Rights and Obligations	Valuation/Allocation	Accounting Procedures	Material Item Setup	Receipt of Goods	Storage of Goods	Goods Movement	Shipping	Reverse Logistics	Repairs & Scrap
1	Inappropriate system access to inventory master file and item setups		X	X	X		X	X	X	X	X	X	X
2	Inconsistent setup or usage of costing methods, due to inaccurate data entry, outdated cost sheets, or other causes			X	X	X	X				X		
3	Inaccurate calculation, allocation, and recording of variances, e.g., those for cost, quantities ordered and received, and quantities planned and actually used			X	X	X		X		X			
4	Inventory and Cost of Sales not appropriately updated when goods are shipped (e.g., cutoff issues)				X	X					X		
5	Perpetual inventory records do not represent the actual quantity or amount on hand.			X				X	X	X			
6	Inappropriate access to inventory cycle count adjustments			X					X				
7	Inventory adjustments are incorrectly posted.					X			X			X	X
8	Costs do not accurately flow through the system because production activity (raw materials to work-in-progress to finished goods) was not properly recorded.		X			X				X			
9	Inventory subledger does not agree with general ledger.		X							X			
10	Inventory identified as returns, repair, warranty, obsolete, or scrap are not appropriately identified and the financial records are not appropriately updated.				X	X						X	X

the company needs to ensure that only appropriate individuals have access to add, change, or delete information in the inventory master file. The inventory master file includes information such as inventory item, description, and cost. If this data were inappropriately entered or modified with inappropriate information, then this information could be processed through the system, which could cause costing issues and ultimately incorrect financial information.

Inadequate system access could result in inventory master files with incomplete data or erroneous information. IT application controls that can help prevent the inaccurate information could include edit checks, reasonableness checks, and validity checks. For example, the system could have popup screens that provide a warning (soft or hard) if numerical data is being entered in a field that requires alphabetic entry, or vice versa. There could be a control that indicates when the item has already been set up in the system to avoid duplication.

System controls should be enabled to specify the access of who can enter data, change data, or delete data within the system. This would also include who has override or workflow authority approvals. When we are setting up an inventory master file or item card, we need to ensure that only appropriate individuals have this access. This control can be reviewed by looking at the access listings to see who has been assigned these access rights. Other access considerations could be for overrides when an item card or master file is changed. Some systems will generate a report, which we refer to as an IT-dependent manual control that would notify management of when there has been a change to the master file. Alternatively, there could be a popup screen that requires an authorized approver's password to enable the change on the master file.

The ability to override the item costs, costing method, and variances could affect how the financial information is valued in the system, processed, and allocated. Once again, logical security controls and inventory setup security is paramount.

Microsoft Great Plains Dynamics (GPD) has robust capabilities around inventory management security and item setup. Figure 7.5 demonstrates the screen where one can configure the ability to allow for adjustment overrides, variance overrides, and transfer overrides. The auditor should note whether overrides are allowed.

Figure 7.6 demonstrates inventory setup in QB. Choosing the dropdown menu "Edit" and selecting the last item, "Preferences," will bring up this screen. Selecting "Items & Inventory" on the side blue select menu will show QB's settings for its hard and soft controls. The options include whether to account for inventory. Checking this first box will place the purchase orders and receiving icons on the home screen. Again, QB uses purchases and sales to track inventory, rather than using a POS system or a manual system. This preference screen is a major lack of controls over inventory. QB should use hard controls and remove the option to toggle them off in order to strengthen controls within the accounting system.

The other preferences on this screen allow for the user to toggle on and off the soft controls QB uses for inventory. The first soft control option is for "warnings about duplicate purchase order numbers." The second option deals with the computation of quantity available, and whether the user wants to deduct quantity reserved for pending builds (manufacturing company) and whether to deduct quantity on sales orders. Lastly, there is an option to toggle the warning for not enough inventory to

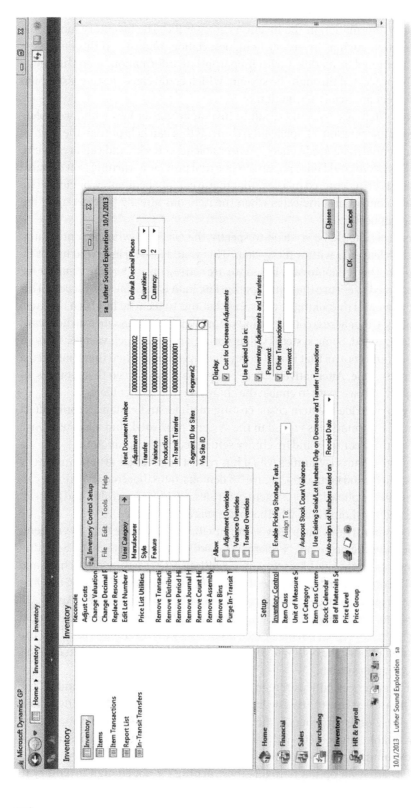

FIGURE 7.5 GPD Inventory Control Setup

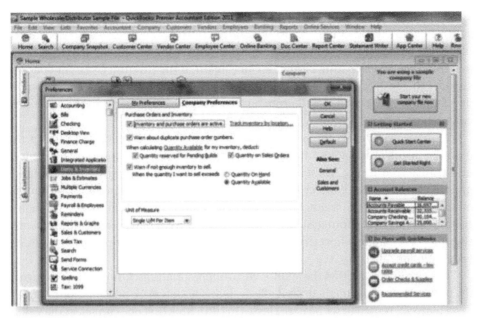

FIGURE 7.6   QB Inventory Setup

sell, when the quantity the user wants to sell exceeds either quantity on hand or quantity available.

Inconsistent Setup or Usage of Costing Methods Due to Inaccurate Data Entry, Outdated Cost Sheets, or Other Causes

Incorrect or incomplete costing information could be entered into the system, resulting in inaccurate cost processing throughout the system. This could include things such as the inappropriate selection of costing methods or inaccurate data entry due to reliance on outdated cost sheets. Within the system, there are controls that could help prevent inaccurate information from being captured and going undetected. For instance, while human error is a major factor in erroneous data entry, system reports can be used to review the data entered into the system to validate accuracy. In addition, some systems may have a tolerance level setup that prevents inaccurate data entry if the tolerance level is exceeded. Some systems may not have all inventory costing methods available for the company to choose. For example, QB is limited in the inventory costing methods available for use, which sometimes results in companies selecting alternative third-party software packages to manage the manufacturing and cost accumulation processes.

The incorrect data entry could result in a system value that provides an erroneous inventory value. The erroneous selection of a costing method or inconsistent selection of costing method (that is, changing the costing method in the system without considering the full impacts to the inventory balances, e.g., do we need to make an adjusting entry?) could result in the inaccurate valuation of the inventory balance.

Review of security reports and/or analysis of logical access controls indicate the existence and/or source of changes to costing information. Ideally, the system should warn the user before costing methods are changed, by either a soft control (a warning popup screen) or a hard control that requires an approver's password. If a system does not include these features, the auditor will need to perform a manual review of costing changes. Once again, if the inventory system does not support the desired costing method, then third-party software (or an internally developed spreadsheet file) will probably be used in order to perform the necessary calculations.

Management needs to ensure that the costs that are generated during the manufacturing process (e.g., direct labor, overhead, etc.) are appropriately captured and transferred to FG. The cost accumulation process affects the cost of goods manufactured (COGM) and cost of goods sold (COGS) calculations that ultimately are represented on the financial statements. Within the system, the costs should transfer during the manufacturing process to the COGM; however, in some systems, this may be a manual effort that requires a journal entry to ensure appropriate cost accumulation.

It is also important that the auditor ensure appropriate disclosure of any change in the company's costing methods that affects financial statement presentation.

Figure 7.7 is used to set up item classes in GPD. Note that one can select the valuation method. See also Figures 7.8 and 7.9.

It appears that QB has limitations around the number of units of inventory within the system (e.g., max of 14,500 units). Also, only the weighted average method can be used. If a company wants to use an alternative costing method, then an external process outside the system will need to be adopted.

Inaccurate Calculation, Allocation, and Recording of Variances

During the acquisition of raw materials or usage of the raw materials, variances can occur for a variety of reasons. Variances include order and receipt quantities, vendor prices, usage, and any other deviation from planned, promised, or budgeted quantities. Here, again owing to the inherent complexity of possible interrelationships within the inventory cycle, many companies perform the calculations in a spreadsheet and input adjusting or correcting entries as required. When variances occur, management needs to track the variances and apply the appropriate accounting treatment to dispose of the variances.

Variances should have tolerance levels set up that require management approvals if the configured threshold needs to be exceeded. Some systems will enable the automatic processing of activity if the variances are within a tolerable range (i.e., within the range of the tolerance setting). However, if the tolerance level needs to be exceeded, this is where a workflow rule should be configured that would not allow the further processing of the activity without management approval. This would be a preventive control and configured in the system.

Management could also print reports that show variances and their actual or planned disposition. This can be a good detective control for management to monitor variances and help ensure that approvals are being obtained when necessary.

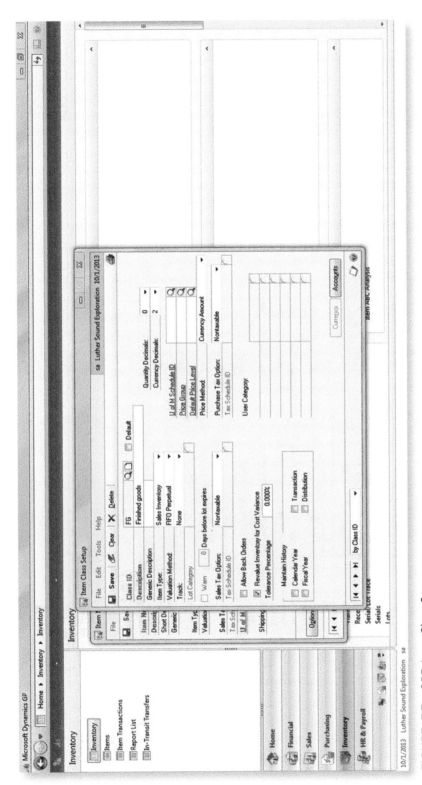

FIGURE 7.7 GPD Item Class Setup

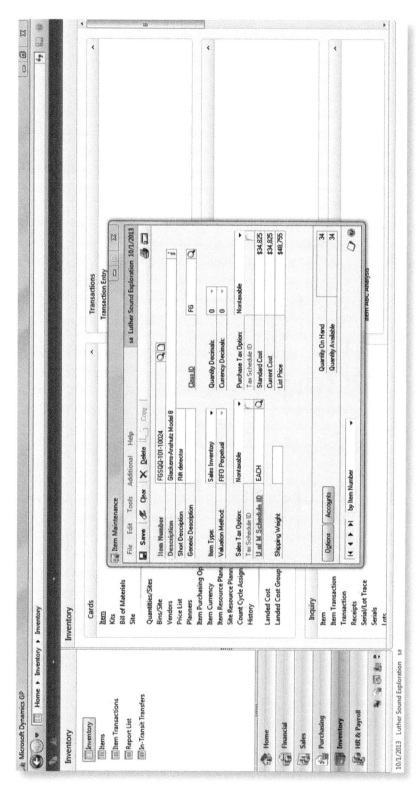

FIGURE 7.8 GPD Item Maintenance

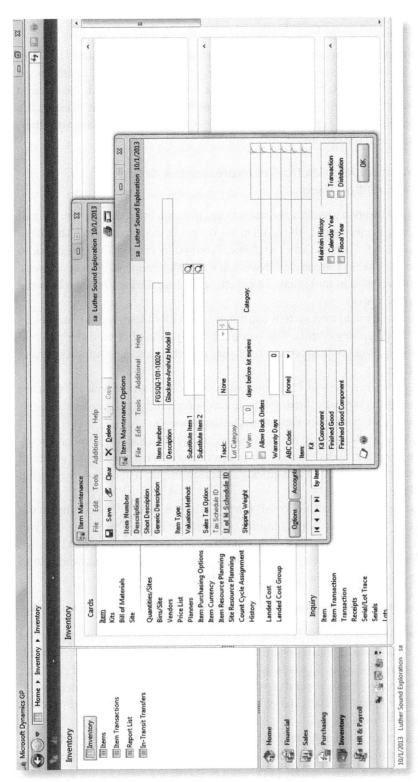

FIGURE 7.9 GPD Item Maintenance Options

153

Inventory and Cost of Sales Not Appropriately Updated When Goods Are Shipped (e.g., Cutoff Issues)

When goods are shipped out of the warehouse, the system needs to be updated to reflect the shipment of goods. The shipment would trigger revenue recognition, which affects the revenue cycle. When the goods are shipped, the costs associated with the FG need to be transferred to the cost of goods sold. The system should automatically transfer the costs, but the company can ensure this happens by looking at system settings or inherent controls built into the system.

Perpetual Inventory Records Do Not Represent the Actual Quantity or Amount on Hand

When auditing the inventory records, the auditor needs to ensure that the quantity of goods physically on hand is equivalent to the goods in the system. In many businesses, the inventory records do get out of balance between physical and system counts. This may be due to the inadvertent movement of physical goods without appropriately updating the system (e.g., shipped, but not recorded in the system; loss; theft) or because the incorrect goods record was updated in the system.

Variances in physical and system counts are typically identified through cycle counting or full inventory counts. The reconciliation process between the physical goods and the system goods is necessary to ensure that the books appropriately reflect the goods on hand.

Within the computer system, IT-dependent manual controls that typically exist are reports. These reports typically illustrate the quantity on hand per the system. Reports can be generated that can help in the reconciliation process.

In this Edit List menu, one can copy and paste directly from Excel or another spreadsheet program into QB to update the detail inventory records. This represents a potential control deficiency in that the user can quickly and easily import a new inventory listing from an Excel file at any time.

One of the few examples of hard controls in QB is in this view: When editing inventory listing, the "Total Value" and "Quantity on Hand" fields are grayed out. One can edit the "Cost Per Item" and the "Sales Price" per item, but these columns don't change the "Total Value" column. When goods are shipped out of the warehouse, the system needs to be updated to reflect the shipment of goods.

Inappropriate Access to Inventory Cycle Count Adjustments

After the physical counts have been made in the cycle count process, adjustments need to be made in the system to get the system up-to-date with the actual quantity on hand. Management may also want to investigate the variances to understand if theft has occurred or there was simple human error in the data entry of goods movement in the system. Therefore, logical access in the system to update system records with the revised quantity on hand is important.

If access is not appropriately controlled, then a user with access to the cycle count adjustments could inappropriately modify the number of goods on hand and then physically take the goods for inappropriate purposes (i.e., theft).

There are typically reports in systems that enable management to review any adjustments to the system quantities. This is a good detective control that will enable management to review and determine if system changes to the inventory quantities were appropriate or need further investigation. In GPD, one can determine the user who has the ability to update the quantity of goods noted in the system based on the physical counts.

Inventory Adjustments Are Incorrectly Posted

When inventory adjustments are necessary based on physical counts, management needs to ensure that the updated system quantities are posted to the correct account and in the correct accounting period. Management can review reports that show the updates to the system. This would be a detective control.

Controls around closing the books to prevent the unintentional booking of the adjustment in prior accounting periods are discussed further in the financial reporting chapter.

Costs Do Not Accurately Flow through the System because Production Activity Was Not Properly Recorded

The costs of goods manufactured (COGM) for the FG needs to include the costs associated with direct materials, direct labor, and overhead. Therefore, the system needs to provide a mechanism to appropriately capture the various costs and transfer to the FG account. This is important when the FG are sold, so the appropriate costs can be released to the cost of goods sold (COGS).

Depending on the system used, the various costs may be captured within the system and the costs would flow to the appropriate accounts based on the movement of goods within the system. However, some systems may not have robust capabilities and management may have to track costs associated with labor and overhead within the system, alternative systems, or spreadsheets, and then the costs have to be calculated and a manual journal entry made to the appropriate accounts to transfer the costs to the FG account and ultimately to the cost of goods sold when the goods are sold.

From a completeness assertion standpoint, if the system automatically transfers the costs to the FG account (COGM) and then the COGS account, this is typically defined in the setup of the inventory module as a configuration setting or is inherently configured in the system.

Although QB does not track physical internal control processes like requisitions from the warehouse or transfers between departments, the application does have a "Custom Field" option to record the location of inventory for both "Shelf" and "Warehouse" categories.

QB tracks inventory by reconciling the quantity on hand, the amount purchased, and the amount on sales order. As you can see, the example purchase order was not updated to "inventory on hand"; it was placed in the "on purchase order" field. Although the inventory account increased, purchase orders create nonposting entries in QB, meaning the net inventory account isn't updated. The actual inventory on hand is updated after the inventory is received and posted in QB.

This screen pops up after clicking the receive inventory icon on the home page. The receiving input screen allows one to click "Select Purchase Order" and choose the vendor and the purchase order that matches the good received. This represents a control deficiency in that the data provided by the user when inputting the purchase order is automatically populated into the receiving screen. This is only an option; however, it is much more efficient than entering data off the bill, and it is unlikely the accountant will manually enter the data given this option.

Potential issues with QB recording of billings for inventory arise when either the goods arrive before the bill, or the bill arrives before the goods. In the case of goods arriving first, one writer recommends that the user record a "pretend" bill in order to update the inventory-on-hand quantities.* It is important for the user to remember that the pretend bill must be labeled as such in order to avoid misstating the Accounts Payable account in the financial statements. This is clearly a control deficiency, where the user needs to manipulate the QB options to account for very common business occurrences.

In the case of the bill arriving before the goods, it is proper to record that bill and recognize inventory if the terms are "freight on board" shipping point. If they are not, the user must again mark the bill "Pretend" and wait for the receipt of goods to fully account for that billing. After updating the Receiving Inventory page for the sample purchase order created, QB automatically reclassifies the inventory from "On Purchase" to "On Hand."

Inventory Subledger Does Not Agree with General Ledger

The transfer of information between the subledger inventory records and the general ledger helps ensure that the books remain in balance and all appropriate data has been captured by the general ledger. Depending on the system used, the subledger information may be updated to the general ledger in real time (automatically and immediately) or via a batch process, which may be initiated automatically based on configuration settings, or manually.

The controls are typically built into the system and these inherent controls do not need further configuration by the user; however, if management is using a batch system, configuration settings are typically set that require management to indicate which subledgers update the general ledger and in what order. For example, one may want one subledger (xxxx) to update the general ledger before another (yyyy).

Inventory Identified as Returns, Repair, Warranty, Obsolete, or Scrap Are Not Appropriately Identified and the Financial Records Are Not Appropriately Updated

During the manufacturing process, or storage of goods, or even after the shipment of goods and recording of revenue, a company may experience the need to adjust inventory records to account for returns, repairs, warranty, obsolete, or scrap inventory.

After raw materials are received from the vendor, some raw materials may experience damage during the storage or manufacturing process. This may result in the need

---

* Bonnie Biafore, *QuickBooks 2011—the Missing Manual* (Sebastopol, CA: O'Reilly Media, 2010).

for management to return the goods to the vendor, if able; repair the goods for future use; or scrap the goods if not salvageable. Depending on which path is taken, the system records need to be appropriately updated to ensure that the financial records are correct. In addition, goods waiting for use in the manufacturing process or FG waiting to be sold may have a shelf-life. In this case, the goods may have to be identified as obsolete and written off the books.

After FG are sold to the customer, the customer may experience quality issues, which may result in a return from the customer for a refund or for repair, which may be covered under warranty. When goods are returned from the customer, appropriate return authorization documentation should be completed in the system (or external manual process) to ensure the appropriate return of goods. When goods are returned and are being worked upon, the accounting records need to be appropriately updated to reflect the costs accumulated with these activities.

If goods are returned for a refund, management should ensure that the system does not allow for a return to be processed without appropriate workflow approval. Most systems have controls in place that will prevent the return of sold goods without an approver. In addition, most systems will enable management to print reports that will show sold goods that were returned or had their values adjusted in the system. This is called an IT-dependent manual control and is an effective detective control when utilized.

If goods are returned and are repaired, the related costs need to be accumulated. The costs either will be charged back to the vendor of the raw materials (if a warranty issue can be traced to the vendor), or will be absorbed internally (if the costs are associated with the quality of the manufactured product). The costs will need to be captured and should be either transferred to the FG account to increase the cost of goods manufactured, or expensed as a period cost (depending on the value of the repair and internal accounting policies).

From an accounting procedure assertion standpoint, reports can be generated within the system to analyze the impact on the accounting records.

SUMMARY

Now that we have reviewed the inventory cycle, you should have a better understanding of the risks and controls that affect the subcycles. It is important to remember that inventory makes up a material value on most financial statements; therefore, it is imperative for the inventory cycle to have robust controls built into the financial application and monitoring controls outside the application to ensure that inventory data is correct.

CHAPTER EIGHT

The Payroll Cycle

THE PAYROLL CYCLE ENCOMPASSES ALL processes, personnel, and activities that relate to the acquisition (hiring), maintenance (employee management and payroll processing), and termination (firing, retiring) of employees and contractors. Note that in some companies, contractors may bypass the payroll process and be paid through accounts payable. Additionally, some companies also have a separate human resources (HR) cycle that may include some of the payroll cycle activities discussed in this chapter. We focus our discussion on common-law employees and leave contractors as a special case within the purchasing system.

Payroll processes are highly affected by compliance burdens for local, state, and federal taxation as well as employment laws. Additionally, many small and medium-sized entities outsource payroll and/or associated HR recordkeeping to third-party providers. However, this does not eliminate the organization's requirement to maintain a strong control environment. Regardless of whether the entity performs payroll tasks in-house, it is essential to manage the controls within the process.

RISK EXPOSURES AND SUBPROCESSES

The payroll cycle contains several risk exposures. These include:

- **Setup and maintenance:** Are employees set up in the system consistent with their pay status, pay rates, and other vital information? Who has access to add, change, or delete payroll master file information? What prevents ghost employees from being set up and subsequently paid?

- **Calculations:** Are tax tables updated appropriately to ensure tax calculations reflect the current tax rates based on jurisdiction? What ensures the time was captured and entered into the system appropriately? Was the time extended to the pay rate so the appropriate pay was calculated? Was the third-party payroll processor provided with correct payroll information for calculations?

- **Processing:** Are there variance tolerance levels set up in the system? What ensures that the amounts scheduled to be paid are paid? Does segregation of duties exist in the payroll processing process? Are signature approvals captured and are digital signatures protected? Is electronic check stock protected? Was the third-party payroll processor provided with correct payroll information for processing?

- **Disbursements:** Are completed checks secured for disbursement? Do controls exist that ensure that direct deposits were made to the right account and complete?

- **Reconciliations:** Do reports appropriately reflect the payroll that was scheduled to be disbursed and that was actually disbursed? What reports exist in the system for review?

- **Accruals and adjustments:** Are accruals and adjustments to payroll, benefits, and taxes calculated so the financial records can be updated? Are payments made to the tax authorities for the tax liability? Are benefit accounts updated for the benefits liability?

These risk exposures can affect the financial audit in a number of ways, and each risk exposure relates to one or more cycle subprocesses. Table 8.2 in the next section illustrates these links at a high level, showing, for each of several illustrative risks, the potential impact on one or more of the assertions underlying the financial statements. The table also ties these risks to specific revenue cycle subprocesses.

Application controls can mitigate these exposures, and it is thus important for the auditor to have a working knowledge of what these controls are, how they should function, and points of vulnerability. The numbered references in Figure 8.1 identify locations of specific risks discussed in the next section.

There are several subprocesses within the payroll cycle. These include:

- **Payroll master file maintenance:** This subprocess follows the employee life cycle from initial hiring to maintenance to termination. Activities include preparation of employee records (including personal [HR] information, salary, job classification, exempt/nonexempt status), taxes and other contributions (voluntary or imposed, e.g., closed shop union dues); classification as common-law employee or contractor; and other information required by the particular operations of the business.

- **Tax records and calculations:** This subprocess involves the updating of tax information in the system to ensure the appropriate tax rates are being used in the payroll processing. Tax tables are obtained from various taxation authorities and need to be updated in the payroll system.

- **Time and attendance:** This subprocess involves the capture of time and attendance so the appropriate payments can be made to employees. Companies may use third-party software or manual processes to capture time and attendance, and

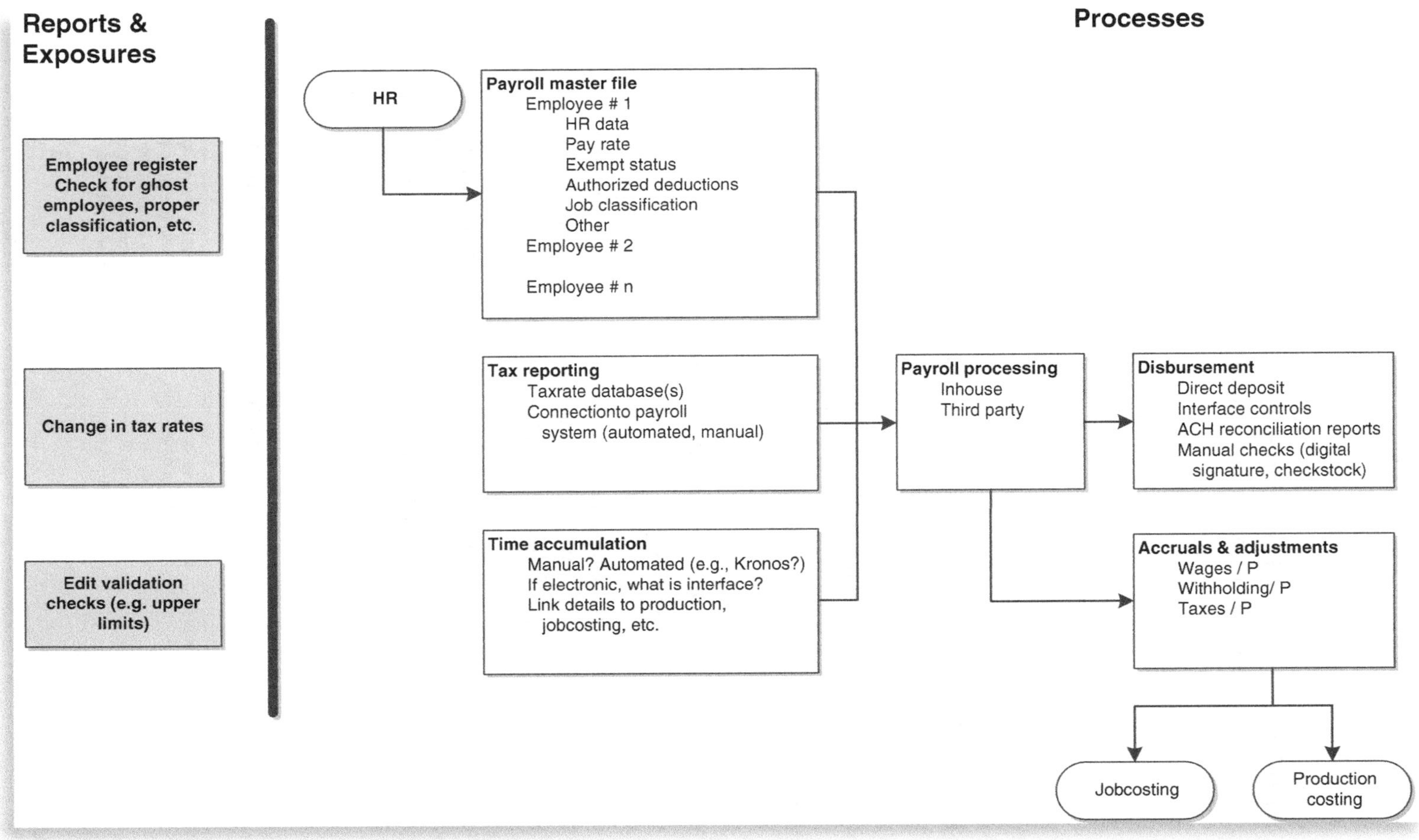

Processes

```
                    ┌─────────────────────────┐
                    │ Payroll master file     │
                    │ Employee # 1            │
                    │   HR data               │
                    │   Pay rate              │
          ┌────────▶│   Exempt status         │─────┐
┌────┐    │         │   Authorized deductions │     │
│ HR │────┘         │   Job classification    │     │
└────┘              │   Other                 │     │
                    │ Employee # 2            │     │
                    │ Employee # n            │     │
                    └─────────────────────────┘     │
                                                     │
                    ┌─────────────────────────┐     │      ┌──────────────────┐
                    │ Tax reporting           │     │      │ Payroll processing│
                    │ Tax rate database(s)    │     ├─────▶│ Inhouse           │
                    │ Connection to payroll   │─────┤      │ Third party       │
                    │ system (automated,      │     │      └──────────────────┘
                    │ manual)                 │     │
                    └─────────────────────────┘     │
                                                     │
                    ┌─────────────────────────┐     │
                    │ Time accumulation       │     │
                    │ Manual? Automated       │     │
                    │ (e.g., Kronos?)         │─────┘
                    │ If electronic, what is  │
                    │ interface?              │
                    │ Link details to         │
                    │ production, jobcosting, │
                    │ etc.                    │
                    └─────────────────────────┘
```

Disbursement
Direct deposit
Interface controls
ACH reconciliation reports
Manual checks (digital signature, checkstock)

Accruals & adjustments
Wages / P
Withholding/ P
Taxes / P

Jobcosting

Production costing

Reports & Exposures

Employee register
Check for ghost employees, proper classification, etc.

Change in tax rates

Edit validation checks (e.g. upper limits)

FIGURE 8.1 Payroll Cycle

161

the payroll module may need to have manual data entry to acknowledge the time spent by the employee. Ultimately, access to the entry of time is critical. System controls could be in place to prevent or flag the unusual documentation of time (e.g., working 25 hours in a day, or working on weekends when the company is closed).

◼ **Payroll preparation and processing:** This subprocess involves the preparation of payroll registers and cash requirements journals to identify the payroll to be processed and the cash requirements. Payroll reports are typically reviewed to ensure adequate payments. Payroll needs are then processed in the system or the data is given to the third-party payroll provider for processing. During the processing phase, the checks are produced for disbursement. Controls around check stock and signature stamps (either manual or electronic signatures) should be safeguarded to prevent unauthorized checks. Dual signatures for payroll checks over certain dollar amounts may also be utilized. System controls could be in place to prevent unauthorized payments.

◼ **Payroll disbursement and reconciliation:** This subprocess involves the disbursement of checks or direct deposits of the payroll. Manual and system controls provide management with safeguards to ensure appropriate disbursement of payroll. Direct deposit controls could include notification from the bank that the dollar amount and number of payroll transactions have occurred. Reconciliation reports provide management with an IT-dependent manual and detective control that enables management to reconcile the paid payroll with what was supposed to be paid.

◼ **Accruals and adjustments associated with payroll, benefits, and tax payments:** This subprocess includes the calculations of payroll accruals associated with salaries payable, benefits due to the employee, and taxes payable. The company needs to ensure adequate calculations and remittance to the appropriate authorities to be in compliance with laws and regulations. System controls should be in place to provide reporting capabilities and calculations of payments.

Figure 8.2 illustrates a typical HR cycle for a small or medium-sized enterprise. The drawings are not intended to be comprehensive or applicable to all business models; rather, the intent is to highlight the broad relationships between common processes and frequently occurring risks.

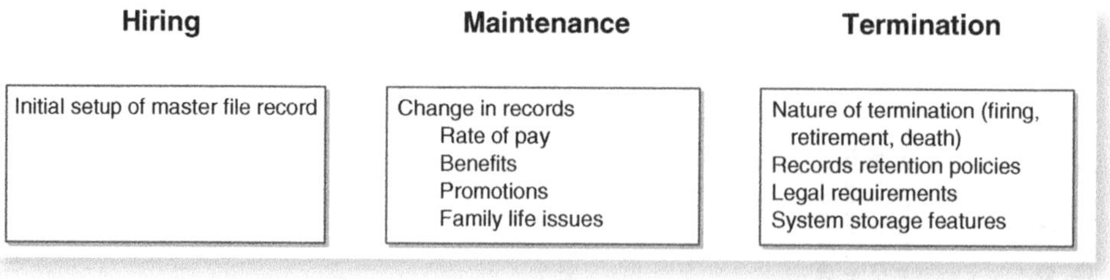

Hiring	**Maintenance**	**Termination**

Initial setup of master file record	Change in records
	    Rate of pay
	    Benefits
	    Promotions
	    Family life issues
		Nature of termination (firing,
		    retirement, death)
		Records retention policies
		Legal requirements
		System storage features

FIGURE 8.2 HR Cycle

The initial setup of an employee record through an HR process changes the payroll master file. For processing to occur, two additional and different sources of information are required: current tax rate information for applicable jurisdictions, and some system for maintaining time records. This may be done manually by entity personnel, or involve an automated system such as Kronos. Whether the processing is done in-house or by a third-party vendor, the IT auditor needs to concern herself with the accuracy and reliability of data that enters the processing queue. Thus, for example, the system should generate an employee register that facilitates review for checks on ghost employees or proper job classification. The interface relating to tax rate and tax table information needs to be evaluated: Is the data provided by lookup tables or rekeyed data? Similar concerns obtain for the timekeeping system: Are the interfaces automated or do they rely on a manual process? Does the system contain edit validation checks, such as upper limits on the number of hours that an employee works?

Processing results in two major outputs: disbursement of wage and tax payments, and the accounting information that updates accruals and adjustments.

APPLICATION CONTROLS, PAYROLL CYCLE RISKS, AND RELATED AUDIT PROCEDURES

This section begins with a general introduction to application controls. We then consider an illustrative set of risks that arise in the payroll cycle. These include operational risks (what could go wrong) and financial statement risks. We examine these risks and the controls that should either prevent the problem (preventive controls) or alert personnel to the problem so that it can be remediated (detective controls). Within the context of each risk exposure and related controls we also discuss appropriate IT audit procedures.

Application Controls

Application controls are system-enabled controls within standard business processes. They are designed to enforce specific work requirements and, traditionally, are preventive in nature. Examples of application controls include:

- Logical access controls (i.e., application security)
- Date entry/field validations (e.g., validation of entered salary or tax information)
- Workflow rules (e.g., electronic routing and sign-off of overtime requests)
- Field entries being enforced based on predefined values (e.g., pay rate information)

In discussing application controls, it is useful to observe the distinction between inherent and configurable controls. The former are programmed to perform the control through either custom coding or packaged delivery, while the latter can be modified by the end user.

Table 8.1 provides brief definitions for major control types. All of these general types of control are designed to limit the risk of inappropriate input, processing, or output of data.

TABLE 8.1 Major Application Control Types

Edit Checks	These controls relate to field format. For example, dollar amounts should be entered in numeric format.
Validations	Validation controls depend on the confirmation of a test. This could be the validation when payroll is processed that the employee name is compared to the database of employees to ensure that only authorized employees are being paid.
Calculations	Calculations can be used to ensure that a computation is occurring accurately. Extensions and footings can be cross-checked with one another in order to address the risk that portions of a tax calculation may not be included in the payroll.
Interfaces	Interfaces can be designed to address risks posed by data transfers from one system to another (e.g., counts that verify the number of records uploaded from the payroll module to the third-party payroll processor).
Authorizations	Authorizations that limit access to data are a fundamental building block of control. Roles should be defined within the system and used to restrict the ability to modify records. For example, only the human resources manager should have the ability to add employees to the employee master.

The level of automation associated with a control provides another set of fundamental distinctions. In general, controls can be manual, automated, or IT-dependent manual. This last category refers to controls performed by a person who relies on automated output. Most are detective controls that rely on computer-generated information or computer functionality. For example, management reviews a monthly variance report and follows up on significant variances. Because management relies on the computer-produced report to identify and generate the variances, the IT auditor needs to determine that there are controls in place to ensure that the variance report is complete and accurate.

Risks, Processes, and Application Controls

Table 8.2 provides an illustrative set of risk exposures and the ways in which these both impair the validity of management assertions about the financial statements and involve specific subprocesses.

Unauthorized Changes to Payroll Master File

Unauthorized changes to the payroll master file present a key risk in the payroll cycle. Management needs to ensure that access to the payroll master file is restricted to appropriate personnel. Typically, the human resources manager or payroll manager in a small or medium-sized enterprise will have this type of access right. By having too many or the wrong individuals with access to the payroll master file, the company increases its risk of fraudulent activity. Fraud is not guaranteed to occur, but when individuals have access to manipulate data, then the risk probability increases.

The IT auditor should ensure that logical access setup is appropriately controlled, through either inherent or configurable controls. Updating the payroll master file to

TABLE 8.2 Risks, Assertions, and Subprocesses in the Payroll Cycle

	Illustrative Risks	Existence/Occurrence	Completeness	Rights and Obligations	Valuation/Allocation	Accounting Procedures	Master File Maintenance	Tax Records	Time and Attendance	Processing	Disbursements	Accruals and Adjustment
		Assertions					Cycle Subprocess					
1	Unauthorized changes to payroll master file	×		×			×					
2	Tax records are not updated or calculated correctly		×	×	×			×				
3	Time and attendance are not correctly captured		×		×				×			
4	Payroll is not prepared or processed correctly				×	×				×		
5	Payroll disbursements are unauthorized (fraudulent payments)			×							×	
6	Accruals, benefits, and taxes are incorrectly calculated or paid				×							×
7	Disbursed payroll, accruals, and adjustments are not reviewed					×				×	×	×

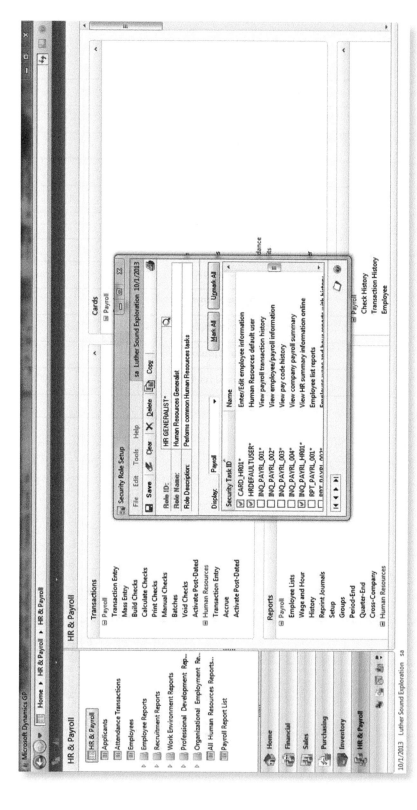

FIGURE 8.3 Security Role Setup (Generalist) in GPD

reflect any payroll changes drives all subsequent activities. Payroll changes include adding new hires, removing terminated employees, changing pay rates, and/or changing discretionary withholdings. Appropriate edit checks to ensure the number of employees actually working and the reasonableness test for the changes being made must also be applied in this step. It is important that the changes are entered before the next pay period because subsequent steps rely on the data provided in the payroll master file. Any errors in the inputs will essentially generate outputs that are not accurate or appropriate. To ensure that the data is accurate, Microsoft Great Plains Dynamics (GPD) consists of many inherent controls as well as configurable controls to help prevent inaccurate data from being entered into the system.

As noted with respect to other cycles, one of the most important controls that mitigate risk of unauthorized changes to the payroll master file is the proper segregation of duties. This control is implemented by granting employees specific permissions to certain functions. For the HR generalist, his or her access to the payroll system may be limited to entering employee information and/or viewing the HR summary. (See Figure 8.3.)

However, a payroll clerk may be granted more access than an HR generalist. These functions can include entering or editing employee information and maintaining payroll deductions and benefits. Depending on the role of the employee, we can apply different levels of security to different positions among payroll personnel to prevent unauthorized access to the payroll master files. (See Figure 8.4.)

The employee maintenance record contains the general information about the employee, including name, Social Security number, contact information, department, and position. In this particular card, the required fields are Employee ID, Last Name, First Name, Social Security Number, Department, and Position. In addition, this card has many inherent controls to help ensure that the information is properly inputted to avoid any problems in subsequent steps. The first control in this particular card is the limit to the number of registered employees. Upon creating an employee exceeding the number allowed, a message pops up as follows: "You have reached your maximum number of registered employees. You cannot add new employees into the system."

Typically GPD requires the company to acquire a license for a specific number of employees. In order to add more employees, the company must purchase another license. The employee ID also uses a lookup button for existing employees that need updates. Instead of having to type in the employee ID, the lookup button helps ensure that the proper employee is selected. The Social Security Number field automatically inserts hyphens so that all employee Social Security numbers are consistent. The Hire Date/Adjusted Hire Date/Last Day Worked must be inputted as DDMMYY or DDMMYYYY. A calendar button is available to avoid inputting the wrong date. The Adjusted Hire Date is automatically inputted as the Hire Date when the Hire Date is entered. In addition, if the Adjusted Hire Date is earlier than the Hire Date, a message pops up stating "The employee's adjusted hire date is earlier than the hire date. Do you want to continue?" Furthermore, if the Last Day Worked as entered is earlier than the Hire Date, a message pops up stating "An employee's hire date must be before the last day worked." This helps prevent human errors in entering the wrong date.

The fields listed in Figure 8.5 (such as Employee ID and Class ID) are foreign keys linked to other cards. If the inputted code does not currently exist for these fields, a message will

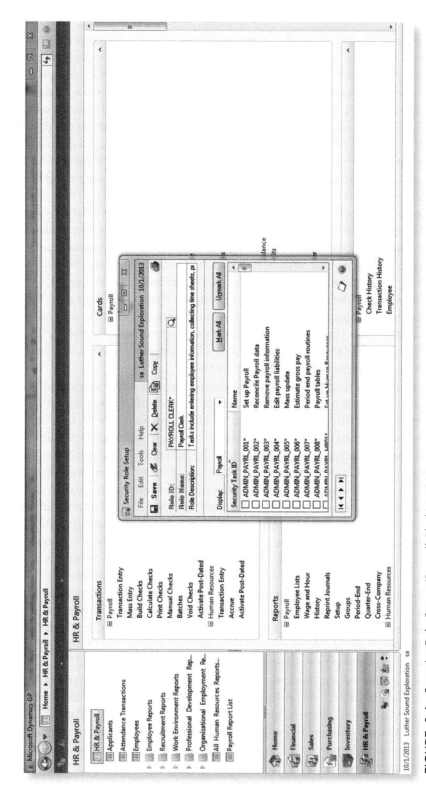

FIGURE 8.4 Security Role Setup (Payroll Clerk) in GPD

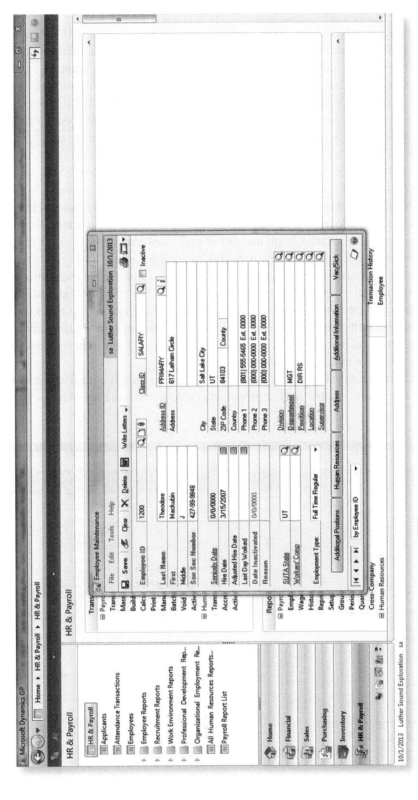

FIGURE 8.5 Employee Maintenance in GPD

169

prompt, stating that the code is nonexistent and asking whether you would like to add the code. Another control would be for the phone number fields where it uses a template such as (XXX) XXX-XXXX Ext. XXXX to prevent inconsistency in entering phone numbers. Furthermore, the card links the user to other multiple cards, including additional positions, human resources, address, personal information, and vacation and sick days. Within these cards are their own separate controls similar to that of this card. Specifically for the vacation and sick days, the user will be prompted if the allowable days available fall below zero.

Auditors should be concerned about the creation, modification, or deletion of employee records. Users can review individual employees' basic information, such as date of hire, contact information, position, and department in the employee maintenance screen. The auditor should ensure that adequate controls exist against the creation of fictitious employees. As shown in Figure 8.6, a GPD screen presents a warning: "You have reached your maximum number of registered employees. You cannot add new employees into the system." Figure 8.7 addresses deletion.

The employee pay code maintenance card links the employees to their pay codes. In this particular card, the required fields are Employee ID, Pay Code, and Unit of Pay. In addition, there are inherent controls. For the Employee ID field, there is a lookup button to ensure that the proper ID is used. After selecting the employee ID, the Name field automatically populates and the field is not editable. However, the name can be edited under the employee maintenance card.

Another control in this particular card is apparent in the pay code where a lookup button is also used to ensure that the proper, available pay code is used. When selecting

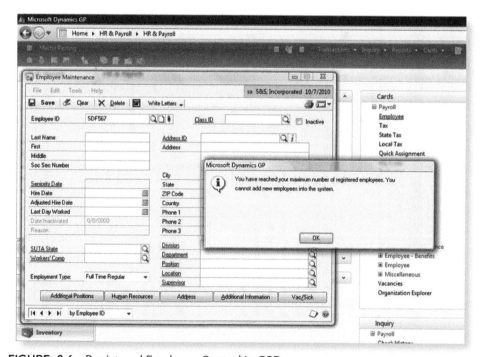

FIGURE 8.6 Registered Employee Control in GPD

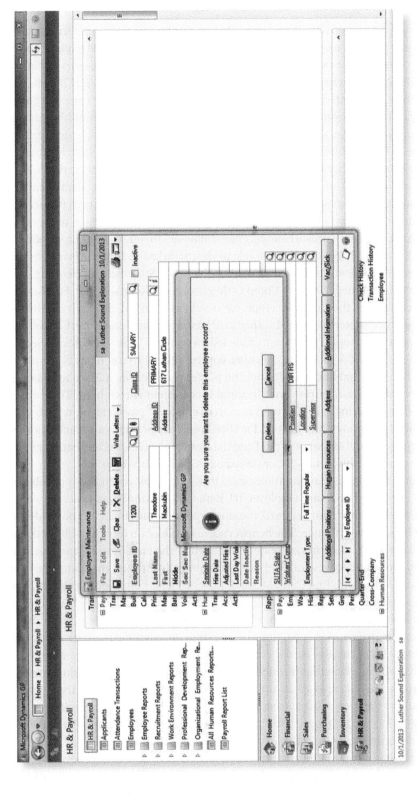

FIGURE 8.7 Employee Deletion Control in GPD

the pay code, a message pops up asking, "Do you want to use default information from the company pay code record?" For salaried and hourly employees, the pay code and pay factor are disabled. For overtime employees, the pay code and pay factors are enabled because these are used in the calculation of the pay per period. In the Pay Rate field, the pay rate must be inputted as $XX.XX automatically. The unit of pay varies for salaried employees with choices including weekly, biweekly, semimonthly, monthly, quarterly, semiannually, annually, and daily. They are automatically inputted as hourly for hourly employees. The Pay Period field is applicable to both salaried and hourly employees where the time frame between each pay period is selected. After inputting the Pay Code, Pay Factor, Pay Rate, Unit of Pay, and Pay Period, the card will automatically calculate the Pay per Period to avoid any human errors. In addition, this ensures the accuracy of the amount to be paid to the employee. Regarding the Shift Code, it allows one to select among different shifts (these can be established through another set of cards). The SUTA State and Worker's Comp Code fields are linked in that the Worker's Comp Code depends on the state that is selected in the SUTA State field. Depending on the state selected, a limited Worker's Comp Code is available to be selected. Furthermore, the card establishes the taxes the employee is subject to using checkboxes. The taxes have already been determined in another card based on downloads from GPD based on governmental numbers. The taxes include federal, state, FUTA, FICA Social Security, local, SUTA, and FICA Medicare. Another control related to the taxes is the input of Flat Tax Rates in that the card inputs the percentage rate as X.XX% to make sure that the percentage is accurate and the input is consistent throughout. This card also links to other cards, including human resources employee pay code, human resources maintenance, summary, and history. Furthermore, they provide summaries as to how much each individual employee is paid and the history of payments and earnings by the employee on a monthly, annually, or period basis. (See Figure 8.8.)

The employee benefit maintenance card links the employee to the applicable benefit codes. Required fields are Employee ID, Benefit Code, and Start Date. As with the employee pay code maintenance card, the employee name automatically populates with entry of the employee ID code. The benefit code uses a lookup tool that allows the user to choose from a predetermined benefits list. When the employee ID and the benefit code have been entered, several fields are automatically filled in, including the benefit Description, Start Date, End Date, Method, Benefit Tiers, Employer Maximum, Maximum Benefits, and W-2. The Start Date and End Date for the benefits use a calendar tool to ensure that the proper date has been selected. For the Deductions fields, the user selects from predetermined deductions by inserting or removing them for the specified employee. In this particular card there is a button that links you to the summary of the employee's benefits, showing the employee's received benefits on an annual, monthly, and quarterly basis. It also states the benefits Year to Date and Life to Date. Furthermore, it allows the user to select from a specific year and displays the results in a clean, non-editable format. Employee benefit maintenance disables certain fields that depend on related requirements until those have been met. (See Figure 8.9.)

The employee post-dated pay rates card is used to update an employee's pay rate when that code becomes effective at a later date. This particular card can be used to enter information about the pay change and it can be activated before the new code becomes

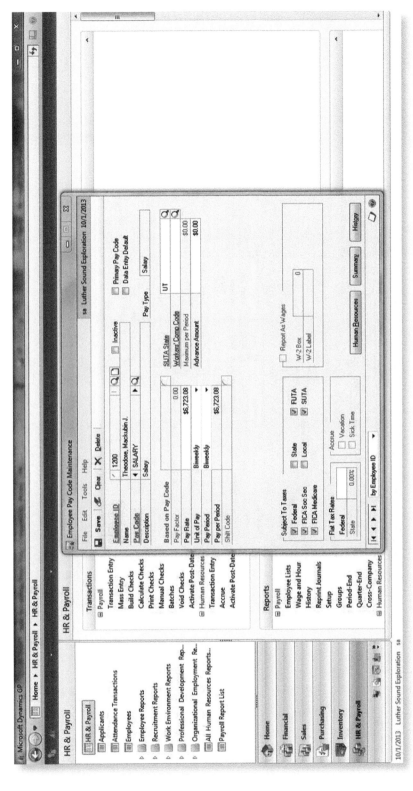

FIGURE 8.8 Employee Pay Code Maintenance in GPD

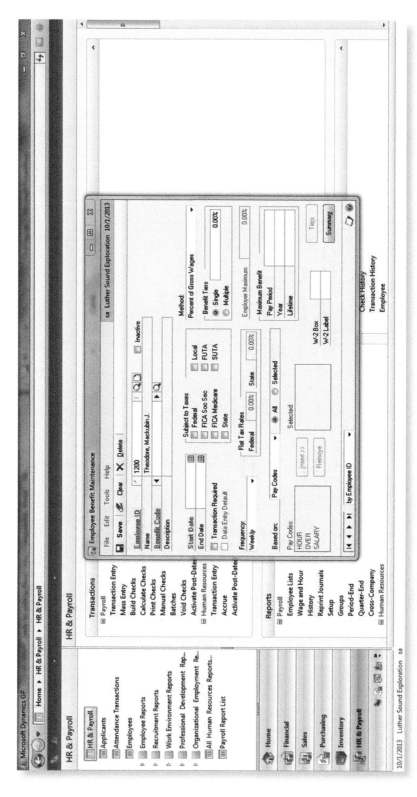

FIGURE 8.9 Employee Benefit Maintenance in GPD

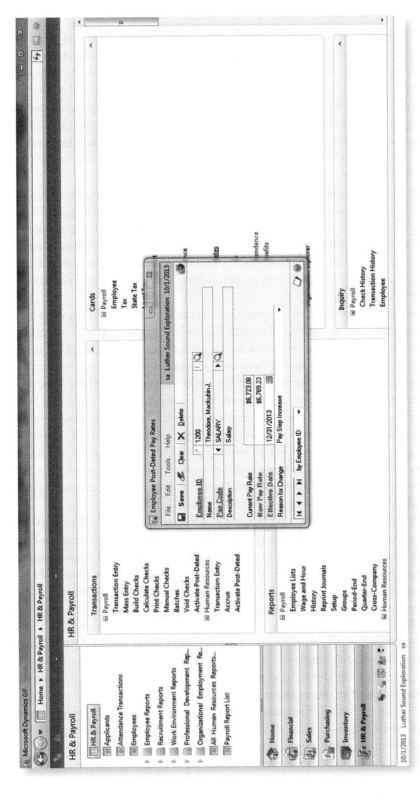

FIGURE 8.10 Employee Post-Dated Pay Rates in GPD

effective. The required fields for the employee post-dated pay rates are Employee ID, Pay Code, New Pay Rate, and Effective Date. Similar to other cards, when the employee ID is entered, the Name field automatically populates. This is also true for the pay code, where the Description field will be entered automatically. Based on the selected employee ID and pay code, the Current Pay Rate will be displayed. This field is not editable; however, it can be updated using the New Pay Rate field and the Effective Date field for when the change should be applied. Furthermore, the card provides a Reason for Change field to notify users who review or use the system to understand why specific changes are made and whether they have been authorized beforehand. (See Figure 8.10.)

The employee direct deposit maintenance card stores information regarding employees' bank accounts and deposit preferences. Employee ID is the required field for this card. After entering the Remainder of Net Line Number several fields are enabled for editing. Required inputs include Bank Number (routing information), Account Number, Check/Savings, Amount, Deduction, Status, and Number. This card uses buttons to add accounts, remove accounts, link predetermined deductions, and undo changes. (See Figure 8.11.)

The human resources management department should be the only department that has update access to the payroll master files for hiring, firing, pay raises, and promotions. As such, the human resources management department should not directly participate in the payroll processing steps or paycheck distribution step. Furthermore, payroll personnel should not be permitted to update the payroll master files. If the proper access controls are not in place to limit the allowable employees from updating the payroll master files, unauthorized changes can create exposures for falsified wages, salaries, commissions, or other base rates used in calculating compensation. In this particular cycle, the segregation of duties is vital in ensuring that changes and updates to the payroll master files are performed by authorized personnel. In addition, any changes to the payroll master files should be authorized and reviewed by separate employees, typically the supervisors of the human resources management department.

The first step of the payroll cycle, updating payroll master files, is subject to threats that include unauthorized changes, stolen confidential information, human errors, and untimely updates. The biggest threat in this payroll cycle would be the unauthorized changes being made to the payroll master file. Weak internal controls could allow unauthorized personnel to gain access rights that might negatively affect the entire payroll process. A second threat associated with the payroll master files is the loss and/or release to unauthorized users of confidential information. As noted above, the master file includes Social Security numbers, banking numbers, addresses, and other sensitive information that exposes employees to the risk of identity theft and other frauds. This is also a potential liability for the company and it is important to ensure that employee information gathered by the company remains secure.

The third threat is due to human errors in recording or updating the payroll master file. The reliability and accuracy of output information from a system depend on the quality and accuracy of the input. Human errors may degrade the quality of input. The auditor should look for and inspect an appropriate supervisory review process for input, assessing both accuracy (to ensure that information is correct) and authorization (to ensure that changes to the payroll master file have been performed by duly authorized

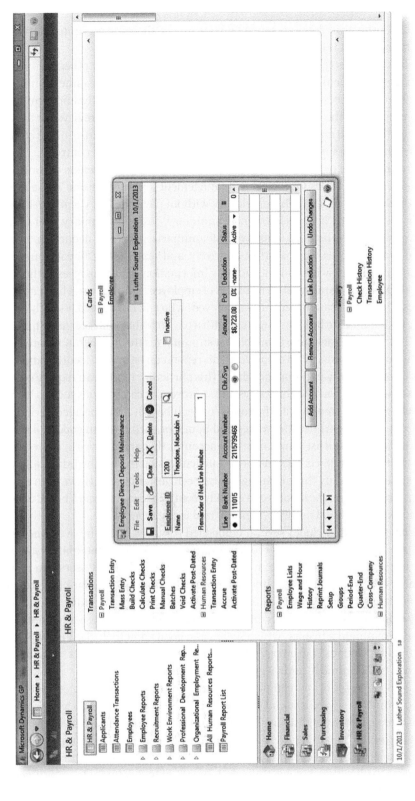

FIGURE 8.11 Employee Direct Deposit Maintenance in GPD

personnel). Untimely updates present a fourth threat: Otherwise accurate information may corrupt a file if it is imported on the wrong date.

The final threat is the overriding of controls by management or other personnel. If the control environment of the company is weak, unauthorized personnel may be able to reconfigure the access rights of certain users and ultimately alter and manipulate the data provided in the system. For this reason, it is important to review not only the changes to the payroll master file, but also the user access rights to ensure that changes to user settings are not made without the proper authorization and controls.

There are several reports that can be used to assess the effectiveness of controls as well as provide summaries for review by management and supervisors. These reports include the detailed employee list, employees without pay code list, vacation/sick time available list, company benefits list, benefit summary, position summary, and detailed direct deposit list. The detailed employee list summarizes the pay, deduction, benefit, state and local tax codes, and monthly, quarterly, and yearly totals for each employee. In addition, it provides wage and withholding information. The employees without pay code list displays the names and ID numbers of employees who have not been assigned pay codes. This report can help identify employees who will not be paid properly or paid at all due to the failure to link the employee with a pay code that will determine his or her net pay. The vacation/sick time available list summarizes the number of vacation/sick days accumulated or used by an employee. This report can be used to identify employees who have not taken any vacation/sick days. This particular report can require employees to take mandatory vacation/sick days and so prevent or catch frauds such as lapping. The benefit summary report lists the totals for each benefit for a specified period. The position summary report lists the wages and hours for each position code in a specific period. The deposit detail list summarizes the accounts that are involved in payroll direct deposit. Overall, the reports related to this particular step review the information put into the system to identify that all changes have been authorized and have been entered correctly. Furthermore, the reports can quickly identify areas of concern based on what is expected and the actual numbers summarized in the reports.

The payroll setup includes several embedded controls. First, the overtime calculation is done automatically, thus reducing human-error computational mistakes as well as the possibility of employee manipulation. Only authorized users can change the number of regular hours required before the overtime calculation kicks in (automatic calculations can be changed during payroll entry to accommodate overtime for biweekly employees who work overtime in one week but not in another). There is also an option to maintain a history, which serves as a good audit tool. (See Figure 8.12.)

Within the "Options" tab on payroll setup there are options for tracking additional information and document control numbers. (See Figure 8.13.)

Figure 8.14 presents an example of a control in the setup for deductions. Family Health Insurance is a fixed amount ($98) and an attempted change to $99 prompts a warning message directing the user to the human resources department. Note that the right to run the update benefit setup would only be permitted to certain employees!

QB prompts for the administrator's password before any new accounts are created. This reduces the likelihood of existing employees simply creating a fake "full-access" account and then tampering with the payroll process. (See Figure 8.15.)

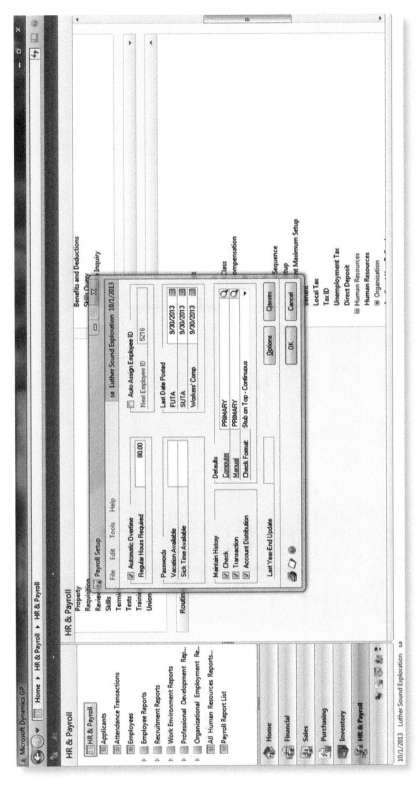

FIGURE 8.12 Payroll Setup in GPD

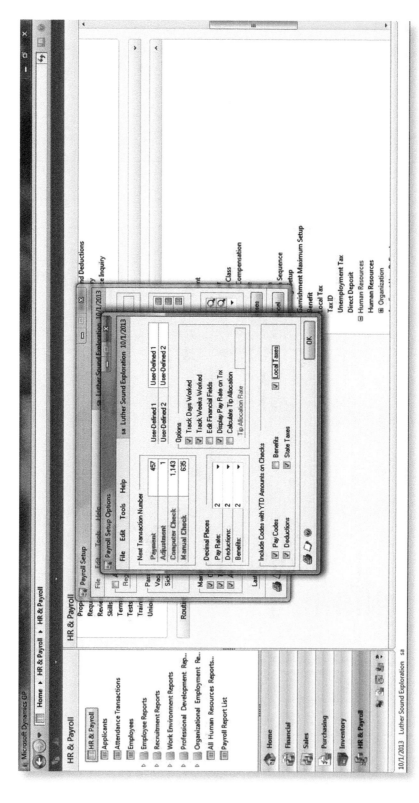

FIGURE 8.13 Payroll Setup Options in GPD

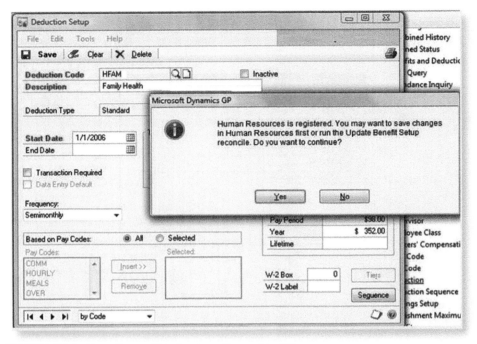

FIGURE 8.14 Benefits and Deductions Control in QB

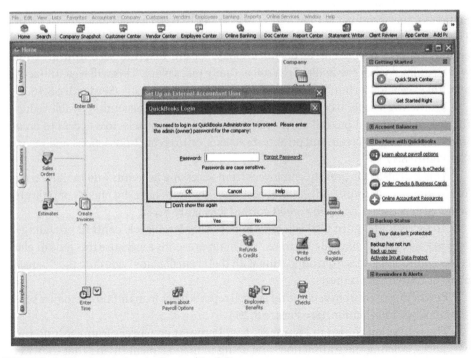

FIGURE 8.15 Admin Login Control in QB

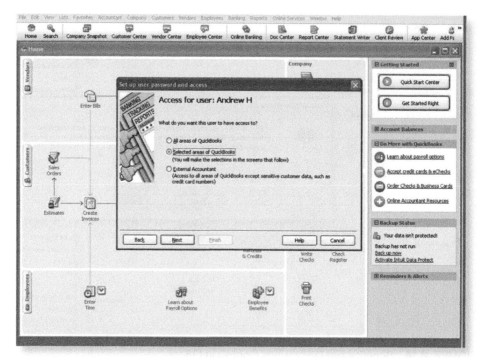

FIGURE 8.16 Set Up User Access in QB

An authenticated user with administrator rights can enter basic employee information for the account. QB then allows him or her to restrict each individual's access. The administrator can select "all areas of QuickBooks" (creating, in essence, another administrator), "selected areas of QuickBooks," or an "external accountant," which will be utilized when the audit of payroll actually takes place. This will be a full-access account except for certain information regarding customer data. (See Figure 8.16.)

Restricting a general employee's access to purchases and accounts payable reduces the risk of fraudulent payroll entries. It is possible to grant selective access to create transactions only, to create and print transactions, or to create transactions and reports. (See Figure 8.17.)

This will also help prevent employees from accessing accounts and making transfers to improper accounts or personal accounts and from printing checks or charging personal expenses to company credit cards. (See Figure 8.18.)

The screen in Figure 8.19 is a very important payroll cycle control: providing or denying access to all payroll functions. The main preventive measure this puts in place is preventing employees from tampering with their benefit plans regarding their pension plans or retirement accounts.

Restricting users from generating payroll reports helps to maintain custody of sensitive employee information. (See Figure 8.20.)

The restriction shown in Figure 8.21 will prevent employees from cashing their paychecks, deleting the transaction, and going to management saying that they were not paid for that period. It will also prevent alterations to the amount of time worked

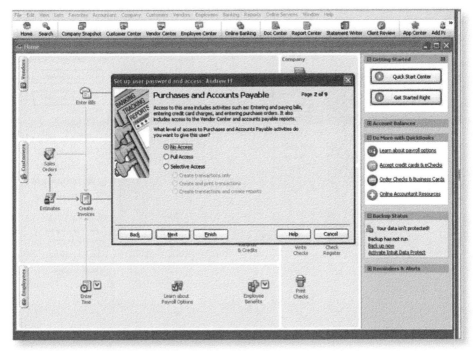

FIGURE 8.17   Set Up Selective User Access in QB

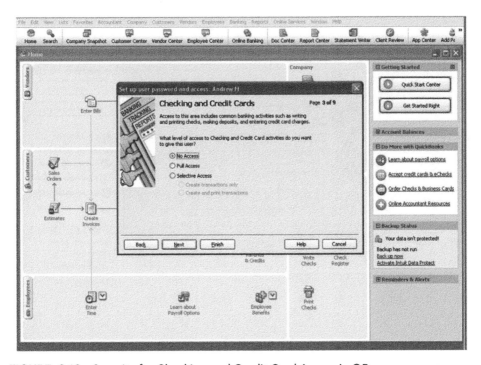

FIGURE 8.18   Security for Checking and Credit Card Access in QB

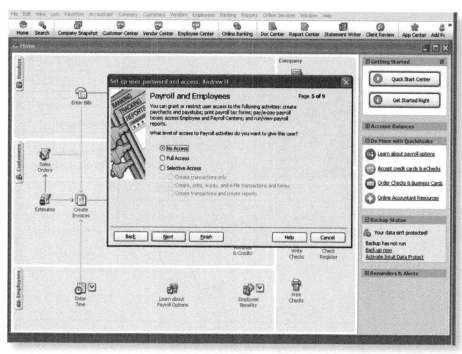

FIGURE 8.19 Security for Payroll Function Access in QB

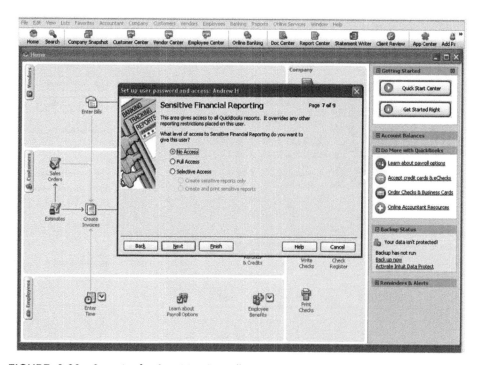

FIGURE 8.20 Security for Sensitive Payroll Reports Access in QB

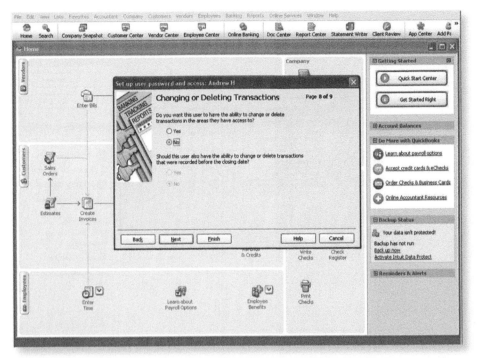

FIGURE 8.21 Security for Changing or Deleting Transactions in QB

during a pay period or changing their pay rate. The only way that these individuals could override this is with the administrative password.

QB provides many prompts to inform the user about setups. The screen in Figure 8.22 shows an overview of restrictions to certain areas of QB. It is a good screen for an auditor to review for a summary of employee access rights within the system.

When creating a company file the accountant should be sure to save it to a secure drive. This will prevent access to the source file so others cannot duplicate, change, or delete it. Ensuring that this master file is backed up on an additional offsite secure server greatly reduces the level of audit risk when assessing a company that uses QB for its payroll cycle. The accountant should be sure to back up the file after every session. (See Figure 8.23.)

QB establishes security protocols after the selection of 1099 or W-2 employee type. The auditor typically would not have to worry about employee tampering for offsite 1099 contractors. Creating W-2 employees allows the accountant to set up customized access profiles. (See Figure 8.24.)

This screen in Figure 8.25 controls for duplicate vendors. This is important if the company sets up employees as vendors for expense reimbursement.

The Employee Setup section provides input lines for W-4 information, pay rate, paycheck deductions, sick or vacation hours, direct deposit information, and hire date. If applicable, an employee's termination date could also be entered here as well. (See Figure 8.26.)

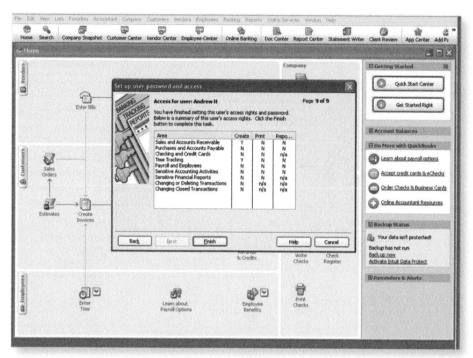

FIGURE 8.22 Summary of Access Rights in QB

Figure 8.27 illustrates an employee summary report. Once the previous information has been entered for an employee, QB brings up a review screen that shows a summary of each employee's payroll information. In this particular screenshot, QB is missing certain required pieces of information on each employee. By double-clicking on a specific employee, you can go through a series of screens and see any information that you forgot to add, or edit any information that was entered incorrectly. You can also click the "Summary" button to bring up a detailed report, listing all the payroll information that was just entered pertaining to an employee, facilitating a final review. (See Figure 8.28.)

Tax Records Are Not Updated or Calculated Correctly

Another risk in the payroll cycle exists with respect to updating and correcting calculations for tax records. From a completeness and valuation/allocation assertion standpoint, within the system, management needs to ensure that tax records are appropriately updated in a timely manner. The tax updates typically occur when management gets the updated tax file from the tax authorities and the data file is loaded into the system. Management should ensure that the data loaded into the system is the same as the tax file being loaded. This is typically accomplished through hash and control totals that ensure that the total number of records and amounts are appropriately transferred. Within the system, management needs to ensure that tax calculations are correct. The calculations functionality is typically an inherent control built into the system. Management can test this functionality by looking at sample transactions and reviewing reports.

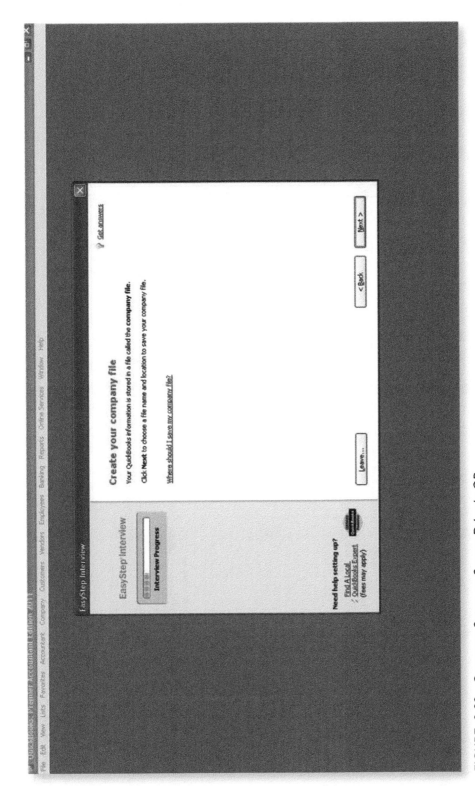

FIGURE 8.23 Company Setup on Secure Drive in QB

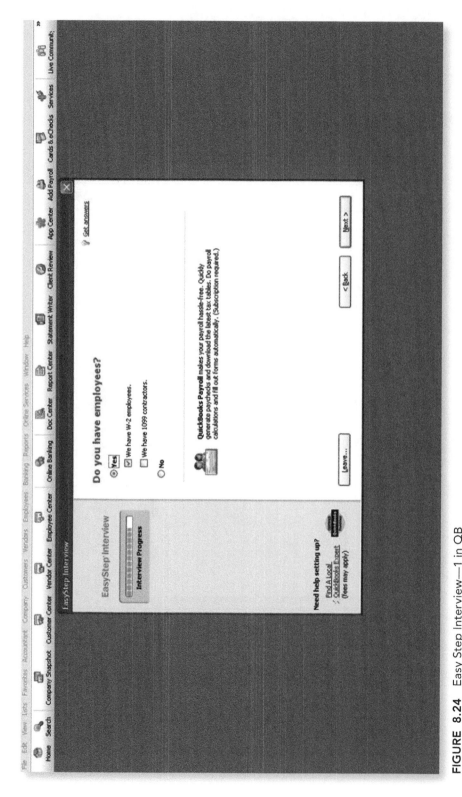

FIGURE 8.24 Easy Step Interview—1 in QB

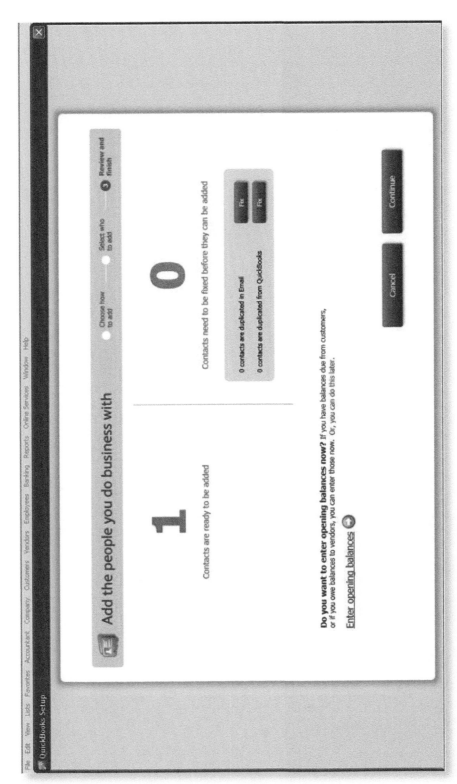

FIGURE 8.25 Easy Step Interview—2 in QB

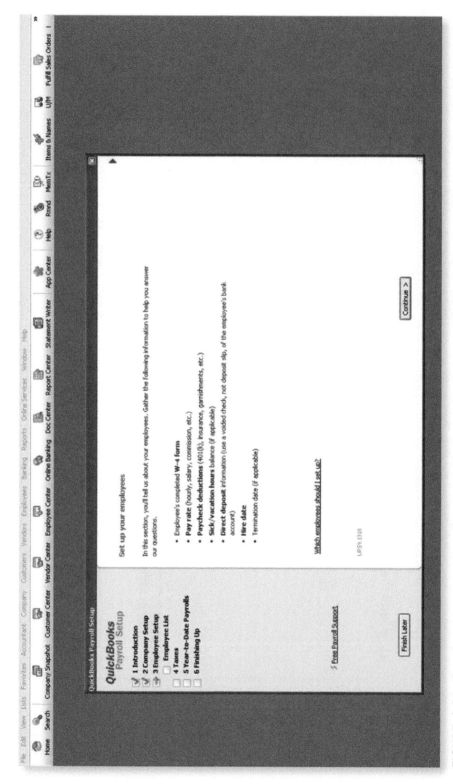

FIGURE 8.26 Easy Step Interview—Payroll

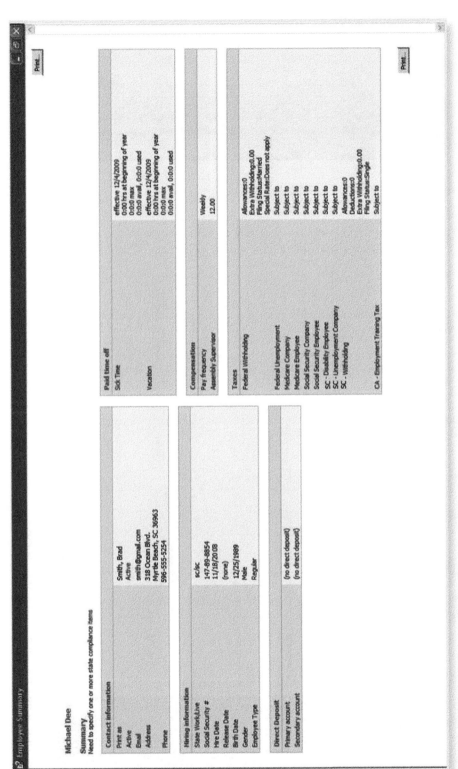

FIGURE 8.27 Sample Detail Payroll Summary View in QB

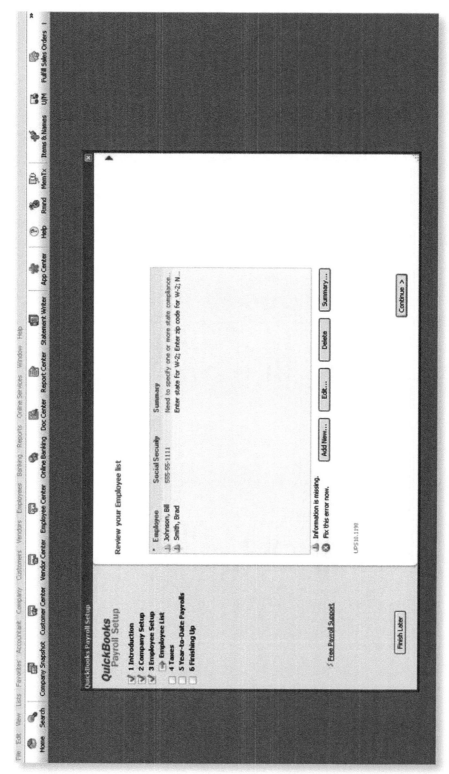

FIGURE 8.28 Payroll Summary View in QB

Within GPD, the human resources management and payroll cycle requires the updating of information about tax rates and other withholdings. Changes occur when the payroll department receives notification of changes in tax rates and other payroll deductions from various government units and insurance companies. The payroll department makes these changes, but the changes should occur infrequently. (See Figure 8.29.)

Setting the tax withholding state establishes the state in which the employee is taxed. The control is configurable, provided that the proper access has been given. Each state has its own rules and therefore has its own separate calculations. (See Figure 8.30.)

Local tax codes must be keyed in and are therefore susceptible to modifications (unlike federal and state rates). Within the payroll department there are threats specific to all the tax maintenance cards. These include errors to the tax rates that could lead to processing errors and, possibly, penalties. In Microsoft Dynamics, the payroll department would have to update tax records by downloading federal and state tax law changes through Great Plains' online payroll subscription service. This is an inherent control that prevents users from modifying any tax rate. However, as stated before, the local tax rates can be changed, which could lead to processing errors in the payroll. (See Figure 8.31.)

The menus in Figures 8.32 and 8.33 features configurable controls with defaults on specific employee deductions subject to certain maximum amounts. The controls include dates, and there is also the potential to set garnishment deductions.

Deduction cards also have the same types of threats that affect tax maintenance cards. Failure to assess accurately garnishments on the employees' wages and remit those funds to the appropriate party can also lead to financial penalties. Take, for example, the deduction sequence card. Improper sequencing of the deduction may cause employees to take incorrect deductions, maybe causing them to lose out on some of the 401(k) benefits. Alternatively, expenses can also increase if deduction base rates such as 401(k) benefits are incorrectly stated. (See Figure 8.34.)

The Payroll Local Tax Set includes controls for local tax codes. If these don't exist in the system, individuals with appropriate access can add a new local tax code. Entry requires a description of the tax code. Without authorized access, selection would be limited to codes provided in the lookup tab.

Federal and state income tax codes are not included in this setup because the tax rates and tables are downloaded from the online payroll tax service. Downloading tax rates directly through the system also controls against manipulations of the rates and selection of incorrect tax rates. (See Figure 8.35.)

Unlike the federal and state tax rates, local tax rates are not downloaded from the online payroll service. This may indicate a potential risk that changes to local tax rates may not be caught by GPD, and thus result in inaccurate local tax withholding. (See Figure 8.36.)

The analogous process in QB involves the setup of appropriate payroll taxes for company employees. QB instructions include a suggested list of information to make setup as simple and streamlined as possible. This includes applicable state unemployment insurance contribution rate, state agency ID number, tax rates, and the company's tax deposit and filing schedule. This screen also provides a link to the QB Tax Information website, which provides FAQ and additional guidance. (See Figure 8.37.)

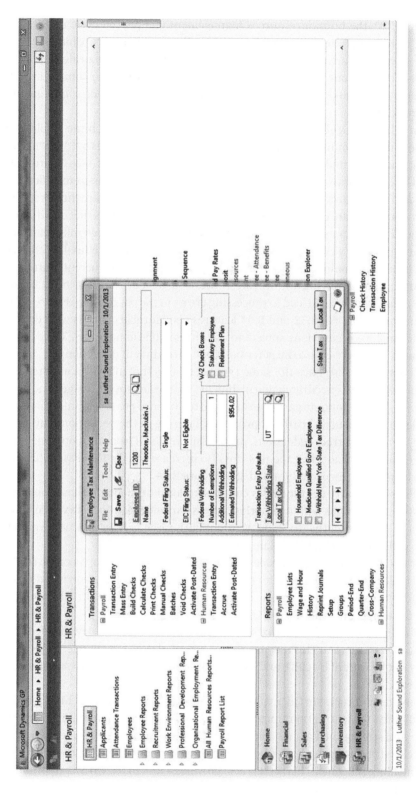

FIGURE 8.29 Employee Federal Tax Maintenance in GPD

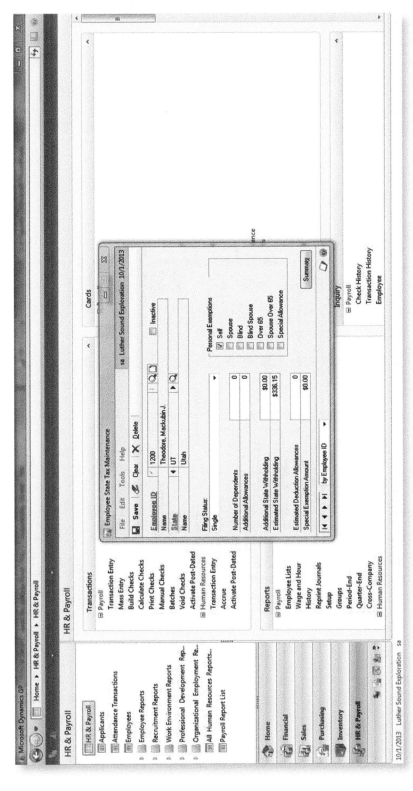

FIGURE 8.30 Employee State Tax Maintenance in GPD

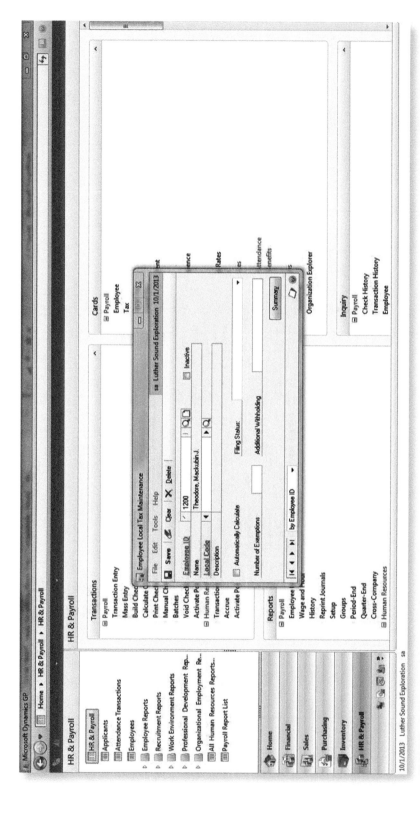

FIGURE 8.31 Employee Local Tax Maintenance in GPD

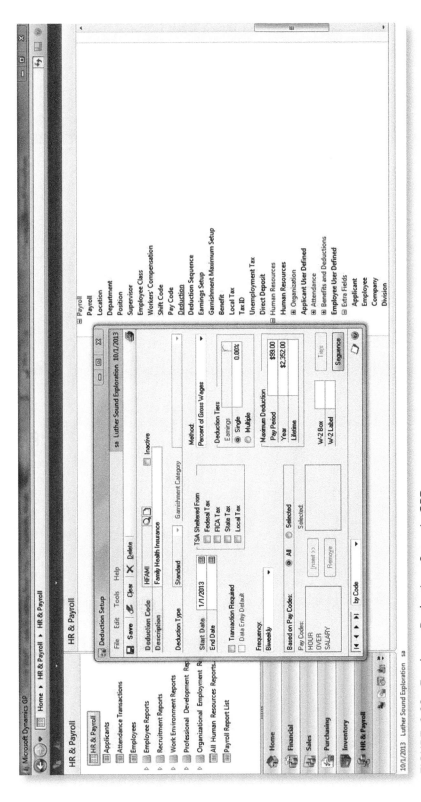

FIGURE 8.32 Employee Deductions Setup in GPD

197

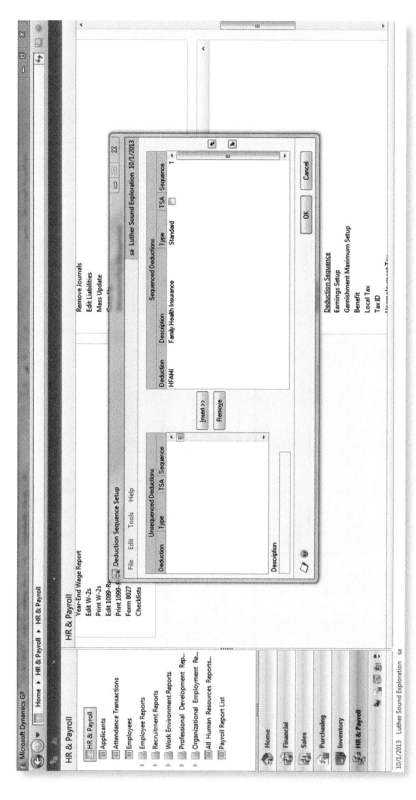

FIGURE 8.33 Employee Deductions Sequence Setup in GPD

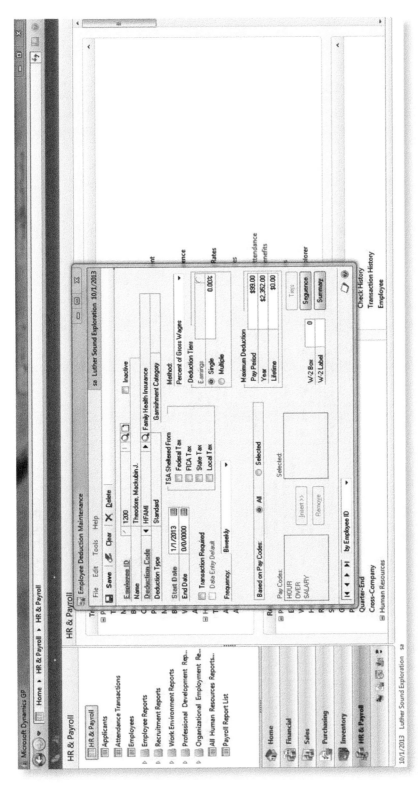

FIGURE 8.34 Employee Deductions Maintenance in GPD

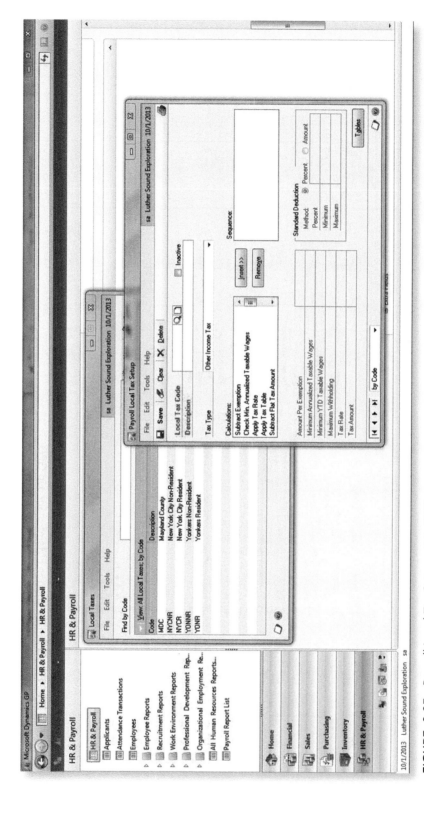

FIGURE 8.35 Payroll Local Tax Setup—1 in GPD

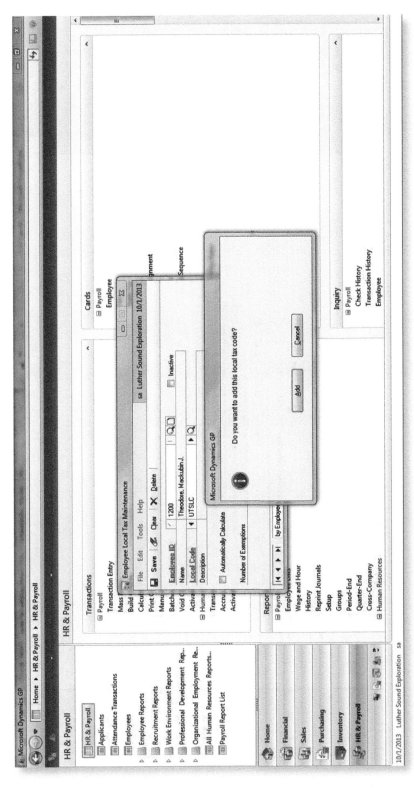

FIGURE 8.36 Payroll Local Tax Setup—2 GPD

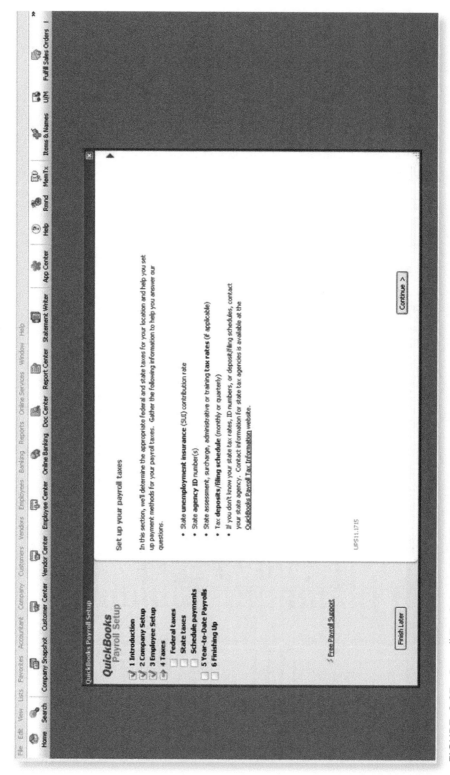

FIGURE 8.37 Payroll Tax Setup—1 in QB

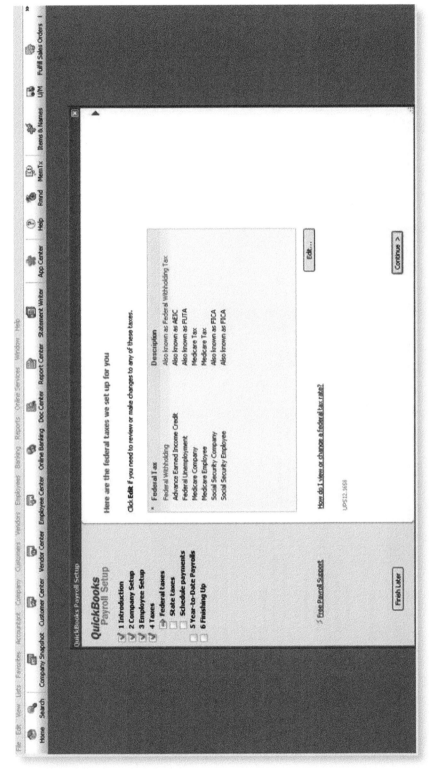

FIGURE 8.38 Payroll Tax Setup—2 in QB

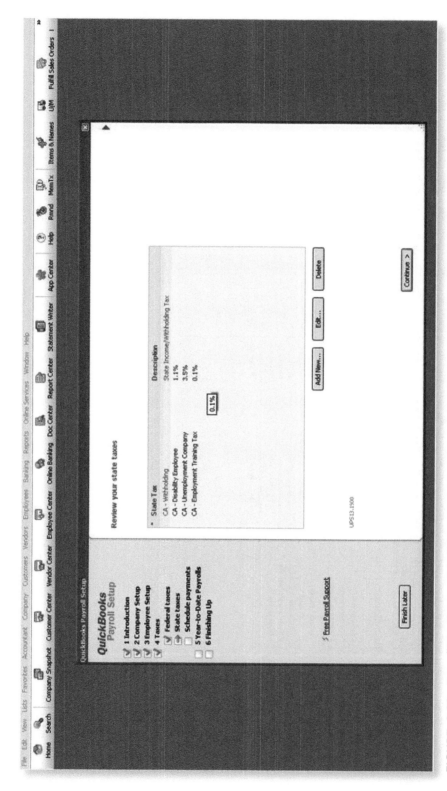

FIGURE 8.39 Payroll Tax Setup—3 in QB

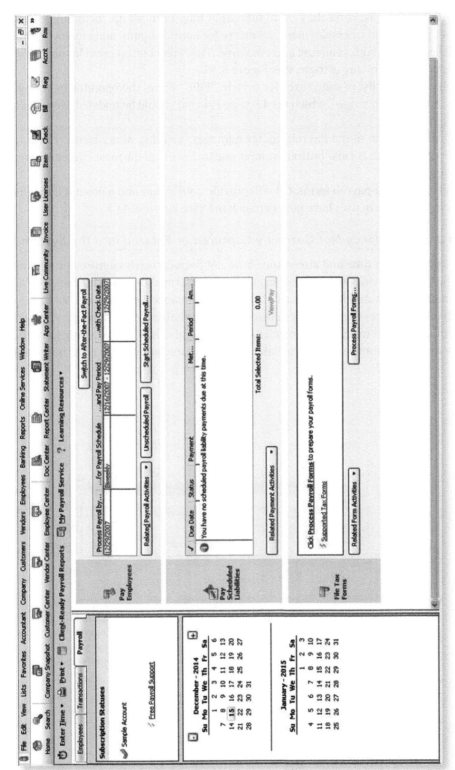

FIGURE 8.40 Processing Payroll Tax Forms in QB

QB provides a list of all the federal taxes that have been set up, including federal withholding, federal unemployment, Medicare for both company and employee, and Social Security for both company and employee. The "Edit" button provides access for review or changes to any of these. (See Figure 8.38.)

QB provides a list of state taxes for review. "Edit" allows the operator to change states, but not the tax rates, which (as discussed ahead) should be updated every year. (See Figure 8.39.)

The last section of the Payroll Center manages the filing of tax forms. Clicking the "Process Payroll Forms" button prompts one to download the most current forms. (See Figure 8.40.)

When creating payroll forms, QB will provide notification and a prompt if the tax tables that the system uses have not been updated. (See Figure 8.41.)

Time and Attendance Not Correctly Captured or Entered into the System

The possibility that time and attendance have not been correctly captured or entered into the system provides another risk. In many small and medium-sized businesses, this information is captured in third-party time and attendance software such as Kronos and then entered into the payroll system for processing either by an electronic interface or through manual rekeying. In some cases the general ledger package may have the ability to track time and attendance. Validation of time and attendance is the heartbeat

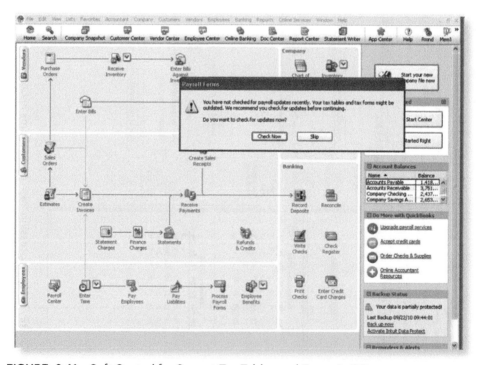

FIGURE 8.41 Soft Control for Current Tax Tables and Forms in QB

of the payroll cycle and the IT auditor should verify that the process includes reasonable controls for accuracy and completeness. (See Figure 8.42.)

The wage and hour report pulls various items of employee information into one location. Reconciling this report to general employee information provides a check on unauthorized changes or deletions.

Within QB, entering time for employees for work completed is accessed from the home screen via the "Enter Time" icon. (See Figures 8.43, 8.44, and 8.45.)

QB enables the user to pick a specific date and employee for this particular activity, enter the customer who was serviced or job that was completed, the rate that will be used for payroll (such as Labor, Supervisor, and Overtime), and the duration. (See Figure 8.46.)

When entering the amount of time that an employee has worked, QB will notify you if you select a payroll item, or rate, that does not exist for that particular employee. This notification serves as a warning if you have accidentally chosen the wrong payroll item for an employee, or have purposely chosen a rate with better pay. In this example, we tried to choose the "installation labor" rate for the employee, Michael Dee, but he does not have a rate set up for installation labor because he works as an assembly supervisor. QB has a great control telling you that a $0.00 rate will be used unless you edit this employee and assign him the chosen rate. Only an administrator would have the ability to do this. (See Figure 8.47.)

In order to change the billing rate for an employee, the administrator would click the "Edit Employee" button in the upper-right of the Employee Center screen. From here you have two options. You can choose to make it a *fixed hourly rate* where the rate you assign (in this case $12.50) will be used for all service items performed by people with this particular rate. You can also choose to make it a *custom hourly rate*, where a different rate can be used for different service items performed by employees. You can also assign the billing rate a name at this time. (See Figure 8.48.)

When you are entering the payroll information for employees, if no withholding amount is specified, QB will have a popup that informs you that the amount is zero and even offer a possible explanation as to why this could occur. (See Figure 8.49.)

Payroll Is Not Prepared or Processed Correctly

Management can review reports within the system to compare what was prepared or processed in the system to the source documents to determine if the payroll is correct.

During the preparation of the payroll, the amounts that get printed on the checks need to be compared against the system reports to ensure that the correct amounts were processed and printed on the checks.

In some circumstances, management may need to review system reports against ACH direct deposits. In this circumstance, management will not have manual checks to review, but instead system reports for the planned payroll against the actual payroll being processed via direct deposit. Note that the report comparison needs to occur prior to the final submission of the payroll.

In other circumstances, management may use a third-party payroll processor that will be responsible for preparing the payroll based on the reported time and attendance. Management should utilize control reports (e.g., "Statements on Controls 1 or 2") to verify the controls in place at the payroll processor.

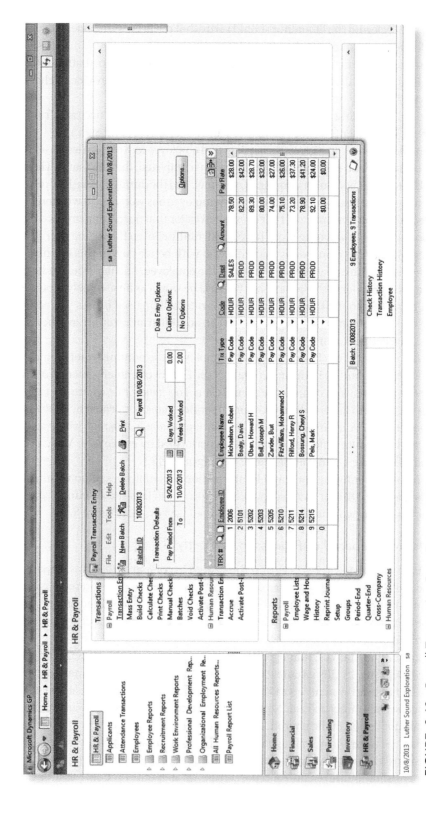

FIGURE 8.42 Payroll Transaction Data Entry in GPD

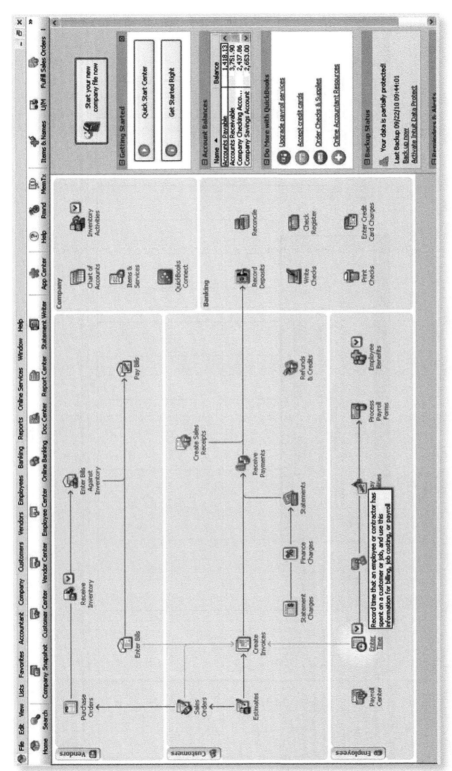

FIGURE 8.43 Payroll Transaction Data Entry in QB

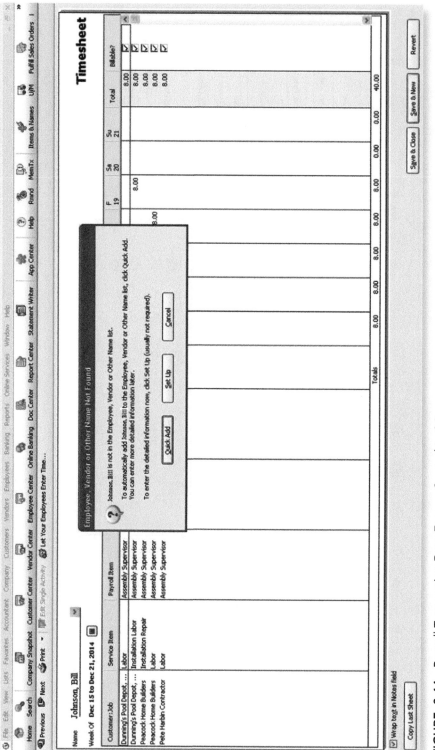

FIGURE 8.44 Payroll Transaction Data Entry—Control in QB

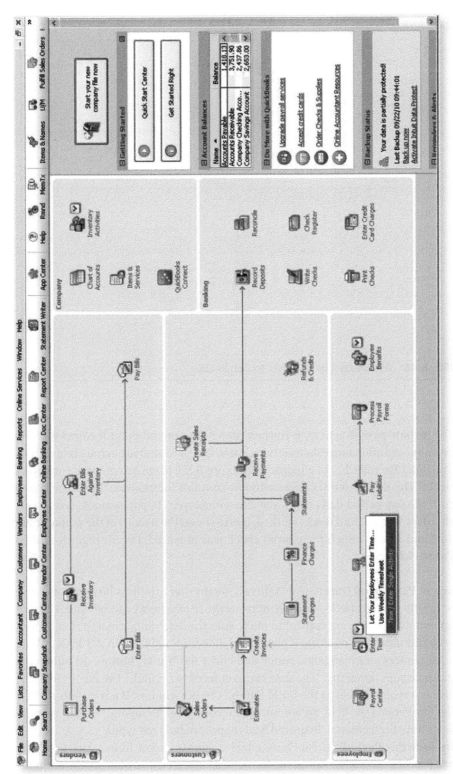

FIGURE 8.45 Payroll Transaction Data Entry—Entered One at a Time in QB

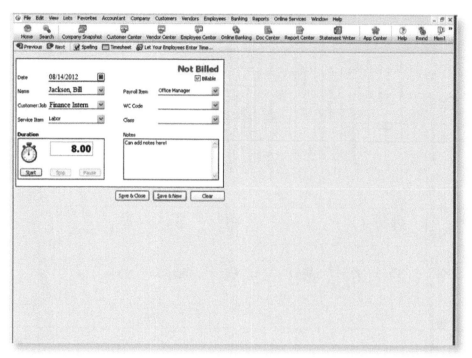

FIGURE 8.46 Assigning Payroll Costs to Job in QB

The prepare payroll activity is the next step in the payroll cycle. It comes after the validate time and attendance data activity, but before the disburse payroll cycle activity.

The Build Payroll Checks window (see Figure 8.50) is used to prepare employees' paychecks. The Build Payroll Checks window contains information about the type of pay run, the pay period date, employee class, employee ID, pay periods, deductions, benefits, days worked, and weeks worked. It also shows the user ID of the preparer and the time and date in which the payroll check was prepared. Details regarding these fields are as follows:

- **Select Pay Period Date:** Great Plains allows the user to build salary payroll checks or hourly payroll checks. Furthermore, advance paychecks can be built. GPD has an automated inherent control to make sure the date range entered is valid (e.g., prohibits user from entering a pay period date from 2/14/XX to 2/13/XX). When a user enters an invalid date range and clicks the "Build" button, an automated message pops up saying "The date range entered isn't valid." The Pay Period Date field is a required field in the Build Payroll Checks window. If a user fails to fill in the Pay Period Date field, an automated message pops up saying: "Not all required fields have been entered. Required fields appear in bold red type."
- **Include Pay Periods:** Great Plains enables users to choose from various pay periods (weekly, biweekly, semimonthly, monthly, quarterly, semiannually, annually, daily/misc.). Biweekly is the default that is checked when the Build Payroll Checks

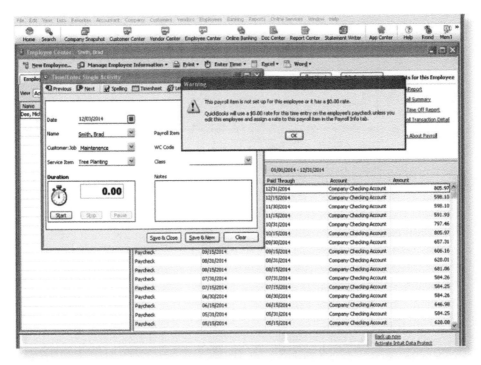

FIGURE 8.47 Payroll Rate Control in QB

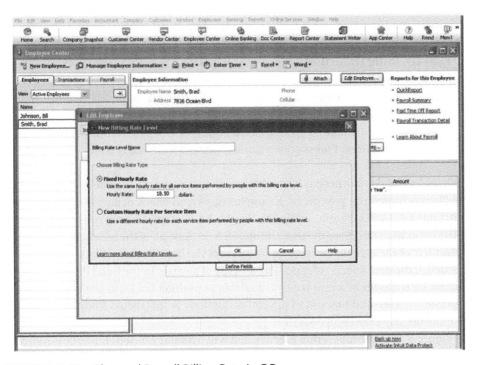

FIGURE 8.48 Changed Payroll Billing Rate in QB

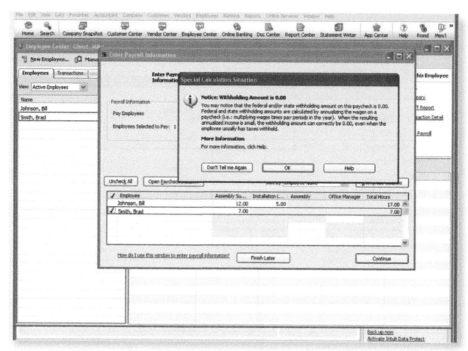

FIGURE 8.49 Soft Control for Withholding in QB

window is first opened. This is because most employees are paid biweekly. This is an automated inherent control within Great Plains that prevents the user from selecting a pay type that is not listed here.

▪ **User ID, Build Date, Build Time, Description:** These fields cannot be modified by the user while building payroll checks. This is an inherent control in GPD so that users do not alter the date or time that the checks are being built. For instance, management may want to alter the date and time a payroll check is created to pay an employee late, but make it appear that the employee was paid on time. This inherent control within Great Plains prevents management from doing this.

In order to calculate net pay, Great Plains allows the user to include deductions and benefits when creating paychecks. Examples of payroll check deductions are 401(k), Contributions, Health Family, or Health Single. An example of a payroll check benefit is 401(k). Great Plains gives the user the option to include all of the benefits/deductions, a select few of the benefits/deductions, or none of the benefits/deductions from the list provided. If the user selects Advance Pay for type of pay run in the Build Payroll Checks window, GPD has an inherent control available to prohibit the inclusion of deductions and benefits. The total amount of payroll deductions is subtracted from gross pay to calculate net pay. (See Figure 8.51.)

Figure 8.52 is the report that is generated when a salary-based employee paycheck is being built. As we attempted to calculate the paychecks, one of Great Plains' controls popped up and would not allow payroll calculation while year-end closing was in

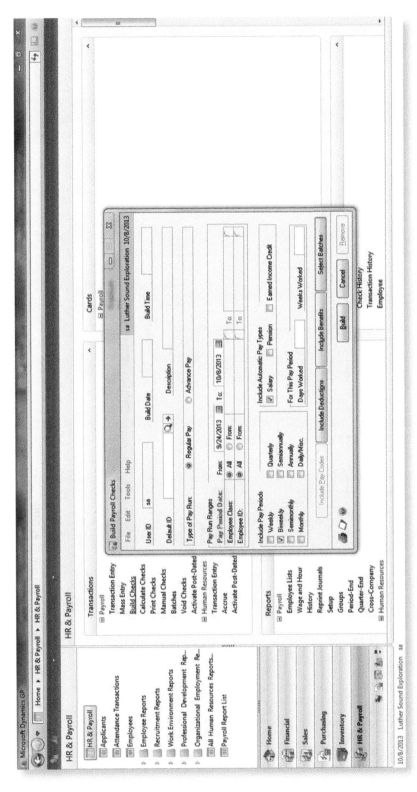

FIGURE 8.50 Build Payroll Checks in GPD

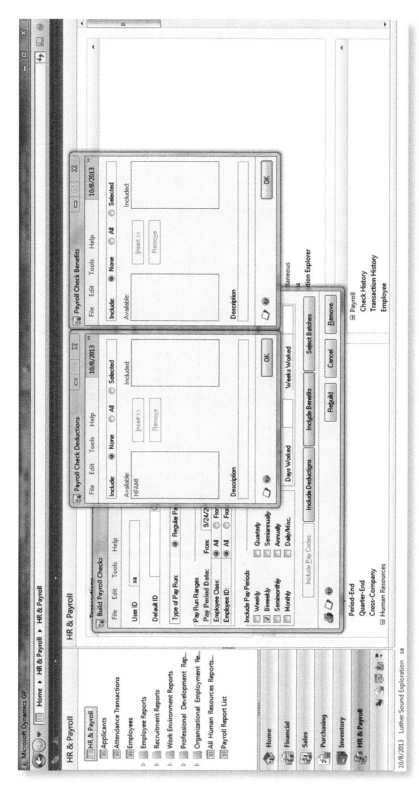

FIGURE 8.51 Payroll Check Deductions in GPD

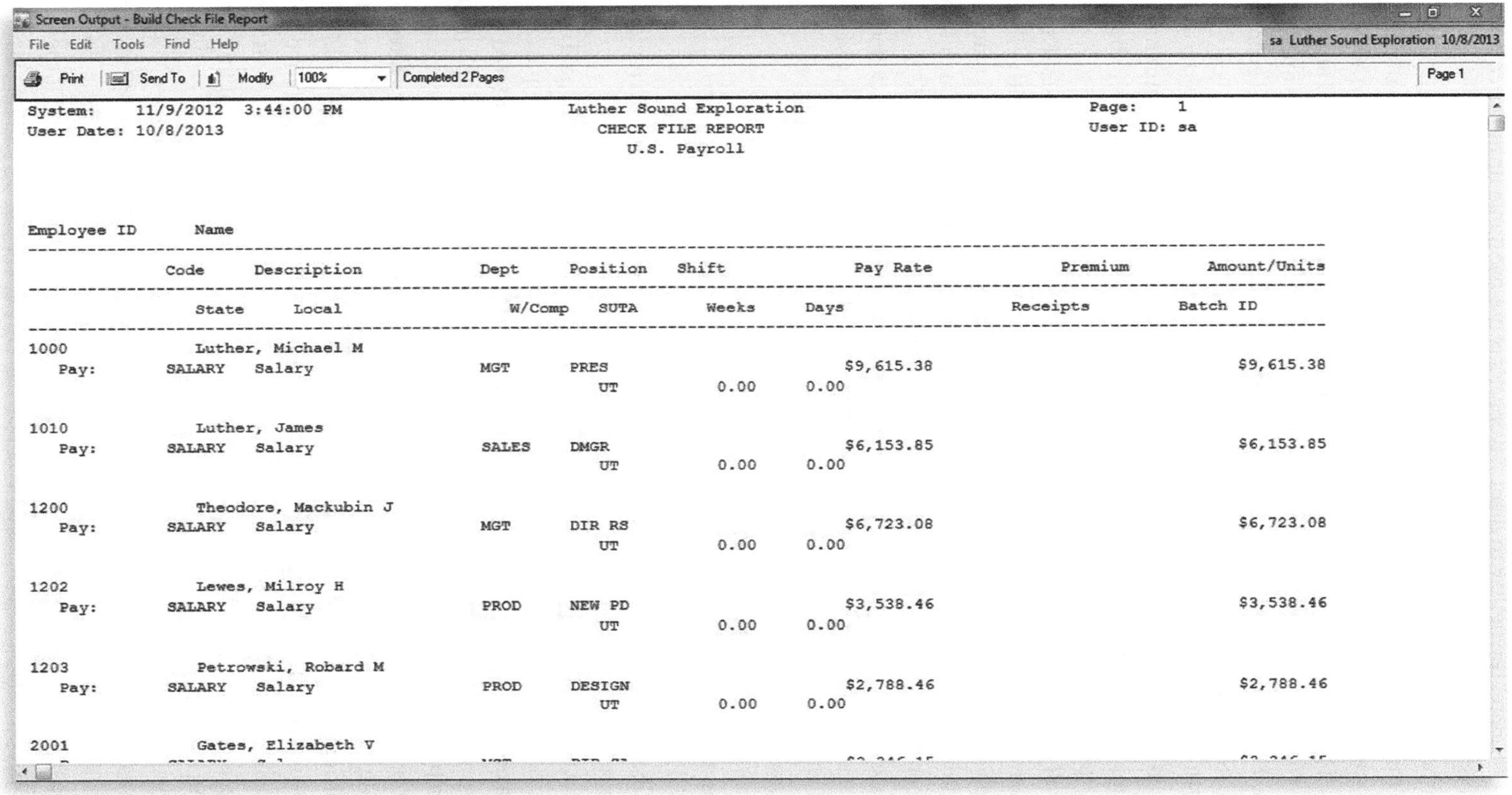

```
System:      11/9/2012   3:44:00 PM              Luther Sound Exploration              Page:    1
User Date: 10/8/2013                               CHECK FILE REPORT                   User ID: sa
                                                     U.S. Payroll


Employee ID      Name
-----------------------------------------------------------------------------------------------------------
    Code      Description      Dept   Position  Shift   Weeks    Days      Pay Rate      Premium    Amount/Units
              State    Local          W/Comp    SUTA                                     Receipts   Batch ID
-----------------------------------------------------------------------------------------------------------
1000          Luther, Michael M
    Pay:      SALARY   Salary   MGT    PRES                0.00    0.00      $9,615.38                 $9,615.38
                                       UT

1010          Luther, James
    Pay:      SALARY   Salary   SALES  DMGR               0.00    0.00      $6,153.85                 $6,153.85
                                       UT

1200          Theodore, Mackubin J
    Pay:      SALARY   Salary   MGT    DIR RS             0.00    0.00      $6,723.08                 $6,723.08
                                       UT

1202          Lewes, Milroy H
    Pay:      SALARY   Salary   PROD   NEW PD             0.00    0.00      $3,538.46                 $3,538.46
                                       UT

1203          Petrowski, Robard M
    Pay:      SALARY   Salary   PROD   DESIGN             0.00    0.00      $2,788.46                 $2,788.46
                                       UT

2001          Gates, Elizabeth V
```

FIGURE 8.52   Payroll Check Report in GPD

217

process. Therefore, the ability to print paychecks is not available until the calculation report is compiled.

After building the checks, it is necessary to calculate them. The Calculate Payroll Checks window is a report that is generated after the checks are built. It lists the user ID, the build status (indicates if any errors are contained in the Build Checks window), the type of pay run, the build date, and the build time, and will also indicate if any warnings or errors exist. Great Plains enables users to print this report for documentation purposes. This report is used as a control in order to make sure that payroll is properly prepared. (See Figure 8.53.)

The HR department can enter employees' pay rates and hours worked in the payroll transaction entry. Batch ID determines whether it is a commission or a regular salary. By selecting the range of pay period and days worked, a total pay amount will be automatically generated. (See Figure 8.54.)

Payroll transaction entry also allows payroll personnel to track expenses. Expense reimbursements are displayed corresponding to individual employees with different codes applied. Most of the reimbursements are related to travels, meals, and entertainments. After inputting all expenses, the payroll transaction entry gives a batch total of the number of employees and transactions. (See Figures 8.55, 8.56, and 8.57.)

Changes made to the employee database can be tracked in the payroll transaction audit list. The list is organized with different letters indicating different types of changes, as follows:

- *A* represents new transactions.
- *D* represents deleted transactions.
- *X* stands for no transaction created.

This list serves as an audit tool to ensure that the payroll personnel can review the changes and make corrections to human errors. (See Figure 8.58.)

In the QB payroll setup, the system asks whether any employee has been paid during the year prior to the setup date. If so, the user will be prompted to enter any paychecks, payroll taxes, and other payroll deductions and contributions already entered in the current year. The purpose of this is to ensure accuracy of future paychecks and payroll tax payments. (See Figure 8.59.)

After providing a review screen, QB informs the user that the paychecks have been successfully created and permits printing directly from the program. (See Figure 8.60.)

QB provides a prompt if the user has added a paycheck to an employee who has already been generated a paycheck for the current pay period. The only negative is that an option for "Don't tell me again" exists, and if it were erroneously selected, it would take time to search for the option to undo it and preserve this very helpful and error-preventing feature. (See Figure 8.61.)

The option in Figure 8.62 is allowed only to those with the proper access. Voiding a paycheck cannot be undone, so it should be done only if absolutely needed. For instance, if you mistakenly created a duplicate paycheck as discussed earlier, this is how you would delete it. When editing, you can lock the net pay for the employee if the check has already been written. This will prevent accidental changes to the total wages or net check amount, which could result in discrepancies when reconciling.

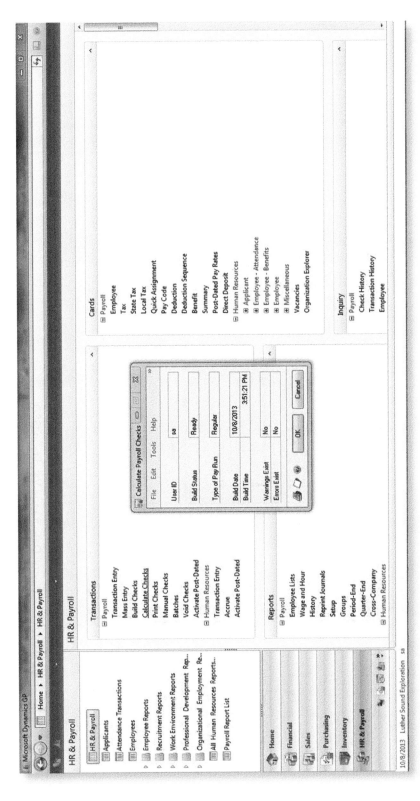

FIGURE 8.53 Payroll Check Calculation in GPD

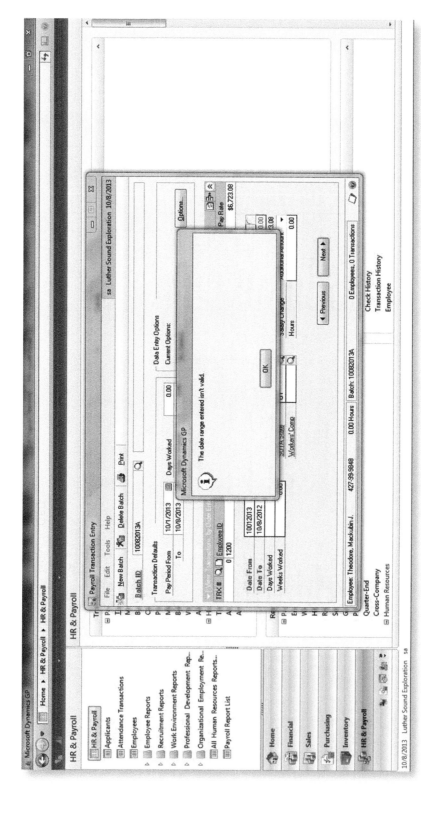

FIGURE 8.54 Hard Control for Payroll Date Range Validity in GPD

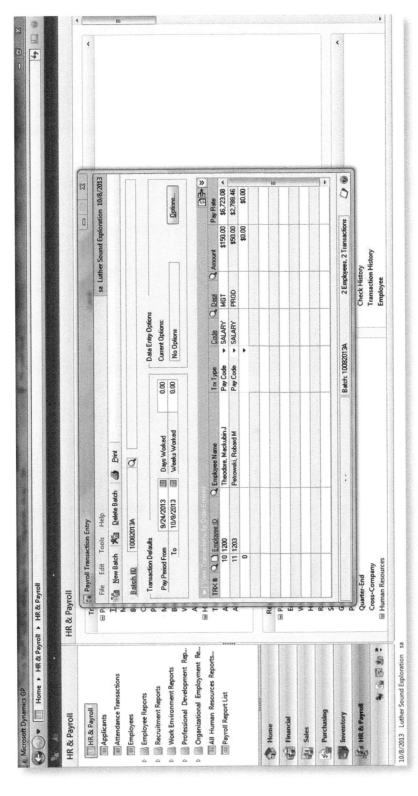

FIGURE 8.55 Employee Expense Tracking in GPD

221

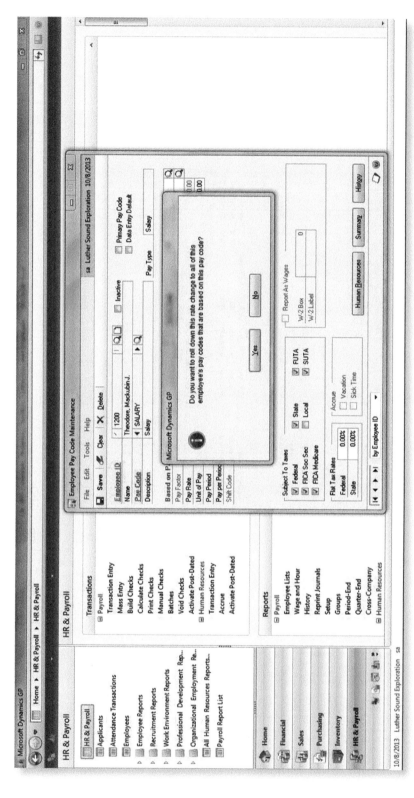

FIGURE 8.56 Employee Pay Code Maintenance in GPD

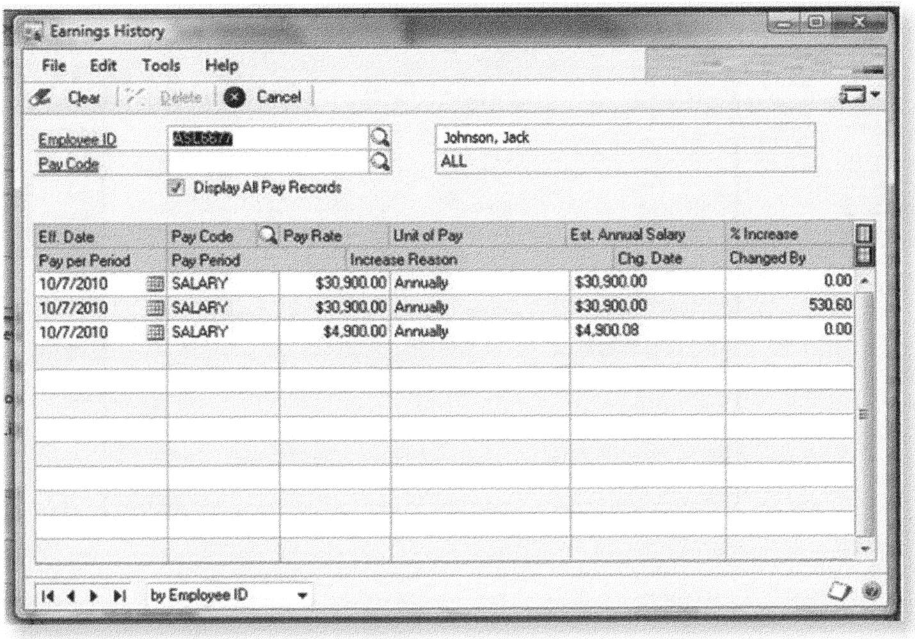

FIGURE 8.57 Earnings History in GPD

Under the Pay Scheduled Liabilities section, we went through and "checked" each payment that we wanted to view. By clicking "View/Pay" we can then review the details of each payment and submit a payment if desired. (See Figure 8.63.)

Figure 8.64 is a summary of all the payroll liabilities that we just submitted payment for. It lists "Payment, Payee, Period, Amount, Method, Status, Withdrawn On, and Tracking #." The total for these payments is also listed at the bottom.

When the "Pay Scheduled Liabilities" menu indicates that there are no more scheduled payments due at this time, the Total Selected Items will be zero. This is a good control for accuracy and completeness.

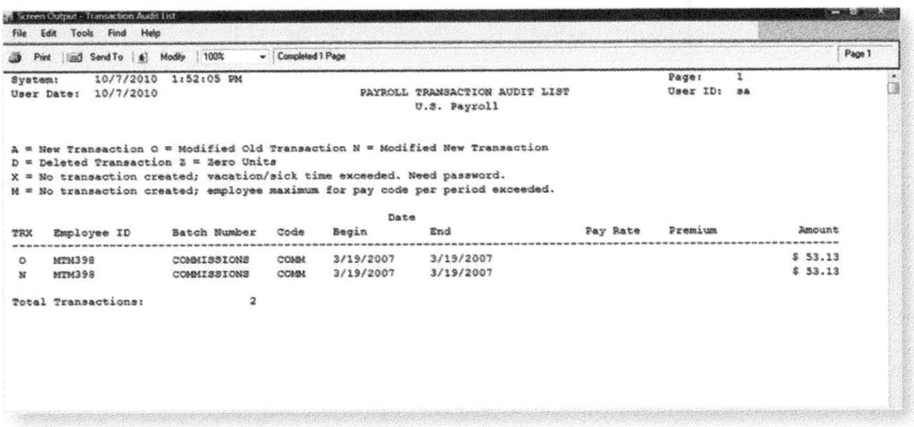

FIGURE 8.58 Payroll History Audit List in GPD

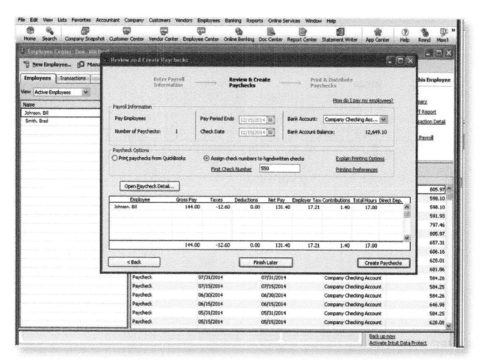

FIGURE 8.59 Review and Create Paychecks in QB

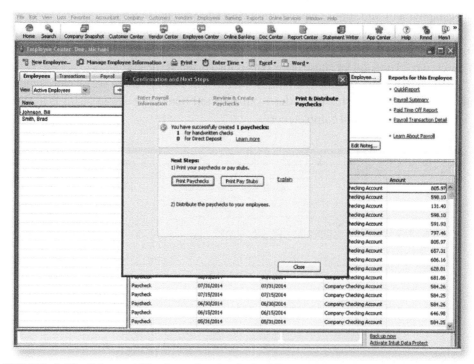

FIGURE 8.60 Print and Distribute Paychecks in QB

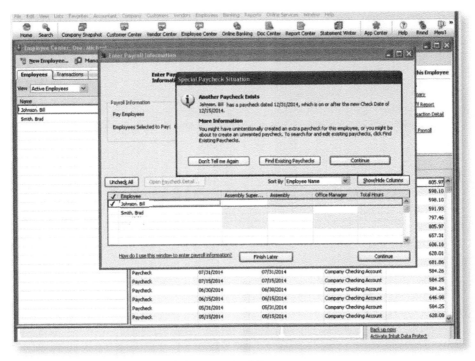

FIGURE 8.61   Special Paycheck Situation in QB

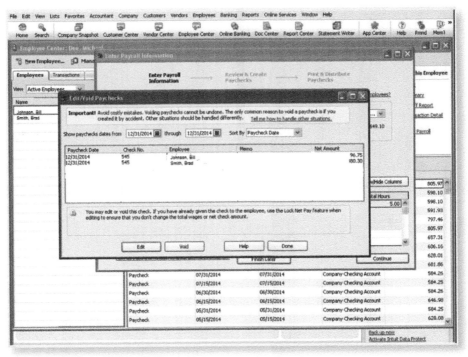

FIGURE 8.62   Void Paycheck in QB

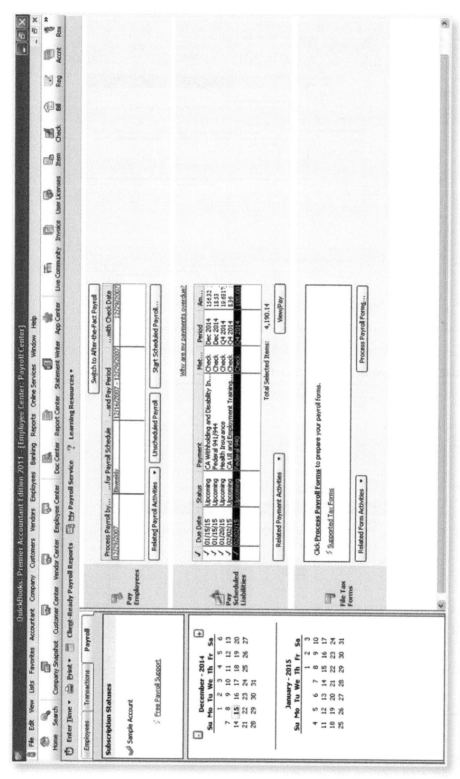

FIGURE 8.63 View/Pay in QB

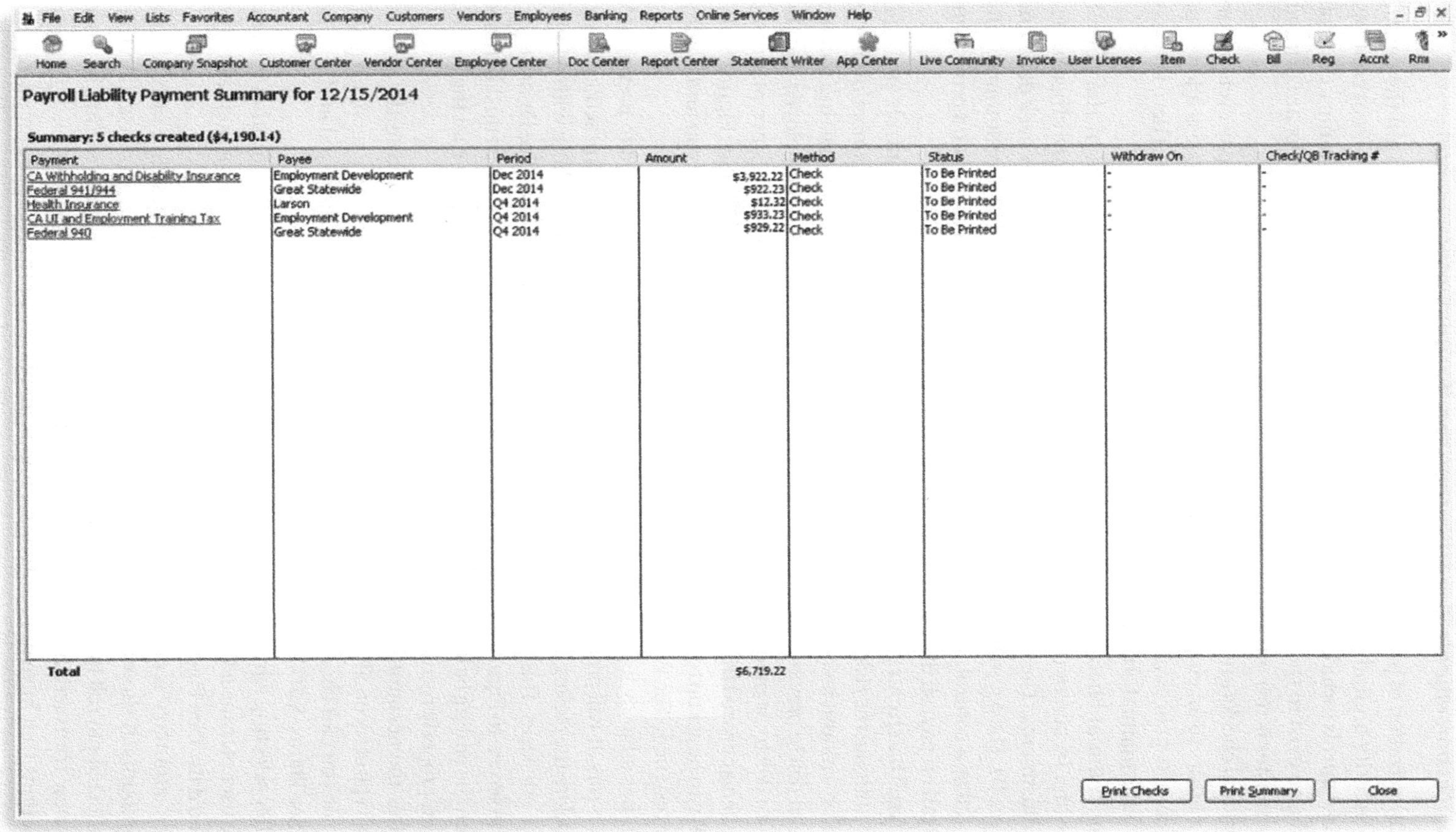
File Edit View Lists Favorites Accountant Company Customers Vendors Employees Banking Reports Online Services Window Help
Home Search Company Snapshot Customer Center Vendor Center Employee Center Doc Center Report Center Statement Writer App Center Live Community Invoice User Licenses Item Check Bill Reg Accnt Rmi
Payroll Liability Payment Summary for 12/15/2014
Summary: 5 checks created ($4,190.14)
Payment | Payee | Period | Amount | Method | Status | Withdraw On | Check/QB Tracking #
CA Withholding and Disability Insurance | Employment Development | Dec 2014 | $3,922.22 | Check | To Be Printed | - | -
Federal 941/944 | Great Statewide | Dec 2014 | $922.23 | Check | To Be Printed | - | -
Health Insurance | Larson | Q4 2014 | $12.32 | Check | To Be Printed | - | -
CA UI and Employment Training Tax | Employment Development | Q4 2014 | $933.23 | Check | To Be Printed | - | -
Federal 940 | Great Statewide | Q4 2014 | $929.22 | Check | To Be Printed | - | -
Total $6,719.22
Print Checks
Print Summary
Close

FIGURE 8.64 Payroll Liability Summary in QB

Payroll Disbursements Are Unauthorized (Fraudulent Payments)

The authorization of payroll disbursements is an important control within the payroll cycle. Security around payroll involves a combination of manual and system controls. Manual controls include physical security of check stock and signature stamps. Controls should also exist in the system to protect digital signatures. Once checks are printed, the paymaster is responsible for disbursing checks to employees.

Manual checks are available for odd situations (e.g., the middle of a pay cycle or correcting errors to an employee's paycheck). The manual check entry process allows one to cancel a lost check and replace it by adding a new check to the batch. There is risk of abuse if the manual check is accessed by unauthorized employees.

The manual check adjustment in GPD is used to fix any errors in the payroll processing. In addition, manual checks can be built for bonuses or any other necessary adjustments. The required fields include the prenumbered check, check date, and employee ID. The payment number, checkbook ID, and account name are automatically prompted as a control. The purpose of these prompts is to keep a record and provide an audit trail on payroll disbursements. (See Figure 8.65.)

Payroll batch entry posts the payroll checks to the general ledger. Controls are available to mitigate the risk of theft. These controls include specifying the number of checks or a dollar amount before processing each batch. This step can modify existing batches and even delete previous batches. This could be a control risk if any employee had the ability to delete or modify batches. However, since the payroll batches are processed only when approved through password entry, the threat is mitigated. (See Figure 8.66.)

QB can be set up to pay employees regularly by printing checks for you and having them presigned. (See Figure 8.67.)

QB has a handy feature if you are trying to reconcile a closed period to prevent tax return errors. It will prompt you for a closing date password to protect transactions dated on or before the closing date. This will cause them to be locked to even those with administrative privileges. This will prevent any errors in future reconciliations. (See Figure 8.68.)

The screen in Figure 8.69 shows that in the example company there is no difference between the ending balance and cleared balance, proving to the auditor that the payroll has been properly reconciled.

After the account has been balanced, QB displays a message asking the user to select a type of reconciliation report. There are three options: a summary report, a detail report, or you can choose to have both of those previous reports displayed at the same time. (See Figure 8.70.)

After selecting which type of report to display, QB has a popup notification informing the user of transactions that were not cleared and of any new transactions after the specified date. (See Figure 8.71.)

The summary report is a brief overview of payroll's liabilities that only shows total amounts. It shows how many items are included in each type of transaction that have affected payroll liabilities and the register balance as well as the ending balance due to new transactions. The detail report of payroll liabilities displays each of those transactions that have not cleared yet, and is much longer than the summary report. (See Figure 8.72.)

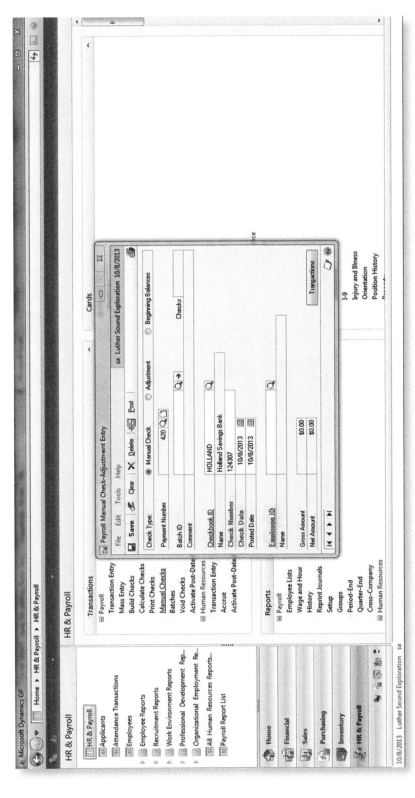

FIGURE 8.65 Payroll Manual Check Adjustment Entry in GPD

229

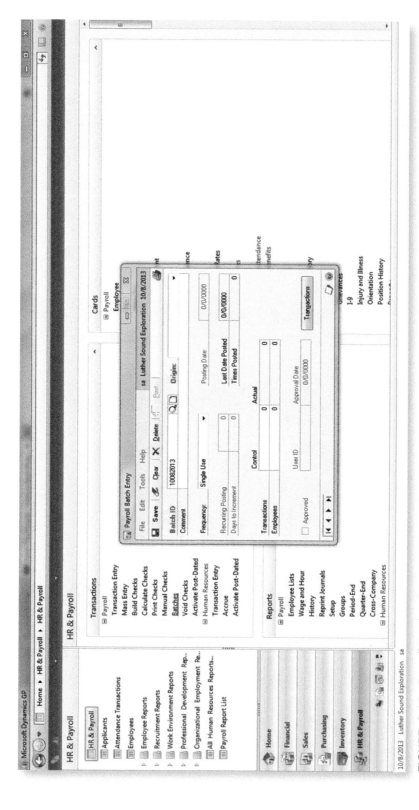

FIGURE 8.66 Payroll Batch Entry in GPD

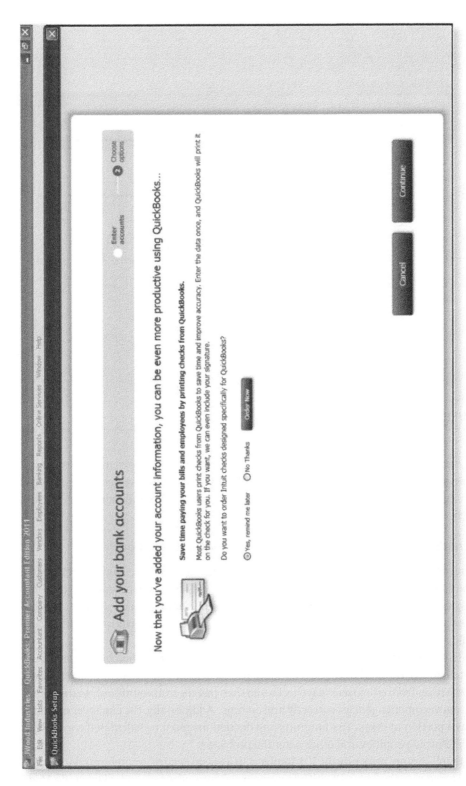

FIGURE 8.67 Add Bank Account in QB

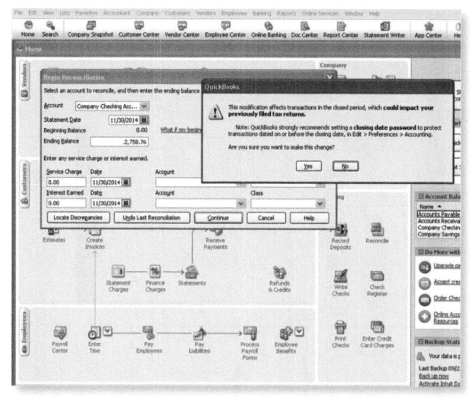

FIGURE 8.68 Reconciliation—1 in QB

An important part of auditing payroll is to make sure that no ex-employees are still receiving paychecks. QB lets you see the list of employees that have been released, and you can then check through those names to see if any of these individuals are getting paychecks. (See Figure 8.73.)

Accruals, Benefits, and Taxes Are Incorrectly Calculated or Paid

Management needs to ensure that accruals, benefits, and taxes are paid correctly. Most of the controls for this step in the payroll activities cycles deal with access controls. Only the system administrator or human resources management should have the ability to access and update these forms and calculations—a point that merits investigation and verification by the IT auditor.

The responsibility for payroll taxes carries on even after the checks have been printed and distributed to employees. Employers are required to withhold appropriate income taxes from employees' paychecks and then pay these amounts over to the appropriate government agencies correctly and on time. Additionally, the employer must pay its own portion of taxes. Tax amounts and deductions must be calculated correctly in order to avoid penalties and other potential problems.

Employers are presently (in 2013) subject to a Social Security matching contribution of 6.2 percent on the first $106,800 of an employee's annual wages and salary, and a Medicare matching tax equal to 1.45 percent of every dollar of each employee's annual wages.

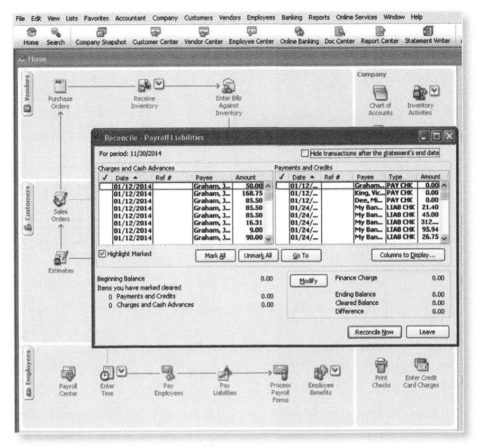

FIGURE 8.69 Reconciliation—2 in QB

For unemployment taxes, the state governments determine the state unemployment tax rate for each employer. The percentage is taken from an employee's annual salary and wages. The rate is usually based on an employer's unemployment history and business type and it is usually capped after reaching an annual limit on gross wages. Even though it is based on the employee's wages, this entire tax is paid by the employer. In addition, the federal government mandates that employers pay a federal unemployment tax of 0.8 percent on each employee's first $7,000 of annual wages. State law usually requires that employers carry Worker's Compensation insurance for employees who are injured on the job. Worker's Compensation insurance rates are determined from many variables. Once a rate is arrived at, it is applied to the wages and salaries of the employees to arrive at the worker's compensation insurance premiums or costs. The employer's net cost for insurance is simply the total amount of premiums paid to the insurance company minus the portion of the cost the employer collects from its employees. The 401(k), savings plans, and profit sharing plans contributions by the employer should appear as an expense in the period when the employee earned the company contribution.

Correct calculation of the employer's taxes and benefits starts with the payroll setup process and the preferences selected for the company. The card in Figure 8.74 shows the

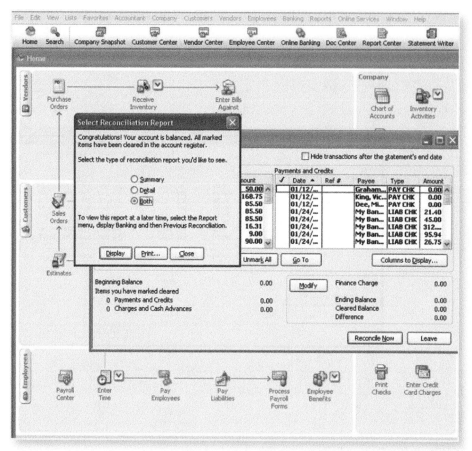

FIGURE 8.70 Reconciliation Report—1 in QB

pay code setup for hourly employees. Available options include Commission Payments, Hourly Employees, Meal Expense Reimbursement, Overtime Pay, and Salaried Employees & Travel Expense. These codes can be used as default entries for setting up employee pay codes. The pay types that a company decides to assign to a pay code will depend on how that specific pay code is being used. For example, an overtime pay code would not typically be used in connection with a pay code for salaried employees.

Other inputs on this card include taxes and pay period. Preferences for these inputs are established for the entire company and then modified for each individual employee. This reduces the setup time and simplifies the process. The required fields include only the pay code (selected from a lookup field) and the unit of pay. Other fields on this form include taxes that the employees are subject to, and codes for shifts and pay period, all of which are set once for the company and then adjusted for specific employees.

The Unemployment Tax Setup window is used to create, maintain, and delete information about state and federal unemployment taxes throughout the payroll module. The initial setup is made for the entire company and then modified as needed for individual employees. Users can download the latest payroll tax update for current state

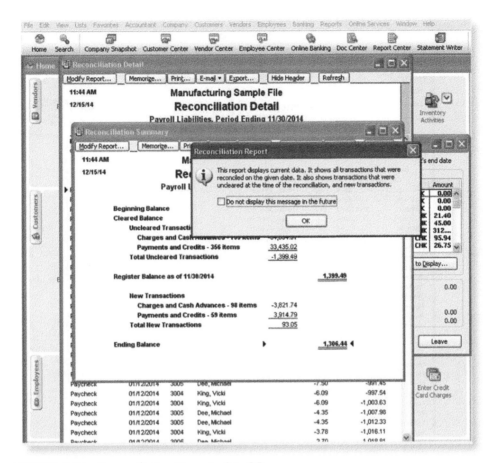

FIGURE 8.71 Reconciliation Report—2 in QB

and federal tax rates. The only required field on this form is the Tax Code. Entering unemployment tax is via abbreviation for the state and FED for federal unemployment tax. This form also provides an option to include previous state wages and tax-sheltered annuities. (See Figure 8.75.)

Required fields for the Worker's Compensation (WC) Setup window include the WC code, a job description, the company's state, and the tax rate percent. GPD allows users to determine the calculation method for worker's compensation insurance, with choices that include percent of gross income, fixed amount, and number of hours or number of days worked. If selecting Fixed Amount, enter the tax rate amount. If selecting Number of Hours/Units, enter the tax rate per unit. If selecting Days Worked, enter the tax rate per day. When a user chooses percent of gross income there is an inherent control that allows entry of a maximum wage limit. A soft control exists for the absence of an amount entered when Fixed Amount is chosen. (See Figure 8.76.)

The employee benefit window is used to create, maintain, and delete benefit information for a company. This card is created for the company as a whole and modified for individual employees. For each benefit entered into GPD, the user decides how the

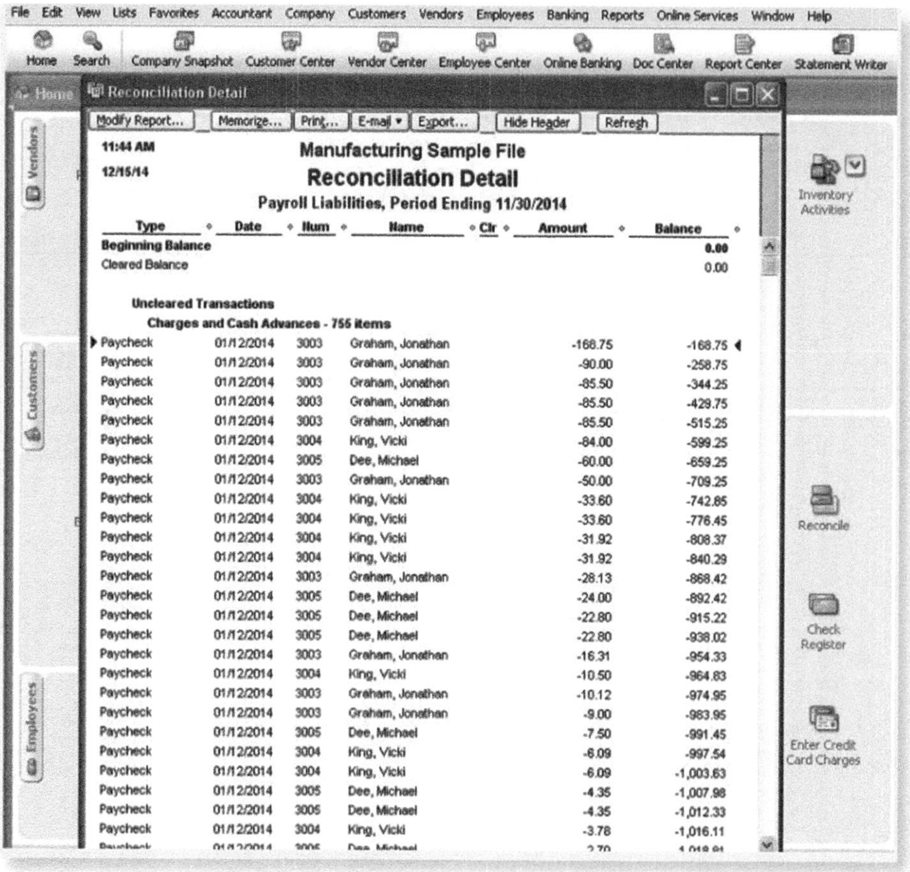

FIGURE 8.72 Reconciliation Detail in QB

benefit should be calculated, the maximum benefits for an employee, and the start and end dates. Benefits can be calculated as Percent of Gross Wages, Percent of Net Wages (gross wage less taxes), Percent of Deduction, Fixed Amount (benefits entered as a fixed amount) or Amount per Unit (benefit based on piecework, hourly, or overtime wages).

Controls in the Benefits Setup form include start and end date for the benefit and should include the start date taking place before the end date (if this is not true, the benefit won't be calculated) and the checkbox for Transaction Required. If the dollar amount or percentage of the benefit varies each time it's calculated, this box should be checked. Note that for any benefit zero is a valid amount. If selected in setup, zero would be the default for new employee records. (See Figure 8.77.)

The Payroll Tax Identification Setup window is designed to assign federal and state tax identification numbers and thus ensure that these numbers are printed correctly on forms such as those generated for the payroll year-end processes. (See Figure 8.78.)

The Employee Benefit Maintenance window allows users to select individual employee cards and apply benefits at the default amount previously set or by entering in a specific amount for that individual employee. Benefits can be based on a variety

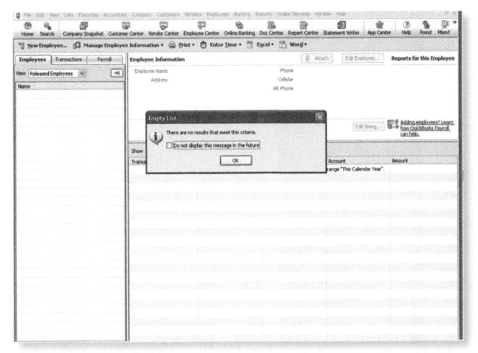

FIGURE 8.73 Searching Released Employees in QB

of measurements, including a fixed amount, net wages, gross wages, a deduction, or amount per unit. One common example of an employee benefit is the 401(k) contributions made by the company on behalf of an employee. (See Figure 8.79.)

Disbursed Payroll, Accruals, and Adjustments Are Not Reviewed

After payroll, accruals, and adjustments are processed, management needs to implement a process in which reports are reviewed. This is considered an IT-dependent manual control.

The final activity of the payroll cycle is to disburse payroll taxes and miscellaneous deductions. Some examples of these deductions include retirement plans, health insurance, and other savings plans available to employees. The employee federal income tax, Social Security, and Medicare withholdings are due three days after issuing payroll checks. The employer's contributions to Social Security and Medicare taxes are also due at the same time. Five days after month-end, employee state and local income tax withholdings are due. Five days after the end of a quarter, employer federal and state unemployment taxes are due. Fifteen days after month-end, employee 401(k) deductions and matching employer contributions are due. Fifteen days after June 30 and December 31, employer state worker's compensation taxes are due. Employee health insurance deductions are due at the time specified in the health insurance contract. It is extremely important to keep track of these dates because failure to meet the deadlines could lead to penalties and hefty fines. This is why GPD has the ability to run reports for different taxes and deductions. Also, this is why the period-end report can cover any length of time.

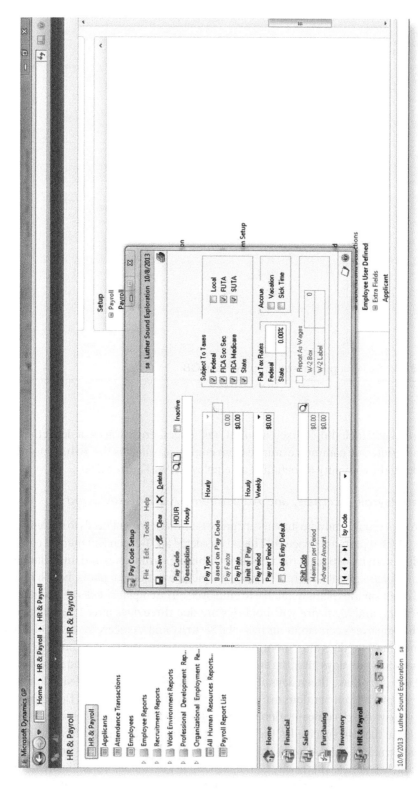

FIGURE 8.74 Pay Code Setup in GPD

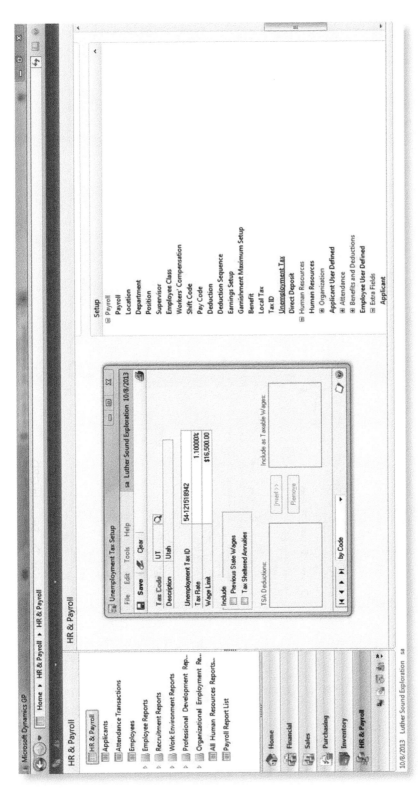

FIGURE 8.75 Unemployment Tax Setup in GPD

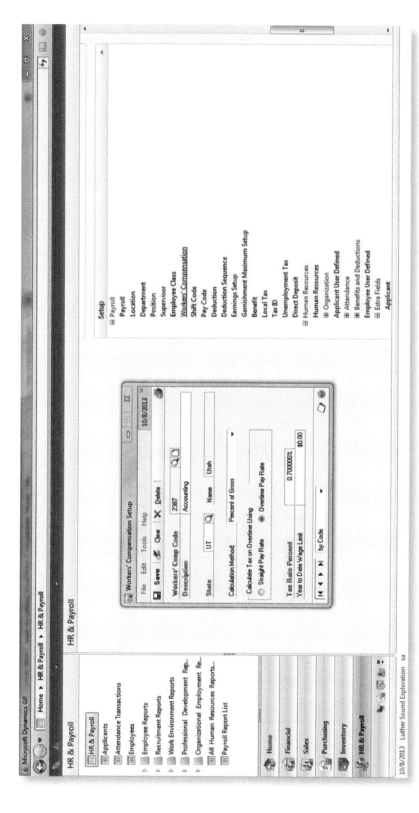

FIGURE 8.76 Worker's Compensation Tax Setup in GPD

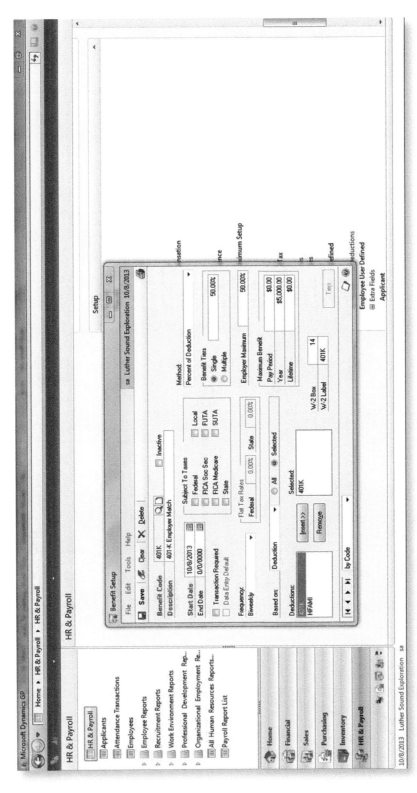

FIGURE 8.77 Benefit Setup in GPD

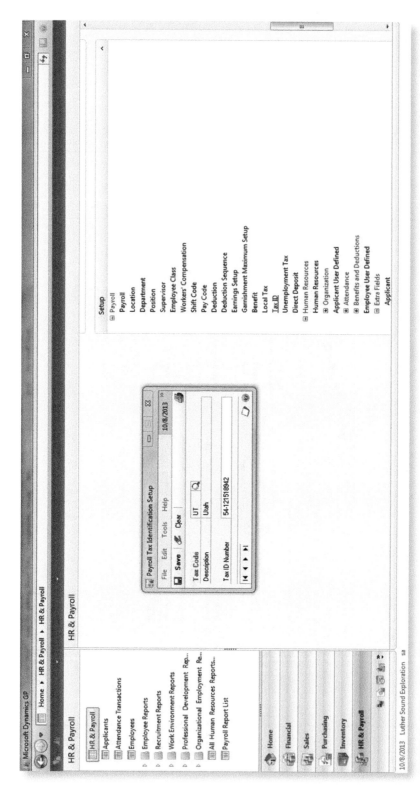

FIGURE 8.78 Payroll Tax ID Setup in GPD

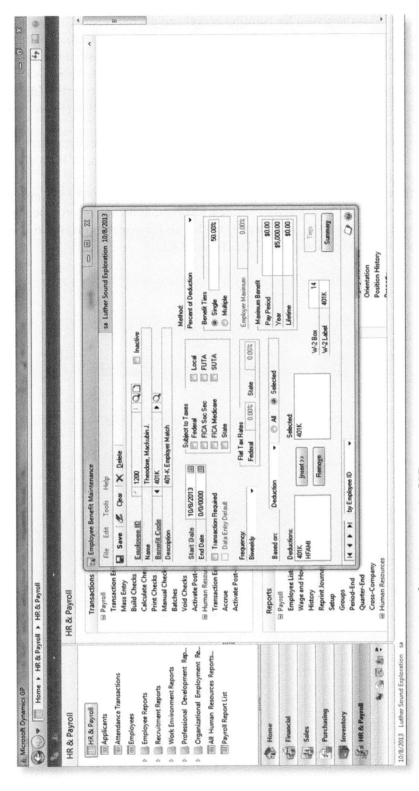

FIGURE 8.79 Employee Benefit Maintenance in GPD

Figure 8.80 is the screen for running period-end payroll reports. These can be weekly, monthly, quarterly, and yearly reports. Types of reports include payroll summary, state and local tax summary, FUTA summary, worker's compensation summary, and benefit summary, just to name a few. It allows the company to keep track of its payroll liabilities. There is very little input necessary to run these reports. This helps minimize the risk of mistakes or errors. In addition, this window allows the company to post the FUTA, SUTA, and worker's compensation liabilities.

Figure 8.81 is the type of report that would be used to summarize payroll deduction liabilities. This report is merely a deduction summary and includes the 401(k) and other health plan deductions chosen by the employees.

The IRS requires quarterly payments and the filing of Form 941. The 941 preparation report and the 941 Schedule B preparation report are audit trail reports and should be kept on file. The Form 941 and Form 941 Schedule B are sent to the IRS to ensure compliance with federal payroll taxes. (See Figure 8.82.)

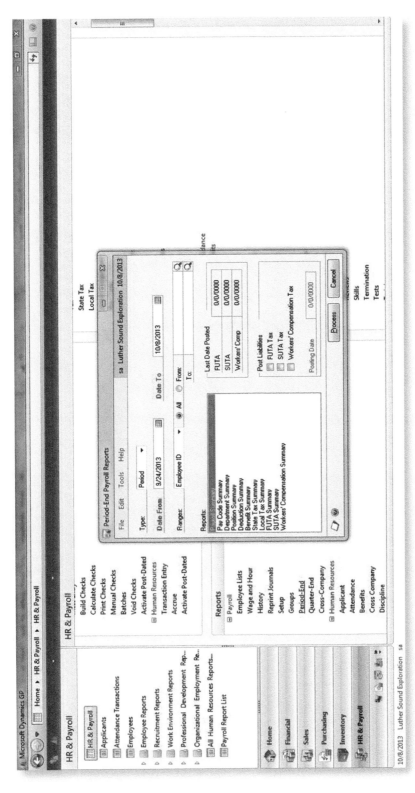

FIGURE 8.80 Period-End Payroll Reports

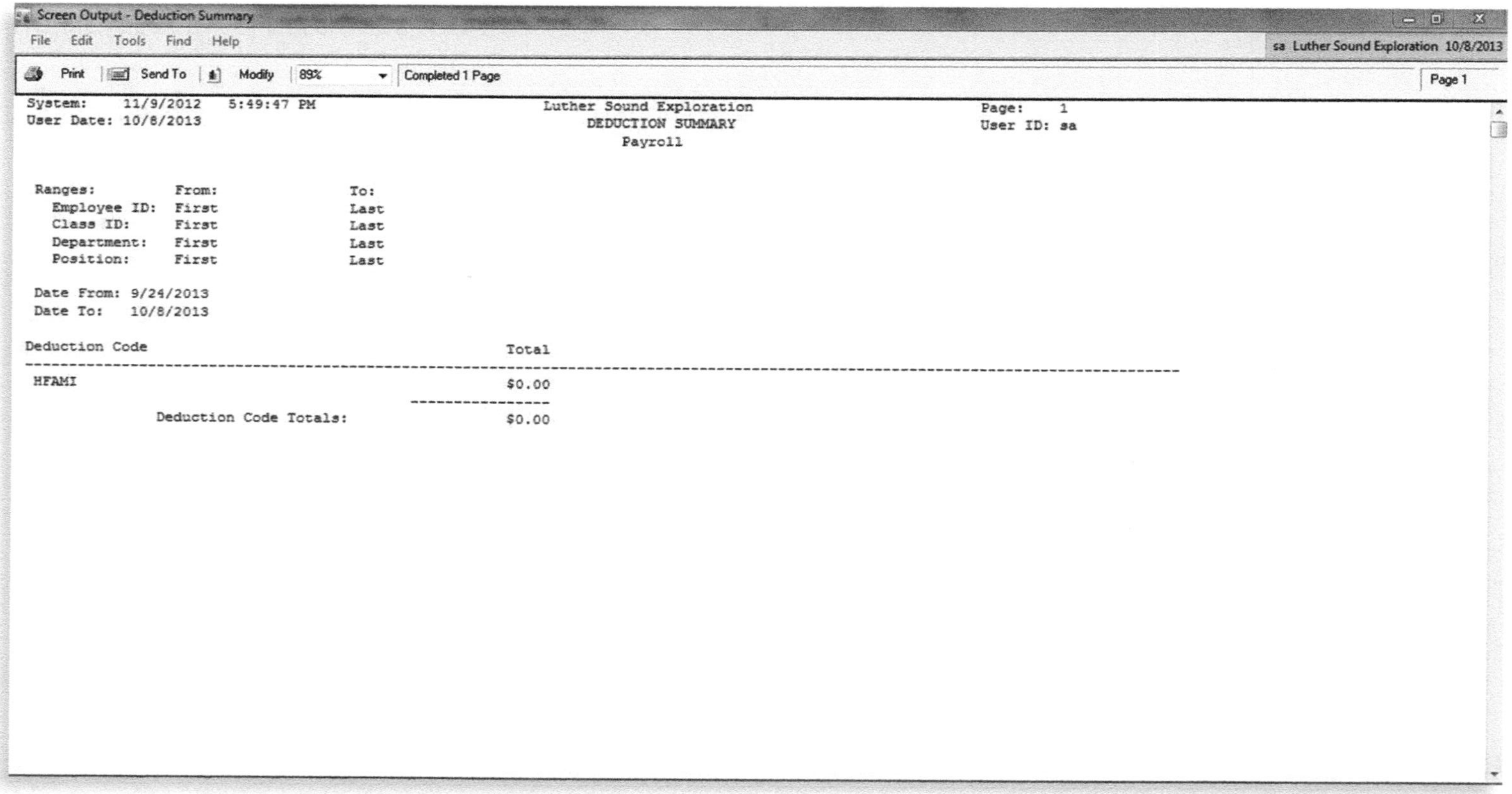

FIGURE 8.81 Period-End Payroll Reports—Summary

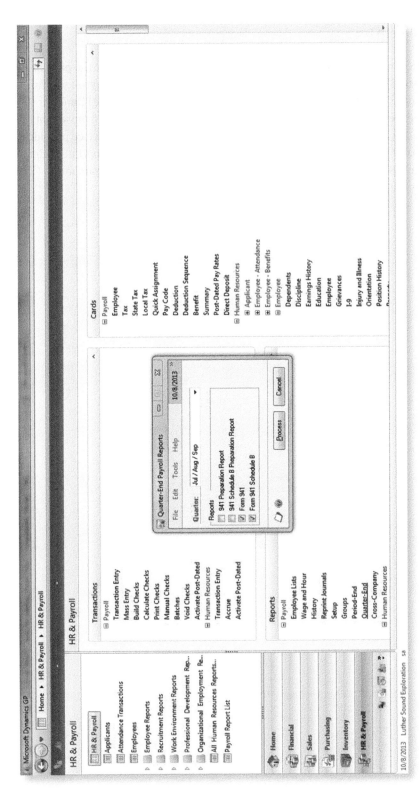

FIGURE 8.82 Quarter-End Payroll Reports

SUMMARY

Compliance burdens create a unique set of challenges and issues for the payroll cycle, whether the SME performs this work in-house or contracts it to a payroll specialist. In the latter case, even though the processing is done by a third party, the IT auditor should consider and evaluate controls that are purely internal to the SME and those that reflect the hand-off of data and information from the SME to the payroll service provider. If a third-party provider is used, the company should ensure that an appropriate Statements on Standards for Attestation Engagements (SSAE) 16 or a Service Organization Control (SOC) report is obtained.

Risk, Controls, Financial Reporting, and an Overlay of COSO on COBIT

N THE PAST DECADE, GUIDELINES for IT auditing and controls emerged from the Committee of Sponsoring Organizations (COSO), the Public Company Accounting Oversight Board (PCAOB), and Information Systems Audit and Control Association (ISACA). Given the mission of the organization, ISACA has been involved with IT auditing and controls as its primary mission for several decades while IT auditing and control is a topic or subtopic within COSO and the PCAOB. COSO has issued guidance specifically for the public small- and mid-sized enterprise (SME) in its *Internal Control over Financial Reporting: Guidance for Smaller Public Companies* (2007) for financial reporting. More recently, COSO has released guidelines in its *2013 Internal Control—Integrated Framework* (2013). The COSO guidelines reference IT controls as part of a larger discussion on financial controls for the entire enterprise. The question is how to make sense of the guidelines from these organizations in the larger context of auditing the financial statements for SMEs.

This chapter will reconcile the guidelines and emerge with a better understanding of the differences a financial auditor can recognize and implement. SMEs are by nature higher risk while at the same time the zeal of various regulatory agencies (e.g., the PCAOB) appears to be increasing. *Internal Control over Financial Reporting: Guidance for Smaller Public Companies* (COSO 2007) specifically mentions fraud as a risk for the public SME. Consistent with the theme of higher risk for the SME, the balance sheet and management maturity are frequently more vulnerable than for a large, mature enterprise. Aside from technology, recognizing, assessing, and assimilating risk in the assurance process are perhaps the most significant differentiators between an auditor today and 20 years ago. As such, controls take on an added dimension in the auditor's assessment of the SME. Therefore, whereas this chapter covers considerable ground because it must, the reader should fully appreciate the complexity of the environment.

Given the advances in technology and its continued expansion, the audit landscape will grow more complex. This chapter will touch on history to gain a perspective of auditing changes and identify emerging trends to provide reference to emerging frameworks that should assist the financial auditor in his or her understanding of IT auditing in the financial audit process. Chapter 10 is an extension of Chapter 9 and cross-references Control Objectives for Information and related Technology (COBIT) to COSO and the PCAOB. In particular, Chapter 10 discusses IT audit risk in more depth, which is integral to the PCAOB, COSO, and COBIT.

 ## PCAOB WARNINGS: INSUFFICIENT EVIDENCE TO SUPPORT OPINIONS

Auditors are making too many mistakes in their audits of internal control over financial reporting, prompting warnings from the PCAOB (PCAOB 2012; Whitehouse 2012). The PCAOB warns that auditors should comply with existing auditing standards and their firms' own audit methodologies. While this book addresses SMEs whether they are public or private and the PCAOB addresses audit firms that audit public companies, there is reason to believe that the observations by the PCAOB carry over to all audit firms that evaluate internal controls.

Arguably, it is very probable that audit firms not regulated by the PCAOB are likely to fail at least at the same rate as firms regulated by the PCAOB. It is also indeed likely that unregulated audit firms are failing at a higher rate with the lack of oversight from a regulatory authority. Moreover, SMEs are likely to have more inherent risk for numerous reasons, including weaker balance sheets, lower quality of earnings, fewer resources to attract qualified staff, and so forth.

According to the PCAOB's inspection findings (PCAOB 2012; Whitehouse 2012), the PCAOB found problems with the audit of internal controls for financial reporting in 15 percent of all audits in its 2010 inspection cycle, which focused on 2009 financial statements. The failure rate is even higher in the PCAOB's 2011 inspection cycle, at 22 percent. The board noted deficiencies in six separate areas: (1) identifying and testing controls that address the risk of material misstatement, (2) testing the design and operating effectiveness of management review controls, (3) obtaining sufficient evidence to test controls from an interim date to the year-end date, (4) testing system-generated data and reports that support key controls, (5) performing adequate procedures on the work of others, and (6) evaluating identified control deficiencies to consider what effect they might have on the financial statement audit and the audit of internal control. The trend in the error rates among these six separate areas suggests numerous deficiencies ranging from inappropriate application of auditing standards to ineffective training and guidance. According to the PCAOB (2012), the root causes of deficiencies include:

- Improper application of the top-down approach to the audit of internal control as required by Auditing Standard (AS) No. 5
- Decreases in audit firm staffing through attrition or other reductions, and related workload pressures
- Insufficient firm training and guidance, including the application of PCAOB standards and the audit firm's methodology
- Ineffective communication with the firm's IT specialists on the engagement team

Workload staffing, attrition, the firms' training and guidance, and ineffective communications are beyond the scope of this text; however, AS No. 5, COSO, and COBIT *are* within the scope of this text. This chapter will address AS No. 5, COSO, and COBIT. In particular, this chapter will review COSO for small public companies, *Internal Control over Financial Reporting: Guidance for Smaller Public Companies* (2007), cross-reference COBIT 4.1 to COSO, and reference COBIT 5.0 as the next framework of IT governance.

HOW WE GOT HERE: A HISTORICAL PERSPECTIVE

It is useful to review audit adjustments of the 1980s and 1990s in connection with financial reporting before COSO was adopted in 1992 and large-scale IT applications became almost ubiquitous by 2000. Though no research is available, the authors believe that many audits for SMEs in 2013 are conducted using the framework promulgated by the AICPA and other professional standards of the 1980s and 1990s. The audit procedures and evidence outlined in Table 9.2 are representative of auditing standards from the 1980s when the audit process was reasonably simple: (a) plan the audit, (b) review and test the internal controls through query and observation, (c) test cash and accounts receivables, (d) observe inventory, (e) expand analytical review as necessary depending on the quality of the internal controls, and (e) deliver an audit opinion. This simplistic process reflects a *transaction-based* versus a *risk-based* audit approach.

During the 1980s, comparatively speaking, IT was in its infancy as it was centered in large black-box mainframe computers with networks of dumb terminals providing limited access to the data. Lotus 1-2-3 led the way in spreadsheet technology until 1988, when Excel became the new leader as Microsoft Windows gained market share. In 1990, Tim Berners-Lee introduced HyperText Markup Language (HTML) and later added the World Wide Web (WWW) in August 1991. By the end of 2010, the end user had taken control of the once-impenetrable black box with powerful applications residing on high-performance personal computers. The financial audit process has significantly evolved to a *risk-based* process to meet the needs of a dramatically different audit environment.

Ten years after COSO, the U.S. Congress enacted the Sarbanes-Oxley Act of 2002 (SOx) and the 11 sections that define *auditor* and *corporate responsibilities*, *expectations of financial disclosures*, and *strong penalties for white-collar crimes*. Key sections of SOx compliance that directly involve IT include Sections 302, 404, 409, and 802 (Public Law 107–204, 2002). Section 302 requires officers of a company to make representations related to the disclosure of internal controls, procedures, and assurance from fraud. Section 404 requires an annual assessment of the effectiveness of internal controls. Section 409 requires disclosures to the public on a "rapid and current basis" of material changes to the firm's financial condition. Section 802 requires authentic and immutable record retention.

The AICPA played catch-up to ISACA as it relates to IT and the role IT auditing plays in the contemporary financial audit. ISACA released numerous guidelines, including COBIT 4, well before the AICPA began an internal initiative for the Certified Informational Technology Professional (CITP). ISACA was founded in 1967 (ISACA 2012a), when a group of individuals with jobs auditing controls in the computer systems, who were becoming increasingly critical to the operations of their organizations, recognized the need for a centralized source of information and guidance in the field. In 1976, the association formed an education foundation to undertake large-scale research efforts to expand the knowledge and value of the IT governance and control field. Financial statement auditing in the 1980s and 1990s mentioned little about IT controls and their consequences to the financial statements.

A basic premise of auditing theory and practice in the 1980s was that if prior-year's audit working papers were a good source of information for planning the current-year audit (Arens and Loebbecke 1980), a presumption was made that key environmental characteristics of the audit client must be fairly stable over time (Ham, Losell, and Smieliauskas 1985). Ham et al. also concluded that audit firms may achieve audit efficiencies by having repeat audit engagements since error rates driving audit adjustments remained relatively stable in their sample data. Consistent with earlier research by Arens and Loebbecke, Wright and Ashton (1989) did not mention IT or anything related to IT as causes of audit adjustments to the financial statements in their 1989 report (see Tables 9.1 and 9.2).

The reasons cited in Table 9.1 for financial reporting problems are also critical to IT control problems, including underqualified personnel, insufficient knowledge or undertrained personnel, cutoff or accrual procedures, mechanical, or inadequate control. Noticeably absent are references to technology, governance, management, monitoring, rapid growth, new technology, new business models, products or activities, expanded foreign operations, new accounting pronouncements, or changes in economic conditions, all of which are frequently mentioned by the Financial Accounting Standards Board (FASB 2010) as risks in contemporaneous financial reporting.

Though no research is available, the authors believe that many audits for SMEs in 2013 are conducted using the framework promulgated by the AICPA and other professional standards of the 1980s and 1990s. The audit procedures and evidence outlined in Table 9.2 are representative of auditing standards from the 1980s when the audit process was reasonably simple:

▪ Plan the audit.
▪ Review and test the internal controls through query and observation.
▪ Test cash and accounts receivables.
▪ Observe inventory.
▪ Expand analytical review as necessary, depending on the quality of the internal controls.
▪ Deliver an audit opinion.

This simplistic process reflects a *transaction-based* versus a *risk-based* audit approach.

It is notable in Table 9.2 that *analytical review, analysis and review,* and *review and performing procedures* played significant roles in identifying audit adjustments to the financial statements. In the contemporary audit, numerous audit tools are available to expedite and provide more in-depth coverage of the potential adjustments to the financial statements. It is also noteworthy that few adjustments arose from the

TABLE 9.1 Causes of Audit Adjustments from Audit Samples in 1984 and 1985

Cause	Total (n = 334)	Small (n = 236)	Medium (n = 50)	Large (n = 48)
			Adjustments	
Personnel problems	6.3 (26.3)	7.2%	6.0%	2.1%
Insufficient accounting knowledge	28.6 (15.0)	26.8	36.0	31.2
Judgment	20.1 (15.3)	22.9	10.0	16.7
Cutoff or accrual	18.6 (38.1)	17.8	20.0	20.8
Mechanical	12.9 (12.5)	12.7	16.0	10.4
Inadequate control, follow-up, or review	12.6 (9.3)	11.4	12.0	18.8
Other	0.9 (19.2)	1.2	—	—

Source: Wright and Ashton (1989).

TABLE 9.2 Procedures and Evidence: Audit Samples in 1984 and 1985

Procedures and Evidence	Adjustments
Form of Evidence:	
Prior-year correspondence files	1.4%
Prior-year working paper schedules	22.5
Notes for subsequent audit	0
Prior audit differences	71.9
Prior financial statements	2.8
Other	1.4
Procedure Originally Signaling the Error in the Prior Year:	
Analytical review	11.6%
Analysis and review	40.7
Mathematical checks	1.4
Documentation	11.6
Confirmation	2.9
Inventory observation	7.2
Client inquiry	14.5
Other procedure	8.7
Don't know	1.4
Phase of Audit When Error Was Detected:	
Initial planning	20.5%
Evaluation of internal control	0

(continued)

TABLE 9.2 (*continued*)

Procedures and Evidence	Adjustments
Phase of Audit When Error Was Detected:	
Preparing audit program	1.3
Performing procedures	66.7
Evaluating results of procedures	5.1
Review of Fieldwork:	
By assistant staff	0%
By senior	1.3
By manager	5.1
By partner or second partner	0
Person Initially Detecting Error:	
Assistant/staff	30.8%
Assistant/staff-in-charge	15.4
Senior	42.3
Manager	7.7
Partner	3.8
Industry Experience of That Person:	
Extensive (more than four prior engagements)	16.7%
Moderate (two to four engagements)	48.7
Little (one engagement)	19.2
No experience	15.4
Average experience in public accounting	3.6 years

review of internal control. COSO's *Internal Control over Financial Reporting: Guidance for Smaller Public Companies* (2007) centers on internal control using a risk assessment process. Also noteworthy is the complete absence of any mention of IT controls in connection with financial reporting adjustments.

The pervasiveness of IT unfolded rapidly in the 1990s with the widespread adoption of Excel and new financial system applications, followed by the widespread adoption of enterprise resource planning (ERP) systems in anticipation of Y2K. Fast-forward with new technologies, COSO, and now Sarbanes-Oxley: What would an auditor discover in material weaknesses in connection with the financial reporting?

Klamm and Watson (2009) examined 490 firms reporting material weaknesses in the first year of SOx to evaluate the interrelatedness of weak COSO components and IT controls. The COSO framework includes five interrelated components:

1. Control environment
2. Risk assessment
3. Control activities
4. Information and communication
5. Monitoring

Klamm and Watson (2009) identified relationships between the reported material weakness and the five components of COSO, including:

- A weak control environment has a positive association with the remaining four weak COSO components (i.e., COSO components are likely to affect each other).
- IT-related weak COSO components frequently spill over to create more non-IT-related material weaknesses and misstatements.
- IT-related weak COSO components negatively affect reporting reliability and add to the number of non-IT material weaknesses reported.

Moreover, the conclusion from Klamm and Watson's research is that the IT domain appears to affect overall control effectiveness and, of course, financial reporting. Several research reports (Ge and McVacy 2005) reported at least one material weakness that was highly correlated to firms that were smaller, younger, riskier, more complex, financially weaker, and with poorer accrual earnings quality. Smaller, younger, riskier, and financially weaker firms meet the definition of an SME for the purposes of this book.

The PCAOB in Auditing Standard (AS) No. 5 identifies the significance of the risk assessment in the audit process that should underlie the entire audit process, including the determination of significant accounts, disclosures, and relevant assertions, the selection of controls to test, and the determination of the evidence necessary for a given control (PCAOB 2013a):

> A direct relationship exists between the degree of risk that a material weakness could exist in a particular area of the company's internal control over financial reporting and the amount of audit attention that should be devoted to that area. In addition, the risk that a company's internal control over financial reporting will fail to prevent or detect misstatement caused by fraud usually is higher than the risk of failure to prevent or detect error. The auditor should focus more of his or her attention on the areas of highest risk. On the other hand, it is not necessary to test controls that, even if deficient, would not present a reasonable possibility of material misstatement to the financial statements.

According to the PCAOB, the complexity of the organization, business unit, or process should play an important role in the auditor's risk assessment and the determination of the necessary procedures. Per Klamm and Watson (2009), the control environment has a positive association with the remaining four weak COSO components and thus should play a significant role in the risk assessment process. In addition, according to Klamm and Watson, weak IT controls spill over to other COSO components. Using a cause-and-effect model in the risk assessment process, an auditor should examine the control environment and IT controls as leading indicators of risk.

Is there a difference in either quantitative or qualitative financial reporting standards for large public companies with broad international equity distribution (e.g., Apple Inc.) versus a dry cleaning company establishment with one retail location in Des Moines, Iowa, with two owners? A clear and concise answer has been a struggle for FASB with a long series of committee initiatives to differentiate GAAP for the large enterprise and GAAP for the SME (Kamnikar, Kamnikar, and Burrowes 2012). The

International Accounting Standards Board (IASB) and FASB concluded that the objective of general-purpose external financial reporting should be the same irrespective of the equity characteristics of the enterprise. The boards also recommended that users of the financial reports for smaller, closely held entities may be able to specify and receive the information they need versus a request for a general-purpose external financial report. *Internal Control over Financial Reporting: Guidance for Smaller Public Companies* (COSO 2007) is relevant for SMEs who are either non-public or private.

Li et al. (2011) found evidence that firms with IT material weaknesses in their financial reporting systems had less accurate management forecasts for internal management purposes. While the purpose of this chapter is to discuss the implications of IT in financial audits, weak IT controls have a pervasive impact on all management reporting. The problems related to data processing issues and weak IT controls are directly associated with the quality of decision making for anyone involved with management or governance. Ineffective IT controls can cause material errors or other significant issues in day-to-day operations (see Table 9.3).

TABLE 9.3 Examples of SOx IT Internal Control Weaknesses

Examples from the SOx 404 Management's Report on IT Internal Control	
Data Processing Integrity	▪ Reopening or changing closed accounting periods
	▪ Deletion of accounts in the system
	▪ Data or program changes lacking user review/approval/authorization/testing
	▪ Improper maintenance of master files (e.g., vendor, price, inventory)
	▪ Inadequate development and maintenance (e.g., new system, updates)
	▪ Inadequate IS/IT support staff
	▪ Inadequate support for business processes (includes manually intense processes)
	▪ Integrity of computer data not verified (e.g., accuracy, validity, completeness)
	▪ Lack of IT controls
	▪ Lack of IT controls over the subsidiary/foreign operations
	▪ Inadequate IT skills
	▪ Program change controls missing or inadequate
	▪ Programming errors
	▪ Relying on systems of others (outsourcing) where controls not verified
	▪ Spreadsheet(s), lack of controls over input, processing, and outpput
	▪ Functionally complex systems
	▪ Nonexistent or weak application controls
	▪ Nonexistent or weak general controls
	▪ Nonexistent or weak IT control activities
	▪ Weak IT control environment
	▪ Weak IT risk assessment

TABLE 9.3 (continued)

IT Security	▪ Weak IT monitoring
	▪ Nonexistent or weak implementation of segregation of duties
	▪ Inadequate records and storage retention
	▪ Nonexistent disaster recovery plan for IT
	▪ Improper segregation of IT personnel access
	▪ Logical access issues
	▪ Security issues
IT Structure	▪ Decentralized systems
	▪ Disparate or nonintegrated systems
	▪ Insufficient IT training
	▪ Lack of system documentation, policies, procedures
	▪ Weak information and communication

Source: Adapted from Li, Peters, Richardson, and Watson 2012.

As noted earlier, the key sections of SOx compliance that directly involve *external reporting* include Sections 302, 404, 409, and 802 (107th Congress 2002). Specific reference to the financial reporting in the context of SOx compliance is in the first column of Table 9.4. *Data processing integrity*, *IT security*, and *IT structure* refer to specific business processes or the general controls of the business process itself used for the preparation of the financial statements.

The same control categories of data processing integrity, access and security, and structure and usage cited in Tables 9.3 and 9.4 affected both internal and external reporting. In many of these companies subsequent to the reported failures of internal control in SEC filings, management changes were made in both the accounting and information technology organizations. For many of the companies cited in Table 9.4, the board of directors replaced the chief financial officer and/or the chief information officer following the announcement of the internal control failures. In some cases, the stock price of the company fell precipitously following the external reporting of the internal control failures. Comprehensive research on the fallout of reported failures of internal controls is not available. It is unlikely that the board of directors of a public company will sit idly given the potential for investor lawsuits and punitive measures by regulatory authorities.

The SME audit environment can present risks that are much higher than for mature enterprises with high-quality balance sheets with predictable earnings. The risks, once identified and isolated, can be linked together, forming a triad of linking accounts, risks, and assertions. (See Figure 9.1.) At the bottom of Figure 9.1, risk assessment documents are the ultimate product. (See Figure 9.2.)

The emphasis in this chapter will be the IT control environment, IT controls, and IT monitoring for the SME that set the stage for Chapter 10, which will fully integrate the IT audit into the financial audit with a cross-reference of COBIT to the PCAOB and COSO guidelines.

TABLE 9.4 Publicly Reported IT Control Issues

Firm and Year	Text from SOx 404 Report	Control Issue
BioScrip 2005	"Inadequate system and manual controls to prevent the potential overstatement of revenue for canceled orders and other nonstandard transactions in our community pharmacies."	Inadequate system to support business processes
Flowserve Corp. 2004	". . . not achieving operating effectiveness over controls in . . . software change management."	Program change controls missing
MGP Ingredients 2006	"Management has identified a programming error in the software application (CMMS) formerly utilized for processing purchasing, receiving, and materials maintenance transactions at the Atchison, Kansas facility . . ."	Programming errors
Online Resources Corporation 2007	"The Company's procedures for the supervisory review of the performance by Company personnel of manual controls associated with account analysis and the verification of the accuracy of electronic spreadsheets that support financial reporting were ineffective."	Spreadsheet(s), lack of controls
Barrett Business Services Inc. 2008	"Our Company did not maintain effective controls over information technology (IT); specifically, general IT controls over program changes and program development were ineffectively designed and/or operating as of December 31, 2008."	Program change controls missing
TRC Companies 2006	"The Company did not adequately design controls to maintain appropriate segregation of duties in its manual and computer-based business processes which could affect the Company's purchasing controls, the limits on the delegation of authority for expenditures, and the proper review of manual journal entries."	Segregation of duties not implemented in system
Ceridian Corp. 2004	"Security control deficiencies surrounding the use of certain information technology applications."	Security issues
Integra Life-Sciences Holding Corporation 2007	"The Company lacked adequate internal access security policies and procedures."	Logical access and security issues
Digimarc Co. 2004	"Implementation of the new accounting system also was flawed because some of our accounting, finance, and operations employees were not properly trained in the use of the new accounting system."	Insufficient training on system
Online Resources Corp. 2006	"While preparing its December 31, 2006, financial statements, the Company discovered that it needed to correct errors, primarily related to the Princeton acquisition and the integration of that company's accounting system and processes."	Disparate (non-integrated) systems
Federal National Mortgage Association 2004	"We did not maintain and clearly communicate information technology policies and procedures. This weakness contributed to our inadequate internal control over financial reporting systems."	Weak information and communication

Source: Li, Peters, Richardson, and Watson 2012.

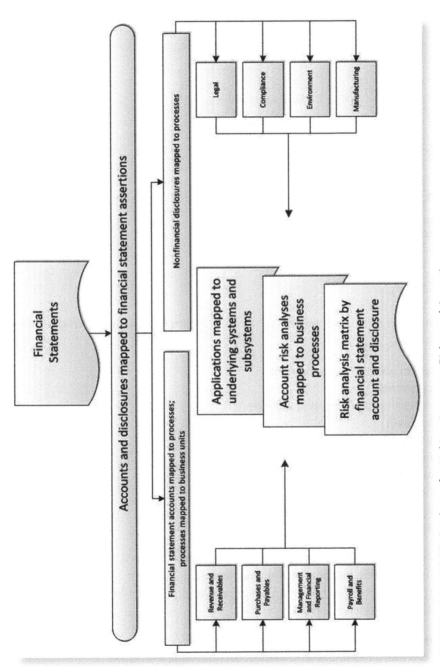

FIGURE 9.1 COSO Guidance for Linking Accounts, Risks, and Assertions

Source: Adapted from COSO 2007, *Internal Control over Financial Reporting: Guidance for Smaller Public Companies.*

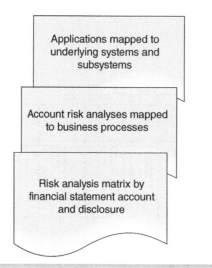

FIGURE 9.2 Ultimate Product of Linking Accounts, Risks, and Assertions

Source: Adapted from COSO 2007, *Internal Control Over Financial Reporting: Guidance for Smaller Public Companies.*

 RISK

The Statement on Auditing Standards (SAS No. 122) cites the risks of financial reporting to include:

- Changes in operating environment
- New personnel
- New or revamped information systems
- Rapid growth
- New technology
- New business models, products, or activities
- Corporate restructurings
- Expanded foreign operations
- New accounting pronouncements
- Changes in economic conditions

Each of these risks directly affects the integrated process of risks, control environment, control activities, information, and monitoring.

COSO (*Internal Control over Financial Reporting: Guidance for Smaller Public Companies*) identified the risks associated with the SME as:

- **Business processes:** Risk identification includes consideration of the business processes that affect financial statement accounts and disclosures.
- **Personnel:** Risk identification and assessment addresses the competency of company personnel supporting the financial reporting objectives.

- **IT:** Personnel supporting IT and the information technology infrastructure and processes supporting the financial reporting objectives are included in the financial reporting risk assessment.
- **Appropriate levels of management:** The organization puts into place effective risk assessment mechanisms that involve appropriate levels of management. Risk identification considers both internal and external factors and their impacts on the achievement of financial reporting objectives.
- **Estimates of likelihood and impact:** Identified risks are analyzed through a process that includes estimating the likelihood of occurrence and potential impact of the risk.
- **Triggers for reassessment:** Management establishes triggers for reassessing risks as changes occur that may affect financial reporting objectives.

While the COSO discussion is helpful, a very small SME may not have layers of management to implement risk assessment mechanisms or create estimates of likelihood and impact, nor will it have the systems to trigger reassessments because the personnel simply doesn't exist. For the small SME, the accounting personnel may also be the same personnel managing the IT financial reporting application. It is very likely that an outside accounting firm or senior management has a significant role to play in the six attributes described by COSO. An active and meaningful board must play some role in the assessment of management, estimates of likelihood and impact, and triggers for reassessment. In a small SME, the role must be much more significant. An SME with several hundred employees would likely have the opportunity to implement the six attributes described by COSO without participation from outside personnel. Given the potential that some of the attributes described by COSO are missing or incomplete, the financial reporting risks are defined accordingly. *So, what is the appropriate level of control activities for SMEs? Moreover, where do we go from here?*

AU-C Section 315 (SAS No. 122) notes that while information systems in smaller, less complex organizations are likely to be less formal than in larger organizations, management's or the owner's role is just as significant as it is in smaller entities with active management involvement that may not need extensive descriptions of accounting procedures, sophisticated accounting records, or written policies. AU-C Section 315 notes that management's monitoring of controls often is accomplished by management's or the owner-manager's close involvement in operations. This involvement often identifies significant variances from expectations and inaccuracies in financial data leading to remedial action to the control. For example, smaller, less complex entities may not have an independent or outside member on the board of directors.

RISK AND FRAUD

Fraud for the SME is both a serious financial risk and a significant financial reporting risk. According to a recent study by the Association of Certified Fraud Examiners (ACFE 2012), businesses with fewer than 100 employees often lacked formal controls and were shown to be three times more likely than their larger counterparts to discover fraud by accident. Smaller businesses were almost twice as likely to discover fraud when police were involved and were not nearly as likely to uncover fraud through an internal audit. Research by the ACFE concluded that compared to large organizations, small businesses (those with fewer than 100 employees) have far fewer antifraud controls in place than do larger organizations. Furthermore, small organizations were victimized by fraud more frequently than larger organizations and they suffered a disproportionately large median loss of $147,000.

Research by the ACFE has consistently reinforced the idea that fraud schemes fall into three primary categories. The first is asset misappropriation schemes (see Table 9.5). The second category is corruption schemes (e.g., schemes involving bribery or conflicts of interest). The third is financial statement fraud schemes (e.g., recording fictitious revenues, understating reported expenses, or artificially inflating reported assets). The third category directly affects the financial auditor.

COSO (2007) recommends several approaches to assessing the fraud risk for the SME, including:

- Conduct fraud assessments across the enterprise to evaluate vulnerabilities that are unique or typical of that industry.
- Consider approaches to circumvent or override controls in identifying, evaluating, and testing the design and operating effectiveness of entity-wide controls that address fraud.
- Use IT tools where practical, including security systems, fraud detection, and monitoring tools, and incident tracking systems to identify and manage fraud risk.
- Develop Incident Investigation and Remediation Processes Management to enable a structured process for incident investigation and remediation.
- Investigate roles and responsibilities with identified processes that include a tracking mechanism that allows management to report on material fraud events.

The ACFE's 2012 *Report to the Nations* (ACFE 2012) recommends relatively low-cost measures such as a code of conduct, employee training programs, and formal management review of controls and processes that can significantly increase prevention and detection of fraud in SMEs. The cost of instituting codes of conduct and management review of controls and processes can be essentially limited to the expenses required for the labor to implement them.

 CONTROLS

COSO views five internal control components as comprising an integrated process, which indeed internal control is (see Figure 9.3), and not focused on any one component. This process highlights the interrelationship of the components, and recognizes that management has flexibility in choosing controls to achieve its objectives and that an organization can adjust and improve its internal control over time. The process cascades from first setting the financial reporting objectives, to identifying the risks for those

TABLE 9.5 Asset Misappropriation and COSO

		Asset Misappropriation by Risk Rating		
Category	Description	Examples	Percentage of All Cases	Illustrative Components from COSO to Prevent or Detect Misappropriation (suggested guidelines from the authors)
Billing	A person causes the employer to issue a payment by submitting invoices for fictitious goods or services, inflated invoices, or invoices for personal purchases.	An employee creates a fictitious company and bills the employer for services not actually rendered. An employee purchases items or services and submits an invoice to the employer for payment.	24.9%	SME higher risk, thus all COSO components are important: control activities, information and communication, control environment, and risk assessment and monitoring.
Noncash misappropriation	An employee steals or misuses noncash assets of the victim organization.	An employee steals inventory from a warehouse or storeroom. An employee steals or misuses confidential customer financial information.	17.2%	SME higher risk, thus all COSO components are important: control activities, information and communication, control environment, and risk assessment and monitoring.
Skimming	Cash is stolen from the enterprise *before* it is recorded on the enterprise's financial records.	An employee deliberately avoids recording a sale and pockets the customer payment.	14.6%	SME higher risk, thus all COSO components are important: control activities, information and communication, control environment, and risk assessment and monitoring.
Expense reimbursement	An employee makes a claim for reimbursement of fictitious or inflated business expenses.	An employee files a fraudulent expense report, claiming personal travel, nonexistent meals, etc.	14.5%	SME higher risk, thus all COSO components are important: control activities, information and communication, control environment, and risk assessment and monitoring.

(continued)

TABLE 9.5 *(continued)*

Check tampering	A person intercepts, forges, or alters a check drawn on one of the enterprise's bank accounts.	An employee steals blank company checks and makes them out to himself/herself or an accomplice. An employee steals an outgoing check to a vendor and deposits it into his or her own bank account.	11.9%	SME higher risk, thus all COSO components are important: control activities, information and communication, control environment, and risk assessment and monitoring.
Misappropriation of cash on hand	The perpetrator misappropriates cash kept on hand at the victim organization's premises.	An employee steals cash from the company's vault.	11.8%	SME higher risk, thus all COSO components are important: control activities, information and communication, control environment, and risk assessment and monitoring.
Cash larceny	Cash is stolen from the enterprise *after* it has been recorded on the enterprise's financial records.	An employee steals cash and checks from daily receipts before the cash is deposited in the bank.	11.0%	
Payroll	An employee causes his or her employer to issue a payment by making false claims for compensation.	An employee claims overtime for hours not worked. An employee adds employees to the payroll.	9.3%	SME lower risk (below 10% of all reported fraud), but control activities, information and communication, control environment, and risk assessment remain important. Cost benefit of the controls becomes more important.
Cash register disbursements	An employee makes false entries on a cash register to conceal the fraudulent removal of cash.	An employee fraudulently voids a sale on his or her cash register and steals the cash.	3.6%	SME lower risk (below 5% of all reported fraud), but control activities, information and communication, control environment, and risk assessment remain important. Cost benefit of the controls becomes more important.

Source: Adapted from ACFE 2012.

financial reporting objectives, assessing the control environment that is shaped by the organization's culture, including the tone at the top, identifying the control activities in that control environment and the information and communication from those activities, and finally monitoring activities.

All five components of internal control set forth in the framework are important to achieving the objective of reliable financial reporting. Determining whether a company's internal control system is effective involves a judgment resulting from an assessment of whether the five components are present and functioning effectively without material weakness. None of the framework's five components is an end in itself. Rather the components are an integrated system working together to reduce risk to reliable financial reporting to an acceptable level.

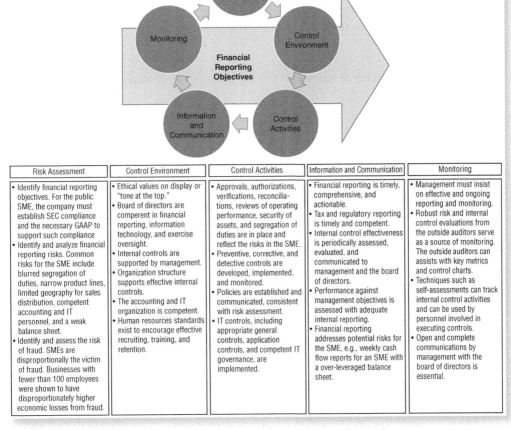

Risk Assessment	Control Environment	Control Activities	Information and Communication	Monitoring
• Identify financial reporting objectives. For the public SME, the company must establish SEC compliance and the necessary GAAP to support such compliance • Identify and analyze financial reporting risks. Common risks for the SME include blurred segregation of duties, narrow product lines, limited geography for sales distribution, competent accounting and IT personnel, and a weak balance sheet. • Identify and assess the risk of fraud. SMEs are disproportionally the victim of fraud. Businesses with fewer than 100 employees were shown to have disproportionately higher economic losses from fraud.	• Ethical values on display or "tone at the top." • Board of directors are comperent in financial reporting, information technology, and exercise oversight. • Internal controls are supported by management. • Organization structure supports effective internal controls. • The accounting and IT organization is competent. • Human resources standards exist to encourage effective recruiting, training, and retention.	• Approvals, authorizations, verifications, reconciliations, reviews of operating performance, security of assets, and segregation of duties are in place and reflect the risks in the SME. • Preventive, corrective, and detective controls are developed, implemented, and monitored. • Policies are established and communicated, consistent with risk assessment. • IT controls, including appropriate general controls, application controls, and competent IT governance, are implemented.	• Financial reporting is timely, comprehensive, and actionable. • Tax and regulatory reporting is timely and competent. • Internal control effectiveness is periodically assessed, evaluated, and communicated to management and the board of directors. • Performance against management objectives is assessed with adequate internal reporting. • Financial reporting addresses potential risks for the SME, e.g., weekly cash flow reports for an SME with a over-leveraged balance sheet.	• Management must insist on effective and ongoing reporting and monitoring. • Robust risk and internal control evaluations from the outside auditors serve as a source of monitoring. The outside auditors can assists with key metrics and control charts. • Techniques such as self-assessments can track internal control activities and can be used by personnel involved in executing controls. • Open and complete communications by management with the board of directors is essential.

FIGURE 9.3 COSO's Five Integrated Components of Internal Control

Source: Adapted from COSO 2007: *Internal Control Over Financial Reporting: Guidance for Smaller Public Companies.*

A weak control environment has a pervasive negative influence on all parts of the COSO internal control process, including risk assessment, control activities, information and communication, and monitoring. As cited earlier, Klamm and Watson (2009) identified relationships between the reported material weaknesses and the five components of COSO, identifying that a weak control environment has a positive association with the remaining four weak COSO components.

The control environment is a pervasive structure that affects many business processes, including management's *integrity and ethical values, operating philosophy,* and *commitment to organizational competence* (Ramos 2004). Tests of the control environment consist of a combination of procedures, including a review of relevant documentation of the design, inquiries of management and employees, and direct observation. COSO identifies seven principles to develop a robust control environment (COSO 2007):

1. Integrity and ethical values
2. Board of directors
3. Management's philosophy and operating style over financial reporting
4. Organizational structure
5. Financial reporting competencies
6. Authority and responsibility
7. Human resources

Integrity and ethical values: COSO suggests three principles for integrity and ethical values:

1. An articulation of the values of senior management espoused throughout the organization
2. Processes in place to monitor adherence to articulated values
3. Variances from integrity and values appropriately addressed and remedied at appropriate levels within the company

In simple terms, management must set the tone for behavior in the enterprise. Management must communicate this tone (e.g., a newsletter) and act upon it in terms and behavior that are consistent with the newsletter and articulated values. If suspected fraud or misbehavior occurs, management should act upon it immediately via the appropriate level of authority, including outside law enforcement.

Board of directors: A meaningful, active, and independent board is essential for a robust control environment in an SME. That board should have a sufficient number of members who are independent and actively evaluate and monitor risks of management override of internal control and consider risks affecting the reliability of financial reporting. The board should retain financial reporting expertise within its ranks, including oversight of the quality and reliability. The board should provide oversight of financial reporting and financial statement preparation. A significant departure from past practice with the passage of SOx and COSO is the oversight of the audit committee and/or board, including the authority to engage, replace, and determine the compensation of the external audit firm. Before SOx, the senior financial staff, including the CFO, typically had the authority to hire and fire the external audit firm.

Management's philosophy and operating style: This practice emphasizes the importance of minimizing risks related to financial reporting and through its dealings with customers, suppliers or distributors, and employees. Documentation and authorizations support all journal entries. Employees recognize the importance of applying appropriate diligence and business judgment in the performance of assigned job responsibilities.

Organizational structure: An organizational chart sets forth roles and respective reporting lines for all employees, including those involved in financial reporting. Management maintains job descriptions for key positions and updates them as conditions and circumstances warrant. Management adopts a structure whereby only three staff layers exist between the CFO and personnel directly involved in the financial reporting process. An internal audit function reports directly to the CEO, with direct access to the audit committee, to maintain independence over financial reporting.

Financial reporting competencies: Management employs or retains individuals who possess the required competencies to support and execute financial reporting. Those same competencies are regularly evaluated and maintained.

Authority and responsibility: The functions of the audit committee and the internal audit function (if one exists) are robust and maintained through defined levels of responsibility and authority. The audit committee oversees management's process for defining responsibilities for key financial reporting roles. The CEO and top management are responsible for internal control over financial reporting, including both initiating and maintaining the internal control system. Senior and functional management are responsible for ensuring all employees understand their responsibilities for achieving financial reporting objectives through adherence to internal control policies and procedures.

Human resources practices: Management establishes practices that maintain a commitment to integrity, ethical behavior, and competence. Those practices support employees by providing tools and training needed to perform their financial reporting roles. Management supports employee performance evaluations and compensation practices that align to the achievement of financial reporting objectives (i.e., management walks the talk and does what it must to maintain the commitment).

Auditors must probe to understand the company's attitude toward internal control over financial reporting. As part of that probe, the auditors should ask management for a self-assessment. Tests that auditors are accustomed to performing, such as walkthroughs, reperformance of the control using a sample, and focusing solely on activity-level controls, are inappropriate.

Under SOx reporting, management is responsible for evaluating and reporting on a company's controls. The external auditors are responsible for auditing management's assertion and independently coming to their own conclusions about the company's internal control effectiveness. They must evaluate management's assessment and perform their own independent tests in many areas, including the control environment.

Control Activities

Control activities include a range of activities that vary in terms of cost and effectiveness, depending on the circumstances.

- ▪ These include approvals, authorizations, verifications, reconciliations, reviews of operating performance, security of assets, and segregation of duties.
- ▪ Management uses an appropriate balance of preventive and detective controls, and an appropriate balance of manual and automated controls, to mitigate risks to the achievement of financial reporting objectives.
- ▪ Duties divide processes to mitigate risks and meet financial reporting objectives.
- ▪ When selecting among alternative control options, management considers the cost of control activities in relation to expected benefits of improved control.

Communication and Monitoring

COSO (2007) emphasizes three major points regarding information and communication and all focus on transparency, timeliness, and redundancy. In an SME these attributes may be much more difficult to achieve than in a larger company where resources are more abundant, competencies are established, and roles are well defined. In an SME where staffing is more limited and roles are more fluid, information and communication are more important than they are in a public enterprise where previously published public information is available and competitive information is widespread and easily accessible.

The first emphasis by COSO is quite simple; if management does not ask for a deliverable, the deliverable will not appear or may never exist. Management must communicate and emphasize that internal control over financial reporting must be taken seriously. Without an emphasis on and commitment to reporting on internal controls, financial management can easily mislead or fail to connect the dots and provide less than a complete picture of internal controls in the SME. A variety of reporting resources are available for even a very small enterprise. With the help of the accounting firm or other outside consultants, control charts and key metrics help track internal control activities. Control charts can track first-level accountability for processes and activities to use in considering whether control performance is on track with deviations and these are being investigated and resolved. Simple techniques such as self-assessments can track internal control activities and can be used by personnel involved in executing controls. Management can periodically test its computer network by performing a penetration test to identify weaknesses in internal controls for both internal and external connectivity. Identified security issues concerning access to financial data are addressed and resolved in a timely manner. Internal audit is a resource that many SMEs cannot afford, but if it is available, the role can provide an objective perspective regarding key elements of the internal control system. Internal audit reports are distributed to senior management and the audit committee.

The second emphasis by COSO is that communication between management and the board of directors must be sufficient so each may fulfil their roles with respect to financial reporting objectives. Board members with experience will know what to expect in information flows in board reporting while newer board members will not have a sense of expectations. Board members being recruited to an SME may not have the depth of experience of a larger enterprise and thus may not be fully aware of what to expect. Particularly relevant to IT, one or more board members should have experience in sophisticated technology installations if the SME is using or attempting to use sophisticated technology.

The board should also have access to the information sources outside of management, including access to the external auditors, the internal auditors, and other relevant parties such as regulatory authorities. If the board does not have regular access to qualified resources, the board members should be able to invite outside resources to board meetings to evaluate certain topics.

Ultimately, control deficiencies should be identified and communicated in a timely manner to those parties responsible for taking corrective action, and to management and the board as appropriate. Outsides resources may be needed for guidance useful in implementing or assessing the application of internal control guidelines.

FINANCIAL REPORTING

Whether or not GAAP compliance occurs for the SME, there is one overriding objective: to create useful information for those who make financial decisions about the enterprise. The balance sheet must report obligations that will be due in the near term and the nature of assets available to satisfy those claims. The income statement must identify income and expenses for the reported period. The cash flow statements must identify the sources of cash and how the cash was used. The disclosures identify pertinent material, qualitative and quantitative information that influences the income statement, balance sheet, and cash flows. Said another way, the financial statements should make it possible for investors and creditors to (FASB 2010):

- Make informed investment, credit, and similar resource allocation decisions.
- Assess the amounts, timing, and uncertainty of the entity's future cash inflows and outflows (the entity's future cash flows). This information is essential in assessing an entity's ability to generate net cash inflows and thus to provide returns to investors and creditors.
- Assess the economic resources of the entity (its assets) and the claims to those resources (its liabilities and equity). Information about the effects of transactions and other events and circumstances that change resources and claims to them is also essential.

COSO describes the financial reporting characteristics associated with the SME:

- Management specifies financial reporting objectives with sufficient clarity and criteria to enable the identification of risks to reliable financial reporting.
- Financial reporting objectives are consistent with GAAP and are appropriate in the circumstances of the SME.

▪ Financial statements are informative for end users and are classified and summarized in a reasonable manner, neither too detailed nor too condensed.
▪ The financial statements reflect the underlying transactions and events in a manner that presents the financial position, results of operations, and cash flows within a range of acceptable limits.

The FASB (2010) cites several qualitative characteristics that are integral to the general-purpose financial report:

▪ **Relevance:** If information is relevant, it is capable of influencing the decisions to evaluate the potential effects of past, present, or future transactions or other events on future cash flows (predictive value) to confirm or correct their previous evaluations (confirmatory value).
▪ **Timeliness:** Timeliness is making information available to decision makers before it loses its capacity to influence decisions.
▪ **Faithful representation:** For information to be faithful, it must be verifiable, neutral, and complete. Information is not neutral when it makes a company's position look better or worse under a set of circumstances.
▪ **Consistency:** Consistency refers to use of the same accounting policies and procedures, either from period to period within an entity or in a single period across entities. Consistency enables comparability of financial statements.
▪ **Understandability:** Financial reporting must be understandable and comprehensible for those who are willing to spend reasonable time to understand the reports.
▪ **Conservatism:** Conservatism is the practice of using the least optimistic estimate when two or more estimates are equally likely.
▪ **Materiality:** Materiality is an amount that affects a decision. Adding immaterial information to a financial report can mask, reduce, or hide the impact of material information.

Management is ultimately responsible for the fair presentation of financial statements that reflect the nature and operations of the entity. In the case of an SME, it is very likely that management and significant equity holders of the enterprise are the same individuals. As such, it is common that the personality of the manager is often inseparable from the operations of the business and thus is a motivating factor for an outcome that favorably represents the business.

Financial Reporting Assertions

Figure 9.3, COSO's guidance for linking accounts, risks, and assertions, maps the relationship between financial accounts, risks, and assertions, and defines the process from financial reporting requirements (e.g., the 10-K) and walks through the financial accounts and nonfinancial disclosures to define audit risks. Inherent in that diagram are both the financial audit and IT audit risks. So, what are the IT audit risks?

To answer that question, we must understand the control objectives for each of the major account and subaccount groups and the assertions made. Financial assertions of completeness, existence, and/or valuation are made for each of the major subaccounts in the normal course of the financial reporting. Table 9.6 defines the objectives and

TABLE 9.6 Control Objectives and Financial Assertions of the Financial Close Cycle

Illustrative Control Objectives from COBIT 4.1	Financial Assertions
Entries booked in the close process are complete and accurate.	Completeness Existence
Automated amortization timing, periods, and methods are appropriate and accurately entered.	Valuation Existence
Variance reports identify posting errors/out-of-balance conditions.	Completeness Existence Valuation
Standard, recurring period-end journal entries submitted from subsidiary ledger systems are automated, appropriately approved, and entered accurately.	Completeness Existence Valuation
Systems generate reports of all recurring and nonrecurring journal entries.	Completeness Existence
Track all nonstandard journal entries.	Completeness Existence
Account codes and transaction amounts are accurate and complete, with exceptions reported.	Completeness Existence
General ledger balances reconcile to subledger balances.	Completeness Existence
Recorded amounts undergo an automated comparison to predicted amounts.	Completeness Existence
Prohibit out-of-balance entries.	Completeness Existence
Enterprise-wide consolidation, including standard intercompany eliminations, is automated/performed using a third-party software product.	Completeness Existence Valuation
System functionality supports the segregation of the posting and approval functions.	Existence
Access to general ledger records is appropriate and authorized.	Completeness Existence Valuation
Recording of transactions outside of financial close cutoff requirements is prohibited.	Completeness Existence Valuation
Annually approved recurring accruals are accurately booked in the appropriate periods.	Completeness Existence Valuation
System controls are in place for appropriate approval of write-offs.	Existence
Interrelated balance sheets and income statement accounts undergo automated reconciliation.	Completeness Existence
The sources of all entries are readily identifiable.	Existence
In the event of data exceptions, rejections and exceptions occur.	Completeness Existence
Account mappings are up to date.	Existence

Source: COBIT 4.1 © 2007 IT Governance Institute. All rights reserved. Used by permission.

assertions for the financial close cycle; the control objectives define major subaccounts in the next section, control objectives for applications. With a clear understanding of the control objectives, the audit IT audit plan includes the appropriate control objectives. Moreover, by mapping the control objectives by subaccounts, the IT auditor creates the control requirements for each major IT application (e.g., Payroll, Inventory, etc.).

Control Objectives for Applications

Six different transaction errors can occur in financial assertions:

1. Recorded transaction(s) are not real.
2. Transaction(s) are real but not recorded.
3. Transaction(s) are posted in the wrong amount.
4. Transaction(s) are posted to the wrong account.
5. Transaction(s) are posted to the wrong period.
6. Unauthorized transaction(s) occur.

Control objectives and the supporting actions manage the various types of transaction errors. (See Figure 9.4.)

Application control objectives 1 through 6 as described for the general ledger in Chapter 4 are appropriate for revenue, purchasing, inventory, fixed assets, human resources, payroll, and taxes.

1. **COBIT 4.1 Application Control: *Source Data Preparation and Authorization:*** This application control ensures that source documents for journal entries or other changes and entries to revenue, purchasing, inventory, fixed assets, human resources, payroll, and taxes are prepared by authorized and qualified personnel, following established procedures, taking into account adequate segregation

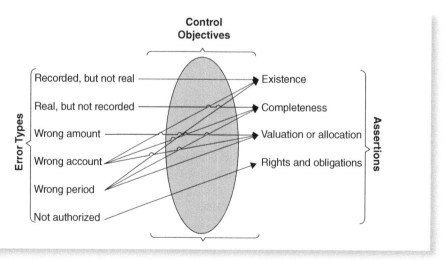

FIGURE 9.4   Relationships of Transaction Errors to Assertions

of duties regarding the origination and approval of these documents. Input and design reduce errors and omissions. A more complete description is in Chapter 4.

2. **COBIT 4.1 Application Control:** *Source Data Collection and Entry:* This application control ensures that data input for revenue, purchasing, inventory, fixed assets, human resources, payroll, and taxes is performed in a timely manner by authorized and qualified staff. Correction and resubmission of data should be performed without compromising original transaction authorization levels. Original source documents are retained for the appropriate amount of time. A more complete description is in Chapter 4.

3. **COBIT 4.1 Application Control:** *Accuracy, Completeness, and Authenticity Checks:* Revenue, purchasing, inventory, fixed assets, human resources, payroll, and tax transactions should be accurate, complete, and valid. Data corrections occur next to the point of origination. A more complete description is in Chapter 4.

4. **COBIT 4.1 Application Control:** *Processing Integrity and Validity:* This application control maintains the integrity and validity of data for revenue, purchasing, inventory, fixed assets, human resources, payroll, and taxes throughout the processing cycle. Application controls ensure that detection of erroneous transactions does not disrupt the processing of valid transactions. A more complete description is in Chapter 4.

5. **COBIT 4.1 Application Control:** *Output Review, Reconciliation, and Error Handling:* Procedures and associated responsibilities for revenue, purchasing, inventory, fixed assets, human resources, payroll, and taxes, including financial statements, are handled in an authorized manner, delivered to the appropriate recipient, and protected during transmission. A more complete description is in Chapter 4.

6. **COBIT 4.1 Application Control:** *Transaction Authentication and Integrity:* Before passing transaction data between internal applications and business operational functions (in or outside the enterprise), check the data for proper authenticity of origin and integrity of content. Maintain authenticity and integrity during transmission or transport. A more complete description is in Chapter 4.

For revenue, the application controls (adapted from COBIT 4.1) should ensure that:

- Orders are processed only within approved customer credit limits. [Threat: Orders are processed with more generous credit terms than approved by management.]
- Orders are approved by management as to prices and terms of sale. [Threat: Orders are processed but prices and terms of sale are not approved by management, leading to lost revenue.]
- Orders and cancellations of orders are input accurately. [Threat: Orders and cancellations are inaccurately input, leading to adverse customer relations and potentially lost revenue.]
- Order entry data is transferred completely and accurately to the shipping and invoicing activities. [Threat: Orders are received and processed accurately but shipped and invoiced inaccurately, leading to lost revenues and potentially higher cost of sales.]
- All orders received from customers are input and processed. [Threat: Orders are lost or input into the order processing system inaccurately, leading to misstated revenue and adverse customer relationships.]

- Only valid orders are input and processed. [Threat: Invalid orders are input, leading to invalid shipments and potentially unrecoverable product shipments.]
- Invoices are generated using authorized terms and prices. [Threat: Invoices are generated using unauthorized terms and prices, leading to potentially lost revenues, higher cost of sales, and receivables.]
- Invoices are accurately calculated and recorded. [Threat: Inaccurate invoices are generated and recorded, leading to inaccurate revenues, cost of sales, and receivables.]
- Credit notes and adjustments to accounts receivable are accurately calculated and recorded. [Threat: Credit notes are calculated inaccurately, leading to inaccurate credit notes receivables and potentially lost interest revenues.]
- All goods shipped are invoiced. [Threat: Product is shipped but revenue is not recognized and revenue is ultimately lost.]
- Credit notes for all goods returned and adjustments to accounts receivable are issued in accordance with organization policy and in the appropriate reporting period. [Threat: Credit note receivables do not reflect organizational policy, leading to misstated balances in any one particular period.]
- Invoices relate to valid shipments. [Threat: Revenue is not supported by valid shipments.]
- All credit notes relate to a return of goods or other valid adjustments. [Threat: Revenue credits are not supported by valid returns.]
- All invoices issued are recorded. [Threat: Revenue is understated.]
- All credit notes issued are recorded. [Threat: Credit notes are not recorded, leading to receivable balances that are understated.]
- Invoices are recorded in the appropriate period. [Threat: Revenue is misstated in a particular reporting period.]
- Cash receipts are recorded in the period in which they are received. [Threat: Revenue is misstated in a particular reporting period.]
- Cash receipts data is entered for processing accurately. [Threat: Cash is misstated in a particular reporting period.]
- All cash receipts data is entered for processing. [Threat: An incomplete audit trail is created and revenue is misstated.]
- Cash receipts data is valid and entered for processing only once. [Threat: Cash receipts data is not valid and revenue is misstated.]
- Cash discounts are accurately calculated and recorded. [Threat: Cash discounts are inaccurate, leading to potentially misstated net revenue, margins, and lost revenues.]
- Timely collection of accounts receivable is monitored. [Threat: Receivables are not monitored, leading to aged and uncollected receivables and ultimately lost revenue.]
- The customer master file is maintained. [Threat: Master file is inaccurate, leading to inaccurate shipping, invoicing, credit terms, and potentially lost or misstated revenue.]
- Only valid changes are made to the customer master file. [Threat: Invalid changes are made to master file, leading to inaccurate shipping, invoicing, credit terms, and potentially misstated revenue.]

- Changes to the customer master file are processed in a timely manner. [Threat: Delays in maintenance lead to inaccurate shipping, invoicing, credit terms, and potentially misstated revenue.]

For purchasing, the application control objectives (adapted from COBIT 4.1) should ensure that:

- Purchase orders are placed only for approved requisitions. [Threat: Unauthorized requisitions lead to unauthorized expenses and capital acquisitions.]
- Purchase orders are accurately entered. [Threat: Poorly executed purchase orders lead to unauthorized expenses and capital acquisitions.]
- All purchase orders issued are input and processed. [Threat: Lost or poorly executed purchase orders lead to delays in products and services and ultimately additional expenses.]
- Amounts posted to accounts payable represent goods or services received. [Threat: Postings to accounts payable do not have an adequate audit trail and cannot be supported.]
- Accounts payable amounts are accurately calculated and recorded. [Threat: Postings to accounts payable are inaccurate, leading to under- or overpayment to vendors.]
- All amounts for goods or services received are input and processed to accounts payable. [Threat: Amounts for goods and services are not input or processed, leading to underpayment to vendors.]
- Amounts for goods or services received are recorded in the appropriate period. [Threat: Amounts for goods and services are not posted to the appropriate period, leading to misstated payables for any particular reporting period.]
- Accounts payable are adjusted only for valid reasons. [Threat: Amounts are posted for invalid reasons, leading to misstated payments, unauthorized expenses, and potentially misstated payables.]
- Credit notes and other adjustments are accurately calculated and recorded. [Threat: Amounts are posted for invalid reasons, leading to misstated payments and credit notes payables.]
- All valid credit notes and other adjustments related to accounts payable are input and processed. [Threat: Credit notes are not appropriately posted to accounts payable, leading to potential underpayment.]
- Credit notes and other adjustments are recorded in the appropriate period. [Threat: Credit notes are not appropriately posted to the correct periods, leading to an under- or overstatement of credit note balances for any particular period.]
- Disbursements are made only for goods and services received. [Threat: Disbursements are made for goods and services that have not been received.]
- Disbursements are distributed to the appropriate suppliers. [Threat: Disbursements are made to inappropriate suppliers, leading to purchases that do not meet specifications and potentially unauthorized expenses.]
- Disbursements are accurately calculated and recorded. [Threat: Disbursements are inaccurately calculated and recorded, leading to under- or overstated expenses.]
- All disbursements are recorded. [Threat: Disbursements are not recorded with the potential that expenses will not be recognized.]

- Disbursements are recorded in the period in which they are issued. [Threat: Disbursements are not recorded in the appropriate period, leading to over- or understated expenses in any particular period.]
- Only valid changes are made to the supplier master file. [Threat: Invalid changes are made to supplier master list, potentially leading to unauthorized expenses, misstated payables, and misstated expenses.]

For inventory, the application control objectives (adapted from COBIT 4.1) should ensure that:

- Adjustments to inventory prices or quantities are recorded promptly and in the appropriate period. [Threat: Delayed postings for prices or quantities may lead to poorly executed inventory and product planning.]
- Adjustments to inventory prices or quantities are recorded accurately. [Threat: Inaccurate adjustments to prices and quantities may lead to poorly executed inventory and product planning, leading to lower gross margins and delayed production.]
- Raw materials are received and accepted only if they have valid purchase orders. [Threat: Materials may be received without purchase orders, leading to poorly executed inventory and product planning and in turn leading to lower gross margins, potentially delayed production, and poor use of cash resources.]
- Raw materials received are recorded accurately. [Threat: Raw materials being recorded inaccurately may lead to poorly executed inventory and product planning, leading to lower gross margins and delayed production.]
- All raw materials received are recorded. [Threat: Raw materials being received inaccurately may lead to poorly executed inventory and product planning, leading to lower gross margins and delayed production.]
- Receipts of raw materials are recorded promptly and in the appropriate period. [Threat: Raw materials being delayed may lead to poorly executed inventory and product planning, in turn leading to lower gross margins and delayed production.]
- Defective raw materials are returned promptly to suppliers. [Threat: Defective raw materials not being returned on a timely basis may lead to cash being committed to unproductive resources and ultimately lower gross margins.]
- All transfers of raw materials to production are recorded accurately and in the appropriate period. [Threat: Transfers of materials not being recorded accurately or in the correct period may lead to misstated product costs and misstated margins in particular periods.]
- All direct and indirect expenses associated with production are recorded accurately and in the appropriate period. [Threat: Direct and indirect expenses are recorded inaccurately and in the wrong period, leading to misstated financial statements.]
- All transfers of completed units of production to finished goods inventory are recorded completely and accurately in the appropriate period. [Threat: Transfers are not stated accurately, leading to poor production planning and potentially lost sales opportunities.]
- Finished goods returned by customers are recorded completely and accurately in the appropriate period. [Threat: Returns are not stated accurately, leading to misstated sales and finished goods inventory balances.]

- Finished goods received from production are recorded completely and accurately in the appropriate period. [Threat: Finished goods are not recorded accurately, leading to poor production planning and inaccurate inventory balances.]
- All shipments are recorded. [Threat: Shipments not recorded lead to poor production planning, inaccurate inventory balances, and inaccurate sales.]
- Shipments are recorded accurately. [Threat: Shipments are recorded inaccurately, leading to poor production planning, inaccurate inventory balances, and inaccurate sales.]
- Costs of shipped inventory are transferred from inventory to cost of sales. [Threat: Costs of shipped inventory are not transferred to cost of sales, leading to poor production planning, inaccurate inventory balances, inaccurate cost of sales, and inaccurate margins.]
- Costs of shipped inventory are accurately recorded. [Threat: Costs of shipped inventory are not transferred accurately to cost of sales, leading to poor production planning, inaccurate inventory balances, inaccurate cost of sales, and inaccurate margins.]
- Costs of shipped inventory are transferred from inventory to cost of sales promptly and in the appropriate period. [Threat: Costs of shipped inventory are not transferred accurately to cost of sales in the appropriate period, leading to poor production planning, inaccurate inventory balances, inaccurate cost of sales, and inaccurate margins in any one particular period.]

For payroll and human resources, the application control objectives (adapted from COBIT 4.1) should ensure that:

- Additions to the payroll master files represent valid employees. [Threat: Fraudulent additions to the payroll master file.]
- All new employees are added to the payroll master files, [Threat: New employees are not added to the payroll master, leading to understated payroll expense.]
- Terminated employees are removed from the payroll master files. [Threat: Terminated employees are not removed from the payroll master, leading to unauthorized expense.]
- Time worked is accurately input and processed. [Threat: Inaccurate time is input, leading to misstated payroll expense and potential litigation.]
- Payroll is recorded in the appropriate period. [Threat: Payroll is recorded in the wrong period, leading to over- or understated payroll liabilities for any particular period.]
- Payroll (including compensation and withholdings) is accurately calculated and recorded. [Threat: Payroll is not accurately calculated, leading to an over- or understated payroll expense.]
- Payroll is disbursed to appropriate employees. [Threat: Payroll is disbursed to inappropriate employees, leading to overstated and potentially fraudulent payroll expense.]
- Only valid changes are made to the payroll master files. [Threat: Invalid changes are made to payroll master files, creating the potential of unauthorized payroll expenses.]
- All valid changes to the payroll master files are input and processed. [Threat: Invalid changes are made to payroll, creating the potential of unauthorized payroll expenses.]

- Changes to the payroll master files are accurate. [Threat: Invalid changes are made to payroll master, creating the potential of unauthorized payroll expenses.]
- Changes to the payroll master files are processed in a timely manner. [Threat: Changes made to payroll master files are untimely, creating the potential of unauthorized payroll expenses.]
- Payroll master file data remains up to date. [Threat: Untimely changes are made to payroll master file, creating the potential of unauthorized payroll expenses.]
- Only valid changes are made to the payroll withholding tables. [Threat: Invalid changes are made to payroll, creating the potential of unauthorized payroll expenses.]
- All valid changes to the payroll withholding tables are input and processed. [Threat: Invalid changes are made to payroll withholding files, creating the potential of unauthorized payroll expenses or payroll expenses that do meet legal requirements.]
- Changes to the payroll withholding tables are accurate. [Threat: Invalid changes are made to payroll, creating the potential of unauthorized payroll expenses.]
- Changes to the payroll withholding tables are promptly processed. [Threat: Invalid changes are made to payroll, creating the potential of unauthorized payroll expenses.]
- Payroll withholding table data remains up to date. [Threat: Invalid changes are made to payroll, creating the potential of unauthorized payroll expenses.]

For taxes, the application control objectives (Adapted from COBIT 4.1) should ensure that:

- Tax payments are correctly calculated and recorded to the general ledger. [Threat: Tax payments are inaccurately calculated and recorded, leading to misstated tax expense and tax liabilities on the financial statements.]
- Tax exposures and valuation allowances are correctly calculated and recorded. [Threat: Tax exposures and valuation allowances are inaccurately calculated and recorded, leading to misstated tax expense and tax liabilities on the financial statements.]
- Tax expenses are recorded in the correct periods. [Threat: Tax expenses are recorded in inaccurate periods, leading to an under- or overstatement of tax expense in any particular period.]
- Permanent and temporary differences are identified and recorded accurately. [Threat: Permanent and temporary differences are inaccurately recognized, leading to misstatements in tax expense in the current period and corrections in future periods.]
- Correct book income is used in the tax accrual. [Threat: Inaccurate book income is used in the tax accrual, leading to a misstated tax rate and inaccurate financial statements.]
- Tax assets, liabilities, and expenses are complete and correctly calculated and reported. [Threat: Assets, liabilities, and expenses are misstated, leading to inaccurate financial statements.]
- Depreciation is calculated using appropriate bases, resulting in correct charges and tax ramifications. [Threat: Inappropriate bases are used in the depreciation

calculation, leading to misstated depreciation and in turn leading to misstated financial statements in the current period and future periods.]

▪ Sales and use tax are calculated appropriately, correctly, and in a timely manner. [Threat: Inappropriate sales and use tax are calculated, leading to misstated sales taxes and use tax accruals.]

▪ Transfer pricing policies are up to date and accurately represented in the systems. [Threat: Transfer pricing is not up to date, leading to under- or overstatement of product costs, leading to inaccurate financial statements.]

▪ All tax payments are accurately reflected in the general ledger. [Threat: Tax payments are not accurately reflected in the general ledger, leading to misstated tax payments and potentially inaccurate tax expense on the financial statements.]

▪ Property tax filings are timely and accurate. [Threat: Tax payments are not made on a timely and accurate basis, ultimately leading to tax penalties associated with those payments.]

PCAOB GUIDANCE ON IT CONTROLS

While COBIT remains *the most comprehensive benchmark for IT audit compliance*, guidance from the PCAOB remains a meaningful reference and discusses IT controls for financial reporting in Paragraphs 50 and 53 in PCAOB's AS No. 2 (now superseded by AS No. 5). The PCAOB's AS No. 2, *An Audit of Internal Control over Financial Reporting Performed in Conjunction with an Audit of Financial Statements*, cites the following references:

50. Some controls (such as company-level controls, described in paragraph 53) might have a pervasive effect on the achievement of many overall objectives of the control criteria. For example, information technology general controls over program development, program changes, computer operations, and access to programs and data help ensure that specific controls over the processing of transactions are operating effectively. In contrast, other controls are designed to achieve specific objectives of the control criteria. For example, management generally establishes specific controls, such as accounting for all shipping documents, to ensure that all valid revenue is recorded.

53. Company-level controls are controls such as the following:

▪ Controls within the control environment, including tone at the top, the assignment of authority and responsibility, consistent policies and procedures, and company-wide programs, such as codes of conduct and fraud prevention, that apply to all locations and business units (see paragraphs 113 through 115 for further discussion);

▪ Management's risk assessment process;

▪ Centralized processing and controls, including shared service environments;

▪ Controls to monitor results of operations;

▪ Controls to monitor other controls, including activities of the internal audit function, the audit committee, and self-assessment programs;

- ▪ The period-end financial reporting process; and
- ▪ Board-approved policies that address significant business control and risk management practices.

Particularly noteworthy is the PCAOB's heavy emphasis on entity controls or general controls in Paragraph 53. The PCAOB specifically mentions monitoring, fraud prevention, clear assignment of responsibility and authority, tone at the top, the period-end financial closing process, and board-approved policies. PCAOB references program development but does not provide depth beyond the statements referenced in Paragraph 50. The PCAOB also expects management to complete a risk assessment process such as that discussed in Chapter 10.

 ## INTEGRATING COSO, COBIT, AND THE PCAOB

Why are COBIT 4.0, 4.1, or 5.0 relevant to financial reporting and COSO? While COSO establishes an internal control framework for financial reporting, COBIT establishes an IT governance and assurance framework for control and security and links the requirements, policies, and standards to support a common standard. For that reason, many companies use COBIT to supplement COSO when evaluating IT controls. Its fourth edition (COBIT 4.0) was released in December 2005 and includes important updates for Section 404 and strengthens links to frameworks such as COSO. An updated edition 4.1 was released in May 2007 with the COBIT 4.1 release. COBIT 5.0 was released in 2012 and is considered the next-generation IT framework. So, although COBIT 5.0 was released in 2012, COBIT 4.0 and 4.1 have been widely used for audit frameworks and remain very relevant. For this chapter and the following chapter, COBIT 4.1 identifies audit plans and procedures.

Practitioners describe PCAOB and COSO as high-level concepts that in many instances lack specificity about IT controls and business processes. Despite the lack of specificity, IT audit assessments must comply with the PCAOB, SOx, or any other audit standards. PCAOB AS No. 2 recommends the COSO model for auditing SOx Section 404. An overlay of COSO to COBIT is useful to IT auditors and managers alike in complying with SOx. *IT Control Objectives for Sarbanes-Oxley* (ITGI 2013) maps COSO to COBIT. The authors of this book recommend COBIT as an effective IT audit approach for PCAOB and COSO compliance.

Table 9.7 overlays the COSO framework against COBIT 4.1. The COBIT 4.1 uses four definitions in its framework: (1) Plan and Organize, (2) Acquire and Implement, (3) Delivery and Support, and (4) Monitor and Evaluate. Chapter 10 uses the same definitions. For the presentation in Table 9.7, the five components of COSO, Control Environment, Risk Assessment, Control Activities, Information and Communication, and Monitoring, are used. The presentation illustrates how COBIT fills in the blanks as a supplementary and meaningful framework to create a robust IT auditing approach for either the SME or large enterprise. Chapter 10 builds out the intersections of COSO and COBIT with a suggested audit plan.

TABLE 9.7 Overlay of COSO to COBIT 4.1

		COBIT 4.1 and COSO Frameworks					
			COSO Components				
Entity Level	Activity Level		Control Environment	Risk Assessment	Control Activities	Information and Communication	Monitoring
		COBIT IT Processes					
*		**Plan and Organize (IT Environment)**					
		Define IT strategic planning	*			*	*
		Define the information architecture					
		Determine the technological direction					
*		Define the IT processes, organization, and relationship	*			*	*
		Manage the IT investment					
*		Communicate management aims and direction	*			*	
*		Management of IT human resources	*			*	
*		Management quality	*		*	*	*
*		Assess and manage IT risks		*			
*		Manage projects					
		Acquire and Implement (Program Development and Program Change)					
		Identify automated solutions					
	*	Acquire and maintain application software			*		
	*	Acquire and maintain technology infrastructure			*		
	*	Enable operation and use			*	*	
		Procure IT resources					
	*	Management changes		*	*		*
	*	Install and accredit solutions and changes			*		
		Delivery and Support (Computer Operations and Access to Programs and Data)					
	*	Define and manage service levels	*		*	*	*
	*	Manage third-party services	*	*	*		*
		Manage performance and capacity					
		Ensure continuous service					

(continued)

TABLE 9.7 (continued)

Entity Level	Activity Level		Control Environment	Risk Assessment	Control Activities	Information and Communication	Monitoring
	*	Ensure systems security			*	*	*
		Identify and allocate costs					
*		Educate and train users	*			*	
	*	Manage service desk and incidents			*	*	*
	*	Manage the configuration			*	*	
	*	Manage problems			*	*	
	*	Manage data			*	*	
	*	Manage the physical environment			*	*	
	*	Manage operations			*	*	
		Monitor and Evaluate (IT Environment)					
*		Monitor and evaluate IT performance			*	*	*
*		Monitor and evaluate internal control	*				*
*		Ensure regulatory compliance			*	*	*
*		Provide IT governance	*				*

Source: COBIT 4.1 © 2007 IT Governance Institute. All rights reserved. Used by permission.

As cited earlier, Klamm and Watson (2009) examined 490 firms reporting material weaknesses in the first year of SOx compliance to evaluate the interrelatedness of weak COSO components and IT controls. Their research also examined compliance against COBIT 4.1 as a framework (see Table 9.8). The research cited by Klamm and Watson strongly suggests that a combined approach (i.e., using COBIT in combination with COSO) to evaluate internal controls is an effective approach.

The next step in the risk assessment is to integrate the IT audit risks into the financial audit plan after a comprehensive IT risk assessment. Chapter 10 completes the integration of the IT audit with a discussion of PCAOB IT guidance as well as an in-depth evaluation of COBIT 4.1 as it applies to COSO.

How does the new release of COBIT 5.0 affect the IT audit of the SME? COBIT 5.0 was released in 2012 to provide a combined governance and management framework for enterprise information and related technology, a framework that has evolved from COBIT 1.0, which focused almost entirely on the IT audit released in 1996 (Vander Wal, Lainhart, and Tessin 2012). The goal of COBIT 5.0 is to integrate all other major ISACA frameworks and guidance. COBIT 5.0 provides a comprehensive framework that assists

TABLE 9.8 Comparing SOx Weaknesses to COSO to COBIT 4.1

Examples of SOx 404 Weaknesses Classified by COSO and/or COBIT Component

COSO Component	SOx 404 Internal Control Weakness	COSO or COBIT Classification
Control environment	Ineffective or understaffed audit committee members who likely lack the prerequisite qualifications to be on the audit committee	COSO Framework: Board of directors and audit committee identified as relevant to control environment effectiveness.
	Inadequate IT training	COBIT 4.1: Educate and train users on the system on the control environment.
Risk assessment	Foreign, subsidiary, acquisition, merger, disposal, or reorganization issues	COSO Evaluation Tools, pp. 26–27: Managing change includes handling foreign operations, corporate restructuring as well as new lines, products, activities, and acquisitions.
	Weak or nonexistent (IT) risk assessment	Identified as weak by the firm.
Control activities	Inadequate account reconciliations and segregation of duties	COSO Executive Summary: Control activities include approvals, authorizations, verifications, reconciliations, reviews of operating performance, security of assets, and segregation of duties.
	Logical access and security issues	COBIT 4.1: Identifies ensured IT security, including access rights, as primarily a control activity. COSO Framework: Identifies access to data as a control activity.
Information and communication	Lack of communication	COSO Executive Summary: Effective communication is essential to control objectives.
	Inadequate information flow	COSO Framework: Information should be appropriate, timely, current, accurate, and accessible.
	Weak (IT) information and communication	Identified as weak by the firm.
Monitoring	Lack of supervision or oversight	COSO Executive Summary: Monitoring includes supervisory activities. COSO Framework: "Supervisory activities provide oversight of control functions."
	Weak (IT) monitoring	Identified as weak by the firm.

Source: Adapted from Klamm and Watson 2009.

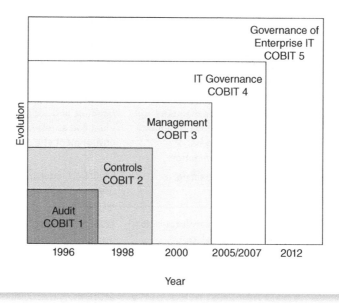

FIGURE 9.5 Evolution of COBIT

Source: Vander Wal, Lainhart, and Tessin 2012.

enterprises to achieve their goals and deliver value through effective governance and management of enterprise IT. (See Figure 9.5.)

COBIT 5.0 reaches beyond a framework for the IT function and treats information and related technologies as core assets to the enterprise in one single integrated framework starting with "meeting shareholder needs" in Step 1 and ending with "separating governance from management" in Step 5 in Figure 9.6. An integrated framework considers all IT-related governance and management enablers to be enterprise-wide and end-to-end, and resembles the same footprint as the financial reporting assertions, as those assertions are enterprise-wide and end-to-end. Efficient and effective governance and management of enterprise IT require a holistic approach, taking into account several interacting components.

COBIT 5 defines a set of enablers to support the implementation of a comprehensive governance and management system for enterprise IT. Enablers are broadly defined as anything that can help to achieve the objectives of the enterprise. The COBIT 5 framework defines seven categories of enablers (see Figure 9.7):

1. Principles, policies, and frameworks
2. Processes
3. Organizational structures
4. Culture, ethics, and behavior
5. Information

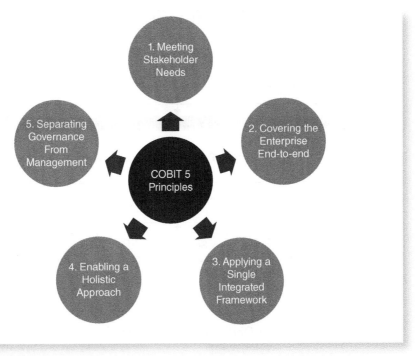

FIGURE 9.6 COBIT 5.0 Principles

Source: ISACA 2012b.

6. Services, infrastructure, and applications
7. People, skills, and competencies

The COBIT 5.0 framework makes a clear distinction between governance and management. These two disciplines encompass different types of activities, require different organizational structures, and serve different purposes. According to COBIT 5.0 (2012b):

> Governance ensures that stakeholder needs, conditions and options are evaluated to determine balanced, agreed-on enterprise objectives to be achieved; setting direction through prioritization and decision making; and monitoring performance and compliance against agreed-on direction and objectives.

And according to COBIT 5.0: "Management plans, builds, runs and monitors activities in alignment with the direction set by the governance body to achieve the enterprise objectives." COBIT 5.0 emphasizes an end-to-end approach using a holistic framework. An in-depth comparison between COSO and COBIT 5.0 is beyond the scope of this text.

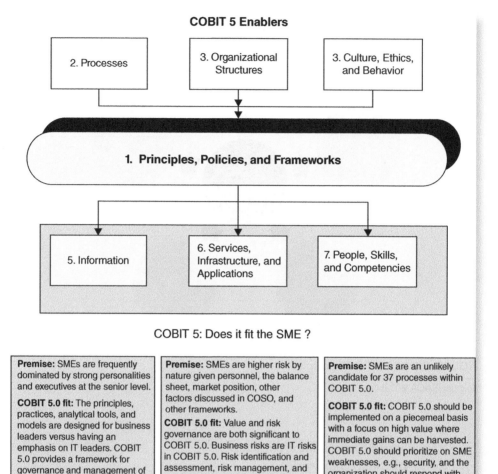

FIGURE 9.7 COBIT 5.0 Enablers

Source: Adapted from ISACA 2012b.

 ## SUMMARY

According to the PCAOB's inspection findings, the PCAOB found problems with the audit of internal controls for financial reporting in 15 percent of all audits in its 2010 inspection cycle and 22 percent of all audits in its 2011 inspection cycle. Workload staffing, attrition, the firms' training and guidance, ineffective communications, and AS No. 5, COSO, and COBIT are contributing factors to the trend. Firms are creating more audit risks for themselves. In combination with SMEs that by their nature have weaker balance sheets, income statements that are more fragile, and management teams that are less seasoned, the SME client base remains in a high-risk environment. As if that were not enough, the expectations for government oversight, globalization of the markets and operations, and rapidly evolving technologies are adding to the complexities and ultimately the audit risks.

While COSO establishes an internal control framework for financial reporting, COBIT establishes an IT framework for control and security and links the requirements, policies, and standards to support a common standard. For that reason, many companies use COBIT to supplement COSO when evaluating IT controls. COSO released an updated *Internal Control—Integrated Framework* in 2013 (COSO 2013). This release formalizes many of the fundamental concepts introduced in the original COSO framework. The five principles of internal control in 2013 were the five concepts of internal control in the previous COSO release. Consistent with earlier frameworks, the internal control principles provide the user assistance in designing and implementing systems of internal control and in understanding requirements for effective internal control. The COSO framework has expanded its discussion of technology but consistent with past releases has declined to address risk associated with specific technologies.

CHAPTER TEN

Integrating the IT Audit into the Financial Audit

W HAT IS THE SCOPE OF the IT audit? How does it relate to Control Objectives for Information and related Technology (COBIT) and the guidelines published by Committee of Sponsoring Organizations of the Treadway Commission (COSO) as discussed in Chapter 9? Moreover, why does it matter, and what is the impact of *IT material weaknesses* (MWs)? The footprint of the IT MWs may be larger than it appears. The audit scope is extremely important to financial reporting.

A risk analysis provides a steering mechanism or direction for the audit while an overlay of COSO against COBIT maps the traversable and relevant audit paths. Like a cross-country trip in an automobile, knowing the path is extremely important. Not all roads on the map are significant and material to the objective. Only roads that are relevant to the material assertions of the financial statements are significant to the auditor.

Research strongly suggests that MWs in IT controls spill over to other areas of the enterprise and may be a harbinger of additional internal control problems in other areas of the enterprise. As earlier chapters cite, Klamm and Watson (2009) identified several relationships between the reported MWs and the five components of COSO, including these three:

1. A weak control environment has a positive association with the remaining four weak COSO components (i.e., COSO components are likely to affect each other).
2. IT-related weak COSO components frequently spill over to create more non-IT-related material weaknesses and misstatements.
3. IT-related weak COSO components negatively affect reporting reliability and add to the number of non-IT MWs reported.

While this chapter provides a structured comparison of COBIT, COSO, and the PCAOB, a handful of questions and simple observations can provide strong clues about the SME IT risk profile at either the entity level or the account or transaction level (Helms 2012; Singleton 2009), including:

- A critical measure of IT risk is the competency of the IT staff; the more competent the IT staff, the lower the risks associated with all elements of IT. [general controls]
- Policies and procedures, IT governance, and project management practices directly affect risk. A brief interview addressing recent projects, key aspects of IT governance, and various policies and procedures can provide considerable insight into IT risk. [general controls]
- Does the IT infrastructure itself present risks to achieving the business goals and objectives? Does the company use the latest versions of software or is it committed to previous releases that may be very outdated and that use custom-coded software? Does the company use software whose resources are readily available to maintain, program, and support in the region? [both general controls and application controls]
- If the IT function writes or modifies code, the degree to which the staff uses best practices of the systems development life cycle (SDLC) reduces risks in the outcomes of the staff and IT. [both general controls and application controls]
- Do access controls sufficiently limit access to systems and information assets by effective authorization and authentication controls? [both general controls and application controls]
- Does the IT management test new systems and applications thoroughly before deployment? Does the enterprise test applications on a standalone basis and subsequently test on interfaces with other applications and whole systems? [both general controls and application controls]
- Does new hardware go through the same process of testing in a staging area? [general controls]
- Can the entity recover from a business interruption or disaster without significant losses? Business continuity, or disaster recovery, is a key aspect of general controls. [general controls]

RISKS, MATURITY, AND ASSESSMENTS

ISACA summarizes inherent risk around the technology, the qualifications and practices of the IT staff, the business processes, and the significance to the financial reports (see Table 10.1). If the technology is complex or unique, then the staff supporting the software should be qualified accordingly. Qualified staff should support complex business processes as some business processes are materially more complex than others. Other factors such as prior experience and the nature of the financial accounts supported by the business process will influence the risk assessment.

Another approach in assessing the qualifications of the IT organization supporting material financial accounts is to develop a *maturity model* (MM). The IT Governance Institute (2007) suggests MM levels of 0 through 5 (see Table 10.2) to outline the relationship of internal controls to the qualifications of the IT personnel supporting

TABLE 10.1 Inherent Risk Considerations

Example Risk Factors	Considerations for Higher Risk	Considerations for Lower Risk
Nature of technology	Complex, unique, customized, developed in-house	Simple, commonly used, not customized, off-the-shelf
Nature of people	Inexperienced, lack of training, limited number of people, high turnover	Experienced, trained, and specialized, sufficient resources, low turnover
Nature of processes	Decentralized, multilocation, ad hoc	Centralized, formalized, consistent
Past experience	History of problems, including processing errors, system outages, data corruption	No history of problems
Significance to the financial reports	Directly used for initiating and recording amounts into the financial reports	Indirectly used for analytical purposes but does not initiate or record amounts into the financial reports

Source: COBIT 4.1 © 2007 IT Governance Institute. All rights reserved. Used by permission.

the business process. The underlying premise of the MM is that if an organization does not have defined and standardized software development processes, it could be unable to provide consistent and reliable controls. The information technology, business operations, and accounting organization must be able to support the internal controls of the organization on a systematic and repeatable level—the controls are integral to the operation of the enterprise. That underlying premise is also applicable to the change management processes to support SOx compliance. An organization with a consistent and reliable development and change management process in IT applications will enable compliant IT implementations and contribute to the company's competitive and strategic advantages.

The MM Levels 0, 1, or 2 for internal controls would not be acceptable for an audit committee, the chief financial officer (CFO), the vice president of internal audit, or the chief executive officer (Table 10.2). An MM Level 1 definition that includes an ad-hoc reaction to control issues and high-level review of internal controls would not meet SOx requirements. Using the guidelines at MM Level 2 (Table 10.2), that "assessment of control needs occurs only when needed for selected IT processes to determine the current level of control maturity" and uses an "informal workshop approach," would not be acceptable by most CFOs and external auditors for SOx compliance. With an emphasis on value and risk drivers, detailed analyses, tools and workshops, full support from business process owners, and accountability, COBIT's MM Levels 3 or 4 for internal controls would be acceptable for an audit committee as an intermediate target if MM Level 5 were the ultimate target. An audit committee or CFO would prefer an MM Level 4 that is reasonably close to an MM Level 5.

After interviewing several organizations that implemented SOx, Ho and Oddo (2007) identified several factors that appeared common to successful SOx implementations. Among the most important, senior management must drive, encourage, and

TABLE 10.2   Maturity Model (MM) for Internal Control

Maturity Level	Status of the Internal Control Environment
Level 0, Nonexistent	▪ There is no recognition of the need for internal control.
	▪ Control is not part of the organization's culture or mission.
Level 1, Ad hoc	▪ There is some recognition of the need for internal control.
	▪ The approach to risk and control is ad hoc.
	▪ There is no communication or monitoring of risks or controls.
Level 2, Repeatable but intuitive	▪ Controls are in place but are not documented.
	▪ Operation is dependent on the knowledge and motivation of individuals.
Level 3, Defined controls are in place and adequately documented.	▪ Controls are in place and adequately documented.
	▪ Operating effectiveness is evaluated on a periodic basis.
	▪ An average number of issues is outstanding.
Level 4, Managed and measurable	▪ A formal, documented evaluation of controls occurs frequently.
	▪ Many controls are automated and regularly reviewed.
	▪ Management is likely to detect most but not all control issues.
Level 5, Optimized	▪ Enterprise-wide risk and control program provides continuous and effective control.
	▪ Internal control and risk management are integrated with enterprise practices.
	▪ Controls are automated using real-time monitoring with full accountability for control monitoring, risk management, and compliance enforcement.

Source: Adapted from IT Governance Institute 2007.

if necessary mandate SOx ownership throughout the organization. Additional factors common to successful SOx implementations described by Ho and Oddo include:

1. Effective documentation with specific emphasis on the documentation of testing guidelines.
2. Maintenance of cost-effectiveness of the SOx implementation.
3. Effective project designs, staffing, and support.

Common to the three factors just cited, effective execution at Level 3 or above (Table 10.2) is essential to support change management and IT controls for SOx compliance. Through a handful of meaningful questions, an auditor can quickly assess whether those factors are in place in a particular enterprise. If those factors are not in place, the enterprise is probably at MM Level 2 or lower and is at higher risk of failed internal controls.

As earlier citations demonstrate, Steps 1 through 7 in Figure 10.1 describe a systematic examination of the financial statements and a risk assessment for financial reporting.

Step 1	Identify significant IT audit risks by considering • Items separately disclosed in the consolidated financial statements • Qualitative and quantitative factors • Materiality at the consolidated financial statement level
Step 2	Identify business processes/cycles and subprocesses/cycles and map to material accounts and disclosures
Step 3	Identify the relevant financial statement assertions for each significant account and disclosure
Step 4	Perform a risk assessment of the business subprocesses/subcycles using a comparision of COBIT versus COSO and PCAOB for guidance on control objectives

Determine Multiple-Location Coverage of Related Entities

Step 5	Obtain a complete listing of locations or business units
Step 6	Identify locations subject to testing and assess coverage
Step 7	Map locations to the business process/cycles and subprocesses/subcycles identified previously

Steps 1 through 7 are consistent with COSO Internal Control over Financial Reporting discussed in Chapter 9

FIGURE 10.1   Scoping the IT Audit Plan for Significant Accounts, Disclosures, and Business Process/Cycles

Source: Adapted from PricewaterhouseCoopers 2004a.

A dashboard for a risk assessment (see Table 10.3) using factors discussed in Tables 10.1, 10.2., and Figure 10.1 can identify the next steps in the risk assessment process. Factors including self-assessment input from management, prior unmediated IT audit issues, and the last year in which an IT audit was conducted can be mapped against material financial accounts and business processes in the enterprise. The column (in Table 10.3) labeled "Self-Assessment" is management's feedback, created through interviews and potentially with the help of the internal audit function, if an internal audit function exists. The nature and qualifications of the support staff can be derived from the MM analysis from Table 10.2. The overall level of the MM can be posted under the column "Maturity Level of Processes." While the grid columns suggest an even weighting between the columns, a history of prior problems, inexperienced or poorly qualified staff, complex systems, or how application data is being used in the financial statements may drive an overweighting of one column versus another.

Ultimately, a decision must be made as to whether the financial audit requires an IT audit as part of its scope given the risk assessments identified in this grid. The column in Table 10.3 labeled "Overall IT Risk Score" is a mathematical accumulation of the weightings used in the prior columns. Scores indicating "low risk" or an average close to "1" should be a low priority for an IT audit. Scores with a "medium" or "high" are high

TABLE 10.3 Sample Risk Assessment Grid for an SME: Luther Sound Exploration Inc.

LSE, Inc. Risk Assessment	Self-assessment	Unremediated Issues	Last Year Audited	Nature of Technology	Nature of Support Staff	Nature of Processes	Significance to Financial Reports	Overall IT Risk Score	Combined Financial and IT Audit
Rating Score, High = 3, Medium = 2, Low = 1									
Report Writers									
Crystal Reports									
Access									
Excel									
Data Base									
MS SQL									
Access									
Operating System									
Win Server									
Windows Vista									
Windows XP									
Software—Applications									
Payroll									
Human Resources									
Accounts Payable									
General Ledger									
Fixed Assets									
Accounts Receivable									
Hardware									
Workstations									
Servers									
Networking									
Firewalls									
WAN									
LAN									
Wireless Devices									
All Other									
Data Center Operations/Computer Rooms									
Help Desk Function									
E-commerce									
E-mail/Encryption									
Backup/Disaster Recovery Plan									
Virus Protection									

on the priority list for an IT audit. After the risk score is calculated, another column (not shown in Table 10.3) should identify application controls and general controls.

CROSS-REFERENCING COBIT TO THE PCAOB AND COSO

Tables 10.4, 10.5, 10.6, and 10.7 cross-reference COBIT to PCAOB and COSO in the categories of Plan and Organize, Program Development and Change, Computer Operations, and Monitor and Evaluate. The analysis in Table 10.3 should point the way for evaluations in the following tables. Financial accounts and nonfinancial disclosures that are material to the financial reporting and are "medium" or "high" risk in Table 10.3 are candidates for active scrutiny by the IT auditor.

IT auditors authored COBIT while financial auditors and regulators authored the COSO and PCAOB guidelines, whose objectives are to maintain the integrity of financial reporting. A visual comparison across the various columns in Table 10.3 will help you to identify different emphases. The information in Tables 10.4 to 10.7 helps the financial auditor to examine COBIT, COSO, and PCAOB guidance simultaneously. The purpose of the comparisons is to identify significant areas within the COBIT framework that could affect financial reporting. The last column summarizes the potential impact to the enterprise reporting a descriptive of either "high" or "medium." The suggested ratings used in the last column are just that; the auditor has the final judgment as to whether a particular rating should be higher or lower than the guidelines suggested in this chapter.

Beyond the guidance provided in the following tables, an in-depth framework for the evaluation and testing of internal controls is provided in a discussion following the tables irrespective of whether the applications are Oracle, Microsoft Dynamics, IBM, QuickBooks, or a custom-written application. A challenging question is: How does an auditor scale the discussions included in the following tables to an SME? The IT audit guidelines support more complex IT environments than QuickBooks, Microsoft Dynamics, or Microsoft Excel. For an SME with 10 employees (e.g., the retail dry cleaner in Des Moines, IA, that uses QuickBooks), can the auditor expect a strategic IT plan with a comprehensive risk assessment? Not likely! While several of the items referenced in COBIT are not scalable in a very small SME, an assessment of the IT personnel and general IT controls remains very relevant. If the general controls have material weaknesses without compensating controls, it is very difficult to maintain the integrity of the application controls. The auditor will rely on very high levels of general controls and application control testing listed in each of these tables for a very small SME. For many companies with 500 or fewer employees, the IT environments can be very complex and, as such, the content in the following tables may all be applicable and material.

The framework in Figure 10.2 walks through the steps of evaluating IT control exceptions or failures in IT control objectives. Assuming a control failure is not isolated, the financial controls team evaluates whether the control is an application control or a general control (ITGC). The financial controls team should assess all material weaknesses in application controls. If an ITGC failure does not have a compensating control(s), the financial controls team should assess whether it affects an application control for financial reporting.

TABLE 10.4 Plan and Organize

Luther Sound Exploration, Inc.				PCAOB References				COSO Reference					
COBIT Objective	Control Objective	COBIT Reference	Access to Programs and Data	Computer Operations	Program Development	Program Change	Control Environment	Risk Assessment	Control Activities	Information and Communication	Monitoring	Impact to LSE Financial Reporting? (High, Medium, Low)	
IT strategic planning	What controls ensure that IT strategies are aligned with business objectives?	PO 01					X	X		X	X	High	
Information architecture	What controls ensure that the information architecture has been defined and executed to ensure quality and integrity?	PO 02							X	X		Medium	
IT organization and relationships	What controls for IT roles, responsibilities, and data ownership have been defined and appropriately segregated?	PO 04					X			X		Medium	
Communication of management aims and direction	What controls for IT governance policies and procedures ensure that appropriate personnel receive communications and directives for compliance?	PO 06					X			X	X	Medium	

Luther Sound Exploration, Inc.

COBIT Objective	Control Objective	COBIT Reference	Access to Programs and Data	Computer Operations	Program Development	Program Change	Control Environment	Risk Assessment	Control Activities	Information and Communication	Monitoring	Impact to LSE Financial Reporting? (High, Medium, Low)
			PCAOB References				COSO Reference					
Management of human resources	What controls ensure appropriate response to job terminations and that the IT organization has adopted and promoted the company's culture of integrity and ethical business practices?	PO 07					X			X		Medium
Compliance with external requirements	What controls ensure that the organization monitors changes in external legal and regulatory requirements?	PO 08								X	X	Medium
Assessment of risks	What controls ensure that a comprehensive IT entity- and activity-level risk assessment framework is used to periodically assess risks?	PO 09						X				Medium
Management of quality	What controls ensure that documentation of all significant IT processes, controls, and activities exist and are maintained in connection with a quality assurance plan for all major IT functions?	PO 11					X		X	X	X	Medium

Source: Adapted from COBIT 4.1 2007.

TABLE 10.5   Program Development and Program Change

| | Luther Sound Exploration, Inc.: Acquire and Implement | | | PCAOB References | | | | COSO Reference | | | | | |
COBIT Objective	Control Objective	COBIT Reference	Access to Programs and Data	Computer Operations	Program Development	Program Change	Control Environment	Risk Assessment	Control Activities	Information and Communication	Monitoring	Impact to LSE Financial Reporting? (High, Medium, Low)
Acquire or develop application software	What controls assure that application and system software is developed to support financial reporting requirements?	AO 02	X	X	X	X			X			High
Acquire or develop technology infrastructure	What controls assure that technology infrastructure, application and system software are developed to support financial reporting requirements?	AO 03	X	X	X	X			X			High
Develop and maintain policies and procedures	What controls assure that policies and procedures exist to define acquisition and maintenance processes?	AO 04	X	X	X	X			X	X		High
Install and test application software and technology infrastructure	What controls assure that the systems are tested and validated prior to being placed into production processes?	AO 05	X	X	X	X			X			High
Manage changes	What controls assure that system changes for financial reporting significance are authorized before being moved to production?	AO 06		X		X			X		X	High

Source: Adapted from COBIT 4.1 2007.

TABLE 10.6   Computer Operations and Access to Programs and Data

			PCAOB References				COSO Reference					
COBIT Objective	Control Objective	COBIT Reference	Access to Programs and Data	Computer Operations	Program Development	Program Change	Control Environment	Risk Assessment	Control Activities	Information and Communication	Monitoring	Impact to LSE Financial Reporting? (High, Medium, Low)
Define and manage service levels	What controls ensure that specified service levels exist and key performance indicators are monitored and evaluated?	DS 01	X	X	X	X	X		X		X	High
Manage third-party service	What controls exist to ensure that qualified third-party providers are selected and that security, availability, and processing integrity are reported systematically?	DS 02	X	X	X	X	X	X	X		X	High
Manage performance and capacity	What controls ensure that IT management monitors system capacity and performance?	DS 03							X		X	Out of Scope
Ensure systems security	What controls ensure that financial systems and subsystems are secured?	DS 05			X	X			X	X	X	High
Educate and train users	What controls provide for identifying and documenting the training needs of personnel?	DS 07					X			X		Out of Scope

Luther Sound Exploration, Inc.

(continued)

TABLE 10.6 *(continued)*

COBIT Objective	Control Objective	COBIT Reference	Access to Programs and Data	Computer Operations	Program Development	Program Change	Control Environment	Risk Assessment	Control Activities	Information and Communication	Monitoring	Impact to LSE Financial Reporting? (High, Medium, Low)
Manage the configuration	What controls ensure security, processing and availability for the IT configuration?	DS 09			X	X			X	X		High
Manage problems and incidents	What controls ensure that incidents are properly resolved and investigated?	DS 10			X				X	X	X	Medium
Manage data	What controls ensure that data remain complete, accurate and valid in the update, storage, and back-up process?	DS 11			X	X			X	X		High
Manage facilities	What controls ensure that facilities are equipped with environmental controls?	DS 12						X				Medium
Manage operations	What controls ensure that programs are executed as planned and deviations are identified and investigated?	DS 13			X	X			X	X		Medium

Source: Adapted from COBIT 4.1 2007.

TABLE 10.7 Monitor and Evaluate

Luther Sound Exploration, Inc.

COBIT Objective	Control Objective	COBIT Reference	PCAOB References					COSO Reference					Impact to LSE Financial Reporting? (High, Medium, Low)
			Access to Programs and Data	Computer Operations	Program Development	Program Change	Control Environment	Risk Assessment	Control Activities	Information and Communication	Monitoring	
Monitoring	What controls ensure that performance indicators have been defined and progress is monitored by management?	MO 01								X	X	High
Adequacy of internal controls	What controls ensure that IT management monitors the design and operating effectiveness of internal controls?	MO 02									X	High
Independent assurance	What controls ensure that independent control reviews are conducted and documented of 3-rd party providers and major IT systems before implementation?	MO 03					X				X	High
Internal audit	What controls ensure that the internal audit plan is based on a risk assessment including IT and covers the full range of IT audit activities?	MO 04									X	High

Source: Adapted from COBIT 4.1 2007.

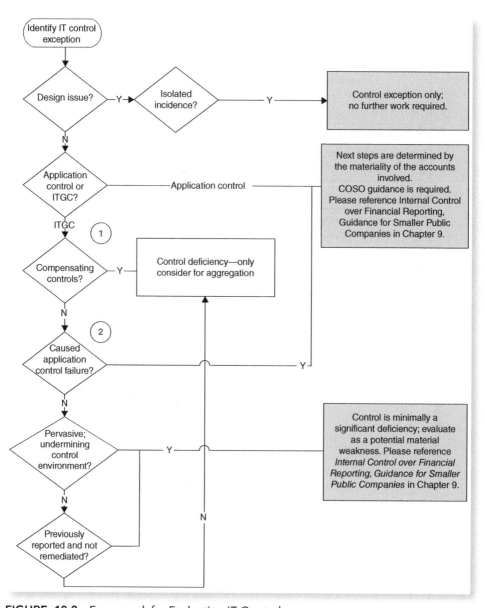

FIGURE 10.2 Framework for Evaluating IT Controls

Source: Adapted from COBIT 4.1 2007.

Not discussed in these tables is how the financial auditor or IT auditor accumulates the appropriate information for the evaluation or testing. The financial auditor or the IT audit team will interview various levels of management, accumulate reports and documentation, and test applications to build understanding of the audit environment. A comprehensive discussion of how the auditor accumulates evidence for evaluating internal controls for IT control objectives is beyond the scope of this text.

PLAN AND ORGANIZE

This section will walk through eight control objectives and their significance to the PCAOB and COSO guidelines. Table 10.4 provides a roadmap for the auditor to determine relevant control objectives in the Plan and Organize section of COBIT. The discussion including the control objective, evaluation, and testing was adapted from ISACA'S COBIT 4.1 audit guidelines (ISACA 2007). This discussion format helps the reader create an audit plan to follow in the course of the IT audit.

It is important to note that several control objectives from the Plan and Organize section of COBIT were not included in Table 10.4 because they were considered less material to the guidelines of the PCAOB or COSO for financial reporting purposes. The significance of COBIT to the PCAOB and COSO guidelines is in the view of the authors and not ISACA; they are included in this book as suggested guidelines.

Luther Sound Exploration Inc.: Plan and Organize*

Control Objective: IT Strategic Planning

What controls and activities ensure that IT management aligns strategies with business objectives using input from senior management, user management, and the IT function?
Evaluating Internal Controls: Structured IT planning process is in place including:

■ Support for the organization's mission and goals with IT initiatives.
■ Feasibility studies of IT initiatives.
■ Risk assessments of all significant IT initiatives.
■ Reengineering of IT initiatives to reflect changes in the enterprise's mission and goals.
■ Alternative strategies for data applications, technology, and organization.

Testing Controls: Evaluate and test:

■ Whether minutes from IT planning/steering committee meetings are consistent with control objectives.
■ Whether planning methodology deliverables exist and are as prescribed.
■ Whether relevant IT initiatives are included in the IT long- and short-range plans.
■ Whether IT long- and short-range plans are consistent with long- and short-range plans and the organization's requirements.
■ Whether IT long-range plans are systematically translated into short-range plans.
■ Whether plans are actionable in an SDLC format.

Control Objective: Information Architecture

What controls and activities ensure the information architecture maintains the quality and integrity of information used for financial and disclosure purposes?

---

* COBIT objectives are adapted from COBIT 4.1 (ISACA 2007).

Evaluating Internal Controls: A structured process maintains the enterprise data dictionary and data syntax rules:

- Classification of data, including security categories and data ownership, and access rules are appropriately defined.
- Standards define the default classification for data assets that do not contain a data classification identifier.

Determine whether IT policies and procedures address that:

- Authorization process is in place requiring the owner of the data, and access to that data and to the security attributes of the data.
- Security levels define each data classification.
- Access levels define each data classification.
- Access to sensitive data requires explicit access levels and data is provided only on a need-to-know basis.

Testing Controls: Test that:

- Existing applications and pending projects use a common enterprise data dictionary.
- Data dictionary documentation adequately defines data attributes and security levels for each data item.
- Data classifications, security levels, access levels, and defaults are appropriate.

Test that each data classification clearly defines:

- Who has access.
- Who determines the level of access.
- Specific approval steps needed for access.
- Special requirements for access (i.e., nondisclosure or confidentiality agreement).

Control Objective: IT Organization and Relationships

What controls and activities for IT roles, responsibilities, and data ownership ensure IT personnel's execution of the defined roles, responsibilities, and data ownership?

Evaluating Internal Controls: Determine that:

- Membership and functions of the IT planning/steering committee exist and responsibilities are identified.
- Policies exist outlining roles and responsibilities for all personnel within the organization for information systems, internal control, and security.
- Regular campaigns exist to enhance internal control, security awareness, and discipline.

- Processes exist within quality assurance to schedule resources and ensure completion of quality assurance testing and signoff before systems or system changes are implemented.
- Management assigns organization-wide responsibility for formulation of internal control and security (both logical and physical) policies.
- Organization's security policy defines responsibilities for information security for each information asset owner.
- Policies and procedures cover data and system ownership for all major data sources and systems.
- Procedures systematically define changes in data and system ownership on a regular basis.
- Policies and procedures describe supervisory practices, and all personnel have sufficient authority and the resources to perform their roles and responsibilities.
- Ensure that segregation of duties maintain the separation of authorization, record keeping, and custody of assets or the equivalent while maintaining an effective technology solution.
- Policies and procedures exist for the evaluation and reevaluation of IT position (job) descriptions.
- Appropriate roles and responsibilities exist for key processes, including SDLC, information security, acquisition, and capacity planning.
- Appropriate and key performance indicators and/or critical success factors are defined.
- IT policies and procedures control the activities of consultants and other contract personnel to ensure the protection of the organization's assets.
- Procedures applicable to contracted IT services for adequacy and consistency with organization acquisition policies are monitored.

Testing Controls: Test that:

- The IT planning/steering committee oversees the IT function.
- The reporting hierarchy for the IT function is appropriate.
- IT function's location in the organization is effective to provide a partnership with senior management.
- Senior IT management monitors, measures, and reports on the IT function's performance.
- There is a process for analyzing actual results against target levels to determine the corrective actions taken.
- Users'/owners' management assesses the IT function's responsiveness and ability to provide timely and substantive IT information technology solutions that meet users'/owners' needs.
- IT management is aware of its roles and responsibilities.
- Sufficient awareness of consistent application of security policies and procedures exist.
- Personnel attend information security and internal control training.
- Data and system ownership exists for all information assets.
- Data and system owners approve changes made to data and systems.

- Ownership exists for all data and systems.
- Asset's owners approve access to all data and the asset.
- Job descriptions delineate authority and responsibility
- Job descriptions describe the required business, relational, and technical competencies.
- Individuals understand their job descriptions.

Control Objective: Communication of Management Aims and Direction

What controls and activities for IT governance policies and procedures ensure that appropriate personnel receive communications and directives for compliance with governing policies and procedures?

Evaluating Internal Controls: Determine whether organization policies and procedures create a framework and awareness program, giving specific attention to:

- Integrity.
- Ethical values.
- Code of conduct.
- Security and internal controls.
- Competence of personnel.
- Management philosophy and operating style.
- Accountability, attention, and direction provided by the board of directors or its equivalent.

Management has accepted full responsibility for formulating, developing, documenting, promulgating, controlling, and regularly reviewing policies governing general aims and directives:

- Formal awareness program exists to provide ongoing communication and training related to management's positive control environment.
- Organization policies and procedures ensure that appropriate and adequate resources are assigned to implement the organization's policies in a timely manner.
- Appropriate procedures ensure that personnel understand the implemented policies and procedures, and that the policies and procedures are being followed.
- IT policies and procedures define, document, and maintain formal policies and objectives governing quality of systems and services produced, which are consistent with the organization's policies and objectives.
- Procedures address the need to periodically review and reapprove key standards, directives, policies, and procedures relating to IT.

Senior management accepts full responsibility for developing a framework for the overall approach to security and internal control. Security and internal control framework specifies the security and internal control policy, purpose and objectives, management structure, scope within the organization, assignment of responsibilities, and definition of penalties and disciplinary actions associated with failing to comply with security and internal control policies.

Formal security and internal control policies identify the organization's internal control process and include control components such as:

- Control environment
- Risk assessment
- Control activities
- Information and communication
- Monitoring

Testing Controls: Test that:

- Management fosters a positive control cover the key aspects, such as integrity, ethical values, code of conduct, security and internal controls, competence of the personnel, management philosophy and operating style, accountability, and attention.
- Employees understand the code of conduct and apply it.
- Management addresses the organization's internal control environment on a regular basis.
- Management formulates, develops, documents, promulgates, and controls policies covering the internal control environment.
- Management conducts regular reviews of standards, directives, policies, and procedures for continued appropriateness and its ability to adapt to changing conditions.
- Management monitors efforts to ensure that appropriate and adequate resources are assigned to implement the organization's policies in a timely manner.
- Management enforces standards, directives, policies, and procedures concerning the internal control environment.
- Selected members of management are involved and understand the contents for security and internal control activities (i.e., exception reports, reconciliations, comparisons, etc.).
- Selected management have individual roles, responsibilities, and authorities that are clearly communicated and understood at all levels of the organization.
- Selected departments assess procedures for routinely monitoring security and internal control activities (i.e., exception reports, reconciliations, comparisons, etc.) and the process for providing feedback to management is occurring.
- Selected system documentation confirms that system-specific management decisions have been documented and approved in compliance with the SDLC.
- Management signs off on activities, applications systems, or technologies.

Control Objective: Management of Human Resources

What controls and activities ensure that the processes exist to support timely and appropriate response to job terminations and job changes, and that the IT organization has adopted and promoted the company's culture of integrity and ethical business practices?

Evaluating Internal Controls: Determine whether:

- Criteria ensure effective processes exist for recruiting and selecting personnel to fill open positions.
- Specifications of required qualifications take into account relevant requirements of professional bodies where appropriate.
- Training programs ensure organization's minimum requirements concerning education and general awareness covering security issues.
- Management ensures adequate personnel training and career development.
- Appropriate actions ensure technical and management skills gaps are filled.
- Ongoing cross-training and backup of staff for critical job functions occurs.
- Enforcement of uninterrupted holiday policy occurs.
- Organization's security clearance process is adequate.
- Employees are evaluated using competency profiles for the position and evaluations.
- Job change and termination processes ensure the protection of the organization's resources.

Testing Controls: Test that:

- Recruiting and/or promotion ensure objectiveness and relevancy to the requirements of the position.
- Personnel have adequate knowledge for their job function or areas of responsibility.
- Position descriptions exist, are reviewed, and are kept up to date.
- Personnel files contain employee acknowledgments of the organization's overall education and general awareness program.
- Ongoing training and education occurs for appropriate personnel assigned to critical functions.
- IT personnel receive proper training in security procedures and techniques.
- IT management and staff are aware of and understand organizational policies and procedures.
- Personnel assigned to critical IT functions understand internal systems security and controls.

Control Objective: Compliance with External Requirements

What controls and activities ensure that the organization monitors changes in external legal and regulatory requirements and processes to support continuous compliance?

Evaluating Internal Controls: Determine whether:

- Policies and procedures ensure appropriate corrective action is undertaken on a timely basis and procedures are in place to ensure continuous compliance.
- Insurers are kept aware of all material changes to the IT environment.

Determine whether security procedures are in accordance with all requirements and are adequately addressed, including:

- Password protection and software to limit access
- Authorization procedures
- Terminal security measures
- Data encryption measures
- Firewall controls
- Virus protection
- Timely follow-up

Testing Controls: Test that:

- External requirements reviews are current, complete, and comprehensive with respect to legal, government, and regulatory issues and result in prompt corrective action.
- IT complies with the documented privacy and security policies and procedures.
- Data transmitted across international borders does not violate export laws.
- Existing contracts with electronic commerce trading partners adequately address the requirements specified in organizational policies and procedures.
- Existing insurance contracts adequately address the requirements specified in organizational policies and procedures.
- Encryption conforms to length of key and other regulatory requirements.
- Where regulations or internal procedures require certain data items to be protected and/or encrypted (e.g., bank PINs, Social Security numbers, tax file numbers, passwords, military intelligence), such protection/encryption is in place.

Control Objective: Assessment of Risks

What controls and activities ensure that a comprehensive IT entity and activity level risk assessment framework is used to periodically assess information risk, including risk assessments, acceptance, and related strategies?

Evaluating Internal Controls: Determine whether:

- A systematic risk assessment framework exists for all financially relevant systems incorporating relevant information risks to the achievement of the organization's objectives and forming a basis for determining how the risks should be managed to an acceptable level.
- The risk assessment approach provides for updated risk assessments.
- Risk assessment procedures ensure that identified risks take into consideration the results of audits, inspections, and identified incidents.
- Procedures for monitoring changes in systems processing activity determine that system risks and exposures are adjusted in a timely manner.
- Procedures exist for monitoring and improving the risk assessment.

Determine whether the risk assessment documentation includes:

- A description of the risk assessment methodology, an identification of significant exposures, the corresponding risks, and corresponding exposures.
- Probability, frequency, and threat analysis definitions and techniques are included in the identification of risks.
- A formal or informal quantitative and/or qualitative (or combined) approach for identifying and measuring risks, threats, and exposures.
- Acceptance of residual risk takes into account: organizational policy risk identification and measurement uncertainty incorporated in the risk assessment approach itself; cost and effectiveness of implementing safeguards and controls.
- Insurance coverage that offsets the residual risk.
- Formal quantitative and/or qualitative approaches to select control measures that maximize return on investment.
- That there is a balance among the detective, preventive, and corrective measures used.

Testing Controls: Test that:

- Risk assessment framework reflects that the risk assessments are regularly updated.
- IT management and staff are aware of and involved in the risk assessment process.
- Management understands risk-related factors and threat probabilities.
- Reports are issued to senior management for review and its concurrence of identified risks.

Priorities from highest to lowest exist, and, for each risk, an appropriate response exists, including:

- Preventive controls
- Detective controls
- Corrective controls

Adequate insurance coverage exists for accepted residual risk and is considered against various threat scenarios, including:

- Fire, flood, earthquake, tornadoes, terrorism, other unforeseeable natural disasters
- Breach of employee responsibilities
- Business interruption—lost revenues, lost customers, etc.
- Other risks not generally covered by insurance

Control Objective: Management of Quality

What controls and activities ensure that documentation of all significant IT processes, controls, and activities exists (and is maintained) in connection with a quality assurance plan for all major IT functions?

Evaluating Internal Controls: Determine whether the quality plan is based on the organization's long- and short-range plans promoting the continuous improvement philosophy and answers the basic questions of *what, who, and how*, and that a standard approach to quality assurance exists, and the approach is:

- Applicable to both general and project-specific quality assurance activities.
- Saleable and applicable to all projects.
- Understood by all individuals involved in a project and quality assurance activities.
- Applied throughout all phases of a project.

Senior management supports IT standards, policies, and procedures, including a formal or appropriately sized SDLC methodology.

The SDLC:

- Governs the process of developing, acquiring, implementing, and maintaining computerized IT, and encourages development/modification efforts that comply with the organization's and IT's long- and short-range plans.
- Requires checkpoints at key decisions.
- Requires authorization to proceed with the project at each checkpoint.
- Is capable of being tailored/scaled to accommodate all types of development occurring within the organization.
- Is applicable to both in-house and purchased software creation and maintenance.

Testing Controls: Test that procedures for developing the IT quality plan include:

- Organization's long- and short-range plans
- IT long- and short-range plans for organization quality policy
- IT organization's quality plan
- IT configuration's management plan

The IT quality plan includes IT long- and short-range plans that define:

- Application systems development efforts and/or acquisitions
- Interfaces with other systems (internal and external)
- IT platform/infrastructure required to support the systems and interfaces
- Resources (both financial and human) to develop/support the targeted IT environment
- Training required to develop and support the targeted IT environment

PROGRAM DEVELOPMENT AND CHANGE

This section walks through five control objectives and their significance to the PCAOB and COSO guidelines. It provides a roadmap for the auditor to determine relevant control objectives in the Program and Development and Change section of COBIT. The discussion including the control objective, evaluation, and testing was adapted from ISACA'S COBIT 4.1 audit guidelines (ISACA 2007). This discussion format literally creates a work paper for the auditor to follow in the course of the IT audit.

It is important to note that several control objectives from the Program and Development and Change section of COBIT were not included in Table 10.5 because they are considered less material to the guidelines of the PCAOB or COSO for financial reporting purposes. The significance of COBIT to the PCAOB and COSO guidelines is in the view of the authors and not ISACA; they are included in this book as suggested guidelines.

Luther Sound Exploration Inc.: Acquire and Implement (Program Development and Program Change)*

Control Objective: Acquire or Develop Acquisition Software

What controls and activities provide reasonable assurance that application and system software effectively support financial reporting requirements?

Evaluating Internal Controls: Determine whether:

- Requirements must exist before development, implementation, or modification is approved.
- Approved user requirements in writing must exist prior to the development, implementation, or modification.
- A cost/benefit analysis ensures a sound economic outcome before programming begins.
- An acceptance plan for specific technology is agreed on with the supplier in the contract and this plan defines the acceptance procedures and criteria.
- Mechanisms exist to assign or maintain security attributes to exported and imported data.
- Testing requires system testing, integration testing, hardware and component testing, procedure testing, load and stress testing, tuning and performance testing, regression testing, user acceptance testing, and, finally, pilot testing of the total system to avoid any unexpected system failure.
- Facilities' acceptance tests guarantee that the requirements specified in the contract.
- Specific technology acceptance tests include inspection and functionality tests that demonstrate sound economic outcomes as well as functional IT controls.
- Software product acquisitions follow the organization's procurement policies, including the request for proposal, the selection of the software product supplier, and the negotiation of the contract.

Testing Controls: Test that:

- The new or modified system satisfies user requirements.
- Solution's functional and operational requirements are met, including performance, reliability, compatibility, and security.

---

* COBIT objectives are adapted from COBIT 4.1 (ISACA 2007).

- System weakness and processing deficiencies are identified, addressed, and resolved by the proposed new or modified system.
- Alternative solutions to satisfy the user requirements have been analyzed.
- Commercial software packages to satisfy the needs of a particular project have been identified and considered.
- All identifiable costs and benefits for each alternative exist and are included as part of the feasibility study.
- A risk analysis report of the security threats, potential vulnerabilities and impacts, and feasible security and internal control safeguards for reducing or eliminating the identified risk is accurate and comprehensive.
- Security and internal control issues are appropriately addressed in the system design documentation.
- Management gives approval that the controls planned and in place are sufficient, with appropriate benefits.
- Adequate mechanisms for audit trails exist or can be developed for the solution identified and selected.
- System design and development of screen layouts, report formats, and online help facilities integrate user-friendly designs to enhance end-user skills.
- IT adheres to common procedures and standards in the procurement of IT-related hardware, software, and services.
- A software purchase agreement allows the user to have a copy of the program source code, if applicable.
- Third-party software maintenance includes requirements for the validation, protection, and maintenance of the software product's technology acceptance plan, including inspections, functionality tests, and workload trials.

Control Objective: Acquire or Develop Technology Infrastructure

What controls and activities provide reasonable assurance that technology infrastructure and application and system software are acquired or developed to support financial reporting requirements?

Evaluating Internal Controls: Determine whether:

- Policies and procedures ensure that the organization's SDLC applies to both the development of new systems and major changes to existing systems, and accounting user participation is required for development.
- Management, user departments, and senior management sign off on design.
- Written program specifications exist for each information development or modification project and these program specifications agree with the system design specifications.
- Adequate mechanisms for ensuring internal control and security requirements exist for each new systems development or modification project.
- The internal control and security requirements include application controls, and guarantee accuracy, completeness, timeliness, and authorization of inputs and outputs.

- Applications program contains provisions that routinely verify the tasks performed by the software and provide the restoration of the integrity through rollback or other means.
- User approves application software after it is tested according to the project test plan using standards adapted before user testing approval.
- Adequate user reference and support manuals exist as part of every systems development or modification process.
- The system design is reassessed whenever significant, technological, and/or logical discrepancies occur during systems development or maintenance.

Testing Controls: Test that:

- The organization's SDLC ensures that all system design issues are addressed.
- System users are involved in the systems design process, design review, and approval process to ensure that all issues have been resolved prior to beginning work on the next phase of the project.
- Major changes to existing systems ensure the SDLC is comparable to the SDLC for the development of new systems.
- Appropriate sign-offs exist before programming starts.
- System file requirements and documentation, as well as the data dictionary, are consistent with standards.
- User sign-off on final file specifications occurs.
- Program specifications agree with systems design specifications.
- Data collection and data entry design specifications match.
- Application control design specifications ensure accuracy, completeness, timeliness, and authorization of inputs and outputs.
- Adequate internal control and security requirements exist in the conceptual design of the system.
- User reference and support materials and an online help facility exists.
- Help desk function assists users with more complex issues.

Control Objective: Develop and Maintain Policies and Procedures

What controls and activities provide reasonable assurance of the existence of policies and procedures that define acquisition and maintenance processes?

Evaluating Internal Controls: Determine whether:

- Evaluation plans exist to assess new hardware and software for impact on the overall performance of the system.
- Thorough testing of system software reflects the SDLC before it is introduced into the production environment.
- Software changes are consistent with the organization's change management procedures.
- Policies and procedures exist for the preventive maintenance of hardware to reduce the frequency and impact of performance failures.

- It adheres to vendor-prescribed preventive maintenance steps and frequency for each hardware device operated.
- Policies and techniques exist for using and monitoring the use of system utilities.
- Programmer responsibilities, including monitoring and logging exist for sensitive software utilities.

Testing Controls: Test that:

- Performance assessment results are compared to system requirements.
- Preventive maintenance schedule ensures that scheduled hardware maintenance will not have a negative impact upon critical or sensitive applications.
- Scheduled maintenance ensures that no conflicts exist with peak workload periods.
- IT operating schedules ensure that there are adequate preparations to accommodate anticipated hardware downtime for unscheduled maintenance.
- System software parameters ensure that the correct ones were chosen by appropriate IT personnel to ensure the integrity of the data and program being stored on the system.
- System software is in accordance with the acquisition and maintenance framework for the technology infrastructure.
- Thorough testing using SDLC occurs for all system software before it's introduced into the production environment.
- All vendor system software installation passwords are changed during installation.
- All system software changes ensure accordance with the organization's change management procedures.
- The addition of new users to the system and networks; database creation and backup; space allocation for data storage; system priorities, and so on are restricted to a limited number of systems operators within the IT organization.

Control Objective: Install and Test Application Software and Technology Infrastructure

What controls and activities provide reasonable assurance that the systems are tested and validated prior to implementation of production processes and the associated controls operate as intended to support financial reporting requirements?

Evaluating Internal Controls: Determine whether:

- An SDLC exists for system installation and accreditation, including a phased approach of training, performance sizing, conversion plan, testing of program, groups of programs and the total system, a parallel or prototype test plan, acceptance testing, security testing and accreditation, operational testing, change controls, implementation and post-implementation review, and modification.
- User training is part of each developmental effort.
- Program/system controls ensure security standards of the organization and IT policies, procedures, and standards.

- Predetermined criteria exist for testing success, failure, and termination of further efforts.
- Quality assurance process includes independent migration of development into production libraries and completeness of required user and operations groups' acceptance.

Testing Controls: Test that:

- A formal training plan supports all new systems development efforts.
- Staff is aware and understands need for SDLC controls and user training.
- Selected users' awareness and understanding of their responsibilities in the system's design, approval, testing, training, conversion, and implementation processes is known and acknowledged.
- Actual costs versus estimated costs and actual performance versus expected performance of new or modified systems are tracked.
- A test plan covering all areas of IT exists—application software, facilities, technology, and users.

Users understand all phases and responsibilities in the SDLC, including:

- Design specifications, including iterations during development
- Cost/benefit analysis and feasibility study
- Approval at each step of the SDLC
- Involvement and assessment of test plan and test results as they occur
- Approval and acceptance of system as it moves through development cycle
- Final approval and acceptance of system
- Assessment of training received for recently delivered systems for sufficiency

Control Objective: Manage Changes

What controls and activities authorize system changes of financial reporting significance before production?

Evaluating Internal Controls: Determine whether:

- Methodology for prioritizing system change requests exists and is in use.
- Emergency change procedures exist and are in use.
- Change control is a formal procedure for both user and development groups.
- Change control logs ensure all changes shown were resolved.
- User is satisfied with turnaround of change requests.

Changes on the change control log ensure that:

- A change that normally should create a new entry in the program and operations log actually occurred.
- Changes were made as documented.

- Current documentation reflects changed environment.
- Change process monitors improvements in acknowledgment, response time, response effectiveness, and user satisfaction.

Testing Controls: Test a sample of changes to ensure that management approves:

- Request for change
- Specification of change
- Access to source program
- Programmer completion of change
- Request to move source into test environment
- Completion of acceptance testing
- Request for compilation and move into production
- Overall and specific security has been determined and accepted
- Existence and deployment of distribution process

Review change control documentation for inclusion of:

- Date of requested change
- Person(s) requesting
- Approval of change request
- Approval of changes made to IT functions
- Approval of changes made originating from users
- Date of documentation update
- Move date into production
- Quality assurance signoff of change
- Acceptance by operations

Analyze types of changes made to system for identification of trends:

- Code check-in and checkout procedures for changes exist.
- Change control log ensures all changes on log were resolved to user satisfaction and that there were no changes made that are not on log.
- Users are aware of and understand need for formal change control procedures.
- Staff enforcement process ensures compliance with change control procedures.

COMPUTER OPERATIONS AND ACCESS TO PROGRAMS AND DATA

This section walks through 10 control objectives and their significance to the PCAOB and COSO guidelines. Table 10.6 provides a road map for the auditor to determine relevant control objectives in the Computer Operations and Access to Programs section of COBIT. The discussion including the control objective, evaluation, and testing was adapted from ISACA'S COBIT audit guidelines (ISACA 2007). This discussion format literally creates a work paper for the auditor to follow in the course of the IT audit.

It is important to note that several control objectives from the Computer Operations and Access to Programs to Programs and Data section of COBIT were not included in Table 10.6 because they were considered less material to the guidelines of the PCAOB or COSO for financial reporting purposes. The significance of COBIT to the PCAOB and COSO guidelines is in the view of the authors and not ISACA; they are included in this book as suggested guidelines.

Luther Sound Exploration Inc.: Computer Operations and Access to Programs and Data*

Control Objective: Define and Manage Service Levels

What controls and activities ensure that specified internal and external service levels exist and key performance indicators are monitored and evaluated regularly?

Evaluating Internal Controls: Determine whether a written service level agreement (SLA) supports an IT service with a third party:

- User participation ensures adequate creation and modification of agreements.
- Responsibilities of users and providers are defined.
- Management monitors and reports on the achievement of the specified service performance criteria and all problems encountered.
- Management reviews all changes.
- Recourse process is identified for nonperformance.

SLAs include but are not limited to:

- Definition of service
- Cost of service
- Quantifiable minimum service level
- Level of IT support
- Availability, reliability, capacity for growth
- Continuity planning
- Security requirements
- Change procedure for any portion of the agreement
- Written and formally approved agreement between provider and user of service
- Effective period and new period review/renewal/nonrenewal
- Content and frequency of performance reporting and payment for services
- Realistic charges compared to history, industry, best practices
- Calculation for services charged
- Service improvement commitment

---

* COBIT objectives are adapted from COBIT 4.1 (ISACA 2007).

Testing Controls: Test for a sample of past and in-person SLAs includes:

- Definition of service
- Cost of service
- Quantifiable minimum service level
- Level of support from the IT function
- Availability, reliability, capacity for growth
- Change procedure for any portion of agreement
- Continuity planning
- Security requirements
- Written and formally approved agreement between provider and user of service
- Effective period and new period review/renewal/nonrenewal
- Content and frequency of performance reporting and payment for services
- Charges that are realistic compared to history, industry, and best practices
- Calculation for SLA charges
- Service improvement commitment
- Both user and provider formal approval
- Appropriate users' are aware and understand SLA processes and procedures
- Users' sufficient level of satisfaction with current service level process and actual agreements

Control Objective: Manage Third-Party Service

What controls and activities exist to ensure that IT management selects qualified third-party service providers? The IT organization has a defined vendor selection policy and reports security, availability, and processing integrity for SLAs on a systematic basis.

Evaluating Internal Controls: Determine that IT policies and procedures relating to third-party relationships exist and are consistent with organizational directives and objectives. Management specifically addresses contracts the definition of what is included in the contracts, and identifies parties to the relationship:

- Contracts represent a full and complete record of third-party supplier relationships.
- Contracts are established for continuity of services specifically, and these contracts include contingency planning by the vendor to ensure continuous service to user of services.

Contract contents include at least the following:

- Formal management and legal approval
- Legal entity providing services
- Services provided
- SLAs, both qualitative and quantitative
- Cost of services and frequency of payment for services
- Resolution of problem process
- Penalties for nonperformance

- Dissolution process
- Modification process
- Reporting of service—content, frequency, and distribution
- Roles between contracting parties during life of contract
- Continuity assurances that services will be provided by vendor
- User of services and provider communications process and frequency
- Duration of contract
- Level of access provided to vendor
- Security requirements
- Nondisclosure guarantees
- Right to access and right to audit

IT management implements escrow agreements where appropriate.

Third parties are properly qualified through an assessment of their capabilities to deliver the required services.

Testing Controls: Test that:

- The list of contracts and the actual contracts in place is accurate and complete.
- No services are being provided by vendors not on the contract list.
- Contract providers actually perform services defined.
- Provider management/owners understand their responsibilities in contracts.
- IT policies and procedures relating to third-party relationships exist and are consistent with organizational directives and policies.
- Policies specifically address need for contracts, definition of content of contracts, owner, or relationship.
- Responsibility is defined as to who is responsible for ensuring contracts are created, maintained, monitored, and renegotiated as required.
- Contracts represent a full and complete record of third-party supplier relationships.

Contracts include at least the following:

- Formal management and legal approval
- Legal entity providing services provided
- SLAs, both qualitative and quantitative
- Cost of services and frequency of payment for services
- Resolution of problem process
- Penalties for nonperformance
- Dissolution process
- Modification process
- Reporting of service
- Roles during life of contract
- Continuity assurances
- User of services and provider communications process and frequency
- Duration of contract
- Level of access provided to vendor

- Security requirements
- Nondisclosure guarantees
- Right to access and right to audit
- Users' awareness and understanding of the need for contract policies and contracts to provide services

Appropriate independence between vendor and organization exists:

- Independence of vendor sourcing and selection processes is occurring.
- Security access lists include only the minimum number of vendor staff based on the least needed.
- Access hardware and software to organization resources are managed and controlled to minimize vendor use.
- Actual level of service performed compares highly to contractual obligations.
- Outsourcing facilities, staff, operations, and controls ensure required level of performance comparable to expectation.
- Continuous monitoring of service delivery by third parties exists.
- Independent audits of contractor operations occur.

Control Objective: Manage Performance and Capacity

What controls and activities ensure that IT management monitors system capacity and performance? IT management should take appropriate corrective action according to specified benchmarks within the SDLC.

Evaluating Internal Controls: Determine that:

- Time frames and levels of service are defined for all services provided by the IT function.
- Time frames and service levels reflect user requirements.
- Time frames and service levels ensure performance expectations of the equipment potentials.
- An availability plan exists, is current, and reflects user requirements.
- Management monitors ongoing performance of all equipment and capacity and lack of performance is addressed.
- Both users and IT review capacity and performance.
- Workload forecasting includes user input on changing demands and from vendors on new technology or current product enhancements.

Testing Controls: Test that:

- Statistics on performance, capacity, and availability reports are accurate, including historical versus forecast performance variance explanation.
- Change process for modifying availability, capacity, workload planning documents reflects changing technology or user requirements.

- Workflow analysis reports address opportunities of additional process efficiencies.
- Performance reporting to users for usage and availability exists, including capacity, workload scheduling, and trends.
- Escalation procedures exist, are being followed, and are appropriate in resolving problems.
- SDLC postimplementation phase includes criteria for determining future growth and changes to performance expectations.
- Levels of support supplied by the IT function are sufficient to support the goals of the organization.

Control Objective: Ensure Systems Security

What controls and activities ensure that IT management secures financial reporting systems and subsystems to prevent unauthorized use, disclosure, modification, damage, or loss of data?

Evaluating Internal Controls: Determine that a security plan is in place providing centralized direction and control over financial information system and subsystem security, along with user security requirements:

- Clear responsibility ensures only appropriate access to system resources.
- Data classification schema is in place and being used, and all system resources have an owner responsible for security and content.
- User security profiles are in place, representing "least access as required," and profiles are regularly reviewed by management for currency.
- Employee training ensures security awareness, ownership responsibility, and virus protection requirements.

Reporting exists for security breaches and formal problem resolution procedures are in place, including:

- Unauthorized attempts to access system
- Unauthorized attempts to access system resources
- Unauthorized attempts to view or change security definitions and rules
- Resource access privileges by user ID
- Authorized security definitions and rule changes
- Authorized access to resources
- Status change of the system security
- Accesses to operating system security parameter tables
- Cryptographic modules and key maintenance procedures, administered centrally and used for all external access and transmission activity
- Cryptographic key management standards for both centralized and user activity
- Formal change control over security software consistent with normal standards of the SDLC

The authentication mechanisms in use provide one or more of the following features:

- Passwords are not reusable.
- Multiple authentication is available.
- Ability exists to specify separate authentication procedures for specific events.
- On-demand authentication is used.
- Limitation set on the number of concurrent sessions belonging to the same user.
- At log-on, an advisory warning message appears to users regarding the appropriate use of the hardware, software, or connection.

Password policy includes:

- Enforced change on first use of password
- A minimum password length
- An appropriate and enforced frequency of password changes
- Password checking against list of not-allowed values exists
- Protection of emergency passwords
- User ID suspended after five unsuccessful log-on attempts
- Date, time of last access, and number of unsuccessful attempts displayed to authorized user at log-on
- Authentication time limited to 5 minutes, after which the session is terminated

Testing Controls: Test that IT function complies with security standards relating to:

- Authentication and access
- Managing user profiles and data security classifications
- Violation and security incident reporting and management review
- Cryptographic key management standards
- Virus detection, resolution, and communication
- Data classification and ownership

Procedures for requesting, establishing, and maintaining user access to system include:

- Procedures for external access to system resources exist (i.e., log-on, ID, password, dial-back).
- Inventory of access devices for completeness is maintained.
- Operating system security parameters are based on vendor/local standards.
- Network security management practices are communicated, understood, and enforced.
- External access provider contracts include consideration of security responsibilities and procedures.
- Actual log-on procedures exist for systems, users, and external vendor access.

- Security reporting occurs for timeliness, accuracy, and management response to incidents.
- Secret keys exist for transmission utilization.

Procedures for protection from malicious software include:

- IT tests all software for viruses prior to installation and use.
- A written policy ensures that guidelines exist for downloading, acceptance, and use of freeware and shareware.
- Users have instructions on the detection and reporting of viruses.
- A policy ensures that diskettes or USB drives brought in from outside the organization are checked.

Firewalls have the following properties:

- All traffic from inside to outside, and vice versa, must pass through the firewall.
- Only authorized traffic, as defined by local security policy, will be allowed to pass.
- The firewall is immune to penetration.
- Traffic is exchanged through the firewall at the application layer only.
- The firewall architecture combines control measures at both the application and network level.
- The firewall architecture enforces a protocol discontinuity at the transportation layer.
- The firewall architecture is configured according to the "minimal art philosophy."
- The firewall architecture deploys strong authentication for management of its components.
- The firewall architecture hides the structure of the internal network.
- The firewall architecture provides an audit trail of all communications to or through the firewall system and generates alarms when suspicious activity is detected.
- Organization's hosts are sitting outside the firewall.

Control Objective: Educate and Train Users

What controls and activities provide for identifying and documenting the training needs of personnel using IT to support business long-term goals and objectives?

Evaluating Internal Controls: Determine that:

- Policies and procedures exist for ongoing security and controls awareness.
- Education/training program focus on information systems security and control principles.
- New employees are aware of security and control responsibilities with respect to using and having custody of IT resources.

There are policies and procedures in effect relating to training and they are current with respect to:

- Technical configuration of IT resources
- In-house training opportunities and frequency of employee attendance [less likely for the SME]

- External technical training opportunities and frequency of employee attendance [more likely for the SME]
- A training function assessment of training needs of IT and user personnel with respect to security and controls, and translating those needs into in-house or external training opportunities

All employees attend security and control awareness training on an ongoing basis, including:

- General system security principles
- Ethical conduct related to IT
- Security practices to protect against harm from failures affecting availability, confidentiality, integrity, and performance of duties in a secure manner
- Responsibilities associated with custody and use of IT resources
- Security of information and information systems when used offsite

Testing Controls: Test to ensure that starting on the first day of employment, new employees have awareness and understanding of security, controls, and fiduciary responsibilities of owning and using IT resources:

- Employee responsibilities exist for confidentiality, integrity, availability, reliability, and security of all IT resources is communicated on an ongoing basis.
- A manager within the IT function has part or all of his or her responsibility for IT training, security and controls awareness, and maintaining continuing education program for professional certifications.
- Ongoing assessment of employee training needs is systematic.

Development or participation in training programs relating to security and controls is part of training requirements:

- Training programs for new and long-term employee security awareness exist.
- Appropriate employees sign confidentiality and conflict-of-interest statements.

Control Objective: Manage the Configuration

What controls and activities provide reasonable assurance of security, processing, and availability for the IT configuration and would prevent any unauthorized changes?

Evaluating Internal Controls: Determine that for configuration inventory—hardware, operating system software, applications software, facilities, and data files—onsite and off-site:

- Organizational policies and procedures exist relating to the acquisition, inventory, and disposition of purchased, rented, and leased computer-related equipment and software.
- Organization policies relate to use of unauthorized software or equipment.
- IT policies and procedures relate specifically to acquisition, disposition, and maintenance of configuration resources.

- IT policies and procedures for the quality assurance and change control functions exist for moving and recording migration of new and modified software development into production status and files.
- Accounting records exist for fixed assets and leases relating to systems resources.
- Reports relate to additions, deletions, and changes to systems configuration.
- Listings exist of various library contents—test, development, and production.
- Inventory exists of offsite storage contents—equipment, files, manuals, and forms—including materials in the possession of vendors.

Testing Controls: Test that:

- Process for creating and controlling configuration baselines exists and is reasonably appropriate.
- Process exists for controlling status accounting of purchased and leased resources.
- Individuals responsible for reviewing configuration control have the appropriate knowledge, skills, and abilities.

Control Objective: Manage Problems and Incidents

What controls and activities provide reasonable assurance that IT management responds to, records, resolves, or investigates for proper resolution problems and/or incidents?

Evaluating Internal Control: Determine that problem management procedures exist for defining and implementing a problem management system and recording, analyzing, and resolving in a timely manner all nonstandard events. In the SME, one individual is typically responsible for problem management and includes:

- Establishing incident reports that are appropriate for the size and scale of the SME.
- Identifying problem types and prioritization methodology allowing for varying resolution efforts based on risk.
- Defining logical and physical control of problem management information.
- Distributing outputs on a need-to-know basis.
- Tracking of problem trends to maximize resources and reduce turnaround.
- Collecting accurate, current, consistent, and usable data inputs to reporting.
- Notifying appropriate level of management for escalation and awareness.
- Determining if management periodically evaluates the problem management process for increased effectiveness and efficiency.
- Existing audit trail for system problems.
- Integration with change, availability, configuration management systems, and personnel.
- Establishing that emergency processing priorities exist, are documented, and require approval by appropriate program and IT management.

Testing Controls: Test that for a selection of problems reported, problem management procedures follow for all nonstandard activities, including:

- Recording of all nonstandard events by process
- Tracking and resolution of each and all events

- Appropriate level of response based on priority of event
- Escalation of problem for critical events
- Appropriate reporting within the IT function and user groups
- Regular review of process effectiveness and efficiency for improvements
- Performance improvement program expectations and success

Control Objective: Manage Data

What controls and activities provide reasonable assurance that data recorded, processed, and reported remain complete, accurate, and valid throughout the update, storage, and backup process?

Evaluating Internal Controls: Determine that:

For data preparation:
- Data preparation procedures ensure completeness, accuracy, and validity.
- Appropriate authorization procedures for all source documents exist.
- Separation of duties between origination, approval, and conversion of source documents into data occurs.
- Authorized data remains complete, accurate, and valid through source document origination.
- Data is transmitted in a timely manner.
- Periodic review of source documents for proper completion and approvals occurs.
- Erroneous source documents are appropriately handled.
- Adequate control over sensitive information exists on source documents for protection from compromise.
- Procedures ensure completeness and accuracy of source documents, proper accounting for source documents, and timely conversion.
- Source document retention ensures reconstruction in event of loss, availability for review and audit, litigation inquiries, or regulatory requirements.

For data input:
- Appropriate source document control ensures appropriate routing for approval prior to entry.
- Proper separation of duties among submission, approval, authorization, and data entry functions.
- Audit trail exists to ensure input.
- Edit checks of inputted data occurs as close as possible to the point of origination.
- Erroneously input data is handled appropriately.
- Responsibility for enforcing authorization over data is clearly delineated.

For data processing:
- Programs contain error prevention, detection, correction routines for all financial and financial subsystems (e.g. revenue, expense, inventory, etc.) in the enterprise.
- Programs must test input for errors (i.e., validation and editing).
- Programs must validate all transactions against a master list of same.
- Programs must disallow override of error conditions.

For error handling:

- Approval for correction and resubmission of errors.
- Individual responsibility for suspense files exists.
- Logs of programs executed and transactions processed/rejected for audit trail exist.
- A control group exists for monitoring entry activity and investigating nonstandard events.
- Counts and control totals exist for all data processed.
- All fields are edited appropriately, even if one field has an error.
- Tables used in validation are reviewed on a frequent basis.
- Written procedures exist for correcting and resubmitting data in error, including a nondisruptive solution to reprocessing.
- Resubmitted transactions are processed exactly as originally processed.

Testing Controls: Test that:

For data preparation:

- For a sample of source documents consistency is evident with respect to stated procedures relating to authorization, approval, accuracy, completeness, and receipt by data entry, and data entry is timely.
- Source, input, and conversion staff are aware of and understand data preparation control requirements.

For data input:

- Submit test data to ensure accuracy, completeness, and authorization-checks are performed.
- For selected transactions, compare master files before and after input.
- Error handling retention, resolution, and appropriate review integrity exists.
- Error handling procedures and actions comply with established policies and controls.

For data processing:

- Run-to-run control totals and master file update controls are effective.
- Test data ensures that data processing validation, authentication, and editing performs as close to the point of origination as possible.
- Error handling process conforms to established procedures and controls.
- Error handling retention, resolution, and appropriate review integrity exist and function appropriately.
- Error handling procedures and actions comply with established procedures and controls.

For data output, interfacing, and distribution:

- Audit trails facilitate the tracing of transaction processing and the reconciliation of disrupted data.
- Report output reviews by the provider and by the user ensure accuracy.

- Error handling procedures comply with established policies and controls.
- Procedures ensure that output reports are secure and awaiting distribution.
- Protection ensures sensitive information during transmission and transport.
- Disposed sensitive information procedures comply with established policies and controls.

Control Objective: Manage Operations

What controls and activities provide reasonable assurance that IT management executes program testing as planned, and identifies and investigates deviations from scheduled processing, including controls over job scheduling, processing, error monitoring, and system availability?

Evaluating Internal Controls: Determine that:

- Completion statistics confirm successful completion of all requirements.
- There are physical and logical separation of source and object, test/development/production libraries, and change control procedures for moving programs among libraries.

Performance statistics for operational activities include but are not limited to:

- Hardware and peripheral capacity, utilization, and performance
- Memory utilization and performance
- Telecommunications utilization and performance
- Extent that performance is matching product performance norms, internally defined performance standards

In addition, user SLA to:

- Maintain and review logs on an ongoing basis.
- Perform maintenance on all equipment in a timely manner.
- Ensure operators are rotating shifts, taking holidays and vacations, and maintaining competencies.

Testing Controls: Test that operations staff members are aware and understand:

- Operating procedures where they are responsible for performance expectations within the IT function
- Emergency program fix, along with restart/recovery procedures
- Operations logging requirements and management review
- Problem escalation procedures
- Turnover procedures for moving development programs into production
- Interaction with remote processing facilities and central processing facilities
- Responsibility for communicating productivity improvement opportunities to management

MONITOR AND EVALUATE

This section walks through four control objectives and their significance to the PCAOB and COSO guidelines. Table 10.7 provides a roadmap for the auditor to determine relevant control objectives in the Monitor and Evaluate section of COBIT. The discussion including the control objective, evaluation, and testing was adapted from ISACA'S COBIT audit guidelines (ISACA 2007). This discussion format literally creates a work paper for the auditor to follow in the course of the IT audit.

It is important to note that several control objectives from the Monitor and Evaluate section of COBIT were not included in Table 10.7 because they were considered less material to the guidelines of the PCAOB or COSO for financial reporting purposes. The significance of COBIT to the PCAOB and COSO guidelines is in the view of the authors and not ISACA; they are included in this book as suggested guidelines.

Luther Sound Exploration Inc.: Plan and Organize*

Control Objective: Monitoring

What controls and activities ensure that IT management defines performance indicators (benchmarks) and reports progress against those benchmarks frequently?

Evaluating Controls: Determine that:

▪ Data identified for monitoring financial and IT resources is appropriate.
▪ Key performance indicators and/or critical success factors measure financial and IT performance against predetermined levels.
▪ Internal reporting of financial and IT resource utilization (people, facilities, applications, technology, and data) is adequate.
▪ Managerial review of IT resource performance exists.
▪ Monitoring controls provide reliable and useful feedback in a timely manner.
▪ Response of organization to quality control, internal audit, and external audit improvement recommendations is appropriate.
▪ Target performance improvement initiatives and results exist.
▪ Organizational performance against stated goals of all groups within the organization is occurring.
▪ User satisfaction analysis exists.
▪ Reliability and usability of performance reporting for nonusers such as external auditor, audit committee, and senior management of the whole organization are sufficient.
▪ Timeliness of reporting allows for rapid response to identified performance shortcomings or exceptions.
▪ Reporting against policies and procedures established for the performance of activities (i.e., performance reporting) is sufficient.

---

* The evaluation and testing controls are adapted from ISACA's COBIT Audit Guidelines (ISACA 2000).

Testing Controls: Test that data performance monitoring reports exist:

- Managerial review of performance monitoring reports and corrective action initiatives is occurring.
- Employees are aware of and understand policies and procedures relating to performance monitoring.

Quality and content of internal reporting relates to:

- Collection of performance monitoring data
- Analysis of performance monitoring data
- Analysis of resource performance data
- Management actions on performance issues
- Analysis of user satisfaction surveys
- Senior management satisfaction with reporting on performance monitoring

Control Objective: Adequacy of Internal Controls

What controls and activities ensure that IT management monitors the design and operating effectiveness of internal controls? This control objective is very relevant to the SME.

Evaluating Controls: Determine that:

- Data identified for monitoring for financial and IT internal controls is appropriate.
- Internal reporting of financial and IT internal control data is adequate.
- Managerial review of financial and IT internal controls exists.
- Monitoring controls exist to provide reliable and useful feedback in a timely manner.
- Response of organization to quality control, internal audit, and external audit improvement recommendations is appropriate.
- Target internal control improvement initiatives and results exist.
- Organizational performance against stated goals of financial and IT internal controls is occurring.
- Information regarding internal control errors, inconsistencies, and exceptions is systematically kept and reported to management.
- Reliability and usability of internal control reporting for nonusers such as external auditor, audit committee, and senior management of the whole organization are sufficient.
- Timeliness of reporting allows for rapid response to identified internal control shortcomings or exceptions.
- Internal control reporting against policies and procedures established for the performance of activities (i.e., internal control reporting) is sufficient.

Testing Controls: Test that:

- Internal control monitoring reports exist.
- Managerial review of internal control reports and corrective action initiatives occurs.
- Employees understand policies and procedures relating to internal control monitoring.

Quality and content of internal reporting relates to:
- Collection of internal control monitoring data
- Internal control compliance performance
- Management actions on internal control issues
- Operational security and internal control assurance
- Senior management satisfaction with reporting on security and internal control monitoring

Performing:
- Benchmarking of internal control assessment against similar organizations or appropriate international standards/recognized industry best practices
- Review of relevancy of data within processes being monitored and in internal controls reporting
- Actual to planned internal control review in all IT areas
- Analysis of extent of accomplishment of internal control goals improvement initiatives
- Review of audit committee's satisfaction with reporting on internal controls
- Analysis of level of implementation of managerial recommendations

Control Objective: Independent Assurance

What controls and activities ensure that appropriate parties conduct and document independent control reviews of third-party service providers and major IT systems before implementation?

Evaluating Controls: Determine that:

- Independent assurance contracts are appropriately executed to ensure adequate review.
- Independent certification/accreditation exists or occurs prior to implementing critical new IT services.
- Independent recertification/reaccreditation of IT services is obtained on a routine cycle after implementation.
- Independent certification/accreditation is obtained prior to using IT service providers.
- Independent recertification/reaccreditation occurs on a routine cycle.
- Independent evaluation of the effectiveness of IT services occurs on a routine cycle.

- Independent evaluation of the effectiveness of IT service providers occurs on a routine cycle.
- Independent reviews of IT compliance with legal and regulatory requirements and contractual commitments occurs on a routine cycle.
- Independent reviews of third-party service providers' compliance with legal and regulatory requirements and contractual commitments occur on a routine cycle.
- Appropriate professional standards provide some level of assurance that the independent assurance staff is competent.
- Management proactively seeks out audit (including the outside financial audit team) involvement prior to finalizing IT service solutions.

Testing Controls: Test that:

- Senior management approves performance of independent assurance entity.
- Independent certification/accreditation occurs prior to implementation of critical new IT services.
- Appropriate to the size and scale of the SME's IT operations, independent recertification/reaccreditation of IT services occurs on a routine cycle after implementation.
- Appropriate to the size and scale of the SME's IT operations, independent certification/accreditation occurs prior to using IT service providers.
- Appropriate to the size and scale of the SME's IT operations, independent recertification/reaccreditation occurs on a routine cycle.
- Appropriate to the size and scale of the SME's IT operations, independent evaluation of the effectiveness of IT services occurs on a routine cycle.
- Independent reviews of third-party service providers' compliance with legal and regulatory requirements and contractual commitments are performed on a routine cycle and are comprehensive, complete, and timely.
- Independent assurance including that of the outside financial auditors are relevant with respect to findings, conclusions, and recommendations.
- Independent assurance function including the outside financial auditors possess the necessary skills and knowledge to perform competent work.

Control Objective: Internal Audit

What controls and activities ensure that the internal audit plan includes a risk assessment including IT and covers the full range of IT audit activities?

Evaluating Controls: Determine that:

- Audit committee exists with qualified personnel who understand financial, IT, and other matters pertinent to the SME.
- Internal audit organization is appropriately established with professional qualifications.
- External audits contribute to the accomplishment of the audit plan.
- Audit plan conforms to a risk assessment methodology.

- Audits are planned and supervised.
- Evidence is commensurate with findings and conclusions.
- Audit staff is competent and performing per the professional background of the auditor and professional financial and IT auditing standards.
- An adequate reporting process exists.
- Follow-up of all control issues is occurring in a timely manner.
- Audit coverage includes the full range of information systems and financial audits including COSO and COBIT.

Testing Controls: Test that:

- Senior management approves the performance of an ongoing independent financial and IT audit function.
- Senior management attitudes are consistent with financial and IT audit charter.
- Internal audit benchmarks against professional financial and IT standards.
- Assignment of auditors assures independence and sufficient skills.
- Ongoing improvements in financial and IT audit staff professional credentials is occurring.
- Audit report content is relevant to the recommendations.
- Follow-up reports summarizing timeliness of implementation exist.

 SUMMARY

In the last decade, the use of IT in enterprises has evolved rapidly from incidental use to pervasive use throughout the enterprise. Instead of a benign mainframe environment, IT now has to support a user-centered environment with multiple devices with access to server-based storage and processing. New development methodologies, integrated package suites, and new technologies create a situation in which IT units may have to interface with over 100 vendors (Rockart, Earl, and Ross 1996). COBIT 5.0 leads the governance discussion about how the successful enterprise must operate with IT leadership at the most senior levels of the enterprise. Effective IT leadership should reside at all levels of the enterprise and not just at the CIO level or lower.

Competent IT staff is essential to the health and well-being of the enterprise. Early in this chapter, the question "What is the competency of the IT staff?" was mentioned as being one of the most relevant questions the financial auditor should ask when discussing IT controls for financial reporting. The topic of IT "competency" has few benchmarks that are either widely accepted in the literature or widely understood. Few research papers exist on the competency of IT staff for the SME. The MM is one of those benchmarks describing business processes and competency and is among the most meaningful. Competency of the IT staff is the *starting point* for the evaluation of internal controls.

For the IT organization to be effective, Rockart et al. (1996) defined eight imperatives for the new IT organization. While an in-depth discussion of the eight imperatives is beyond the scope of this text, these imperatives are essential for an IT organization to be effective. If some or all of these imperatives do not exist or are impaired, it is very likely the internal controls for financial reporting do not exist or are only partially effective. The eight imperatives are:

1. Achieving two-way strategic alignment (i.e., IT strategy and execution aligns with the business strategy)
2. Developing effective relationships with line management
3. Delivering and implementing new systems
4. Building and managing infrastructure
5. Reskilling the IT organization
6. Managing vendor partnerships
7. Building high performance
8. Redesigning and managing the IT organization

Effective IT requires the complete integration and support of senior management as well as working relationships with line management. Without support from senior management, line management, and IT, it is very possible and even likely that the eight imperatives will not be accomplished. As referenced earlier, IT requires leadership at the governance level of the enterprise. Without effective governance, material internal control problems for financial reporting likely exist.

CHAPTER ELEVEN

Spreadsheet and Desktop Tool Risk Exposures

S PREADSHEETS ARE USED BY MOST companies, regardless of size, industry, geography, or the complexity of an entity's business model. While several different spreadsheet programs have been developed and remain in use around the world, Microsoft Excel stands as the dominant package in use as this book goes to press. The control procedures discussed in this chapter are sufficiently general, however, so as to apply to other spreadsheet applications.

While most of this chapter addresses spreadsheet application, we note that the control issues surrounding the development of applications by end users extend to other types of software platforms, such as, end-user databases (EUD) or specialized report writers (collectively referred to as *desktop tools*). In some instances these files have become so large and complex in an organization as to mirror a traditionally developed application.

Spreadsheets are used in everyday business to manage operations, create internal reports, and create primary and secondary external financial reports. Operations personnel use spreadsheets for tasks that might range from quality control, to managing research and development activity, to stochastic modeling, to compliance activities. Financial reporting personnel use spreadsheets to reconcile accounts, create or validate key financial calculations, or perform consolidation activities. Spreadsheet information is frequently uploaded to or downloaded from accounting information systems. Disclosures, footnotes, and supporting journal entries are typically created within spreadsheets. The information that resides within the spreadsheets is typically sensitive, confidential, or proprietary in nature. In addition, the financial information is frequently material in nature, which means that the values created or analyzed are of a significant financial amount that could lead to material misstatement in the event of an error. Thus, companies typically have a significant interest in ensuring the protection and reliability of sensitive spreadsheets.

SPECIFIC TYPES OF RISKS AND EXPOSURES

Spreadsheets create several types of challenges for management and auditors. Spreadsheets are typically user-driven, stored locally, and/or are outside of the control of the information technology (IT) department. This results in an "application" (spreadsheet) that is difficult to secure, audit, and maintain as opposed to a full-fledged software application that may have inherent or configurable controls around security and change management. While there are several frameworks and guidelines relating to spreadsheet use, most of these revolve around a handful of key risk exposures, identified and briefly defined in Table 11.1.

Although spreadsheets are not a risk exposure per se, management should maintain an inventory of spreadsheets that are risk-ranked on the basis of magnitude, materiality, and complexity. The spreadsheet inventory should identify the owner, purpose, location, and other characteristics.

Occasionally problems result from the migration of a file from one spreadsheet package to another (e.g., Lotus or Quattro to Excel). While many of these problems are

TABLE 11.1   Illustrative Spreadsheet Risk Exposures

Risk Exposure	Sample Problems
Logic and formula accuracy	Logic errors in formula construction may result in misleading or erroneous calculated values. Input, logic, and usage errors affect the ability for reliance on the data within the spreadsheet. Logic errors could result from incorrect formulas. The formula may have been incorrect from the beginning or inadvertently altered during a formatting change of the spreadsheet. Usage errors could include the misapplication of the spreadsheet functionality.
Data integrity	Input errors could include excessive manual entries; incorrect links from external sources, pivot tables, or other internal/external spreadsheets; importing incorrect data or wrong parameters; copy-and-paste errors; or unintended changes.
	Data may contain clerical errors. Imported text files may have been imperfectly converted to columns of data. Some numeric values may have been inadvertently formatted as text.
	Values that have been hardcoded into formula expressions (e.g., an embedded tax rate) can easily be overlooked when the spreadsheet is updated.
Versioning	Version control is essential to ensure that the current spreadsheet is updated with the correct information, and to prevent multiple copies of the same spreadsheet from being updated simultaneously, resulting in ambiguity with respect to the question of which version is the current "master" spreadsheet. Poor versioning could result in the use of outdated calculations or stale data.
Fraud	Spreadsheets can be easily manipulated if not protected. If a spreadsheet is not properly controlled, then a fraudster could potentially manipulate and affect the financial reporting process. The changes made by the fraudster may not be detected if spreadsheet changes are not logged or controlled. Note that the separation of data and operating instructions is far less formally defined and controlled in a spreadsheet than in traditional software applications.
Unauthorized users	Access to the spreadsheet needs to be protected to ensure that unauthorized users do not inadvertently change data within the spreadsheets or view the sensitive data within the spreadsheet. Access can be controlled by passwords to ensure that the location of the spreadsheet is protected.

limited to formatting and display issues, the IT auditor should be especially alert to the potential for integrity issues in files of mixed parentage.

RESEARCH ON ERRORS IN SPREADSHEETS

On an anecdotal basis, most spreadsheet users are familiar with the variety of spreadsheet errors and the frequency with which they are encountered in practice. Most of these typically arise from human sources, ranging from clerical miskeying to fundamental errors in logical thinking. As noted the following sidebar, "Material Deficiencies in Internal Control Related to the Use of Spreadsheets," a growing body of literature addresses the prevalence of spreadsheet errors. Groups such as the European Spreadsheet Risks Interest Group* maintain a list of horror stories that include items such as the following:

- "Britain's second largest drug maker AstraZeneca (AZN.L) was forced to reiterate its 2011 and midterm financial forecasts on Monday after inadvertently releasing confidential company information to analysts."
- "The London 2012 [Olympic Games] organizing committee (Locog) . . . [oversold four synchronized swimming sessions by 10,000 tickets] . . . when a member of staff made a single keystroke mistake and entered '20,000' into a spreadsheet rather than the correct figure of 10,000 remaining tickets."
- Other stories include a $6 million misstatement of cash because of a faulty link, underestimation of county tax in Kern County, California, because of "an experienced staffer who used the wrong spreadsheet to calculate Occidental Petroleum Corp.'s tax bill for property it owns in Elk Hills, California," and a $300,000 settlement of a pollution case that was "sparked by a math error" in a spreadsheet.

Material Deficiencies in Internal Control Related to the Use of Spreadsheets

There are material deficiencies in internal control related to the use of spreadsheets. A survey of public domain disclosures suggests the range of potential risk exposures related to the use of spreadsheets in various applications:

- Based on this evaluation under the COSO Framework, management concluded that our internal control over financial reporting was not effective as of December 31, 2007, because of the presence of material weakness. The material weakness relates to a misclassification of cash flows from operating activities, with a corresponding offset to cash flows from investing activities, in the statement of cash flows. The controls over the entry of data into a spreadsheet used in the preparation of the statement of cash flows and the monitoring thereof was not sufficiently precise to prevent the misclassification from occurring.—*Gran Tierra Energy, from Form 10K-A, dated 12/31/2007, Item 9A, Controls and Procedures.*

(continued)

---

*www.eusprig.org.

- The Company's monitoring activities were not effective at identifying, on a timely basis, deficiencies in the operation of controls in the financial statement close process. Specifically, the Company's procedures for the supervisory review of the performance by Company personnel of manual controls associated with account analysis and the verification of the accuracy of electronic spreadsheets that support financial reporting were ineffective. —*Online Resources, from Form 10Q, dated 9/30/2008, Part 1, Item 4, Control and Procedures*

- We failed to maintain proper spreadsheet controls at our Gavitec location. Specifically, critical spreadsheets are password protected and reside on a protected drive, but additional controls, such as critical cell formula testing and locking, logic testing, and input control are missing. Additionally, the Gavitec location did not have the Excel policy adopted last year at our headquarters. —*Neogenomics Inc., from 2007 10-K, dated 12/31/2007, Item 9a, Controls and Procedures*

- We did not maintain effective controls over the determination and reporting of the provision for income taxes and related income tax balances. Specifically, the requisite level of skills and resources in accounting for income taxes was inadequate and our procedures for preparing, analyzing, reconciling, and reviewing our income tax provision and income tax balance sheet accounts did not provide effective internal control. Spreadsheets supporting the calculation of income tax balances were inadequately controlled and were susceptible to manual input errors. —*Neenah Paper Inc., Internal Controls over Financial Reporting, from Form 10Q, dated 9/30/2008, Item 4, Controls and Procedures*

Spreadsheet Risk Vectors

The ease with which spreadsheet information can be manipulated or compromised makes it relatively easy for fraudsters to abuse spreadsheets and potentially remain undetected. Figure 11.1 presents three relatively distinct risk vectors that trail through different types of tasks typically performed through the use of spreadsheets. Spreadsheet risk exposures increase principally because of data features (quantity of data, number of links and references, likelihood of clerical input errors, missing data, etc.) or logical complexity (presence of complex formulas, esoteric functions, VBA code, etc.). Thus, simple invoicing or customer management files (α) require a different IT audit approach (e.g., cross-checks, additional footings,

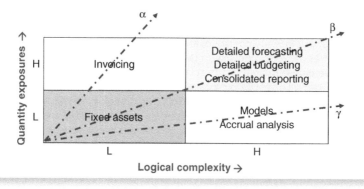

FIGURE 11.1 Spreadsheet Risk Vectors

Factors Affecting the Ability to Detect Spreadsheet Errors*

An extensive body of literature now documents the high likelihood of material errors in end-user spreadsheet models. Experts estimate that as many as one in every three spreadsheets have a major error in them (Creeth 1985). In one case, a Houston consultant found 128 errors in four of his client's multibillion-dollar spreadsheets (Simkin 1987). In another, a clothing manufacturer was lucky enough to discover a mix-up in formulas that resulted in a $1.5 million error (Ditlea 1987). In a third case, an error in a spreadsheet at Fidelity Investments resulted in a multibillion-dollar reporting error (Godfrey 1995). In a fourth case, the spreadsheet error in a Dallas oil and gas company's spreadsheet resulted in million-dollar losses and several executive dismissals (Hayen and Peters 1989).

These are not isolated incidents. In a study of large companies using large spreadsheets, for example, the researchers found that 90 percent of the models contained at least one calculation error (adapted from Freeman, 1996). Similarly, in a study by Galletta, Hartzel, Johnson, and Joseph (1996), 30 CPAs and 30 MBAs collectively missed 35 percent of the mechanical errors and 54 percent of the logical errors built into the six experimental spreadsheets. Summarizing nine studies involving spreadsheet modeling in the past 10 years, Panko (2005) computed an average error rate of 94 percent—that is, 94 percent of the corporate spreadsheet models included in these studies contained one or more material errors in them.

Ironically, the substantive likelihood of errors in spreadsheets is often matched by equally high user confidence that their models are error-free. In one study of 19 commercial spreadsheets, for example, Davis and Ikin (1987) found 4 that contained material errors, even though their developers were "very confident" that their spreadsheets did not contain any. In a second study by Panko (1999), subjects estimated that, on average, there was an 18 percent chance that spreadsheets contained an error, when in fact 86 percent of them contained errors. In a third study by Reithel, Nichols, and Robinson (1996), subjects expressed greater confidence in the accuracy of large, well-formatted spreadsheets over poorly formatted or smaller spreadsheets, despite the intuitive fact that larger spreadsheets are more likely to have errors in them. Finally, when 113 MBA students audited a spreadsheet known to contain exactly eight errors, Galletta et al. (1996) found that on average the subjects were only able to detect half of the mistakes.

The inexorable conclusions to be drawn from these observations are as troubling as they are self-evident: (1) many large spreadsheets are likely to have major errors in them; (2) most spreadsheet users express unfounded confidence in well-formatted spreadsheet models, even if they are seriously flawed; and (3) many spreadsheet users base major decisions on spreadsheet models, regardless of the models' accuracy. These risks are not likely to diminish in the future because the trend is for users to develop larger and more complex spreadsheets (Shaw 2004).

A study by PricewaterhouseCoopers suggests that corporate spreadsheet models are doubling in size and formula content every three years (Whittaker 1999). Although a growing body of research now documents the high incidence of mistakes in even the most critical spreadsheet models, little is known about what types of errors are most common or which individuals are most likely to either discover or overlook them. For example, although formula errors are likely to be the most important in spreadsheets (because they are often copied and therefore systemic), data-entry mistakes, clerical errors, or violations of corporate rules or policies are other examples of problems that can also produce flawed spreadsheet results. Similarly, although it is easy to suspect that novices are more likely to commit or miss errors than veteran users, it has been our experience that the

(continued)

reverse is often true. This is because novices are often more distrustful of spreadsheet results, and their very lack of confidence causes them to be more critical—and therefore more careful—in building or using spreadsheet models.

---

* H. Howe and M. Simkin. 2006. "Factors Affecting the Ability to Detect Spreadsheet Errors." *Decision Sciences Journal of Innovative Education* 4(1).

test decks) than that demanded by proprietary models or highly technical accrual analysis (γ) (e.g., independent verification of model logic by subject matter experts, stress testing, etc.). Some combination of both types of IT audit techniques is required when applications combine large quantities of data (e.g., GL balances from multiple subsidiaries) with logically complex instructions (e.g., VBA code to manage a rollup) (β).

Researchers have developed various taxonomies of spreadsheet errors* but there does not at present appear to be one dominant paradigm for categorizing errors.

Table 11.2 presents several real-world spreadsheet errors documented in public filings by a variety of companies. The defects highlight the intersection of technical and staffing issues.

TABLE 11.2 Sampling of Internal Control Deficiencies Relating to Spreadsheets

Defect	Company/ Source	Comment (text from 10Q or 10K)
Inadequate staffing and supervision	Global Immune Technologies 10Q 12/31/2008	*Lack of review over the financial reporting process that may result in a **failure to detect errors in spreadsheets**, calculations, or assumptions used to compile the financial statements and related disclosures as filed with the SEC.*
Change management	Eastman Kodak 10K 12/31/2005	*The company also reported that it has fully remediated two of the three previously disclosed material weaknesses, namely, the material weakness relating to the company's internal controls surrounding the accounting for pension and other post-retirement benefit plans and the **material weakness relating to the preparation and review of spreadsheets that include new or changed formulas**. The company also reported significant progress in remediating the previously disclosed material weakness surrounding the accounting for income taxes. The company continues to focus on improving its internal controls in this area and will continue to report a material weakness until it is fully remediated.*
Ineffective supervisory review	Online Resources 10Q 9/30/2008	*The Company's monitoring activities were not effective at identifying, on a timely basis, deficiencies in the operation of controls in the financial statement close process. Specifically, the Company's procedures for the supervisory review of the performance by Company personnel of manual controls associated with account analysis and the **verification of the accuracy of electronic spreadsheets** that support financial reporting were ineffective.*

---

* See, e.g., S. Powell, B. Lawson, and K. R. Baker. 2009. "Impact of Errors in Operational Spreadsheets," *Decision Support Systems* 47(2): 126–132, and S. Powell, B. Lawson, and K. R. Baker. 2008. "A Critical Review of the Literature on Spreadsheets," *Decision Support Systems* 46(1): 128–138.

TABLE 11.2 *(Continued)*

Disclosure controls	Carmike Cinemas, Inc. 10Q 9/30/2008	*We did not maintain effective internal control over financial reporting with respect to the application of GAAP as it relates to unusual and non-routine events or transactions such as long-lived asset impairment and GAAP disclosures; had inadequate processes to identify changes in GAAP and the business practices that may affect the method or processes of recording transactions; and had ineffective controls over **critical spreadsheets used in the preparation of accounting and financial information.***
Accounting process	Ceco Environmental 10Q 9/30/2008	*Based on this evaluation, such officers have concluded that these controls and procedures are not effective as of the end of the period covered by this quarterly report on Form 10-Q in ensuring that the information we are required to disclose in reports that we file or submit under the Exchange Act is **recorded, processed, summarized and reported within the time periods specified** in [SEC] rules and forms.*
Remediation via reduced spreadsheet use	Ceco Environmental 10Q 9/30/2008	*The Company has purchased and is in the process of implementing an integrated software system which includes industry standard and current best practice inherent controls. The new system is expected to address and remediate deficiencies including segregation of duties, security (through access restriction limited to job responsibilities), change control procedures, and **reduced use of spreadsheets in preparing financials.***
Disclosure controls	Neogenomics Inc. 10Q 9/30/2008	*. . . concluded that our disclosure controls and procedures were not effective . . . due to the material weaknesses . . . relating to . . . (iii) **failure to maintain proper spreadsheet controls.***
Controls over access and change	Canargo Energy 10Q 9/30/2008	*The Company did not adequately implement certain controls over information technology, including **certain spreadsheets, used in its core business and financial reporting**. These areas included logical access security controls to financial applications, segregation of duties and backup and recovery procedures. signed appropriately. This material weakness affects the Company's ability to prevent improper access and changes to its accounting records and misstatements in the financial statements could occur and not be prevented or detected by the Company's controls in a timely manner. As a result, misappropriation of assets and misstatements in the financial statements could occur and not be prevented or detected by the Company's controls in a timely manner.*
Spreadsheet-based consolidated reporting	Rock of Ages Corporation 10Q 11/7/2008	*Additionally, the Company does not utilize integrated financial reporting software to prepare consolidated period-end results which requires management to rely on **manual spreadsheets**, which are subject to error.*
Synergistic inadequacies in staff skill level and spreadsheet control relating to a specific account	Neenah Paper Inc. 10Q 9/30/2008	*We did not maintain effective controls over the determination and reporting of the provision for income taxes and related income tax balances. Specifically, the **requisite level of skills and resources in accounting for income taxes was inadequate** and our procedures for preparing, analyzing, reconciling and reviewing our income tax provision and income tax balance sheet accounts did not provide effective internal control. **Spreadsheets supporting the calculation of income tax balances were inadequately controlled and were susceptible to manual input errors.***

COMPLIANCE DIMENSIONS OF SPREADSHEET RISK EXPOSURES

Spreadsheet management is imperative for companies to comply with external regulations, minimize risk, and maintain efficient operations. This section briefly reviews some of the major compliance initiatives that a company probably has to consider.

Sarbanes Oxley

Section 404 of the Sarbanes Oxley Act (SOx) requires management to create, document, test, and maintain a system of internal controls for financial reporting. The intent behind this requirement is to reduce the incidence of fraudulent financial reporting. The SEC has encouraged a top-down, risk-based approach. A May 16, 2005, SEC staff paper, the *Statement on Management's Report on Internal Control over Financial Reporting*, states:

> An overall purpose of internal control over financial reporting is to foster the preparation of reliable financial statements. Reliable financial statements must be materially accurate. Therefore, a central purpose of the assessment of internal control over financial reporting is to identify material weaknesses that have, as indicated by their very definition, more than a remote likelihood of leading to a material misstatement in the financial statements. While identifying control deficiencies and significant deficiencies represents an important component of management's assessment, the overall focus of internal control reporting should be on those items that could result in material errors in the financial statements.

Data Privacy

There are several areas of data privacy that potentially interact with the many uses of spreadsheet software. These include the following:

Health Insurance Portability and Accountability Act*

While principally addressed to health plan administrators, health information clearinghouses, and healthcare providers that transmit information electronically, Health Insurance Portability and Accountability Act (HIPAA) "affects all businesses to some degree." "Under the Privacy Rule, covered entities and business associates are required to ensure adequate protection of all [sensitive healthcare] information. Specifically, HIPAA requires these organizations to . . . identify and protect such information

---

*Material in this section is based on M. Simkin and J. H. Yamamura. 2003. "What Businesses Should Know About HIPAA," *CPA Journal*.

[and to] establish policies and procedures to ensure that such information is disclosed only for authorized purposes."

Payment Cards

The Payment Card Industry Data Security Standard (PCI DSS) is an industry-developed standard designed to provide information security for businesses and other entities that process payment cards. Requirements include the use of firewalls, passwords, encryption, and restricted access. While many of these techniques and processes would be applied to customized software systems, the IT auditor should be alert to the role of spreadsheets as a potential weak link in a payment system.

Social Security Numbers

Entities collect Social Security data for purposes that include all aspects of employment (background checks, verification of eligibility), tax compliance, and any company benefit plans. Due to the increased levels of concern over identity theft, many organizations have substantially strengthened policies designed to protect this sensitive information.

While the development of tools that can search drives for potentially sensitive information is beyond the scope of this book, the following quote from a University of Michigan document* throws an interesting light on the challenges of designing and employing such tools:

> The use of tools that recursively traverse file trees, like many of the tools mentioned here, will destroy valuable evidence (file access times, at the very least) if special measures are not taken to protect it. Also, be aware that all of these (and similar) tools are not always accurate. They could find information that is not being sought (false positive), and they could fail to discover information that is being sought (false negative). It is extremely important to understand that simply because a tool appears to have found nothing, it does not mean that the intended information is not present. Additionally, none of these tools are designed to find information that has been obfuscated, encrypted, or intentionally hidden in any manner.

Sensitive Data and Password Protection

Any sensitive data can potentially be used in ways that have a variety of legal and/ or compliance implications—from misappropriated R&D information to earnings projections that might figure in an insider-trading scandal. While protection commands can reduce some of the inherent risks of storing sensitive data in a spreadsheet, they cannot entirely mitigate the exposure. (See Figures 11.2 and 11.3.)

---

*See http://safecomputing.umich.edu/tools/download/ccn-ssn_discovery_tools.pdf.

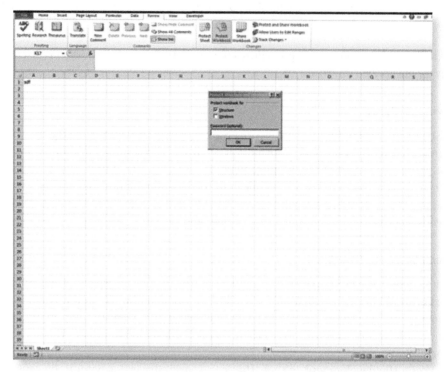

FIGURE 11.2 Applying a Password

Remove Excel Protection and Remove VBA Passwords

Now if you're trying to crack the password that is needed to open the Excel file itself, you will have to try out some other programs, which unfortunately are not free like the one above, however, there are your best chance at getting into that Excel file.

Excel Key recovers all types of passwords for Excel (xls) spreadsheet files including sheet, workbook, file open, etc. This program also works up to Excel 2007. You can download a demo of the program that will only display the first two characters of the password, however, this might be enough to jog some people's memory! If you still can't remember, you can buy it for $45.

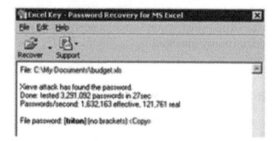

If you need to crack an Excel VBA password, you should check out VBA Key from the same company. It supports all office products including Word, Excel, Access, etc for VBA password recovery. It also supports multilingual passwords. It also costs $45.

Any other Excel password recovery tool you use that you would want to mention? Post a comment! Enjoy!

FIGURE 11.3 Breaking Passwords

Spreadsheet Engineering

The auditor should acquire an understanding of how important spreadsheets are developed within an organization. A framework for researching quality issues in spreadsheet design* suggests an auditing and review protocol for the portfolio of spreadsheets encountered in the field. This sidebar summarizes the major elements of the framework and relates these to audit questions. The framework elements from Grossman's paper are shown in bold type; the IT audit questions are provided in regular type.

■ *Principle 1: Best practices can have large impact.* What best practices in spreadsheet development are particularly relevant to files created for the organization, and how widely are they followed?

■ *Principle 2: Life-cycle planning is important.* Grossman observes that "every piece of software goes through a life cycle, starting with the conception of the software and ending the last time the software is used." Has management chosen a life-cycle model for spreadsheet applications? If not, "failure to choose a life-cycle model is itself a choice, often leading to *de facto* use of the undesirable 'code-and-fix' model with unfortunate and predictable consequences."

■ *Principle 3: A priori requirements specification is beneficial.* Are there mismatches between the requirements put forth by users and the degree of flexibility afforded by the organization's life-cycle model?

■ *Principle 4: Predicting future use is important.* Who is going to be using the model? Will it be used a few times only, by (an) individual(s) with expertise, or repeatedly, by a range of individuals with varying levels of knowledge and skill?

■ *Principle 5: Design matters.* What design principles are employed by individuals who create spreadsheets within the organization? Is there any attempt to design the application before attempting to code it? Is there a review process? What standard protocols are there for naming, use of color, structure, and so on?

■ *Principle 6: Best practices are situation-dependent.* How do specific circumstances within the organization affect best practices?

■ *Principle 7: Programming is a social, not an individual activity.*

■ *Principle 8: Deployment of best practices is difficult and consumes resources.* Grossman cites research supporting the view that "adoption of proven software engineering practices varies widely within and across firms." Does the entity evince a commitment at the managerial level to support a culture of best practices? The IT auditor should evaluate the entity's social environment and factors such as motivation, teamwork, selection, and training.

---

*T. A. Grossman, "Spreadsheet Engineering: A Research Framework," Proceedings of the European Spreadsheet Risks Interest Group Symposium, Cardiff, Wales, 2006.

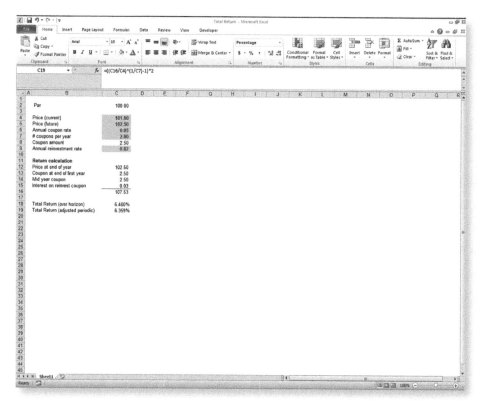

FIGURE 11.4 Sample Worksheet

SPREADSHEET AUDITING TOOLS

Many desktop applications include tools usable by the IT auditor for evaluating the logic and structure of an application. In Excel, the Formula tab provides a "Trace Precedents" function that when activated shows the cells referenced in a formula, as shown in Figure 11.5. The "Show Formulas" function facilitates a quick scan of a worksheet in order to determine which cells or ranges contain data or labels, and which contain formulas, as shown in Figure 11.6. Note that the spreadsheet adheres to a color-coding protocol for data and formulas.

Data cells can be analyzed for dependents with the "Trace Dependent" function, as shown in Figure 11.7.

The judicious use of range names for key cells makes it significantly easier to grasp the logic of a calculation, as suggested by Figure 11.8. Also illustrated in that graphic is the Name Manager, which provides a listing of all named ranges and the option to filter the list by various criteria, as shown in Figure 11.9.

Setting a watch window on a formula in one sheet that depends on inputs from another sheet provides the IT auditor with a tool that may be more efficient than opening multiple windows in order to view different tabs, or working against hard copy, as shown in Figures 11.10 and 11.11

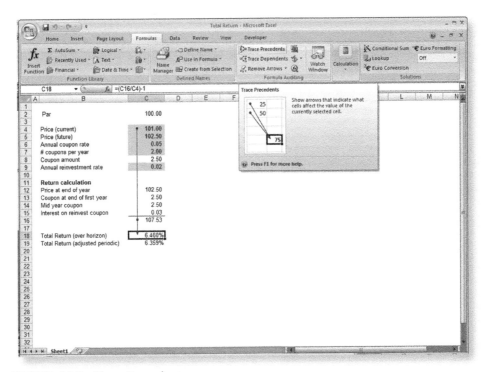

FIGURE 11.5 Show Precedents

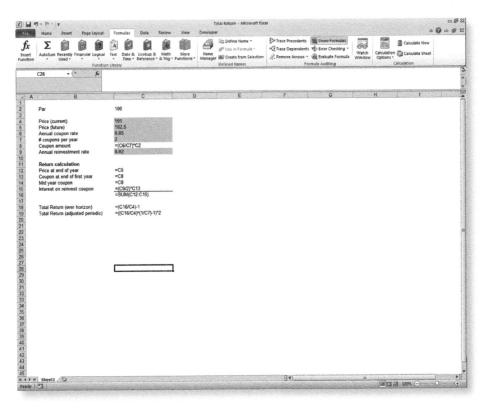

FIGURE 11.6 Show Formulas

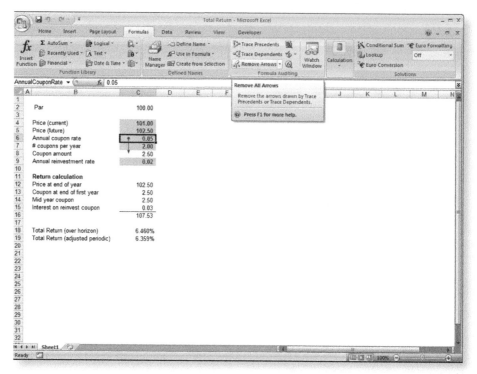

FIGURE 11.7 Show Dependents

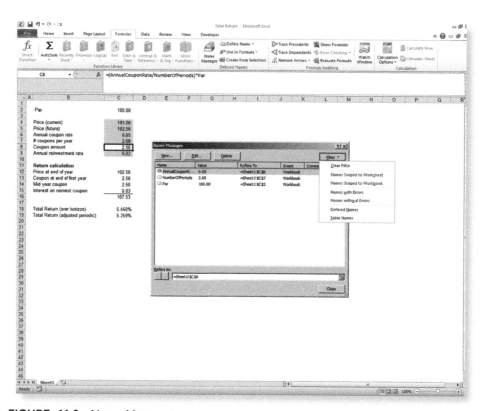

FIGURE 11.8 Name Manager

FILTER NAMES

Use the commands in the **Filter** drop-down list to quickly display a subset of names. Selecting each command toggles the filter operation on or off, which makes it easy to combine or remove different filter operations to get the results that you want.

To filter the list of names, do one or more of the following:

SELECT:	TO:
Names Scoped To Worksheet	Display only those names that are local to a worksheet.
Names Scoped To Workbook	Display only those names that are global to a workbook.
Names With Errors	Display only those names with values that contain errors (such as #REF, #VALUE, or #NAME).
Names Without Errors	Display only those names with values that do not contain errors.
Defined Names	Display only names defined by you or by Excel, such as a print area.
Table Names	Display only table names.

FIGURE 11.9 Filtering Names in Name Manager

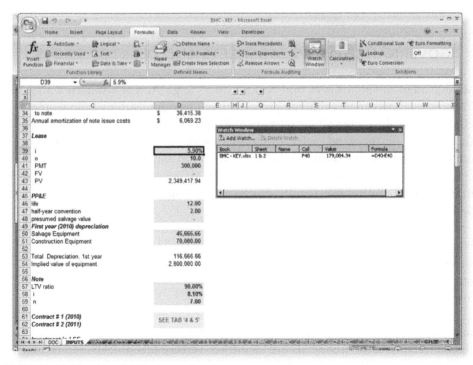

FIGURE 11.10 Watch Window

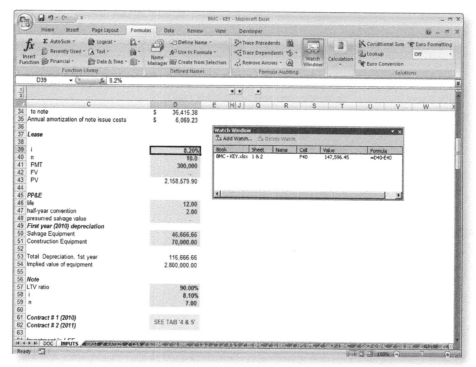

FIGURE 11.11 Watch Window with New Input

 GOVERNANCE OF SPREADSHEETS AND DESKTOP TOOLS

Management of spreadsheet and desktop tools (e.g., Access databases, Crystal Reports, queries) can be a difficult process. In many organizations, management is challenged in identifying all the relevant and critical spreadsheets and desktop tools that support the financial cycles. In some cases, this is because management does not realize that the spreadsheet is being used—for example, an ad hoc spreadsheet could be similar to the old fashion tape register. Management should also consider drafting a policy that specifically discusses the importance of spreadsheet and desktop tools governance.

To begin the process of identifying the spreadsheets and desktop tools that should be considered in-scope, management must first have a good definition of critical spreadsheets and desktop tools. One could define a tool that helps determine transaction amounts on the financial statements or amounts that affect management's decisions and analysis.

When management, the internal auditor, or the external auditor is identifying the scope of the audit, the financial cycles that are considered significant to the materiality of the financials are identified. During this process, management will identify manual controls and information technology controls that support the financial cycle. Just like management needs to identify the relevant information systems that support the financial cycles, management needs to identify the relevant spreadsheets and desktop tools that support the financial cycles. Management can ask the owners of the financial information how the financial information was calculated—that is, manually, via a spreadsheet, or via an application system. For example, in the financial reporting cycle, management may identify spreadsheets that are used to calculate amounts for footnote disclosures or complicated spreadsheets that are used in consolidations.

Management could identify critical spreadsheets and desktop tools that support internal or external financial reporting and safeguarding of assets.

Management would consider the following four questions:

1. Does the output impact financial reporting, budgeting, pricing, or payments?
2. Is the spreadsheet or desktop tool complex in nature?
3. Is the potential size of any error material to the financial statements, budget analysis, or pricing calculation?
4. Does the output have other downstream controls that adequately mitigate the risk of material misstatements?

Providing high-level scrutiny, maintaining logs and versioning records, storage on a separate drive, and other security measures are costly in ways that include direct outlay, use of company resources, and reduced employee productivity. Entities should reserve the high-risk protocols for applications that truly present a high risk, and not burden the security system with excessive procedural requirements. Figure 11.12 shows the decision logic for a sample application control policy for spreadsheets used in financial reporting or planning. While this drawing and the associated commentary focus on Excel files, the general policy could be readily adapted to other desktop applications, such as access interfaces or standalone databases, customized reports, and so forth.

The policy focuses on applications that are used for external reporting or sensitive internal planning processes (first decision node, "FS, B, P?") for financial statements, budgeting, pricing, or calculation support for any process that results in payments, whether these be to external parties (vendors, lenders, etc.) or entity employees. For applications that do not involve the previously mentioned processes, the policies described in Figure 11.12 are not applicable (NA).

The control policy contemplates a "medium" and "high" risk set of protocols. All payment-related processes are defined as high risk without exception or qualification. For the reporting and planning processes, subsequent decision screens evaluate whether the application is complex, whether potential misstatements could be material, and whether downstream controls exist that would detect potential errors. (These decisions might be based on other decision trees, or an overall scoring system, or expert judgment, or some other protocol.) Non complex applications, or those that would not produce material misstatements, or those subject to approved downstream controls would be assigned to the medium-risk category. Complex applications capable of producing material misstatements and not mitigated by approved downstream controls would be assigned to the high-risk category.

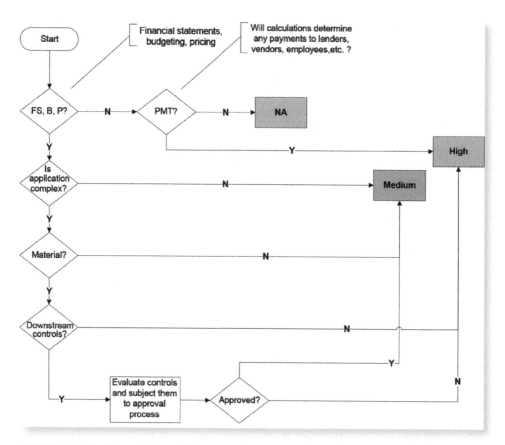

FIGURE 11.12 Sample Spreadsheet Applications Control Policy

The high-risk protocol might include the entire gamut of procedures available to mitigate application risks. A medium- or low-risk protocol would include some subset of these procedures. Not illustrated in Figure 11.12 is the potential use of risk-exposure subcategories. For example, within the medium-risk band there may be some applications that should be subject to segregation and access controls, and other applications where these restrictions would be superfluous or fail a cost/benefit analysis. Likewise, some of the procedures discussed earlier might apply differently for high- and medium-risk exposures. For example, change control for a high-risk application should generally include documentation, extensive testing, protection of sensitive formulas, and password restriction. Some of these procedures might reasonably be handled in a more relaxed manner for lower-risk applications. The IT auditor should assess the overall degree of security required for spreadsheet control policies and the entity resources devoted to these practices. A company policy that sets unrealistically high security levels for all spreadsheet applications may be exposing itself to the risk that not all stipulated policies will be followed because of limited time and staffing.

After management goes through the process of identifying the critical spreadsheets and desktop tools, management can capture the information in a data repository. Within the data repository, example information that should be captured could include:

- Name of spreadsheet or desktop tool
- Specific location of spreadsheet or desktop tool
- Last revision date and history of all changes
- Password used (indicate if a password exists—the actual password does not need to be recorded unless management needs a record of passwords in case personnel change)
- Risk level, including criticality and complexity of spreadsheet or desktop tool
- Purpose of spreadsheet or desktop tool
- Owner of the spreadsheet or desktop tool
- Location of source documents that support the information within the spreadsheet or desktop tool
- Frequency of use (e.g., daily, monthly, quarterly, annually)

After management has identified the spreadsheets and desktop tools, a process needs to be set up to manage the addition or discontinuance of spreadsheets and desktop tools within the organization. Some organizations have used quarterly or annual questionnaire updates to determine whether spreadsheets or desktop tools have been added or discontinued in the financial process. Whichever way management decides to manage this process, it needs to be well controlled, lest critical spreadsheets come to life after the initial inventory, without documented controls.

In addition, management should ensure that each spreadsheet and desktop tool has an owner with defined roles and responsibilities for the management of the spreadsheet or desktop tool. Too often, "applications" come to life without accountability.

CONTROL CONSIDERATIONS

Various organizations have provided thought leadership on risks and controls for spreadsheets and desktop tools. Example risk management guidance and frameworks have been provided by organizations such as:

- PricewaterhouseCoopers (PwC), "The Use of Spreadsheets: Considerations for Section 404 of the Sarbanes-Oxley Act" (2004b)
- Deloitte, "Spreadsheet Management, Not What You Figured" (2008)
- Protiviti, "Spreadsheet Risk Management" (2009)
- Microsoft, "Spreadsheet Compliance in the 2007 Microsoft Office System" (April 2006)
- Panko, "Spreadsheets and Sarbanes-Oxley: Regulations, Risks, and Control Frameworks" (2006)

Even though the guidance previously mentioned primarily focuses on spreadsheets, the same methodology could be extended to desktop tools such as databases. Therefore, the discussion in this chapter takes the generalized approach of using the spreadsheet guidance to apply to spreadsheets and desktop tools. Each of these provides guidance to management in how to govern risk and controls for spreadsheets and desktop tools. By comparing each of the guidance documents, the following control considerations should be evaluated for each critical spreadsheet and desktop tool. These include:

- **Logical security:** What prevents unauthorized access to the spreadsheets? Are passwords used? Is the spreadsheet located in a secure directory?
- **Change management:** What prevents unauthorized changes to spreadsheets? Are changes logged and monitored? How are errors prevented or detected?
- **Operational:** What ensures that the spreadsheets are backed up so they are available? Are spreadsheets appropriately archived in accordance with laws and regulations?
- **Business:** Does adequate documentation exist to support the spreadsheet? Does the spreadsheet support the needs of the business?

The control considerations can be further analyzed to illustrate what management could do to prevent, detect, or minimize the risks. With any risk within an organization, management has to decide if the cost associated with preventing, detecting, or minimizing the risk is in line with the financial wherewithal of the organization or within its risk tolerance levels. Financial information that cannot be secured runs the risk of being unusable to internal or external users without costly auditing and supporting evidence to validate that the data has integrity.

Organizations have also identified and used third-party software to manage spreadsheets and desktop tools. For example, CIMCON Software Inc. has a web-based solution called "SOx-XL" that manages the internal controls for spreadsheets. The software helps implement security and change controls to protect the spreadsheet. Workflow rules and tracking changes help manage the integrity of the spreadsheet. Depending on the third-party solution used by management, management needs to continue to be responsible for the controls around the spreadsheets.

Figure 11.13 depicts how the SOx-XL product manages the spreadsheet controls.

There are also software solutions that help manage desktop tools such as access databases. For example, SOx-XS is a web-based solution for access database controls. Security controls such as role-based signatures enable workflow security and track changes to help manage changes.

 ## AUDITING CONTROLS AND CREATING A BASELINE

After the inventories of spreadsheets and desktop tools have been risk-ranked, management needs to perform audit procedures to validate the logic and controls within the spreadsheet or desktop tool. Depending on the risk ranking, different procedures

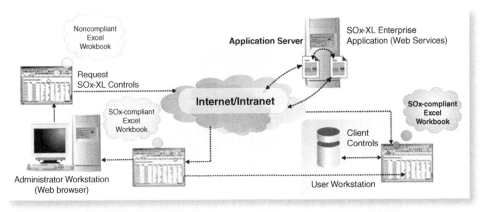

FIGURE 11.13 Web-Based SOx Tool for Spreadsheet Internal Controls

Source: www.sarbox-solutions.com.

may need to be performed. For high-risk spreadsheets or desktop tools, management will apply the maximum procedures to gain assurance that controls are in place. For medium-risk-ranked spreadsheets or desktop tools, fewer procedures will be performed. For low-ranked ones, management may elect not to test, or to perform a basic set of procedures.

Table 11.3 highlights proposed audit tests that could be done based on the risk ranking (the terms are further defined within the sections).

Table 11.3 illustrates the suggested controls and audit tests that should be performed depending on the risk ranking of the spreadsheet. If the spreadsheet (or desktop tool) is ranked as "low," management may decide to do no testing, from a risk acceptance standpoint, but management should consider implementing controls 1 through 5 in the table. If the spreadsheet is ranked as "medium," management should consider implementing controls 1 through 10. If the spreadsheet is ranked as "high," management should consider implementing controls 1 through 13. There may be other controls or tests that management may elect to perform based on internal situations, but these 13 suggested controls provide a baseline to get reasonable comfort with the spreadsheet.

Logical Security

Just like application-level security, security within spreadsheets is critically important to ensure that only authorized individuals have access to view, add, change, or delete data. Controls could include access control, security and integrity of data, segregation of duties, and password protection. The illustrated audit tests in the following include a sampling of potential audit steps that could be performed based on analyzing the various guidance previously mentioned. Management could elect to perform other logical security testing, depending on the overall environment.

As illustrated in Table 11.3, the following logical security controls should be put in place by management depending on the risk level of the spreadsheet or desktop tool:

TABLE 11.3 Audit Tests for Spreadsheet Applications

	Base (Low)	Increased (Medium)	Maximum (High)	Logical Security	Change Management	Operational Controls	Business Controls
1 Password protection	X	X	X	X			
2 Spreadsheet backup and storage	X	X	X	X		X	
3 Spreadsheet access	X	X	X	X			
4 Change approval and documentation	X	X	X		X		
5 Testing of changes	X	X	X		X		
6 Spreadsheet access review		X	X	X			
7 Spreadsheet logic review		X	X		X		
8 Cell protection		X	X	X	X		
9 Historical files		X	X			X	
10 Naming conventions		X	X				X
11 Input fields and formulas			X	X	X		X
12 Access administration			X	X			
13 Testing signoff			X		X		
Counts				7	6	2	2

Source: Adapted from material from Tom Poe, Hudson Consulting Services, 2009.

▪ **Password protection:** This is defined as "Files are password protected (modify) to prevent unauthorized changes." This definition could be extended to mean that the spreadsheet or desktop tool needs to have adequate password security with reasonable password configuration settings to ensure authorized access to the specific file and to key cells or data points within the file. Regardless of the risk ranking of the spreadsheet, passwords should exist to protect the spreadsheet or desktop tool. Many times, passwords in spreadsheets are simple and could be hacked. Management could consider using operating system or windows directory controls to prevent unauthorized access by controlling read/write privileges. Management should also reinforce policies and procedures that underscore the importance of not sharing passwords.

▪ **Spreadsheet backup and storage:** This is defined as "Store spreadsheets in a network folder that is backed up daily." This definition could be extended to mean, from a logical security perspective, that the spreadsheet should be stored in a secure location that can be accessed only by authorized personnel. Some companies have accomplished this by using a common server to house the critical spreadsheets and restricting access rights to that server.

▪ **Spreadsheet access:** This is defined as "Store spreadsheets on limited-access shared drive." This definition could be extended to mean that windows directories could be used to store the spreadsheet and the access to the folders can be restricted to authorized personnel.

▪ **Spreadsheet access review:** This is defined as "Periodically review spreadsheet access." This definition could be extended to mean that management on a quarterly, semiannual, or annual basis should get a listing of the individuals that have system access rights to the spreadsheets to determine if the access is appropriate. To have good segregation of duties to begin with, management needs to ensure that the spreadsheet creators/owners, supervisor reviews, and users of the spreadsheets each have a segregated role. These roles would be reviewed during the periodic review.

▪ **Cell protection:** This is defined as "Maintain cell protection to prevent formula overrides." This definition could be extended to mean the cells need to be protected so inadvertent or purposeful changes are not made. By locking the cells, management can ensure that certain cells cannot be altered without a password. This can help protect sensitive data, formulas, and calculations.

▪ **Input fields and formulas:** This is defined as "Separate and color code input fields and formulas—Break complex calculations into smaller pieces." This definition could be extended to mean that we need to control logical access to who can input data into the fields and alter the formulas.

▪ **Access administration:** This is defined as "Require documented management approval to add/delete/change user access." This definition could be extended to mean that management needs to have a robust process to who has access to the spreadsheets, a robust process for granting initial access to the spreadsheet and removing individuals who no longer need the access. In systems, forms are usually completed with data owners signing off on the access to the data.

The following pages present select security subtopics identified within some of the spreadsheet guidance documents from PwC and Deloitte for further review. The selection of these subtopics does not indicate that these are the only security control considerations, but provides an illustration of security controls that management should consider for further analysis, depending on the risk level of the spreadsheet or desktop tool.

Access Control (PwC, Deloitte)

Access control is simply *how* a company protects access to the spreadsheet or desktop tool. PwC defines it as "Limiting access at the file level to spreadsheets on a central server and assigning appropriate rights" (e.g., Create, Read, Update, and Delete). Spreadsheets can also be password protected to restrict access. Deloitte defines it as "Spreadsheet files should be protected with some form of access control." Users without a business need to open the spreadsheet should be prevented from doing so. This can be done by restricting access to the file itself, or the folder in which the spreadsheet is stored.

When testing for access control, management should ask:

- Who has access to this spreadsheet?
- Is the spreadsheet stored on someone's computer or on the network?
- How is access managed?
- Do you have to know a password to access the spreadsheet? If so, how often is the password changed? Who knows the password?

When testing for access control, management could identify the users that have access to where the spreadsheet resides, and determine if the access is appropriate. For example, some clients will store the spreadsheet on a network folder that is accessible by all employees. When this happens, control is potentially compromised. Management could also attempt to open the spreadsheet without a password. It may be possible to open the file in read-only, save it to a hard-drive, make changes, and then save the file back to the network folder. This circumvents the use of passwords.

Security and Integrity of Data (PwC)

Security and integrity of data is simply the protection of data within a spreadsheet. PwC defines it as "Implementing a process to ensure that data embedded in spreadsheets is current and secure. This can be done by 'locking' or protecting cells to prevent inadvertent or intentional changes to standing data. In addition, the spreadsheets themselves should be stored in protected directories."

When testing for security and integrity of data, management should ask:

- Are cells in the spreadsheets protected?
- Are passwords used to protect the cell?
- Does each person who has access to the spreadsheet know the password for each cell protection, or is this on a need-to-know-basis?

When testing for security and integrity of data, management could identify cells that are cell protected, or attempt to change the cell to see if a password is required.

Segregation of Duties/Roles and Procedures (PwC)

Segregation of duties (SOD) is simply ensuring that only appropriate individuals have access to the spreadsheets or desktop tools. PwC defines it as "Defining and implementing roles, authorities, responsibilities and procedures for issues such as ownership, signoff, segregation of duties and usage."

When testing for segregation of duties/roles and procedures, management should ask:

■ Who manages the process to grant access to this spreadsheet?
■ What roles and procedures have been defined for the use of the spreadsheet?

When testing for segregation of duties/roles and procedures, management could obtain the documentation showing that roles and responsibilities around the spreadsheet have been defined to determine if SOD conflicts exist.

Noninput-Related Spreadsheet Fields Are Password Protected (Deloitte)

Noninput-related spreadsheet fields refers to the protection of cells that perform calculations but do not need to be routinely updated. Deloitte says, "All fields, such as formulas, that do not need to be edited by the end user, but are necessary for the accurate employment of the spreadsheet, should be password protected to prevent unauthorized changes."

When testing for noninput-related spreadsheet fields protection, management should ask:

■ Are cells that do not need editing protected from accidental changes?
■ How does management ensure that cells are protected from accidental changes?

When testing for noninput-related spreadsheet fields protection, management should review the spreadsheet and identify cells that do not need editing and determine whether they are protected from accidental changes.

Change Management

Spreadsheets and desktop tools do not typically have automated mechanisms to control and log changes made. Changes are typically manually recorded. This is where management may elect to use third-party software to manage the changes. If a third-party tool is not used, management needs to implement a process to ensure that only appropriate changes are made and are well-controlled.

As illustrated in Table 11.3, the following change management controls should be put in place by management, depending on the risk level of the spreadsheet or desktop tool:

■ **Change approval and documentation:** This is defined as "Change requirements are formally requested, documented, and approved." This definition could be extended to mean that management needs to ensure that a clear process is documented where any change goes through formal documentation, which requires approval. This is important to ensure an independent approval is obtained to validate the need for changes to high-risk spreadsheets that may contain material formulas or logic.

▪ **Testing of changes:** This is defined as "Changes are independently tested and the test results are documented." This definition could be extended to mean that management should have a process in place to ensure adequate testing of changes made to a spreadsheet prior to the official change. Management could take a copy of the spreadsheet and make the change to see if the change was successful. Then the change could be redone in the production version of the spreadsheet or the test spreadsheet could be copied into production as the new master, assuming no other changes occurred. Management should ensure that adequate testing of changes has occurred in a secured, nonproduction environment, with the changes documented. This means that management should make the changes outside the master spreadsheet first to ensure the changes do not affect the integrity of the spreadsheet or desktop tool. When changes are made, management should update a manual log or automated system log if using third-party software. The log should include the name, date, testing method, and description of the change. This log becomes the history of the spreadsheet or desktop tool. Unfortunately, changes could be made that are not logged and this needs to be mitigated by good review processes of comparing prior spreadsheet or desktop tool versions to current versions for deltas.

▪ **Spreadsheet logic review:** This is defined as "Periodically review spreadsheet calculations to ensure logic is correct." This definition could be extended to mean management should turn on auditing to track changes that could reduce the accidental copy-and-paste errors and enable the reverting back to earlier versions. Auditing could be enabled in some third-party software. For logic inspection control, periodic reviews of the logic should be performed by an independent party to ensure no unauthorized changes have occurred.

▪ **Cell protection:** This is defined as "Maintain cell protection to prevent formula overrides." This definition could be extended to mean that management should ensure the specific protection of specific cells within a spreadsheet. Cell protection is typically seen as a security control, but it could be a change management control in the sense that cells and worksheets on templates that are not to be modified should be locked and only authorized individuals (e.g., spreadsheet creators) should know passwords that could unlock cells.

▪ **Input fields and formulas:** This is defined as "Separate and color code input fields and formulas—Break complex calculations into smaller pieces." This definition could be extended to mean that management should control how data is entered into a spreadsheet to reduce the likelihood of error. Management could consider having standardized templates with formatting, formulas, and logic in place. There could be a tab for all inputs and the following tabs could be the results that are formula driven. This could make data entry simpler, and reduce the risk of error. To validate input control, management should perform reconciliations of data back to source documents. Management needs to ensure that any data transferred between systems is accurate and complete.

- **Testing signoff:** This is defined as "Formal sign-off on testing and results by management prior to implementation." This definition could be extended to mean that testing needs to be signed-off on by the tester and by the end user to ensure that the change meets the need. Sometimes, this may be the same person in small environments.

Next, select change management subtopics were identified within some of the spreadsheet guidance documents from PwC and Deloitte for further review. The selection of these subtopics does not indicate that these are the only change management control considerations, but provides an illustration of the change management controls that management should consider for further analysis, depending on the risk level of the spreadsheet or desktop tool.

Change Control (PwC, Deloitte)

Change control is simply ensuring that only authorized changes have been made to the spreadsheet or desktop tool. PwC defines it as "Maintaining a controlled process for requesting changes to a spreadsheet, making changes and then testing the spreadsheet and obtaining formal signoff from an independent individual that the change is functioning as intended." Deloitte defines it as "All changes to a spreadsheet are reviewed and approved. Someone other than the party making the change should perform this. The review process should guide the reviewer to confirm that the changes are functioning in accordance with management's intentions, and the integrity of the spreadsheet's formulas, data, and results have not been compromised."

When testing for change control, management should ask:

- How are changes to the spreadsheet managed?
- Are only certain people able to make changes?

When changes need to occur, how does management ensure that the changes did not affect the integrity of the spreadsheet? When testing for change control, management could determine:

- Whether management has a listing of changes made to spreadsheets to determine if a change control process was followed
- Whether a listing of changes exists, and obtain support that shows a change process was followed
- Whether a listing is not available, as there will be a need to focus more on analyzing the data within the spreadsheet as if no change controls existed

Version Control (PwC, Deloitte)

Version control is simply ensuring that the master spreadsheet or desktop tool is updated and copies of spreadsheets or desktop tools are not inadvertently updated, resulting in an incomplete master copy. PwC defines it as "Ensuring only current and approved versions of spreadsheets are being used by creating naming conventions and directory structures." Deloitte defines it as "Versioning should be employed in all spreadsheet changes. Changes to a spreadsheet should include some form of unique identifier that can be used by parties to differentiate versions of the spreadsheet."

When testing for version control, management should ask:

- How does management differentiate between versions of the spreadsheets?
- Does management save multiple copies during the creation process?
- If a spreadsheet were to become corrupt, would management have a prior version to rely on?

When testing for version control, management could identify spreadsheets and determine if multiple versions are being used, or identify how management names the various versions. Note that if management does not maintain multiple versions, this does not affect the integrity of the spreadsheet, but poses a risk in case of spreadsheet loss or corruption.

Input Control (PwC, Deloitte)

Input control is simply ensuring that data is input completely and accurately. PwC defines it as "Ensuring that reconciliations occur to make sure that data is inputted completely and accurately. Data may be inputted into spreadsheets manually or systematically through downloads." Deloitte defines it as "The validity of spreadsheet inputs should be ascertained. Whether input data is manually keyed or imported, steps should be taken to confirm input data being imported into the spreadsheet is complete and accurate." Management needs to validate inputs. This involves comparing the input data in the file to the actual source where the data came from to verify that the data made the transition completely and accurately.

When testing for input control, management should ask:

- How does management ensure the integrity of the data being input?
- Are there reviews of data input into spreadsheets for completeness and accuracy?
- If inputs are coming from a system, what does management do to verify that the information coming from the system download was complete and accurate?

When testing for input control, management could review its process for controlling inputs; review reconciliations, if available; or review the controls around any interfaces if the data is input from a non-manual source. Determine the security and change control processes around the interface or system download.

Development Life Cycle (PwC)

Development life cycle is simply ensuring that management has a process to create new spreadsheets or desktop tools to further ensure that they follow a common process. PwC defines it as "Applying a standard software development life cycle to the development process of the more critical and complex spreadsheets covering standard phases: requirements, specification, design, building, testing, and maintenance. Testing is a critical control to ensure that the spreadsheet is producing accurate and complete results."

When testing for software development life cycle, management should ask:

■ Does management have a process in place that governs the creation of new spreadsheets to ensure that adequate controls are installed from the beginning?

When testing for software development life cycle, management could review the policies and procedures regarding new spreadsheet development, or review new spreadsheets to determine if the process was followed.

Logic Inspection (PwC)

Logic inspection is simply ensuring that the formulas and calculations in the spreadsheet are set up correctly. PwC defines it as "Inspecting the logic in critical spreadsheets by someone other than the user or developer of the spreadsheet. This review should be formally documented." Management should verify formulas are functioning in accordance with management's intentions: This is accomplished by first gaining an understanding of the purpose of the various formulas found throughout the spreadsheet, and then examining them to verify that they were configured accurately.

When testing for logic inspection, management should ask:

■ Does management have a process in place that ensures that the formulas, the pivot tables, and so on are correct? That is, was the function used correctly?

When testing for logic inspection, management could review a sample of formulas to determine if the calculation is correct.

Operational Controls

Operational controls are typically in place to support the primary accounting information systems. However, some organizations fail to specifically ensure that the operational controls cover the critical spreadsheets and desktop tools. The operational controls discussed next need to be put in place to protect the spreadsheets and desktop tools.

As illustrated in Table 11.3, the following operational controls should be put in place by management depending on the risk level of the spreadsheet or desktop tool:

■ **Spreadsheet backup and storage:** This is defined as "Store spreadsheets in a network folder that is backed up daily." This definition could be extended to mean, from an operations standpoint, ensuring the continual backup of the spreadsheets so that they are available when needed. Therefore, management should check that backups are performed frequently. Depending on the use of the spreadsheet, management may have various data retention policies to follow (internal or external regulatory). Management can identify the location of the spreadsheet data and ensure that that folder is captured in the backup process. Backups should be done (ideally) on a daily basis.

- **Historical files:** This is defined as "Maintain and segregate historical files from those currently in use." This definition could be extended to mean management needs to have a robust process to segregate retired or previous copies of spreadsheets in a secure location for a designated period of time to meet historical needs or regulatory data retention requirements. The spreadsheets should be maintained in a read-only state so they cannot be manipulated.

In the following pages, select operational controls subtopics were identified within some of the spreadsheet guidance documents from PwC and Deloitte for further review. The selection of these subtopics does not indicate that these are the only operational control considerations, but provides an illustration of operational controls that management should consider for further analysis, depending on the risk level of the spreadsheet or desktop tool.

Backups (PwC, Deloitte)

Backups are a critical operational control. A backup guarantees that the current copy of the data is safeguarded in case of loss or inadvertent change, which results in the need of recovering a copy of the spreadsheet or desktop tool. Backups may be performed for the accounting system, but what happens if a spreadsheet is lost? Does management know which backup tape has the spreadsheet so it can be recovered (assuming it was ever backed up)? PwC defines it as "Implementing a process to back up spreadsheets on a regular basis so that complete and accurate information is available for financial reporting." Deloitte defines it as "Spreadsheet files are backed up to external media. The frequency of the file backups should be sufficient to support business data recovery needs."

When testing for backups, management should ask:

- Where does management back up the spreadsheet?
- Is the backup part of the normal backup procedures?
- Could management easily recover a prior spreadsheet version from a backup if needed?

When testing for backups, management could identify the specific file path where the spreadsheet is located and determine if that particular file path is included in a backup.

Archiving (PwC)

Archiving is the process of keeping historical copies (snapshots) of the spreadsheets or desktop tool data at specified points in time (e.g., monthly, annually) for historical purposes. PwC defines it as "Maintaining historical files no longer available for update in a segregated drive and locking them as read only."

When testing for archiving, management should ask:

- Does management archive old spreadsheets?
- How does management archive old spreadsheets?

When testing for archiving, management could obtain a listing of archived spreadsheets to see if process is followed. Note that even if old spreadsheets are not archived, this does not affect the reliability of current-year spreadsheets.

Spreadsheets Should Reside on File Servers (Deloitte)

The location of the spreadsheet is critical to how it can be managed. Spreadsheets that are located on local hard drives or thumb drives may not have the ability to be secured or backed up in the same manner as a spreadsheet that resides on the server. Deloitte defines it as "Spreadsheets should reside on file servers. The primary copies of critical spreadsheets should not reside on portable or end-user computers." However, the primary purpose here is that the spreadsheet is accessible by those who need it, and is properly backed up.

When testing for file servers, management should ask whether or not:

▪ Management allows spreadsheets to be stored on personal hard drives, or on mobile media.

Note that even if spreadsheets are stored on portable media, the policy should ensure that the spreadsheet is accessible and safe.

Business Controls

Beyond typical information technology (IT) controls of logical security, change control, and operational controls, management needs to ensure that adequate business controls are in place to protect the spreadsheets and desktop tools.

As illustrated in Table 11.3, the following business controls should be put in place by management, depending on the risk level of the spreadsheet or desktop tool:

▪ **Naming conventions:** This is defined as "Implement and maintain spreadsheet naming conventions." This definition could be extended to mean that management needs to enforce common protocols and standards for spreadsheet names to ensure that the titles are easily understood. Some companies use a format that denotes the fiscal year-end at the end of the name. Also to ensure version control, management could use some versioning software or have the naming convention specify the version of the spreadsheet.
▪ **Input fields and formulas:** This is defined as "Separate and color code input fields and formulas—Break complex calculations into smaller pieces." This definition could be extended to mean management could code certain input fields to help with the data entry process. This could help with easier review to identify errors in formulas, logic, or data. This could also help with data analytics in reconciling the data back to source documentation.

In the following sections, select business control subtopics were identified within some of the spreadsheet guidance documents from PwC for further review. The selection of these subtopics does not indicate that these are the only business control considerations, but provides an illustration of business controls that management should consider for further analysis, depending on the risk level of the spreadsheet or desktop tool.

Documentation (PwC)

Documentation is a key part in maintaining the integrity of a spreadsheet or desktop tool. Personnel may change overtime, but the spreadsheet may outlive the creator. Therefore, having adequate documentation is critical during its life cycle. PwC defines it as "Ensuring that the appropriate level of spreadsheet documentation is maintained and kept up-to-date to understand the business objective and specific functions of the spreadsheet."

When testing for documentation, management should ask:

- How does management document the life of the spreadsheet?
- Are there version control logs within the spreadsheet?
- Are inputs color-coded or cell protected? (That is, how does management document the spreadsheets and keep the life cycle of the spreadsheet documented?)

When testing for documentation, management could review the documentation practices and determine if the spreadsheets follow the practice.

Overall Analytics (PwC)

Even if IT controls appear to be effective, management should still continue to perform analytics on the integrity of the spreadsheets and desktop tools. These are referred to as *detective* controls. This provides further assurance that the calculations, footing, and cross-footing are correct. PwC defines it as "Implementing analytics as a detective control to find errors in spreadsheets used for calculations. However, analytics alone are not a sufficient control to completely address the inherent risk of financial amounts generated using spreadsheets." This is where financial auditors get to do what they do best. This is the opportunity to perform analytical procedures to determine if the spreadsheet data is reliable. For example, management can foot, cross-foot, recalculate, or trace numbers back to source documents.

LIFE AFTER THE BASELINE: MAINTAINING SPREADSHEETS AND DESKTOP TOOLS

After management has assessed the spreadsheet and desktop tools for the controls previously described, management will have created a baseline test. The baseline test will give management assurance that the spreadsheet or desktop tool can be relied on, assuming that the controls remain intact. On a periodic basis, management should revisit the controls for each spreadsheet or desktop tool to ensure that the controls are still in place. Organizations typically perform this review on an annual basis; however, management should consider performing the reassessment on a quarterly basis for high-risk spreadsheets or desktop tools. Eventually, management should attempt to move away from spreadsheets and desktop tools into full-fledged IT systems, when appropriate. However, even if management moves into an application, the IT controls still need to be managed and monitored to ensure the integrity of the data.

Downstream Controls and the Risk Acceptance Process

As with any business or financial process that involves risk, management has the responsibility to mitigate, minimize, or accept the risk. The spreadsheet and desktop tools controls discussed could help management mitigate or minimize risks. However, management may decide to rely on downstream controls or accept the risk without any further mitigation or minimization. Downstream controls would refer to other application controls or manual controls that may mitigate or minimize the risk of lack of controls within the spreadsheet or desktop tools. These downstream controls may be in the form of reconciliations, manual review of all journal entries, or other substantive control procedure. As long as the risks are managed somewhere in the overall process, the control does not have to specifically be addressed at the spreadsheet or desktop tool level; however, management that elects to go this route typically spends more time trying to prove negatives (that is, How do we know something did not go wrong?). This approach may indeed prove to be more costly and inefficient; however, the implementation of controls at the spreadsheet or desktop tools level also could prove to be costly and time consuming. Management must make the decision that is the best for the risk environment and company culture. Some companies may elect to accept the risks identified within spreadsheets or desktop tools and opt to not have mitigating or other controls that minimize the overall risk. This approach should be used rarely because management will not be able to gain any comfort that the risks have not negatively impacted internal or external financial reporting or enabled the opportunity for misappropriation of assets.

 ## SUMMARY

The use of spreadsheets is ubiquitous in businesses. Common application areas include operations management, internal reporting, and schedules for primary and secondary external financial reporting. Many exposures arise from two pervasive circumstances: applications created by end users who operate outside a regular system of controls, and applications that contain sensitive data that may not be adequately secured or protected. The IT auditor should obtain a thorough understanding of critical spreadsheet applications and integrate this knowledge with the other aspects of the IT audit.

Just as is the case for a financial application, spreadsheet controls are critical. Many companies, whether SME or Fortune 500, use spreadsheets to manage day-to-day operations. The company does not always know when a spreadsheet is created or used in its organization, or know about the subsequent use of the spreadsheet to make a financial decision or provide data for the financial statements. Given this, spreadsheets should be identified and reviewed for appropriate IT controls.

CHAPTER TWELVE

Key Reports and Report Writers Risk Exposures

K EY REPORTS AND REPORT WRITERS facilitate the flow of information that internal management and external stakeholders rely on to make critical business or investment decisions. Reports can be created as an integrated part of the accounting information system or may be generated through the use of a third-party report writer tool.

 ## HOW REPORTS ARE USED

While accounting information systems such as QuickBooks (QB) or Microsoft Great Plains Dynamics (GPD) come with prebuilt reports that can be useful in making decisions or reporting to external stakeholders, management may also want to create customized or ad hoc reports to facilitate decision making. Reports are used to:

- Display the information from the subledgers and general ledger.
- Display the trial balance information.
- Ultimately display the financial results that help create the internal management reports and/or external financial statements.

Reports are also used in the consolidation process and/or to help create footnotes and disclosures within the financial statements. Management also relies on reports to monitor financial cycle transactions, operational performance, and security settings.

Reports can be broken down into three categories:

1. **Original reports:** Vanilla reports that came with the accounting information system and have not been modified.

2. **Modified reports:** Vanilla reports that came with the accounting information system and have been modified within the application.
3. **New, customized reports:** New reports that have been created either from an original report as the base or a brand-new report created from scratch. Customized reports may originate from within the accounting package or from a separate report writer.

Reports have inherent and configurable control risks similar to those discussed with spreadsheets, and management needs to review reports for potential errors or defects. Audit considerations in reports include:

- **Logical security:** Who can access reports for view, add, modify, and delete functionality? What prevents unauthorized changes to reports? Management and auditors need to ensure that only authorized users have access to reports to prevent unauthorized changes.
- **Change management:** Does management follow a robust change management methodology when creating or modifying reports? Are changes documented in a change log with appropriate approvals? Are changes tested by end users to validate the modification or customization of the report? How does management ensure that reports are modified to reflect changes made to the chart of accounts? How does management validate that all appropriate data sources are being pulled to the right line item within a report? How does management validate the calculations, summations, and other mathematical analysis of a report?
- **Operations:** How does management ensure that the report dictionary is backed up so reports that are customized or modified are not lost in case of a system failure? How does management ensure that reports are available for use after a system failure without having to recreate the report from scratch? For third-party reporting packages, how does management ensure that all data is appropriately transferred between the report writer software and the accounting information system?

Reports are typically user-driven and outside of the control of the information technology (IT) department. The benefits of streamlined and directed information flow provided by report writers are accompanied by several types of potential risk. These are summarized in Table 12.1.

Although doing so is not a risk exposure per se, management should maintain an inventory of key reports that are risk-ranked on the basis of magnitude, materiality, and complexity. The report inventory should identify the owner, purpose, location, and other characteristics.

ORIGINAL REPORTS WITHIN THE APPLICATION

Access to reports can be controlled within the application.

GPD Report Security

Report access controlled in the application is important so only the authorized users have the ability to view, modify, delete, or print the reports. Note that printing reports requires

TABLE 12.1   Key Reports and Report Writer Risk Exposures

Risk Exposure	Sample Problems
Errors in prebuilt and preconfigured reports	Prebuilt and preconfigured reports that come with prepackaged software may not completely and accurately pull information from accounting records if management has modified or customized the chart of accounts. The assumption is that prebuilt and preconfigured reports are free of error, but it is still management's responsibility to perform tests of controls on these reports. However, prebuilt and preconfigured reports can be modified, which could affect the integrity of the report.
Errors in customized reporting	Reports may be designed with flaws that result in incomplete data being pulled to the correct line item, incorrect calculations, or incorrect balancing. The design and construction of reports are typically created by end users who may not fully understand the intricacies of how data is pulled into the reports.
Errors in interfaces and data connections	Some reports may obtain data from other reports or other data sources that may reside in internal data warehouses, internal spreadsheets, or third-party data subscription services. The interfaces or data connections transmit the data via a manual initiation process or have automatic settings where data is transmitted on a periodic basis. The interfaces and data connections could potentially fail to fully transmit all data records, which could result in incomplete and inaccurate data.
Errors in logic and formula accuracy	Logic errors in formula construction may result in misleading or erroneous calculated values. Input, logic, and usage errors affect the ability for reliance on the data within the report. Logic errors could result from incorrect formulas. The formula may have been incorrect from the beginning or inadvertently altered during a design change of the report. Usage errors could include the misapplication of the report functionality.
Lack of data integrity	Input errors could include excessive manual entries; incorrect links from external sources, or other internal/external sources; importing incorrect data or wrong parameters; or unintended changes. Values that have been hardcoded into formula expressions (e.g., an embedded tax rate) can be easily overlooked when the report is updated.
Unauthorized users	Access to the reports needs to be protected to ensure that unauthorized users do not inadvertently change the design of the report. Access can be controlled by passwords and ensuring that the location of the report is protected.

access privileges and these should be assigned to users consistent with the company's overall security policy and assignments. Management or the auditor should review report access in order to ensure compliance with appropriate policies. (See Figure 12.1.)

Accessing Reports in GPD

Access to the report writer in GPD is available via the predefined security task ADMIN_ SYSTEM_008, which can be assigned to an existing role or to a new role designed especially for report writers, as shown in Figure 12.2.*

---

*From the Microsoft GPD reports writer manual.

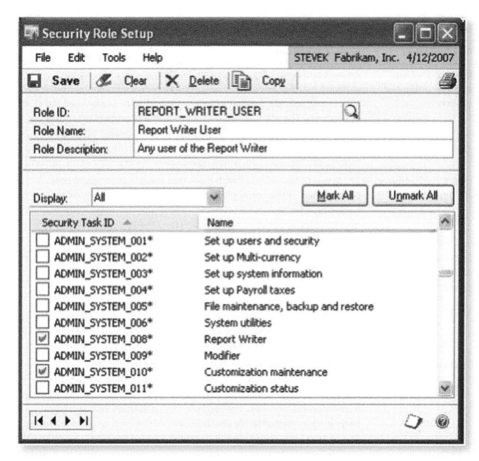

FIGURE 12.1 Accessing Reports in GPD

QB provides similar internal reports, via the Reports tab and "Reports Center" menu option. There are reports relating to all major transaction cycles (Revenue, Purchasing, Inventory, and Payroll) as well as financial statements for external reporting or internal reconciliations (e.g., checking account records). QB supports reports on a yearly, year-to-date, or customized-period basis.

The reports center provides the ability to create graphical presentation of company data. There are set options that allow a user to create accounts receivable graphs, accounts payable graphs, sales graphs, income-and-expense graphs, net-worth graphs, and budget-versus-actual graphs, as shown in Figure 12.2.

Audit Trail Reports

Audit trails can be configured to provide information about changes to any aspects of a company's data, such as amounts, account titling, dates, transactions, adjusting entries, voided or deleted transactions, and so on, along with the identification of the individual who made the change. Activating the QB audit trail feature is accomplished by selecting Edit>Edit Preferences>Accounting>Preferences>Company Preferences and

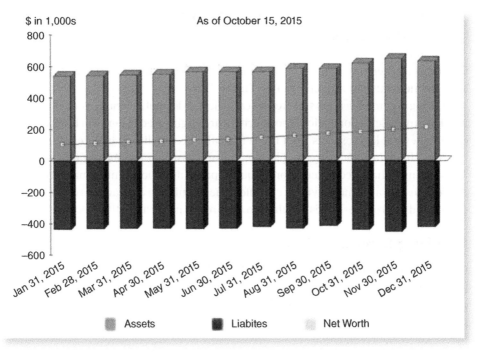

FIGURE 12.2 Net-Worth Presentation

Source: Intuit, Rock Castle.

then checking the "use audit trail" box. Figure 12.3 shows a general audit trail report. At the transaction detail level, a report on voided or deleted transactions that identifies the affected accounts, dates of the transaction and voiding, the individual performing the deletion, explanation of the action, and so on all provide management with a powerful investigative tool.

Rock Castle Construction
Audit Trail
Entered/Last Modified December 2014

Num	Entered/Last Modified	Last modified by	State	Date	Name	Memo	Account	Split	Debit	Credit
Transactions entered or modified by Admin										
Bill										
▸	12/15/2014 02:02:44	Admin	Latest	09/30/2015	Sloan Roofing	Opening Bal...	20000 · Accounts...	54000 · Job E...		500.00 ◂
					Abercrombie, Kris...	Opening Bal...	54000 · Job Expen...	20000 · Acco...	500.00	
	12/15/2013 00:18:22	Admin	Prior	09/30/2014	Sloan Roofing	Opening Bal...	20000 · Accounts...	54000 · Job E...		500.00
					Abercrombie, Kris...	Opening Bal...	54000 · Job Expen...	20000 · Acco...	500.00	
	12/15/2012 13:47:42	Admin	Prior	09/30/2013	Sloan Roofing	Opening Bal...	20000 · Accounts...	54000 · Job E...		500.00
					Abercrombie, Kris...	Opening Bal...	54000 · Job Expen...	20000 · Acco...	500.00	
	12/15/2012 12:49:28	Admin	Prior	09/30/2012	Sloan Roofing	Opening Bal...	20000 · Accounts...	54000 · Job E...		500.00
					Abercrombie, Kris...	Opening Bal...	54000 · Job Expen...	20000 · Acco...	500.00	

FIGURE 12.3 Audit Trail Report

Source: Intuit, Rock Castle.

MODIFIED OR CUSTOMIZED REPORTS WITHIN THE APPLICATION

GPD report writer functionality enables the user to use existing reports, modify reports, or create new, customized reports. (See Figure 12.4.)

Changes or modifications to a report can affect its format, overall layout, data transmission, and calculation logic. Report writers are engineered to perform functions that differ in several key respects from those typically accomplished in spreadsheets, and the powerful data-handling capabilities come at a cost to transparency and flexibility. Thus, changes that affect calculations require special attention. Simple misplacement of a parenthesis or arithmetic symbol can affect the calculation of financial results. Careful design and rigorous testing is required to ensure the integrity of the report.

Modifying Reports in GPD

Original reports within GPD can be modified. The user should first create a copy of the original report prior to modifying the report. The user would select the report and navigate to modify current report. Changes could be made to a specific report or to the global settings that affect all reports. (See Figure 12.5.)

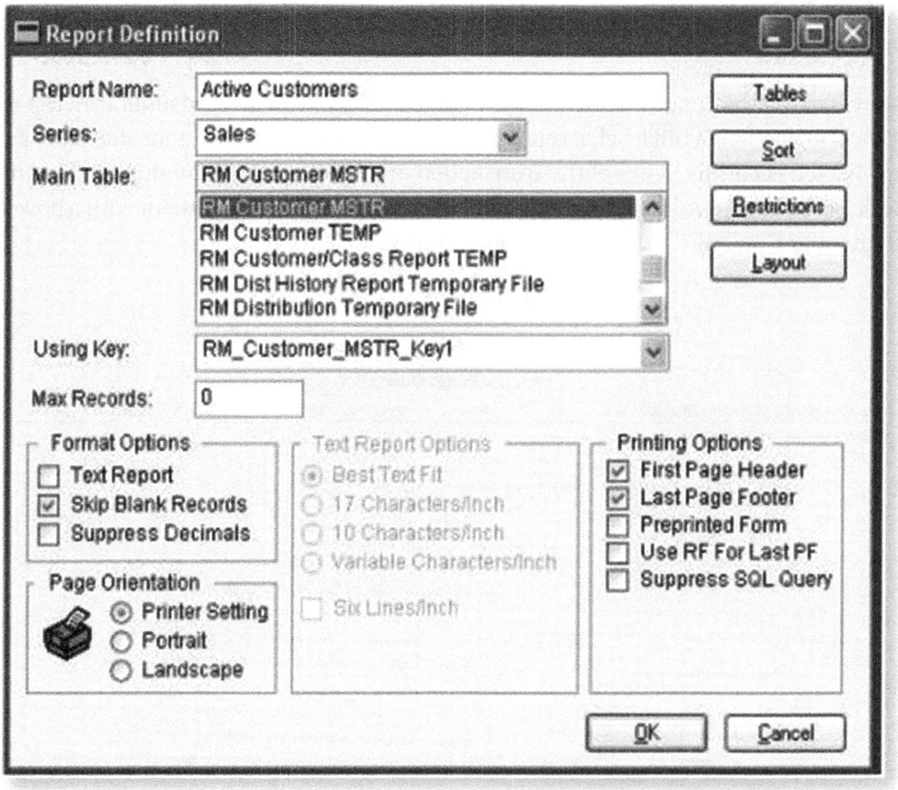

FIGURE 12.4 GPD Report Definition Screen

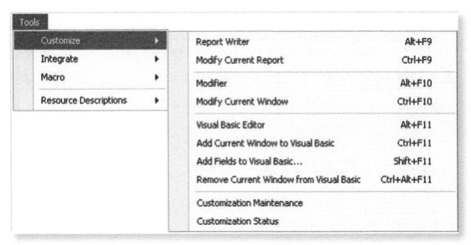

FIGURE 12.5   Modifying Reports

When modifying reports, users may want to, for example, alter the layout of the report or the source from which certain line items pull information. If a new field is added to the report, the user will need to ensure that the appropriate linkages to the data tables are created. If this does not happen, then the user may invalidate the integrity of the report. Any modification of a report should be investigated by management or the auditor to ensure that the report integrity has not been compromised.

Customized Reports in GPD

When management creates new, customized reports, good design protocols need to be in place. Management needs to ensure that the appropriate name is given to the report. Management also has to consider the layout of the report and how data is pulled into the report and calculated (footing, cross-footing, calculations).

Reports, whether modified or custom, are stored in the "reports.dic" file. This is a dictionary file that contains the reports. Management needs to ensure that this file is appropriately backed up to prevent loss of the report designs. In GPD the sequence Tools >Setup>System>Alternate>Modified Forms and Reports brings a window that provides access to all modified reports. (See Figure 12.6.)

The GPD security for customized reports can be accessed via Tools>Setup>System >Security Tasks. The new security task must be named and assigned to appropriate personnel. (See Figure 12.7.)

Aggregating Accounting Data

A commonly desired report modification involves the summary presentation of related account balances. For example, "payroll taxes" may include state and federal unemployment, employer's FICA share, and so on. Rather than presenting each of these as a separate line item on the income statement, management may wish to present one line item balance for all of these related amounts. In QB, the "collapse"

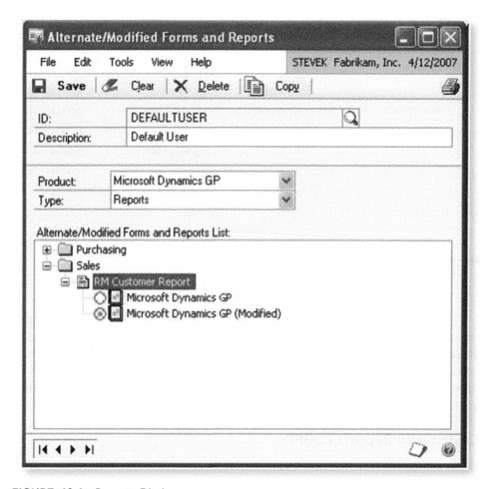

FIGURE 12.6 Reports Dictionary

Source: Microsoft GPD report writer manual.

option on the report screen allows the report writer to accomplish this. Custom report writers such as Microsoft's FRX have more sophisticated tools, as discussed in the following pages. In all instances of a modification that involved aggregating data, there is a risk exposure regarding completeness should the intended accounts not be included.

REPORTS USING THIRD-PARTY PACKAGES

Third-party report-writing packages have been developed for many widely used middle-market accounting packages and embody a wide range of functionalities. These applications generally include a population of predesigned standard reports and the capability to produce a range of custom reports. Microsoft's FRX classifies reports as detail: account

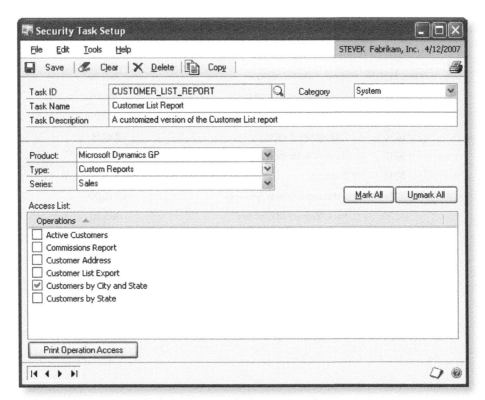

FIGURE 12.7   Security Task Assignment for Customized Reports

Source: Microsoft GPD report writer manual.

focused, detail: transaction focused, and financial. FRX and many other report writers can produce pure or mixed versions of these reports.

Two key IT controls relating to reports are the interrelated topics of security and change management. Read access should be consistent with other security assignments throughout the organization. For instance, in FRX, an optional security system allows the system administrator to limit access to reports and features on an individual or group basis. Change management should follow the same general procedures discussed in Chapter 11 for spreadsheets.

The ability of a report writer to facilitate data export to Excel has two distinct implications. From an IT audit perspective, the accuracy and completeness of data transfer needs to be assured. From a process integrity perspective, the use of Excel as an analytic tool may help management or the external auditor detect unusual or fraudulent behavior through detail analysis of transaction detail. For example, Table 12.2 presents data from a check register. The same data, sorted on payment amounts and supplied with a formula that evaluates whether the amounts in two adjacent rows are identical, readily highlights a potential duplicate payment. The example in Table 12.3 is very simple, but the fact pattern is based on a real fraud.

Figure 12.8 provides a home-page view of a sample third-party package, QReport-Builder, designed expressly for QB.

TABLE 12.2 Check Register Data

3212	Thorpe Supply	16,024.02
3213	Avon First Funding	2,206.50
3214	Park Avenue Microfiber	965.02
3215	J. Wood, LLC	3,500.00
3216	Fitzpatrick Realty	1,820.00
3217	Raspail & Lecter	165.21
3218	Exxon	451.14
3219	Simpson Nuclear Services	4,115.00
3220	Park Avenue Microfiber	965.02
3221	Stevenson Carbonic	311.45
3222	National Helium	197.23
3223	Town of Leicester	1,941.02
3224	Lomborg Sharpening	225.65
3225	Fishman Steel Supply	10,000.00
3226	Schiffman	3,400.00

TABLE 12.3 Check Register Data—Resorted

3217	Raspail & Lecter	165.21	FALSE
3222	National Helium	197.23	FALSE
3224	Lomborg Sharpening	225.65	FALSE
3221	Stevenson Carbonic	311.45	FALSE
3218	Exxon	451.14	FALSE
3214	Park Avenue Microfiber	965.02	FALSE
3220	Park Avenue Microfiber	965.02	TRUE
3216	Fitzpatrick Realty	1,820.00	FALSE
3223	Town of Leicester	1,941.02	FALSE
3213	Avon First Funding	2,206.50	FALSE
3226	Schiffman	3,400.00	FALSE
3215	J. Wood, LLC	3,500.00	FALSE
3219	Simpson Nuclear Services	4,115.00	FALSE
3225	Fishman Steel Supply	10,000.00	FALSE
3212	Thorpe Supply	16,024.02	FALSE

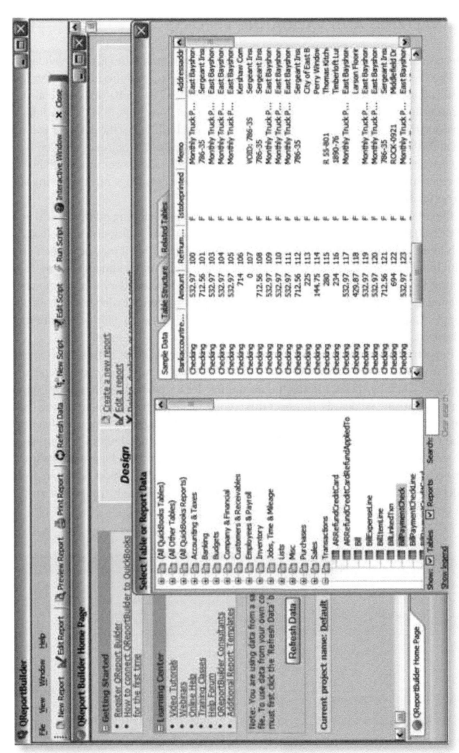

FIGURE 12.8   Third-Party Report Writer for QB

ANALYZING AND VALIDATING REPORTS

Reports are useful only if properly configured and the design of the report is validated.

The "reporting tree" concept in FRX allows users to combine natural account classifications with responsibility centers, for example, 1210-6540-002 as a code for Accounts Receivable (1210) associated with the Buffalo, New York (6540), location for wholesale customers (002). Reports can thus address highly specific detail or roll up data at the location (i.e., all receivables generated by the Buffalo office) or division (i.e., all receivables generated by wholesale operations) levels. The power and flexibility of this reporting capability arrives with the potential risk exposure of misidentifying the sources for data feeds.

Report writers such as FRX allow the use of formulas, including mathematical and IF-THEN-ELSE statements. The IT auditor should evaluate footing and cross-footing totals and evaluate logical formulas for correct implementation. It may be particularly useful to review formulas that control the reporting of normal balances (e.g., positive amounts for income statement credit items and negative amounts for income statement debit items). Inconsistent formulas or balances that swing between debit and credit, for example, "Income Expense (Income)" or "Tax Expense (Benefit)," should be carefully scrutinized.

Report writers such as FRX typically allow the user/designer to link a cell in the report to a range of accounts in the general ledger (GL) package. This can be done in a number of ways: by specifying the full account codes for each account, by specifying ranges, or by using wildcards. However this is done, ensuring that the report draws data from all of the relevant accounts is clearly a key factor in evaluating the completeness of the report. Where specification of a range has been combined with an expression that subtracts references for some part of the range, checking the logic and accuracy of the references is clearly essential. Figure 12.9 (from the FRX report designer/users guide) shows a formula in the formula bar and the choices made by the report writer that generated the formula.

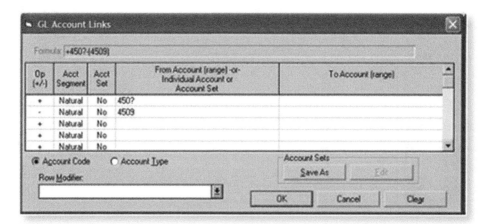

FIGURE 12.9 Formula Bar in FRX Report Writer

Modifiers allow the report user/designer to specify the time period for a report—typically described as *n* number of periods before the current period or year-to-date. These modifiers can be combined into more complex formulas. As with account ranges, the logic and accuracy of these designations should be checked in order to assure that the reports do in fact report the information they purport to provide.

Rounding capabilities in report writers may result in reports that do not foot or cross-foot. The FRX guide previously cited shows an example of the amounts $3,600 and $3,700 each automatically rounded to the nearest thousand: 4. This results in the total of these balances being reported at the anomalous 8. The IT auditor should be aware of rounding protocols used in a particular report.

The power and flexibility of importing data from spreadsheet files along with GL balances come with the potential exposure of misidentifying the files. The IT auditor should review links to ensure not only that the intended files, pages, and ranges have been correctly specified, but also that they tie this work to the review of spreadsheet controls.

Reporting trees can inadvertently lead to incorrect values appearing in a report. The FRX report writer's guide suggests two distinct possibilities:

1. Some rows may have used the full account code and thus pull in every reporting unit with a similar account mask.
2. Use of a GL account mask by the summary units of a reporting tree can result in data being duplicated.

SUMMARY

Report writers are the final mile between transaction processing and the information product delivered to managers, investors, and other statement users. IT audit concerns include access and permissions relating to change management, backups, interfaces, and logic errors that may result in correct data being incorrectly summarized or presented. The IT auditor should be familiar with the scope and variety of available audit trail reports.

Financial reporting drives the organization to demonstrate its performance. Controls around the key reports and report writers are critical to ensure the integrity of financial data being reported.

CHAPTER THIRTEEN

IT Audit Deficiencies

Defining and Evaluating IT Audit Deficiencies

J UST AS RISK IS INEVITABLE in an organization, management is bound to identify opportunities for improvement during routine audits or self-assessments. Organizations typically refer to audit deficiencies as "opportunities for improvement," "audit findings," or "audit issues." Some organizations try to minimize the number of audit findings to prevent possible backlash or repercussions from senior management. This is often where management will water down any audit findings to a degree where the findings become meaningless or are dropped. Other organizations try to maximize the benefits of receiving audit findings to learn from what-went-wrong or what-could-go-wrong scenarios in order to improve the processes and become best-in-class. Most organizations fall in the middle, where they neither seek nor reject audit findings and appreciate the learning opportunity. The auditor needs to be aware of the various dynamics that could be faced when presenting audit findings to management because the company culture will dictate how well received the audit feedback is and what type of corrective action will be taken.

 ## A FRAMEWORK FOR AUDIT DEFICIENCIES

As management or auditors identify IT audit deficiencies, a process needs to be followed to determine the significance of the findings. Even though each organization may have its own definitions for identifying the significance of a particular audit deficiency, such as high, medium, low, verbal, weakness, significant, material, or many other possibilities, the following definitions are based on the definitions used during Sarbanes-Oxley internal control engagements. A framework developed by representatives of the four global firms and several national firms classifies audit deficiencies into one of three categories:

1. A control deficiency
2. A significant deficiency
3. A material weakness

The definitions of these three categories are as follows:*

Control Deficiency
▪ A deficiency in the design or operation of a control that does not allow management or employees, in the normal course of performing their assigned functions, to prevent or detect misstatements on a timely basis.
  ▪ A deficiency in design exists when:
    ▪ A control necessary to meet the control objective is missing, or
    ▪ An existing control is not properly designed so that, even if it operates as designed, the control objective is not always met.
    ▪ A deficiency in operation exists when a properly designed control does not operate as designed, or when the person performing the control does not possess the necessary authority or qualifications to perform the control effectively.

Significant Deficiency
▪ A control deficiency, or combination of control deficiencies, that adversely affects the company's ability to initiate, authorize, record, process, or report external financial data reliably in accordance with generally accepted accounting principles such that there is more than a remote likelihood that a misstatement of the company's annual or interim financial statements that is more than inconsequential will not be prevented or detected.

Material Weakness
▪ A significant deficiency, or combination of significant deficiencies, that results in more than a remote likelihood that a material misstatement of the annual or interim financial statements will not be prevented or detected.

Management and auditors have been challenged to determine the materiality and impact of IT audit deficiencies since many of the deficiencies typically involve more risk management topics and do not tie to specific numbers. With that said, management and auditors can link the IT audit deficiencies with the associated financial processes in order to infer that the financial process would be put at a higher level of risk given the IT audit deficiency.

---

*A Framework for Evaluating Process/Transaction-Level and Information Technology General Control Exceptions and Deficiencies (2004). Participating firms were BDO Seidman LLP; Crowe Chizek and Company LLC; Deloitte & Touche LLP; Ernst & Young LLP; Grant Thornton LLP; Harbinger PLC; KPMG LLP; McGladrey & Pullen LLP; PricewaterhouseCoopers LLP; and Professor William F. Messier, Jr., Georgia State University.

Figure 13.1 is adapted from material in the framework report and illustrates a process that management or the auditor could go through when analyzing IT audit deficiencies.

The decision process starts with a noted deficiency and a review that determines whether additional IT general controls (ITGC) exist that achieve the same control objective (decision node 1). If they do and additional evaluation concludes that the deficiencies are not significant, then the deficiencies are categorized at the lowest level of concern, "deficiency." If additional evaluation concludes that the deficiencies are significant, they are classified at the next higher level of concern, "significant deficiency." A further layer of judgment is required when multiple instances of a deficiency type raise the prospect that the quantity of these related deficiencies exercises a qualitative effect. The drawing in Figure 13.1 shows, in dashed lines, the possible judgment that multiple instances result in an upward revision of the weakness, from deficiency to significant deficiency, or from significant deficiency to material weakness.

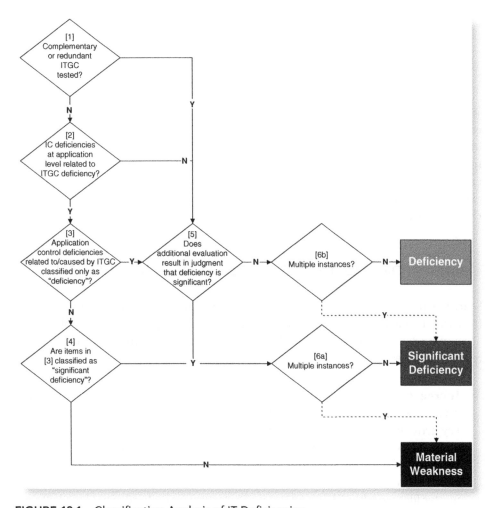

FIGURE 13.1   Classification Analysis of IT Deficiencies

In the absence of additional ITGC, the auditor considers controls at the application level (decision node 2). In their absence, the deficiencies are classified as per the node 5 decision rule. If the application level controls are caused by or related to ITGC deficiencies, the next step in the review process is to determine the classification of the deficiency (decision node 3). A "yes" determination leads to the node 5 decision rule, and a "no" decision leads to the evaluation of whether the deficiency is "significant" or reflects a "material weakness" (decision node 4).

TYPES OF IT AUDIT FAILURES AND ILLUSTRATIVE CASES

Notwithstanding the number of methodologies for evaluating IT controls, many companies still exhibit various deficiencies in this area. Table 13.1 uses publicly available 10-K disclosures to map illustrative examples to an error typology.

Each of the deficiencies in Table 13.2 was classified as a material weakness in a published 10-K report.

USE OF COMPENSATORY CONTROLS

When primary controls fail to achieve the control objective, alternative compensatory controls need to be reviewed to minimize or mitigate the risks associated with not having the primary control operating effectively. Table 13.3 illustrates compensatory controls that could be utilized to minimize or mitigate risk exposures that occur when the primary controls fail. The listing of compensatory controls is illustrative rather than exhaustive. We also reference suggested strategies advocated in Julie Harrer's *Internal Control Strategies: A Mid- to Small Business Guide.*

IDEAS FOR ADDRESSING SEGREGATION-OF-DUTIES ISSUES

Segregation of duties is one of the biggest control problems that small companies face. How can a company have adequate segregation of duties with three people in the accounting department? A few ideas for compensating controls to address limited segregation of duties issues follow:

- **Increase detection controls and monitoring:** Management may consider reviewing reports of detailed transactions that are recorded by staff who perform key activities with limited segregation of duties. The reviews should occur regularly on a timely basis, and questionable transactions should be investigated and corrected. If the accounts payable clerk sets up and maintains all vendor master files, a manager could review a report of all changes and additions made to the master files monthly. The report could be electronic or a hardcopy, signed off and retained for evidence of review.

TABLE 13.1 Illustrative IT Audit Deficiencies and Potential Financial Audit Impact

IT Audit Area	Illustrative IT Audit Deficiency	Potential Financial Audit Impact
Access rights	▪ Three users have inappropriate access to post entries to the general ledger. Management does not have an audit trail in-place to determine who made the entries to the general ledger or if entries were deleted.	▪ The deficiency could enable unauthorized addition or deletion of entries that impair the integrity of the general ledger. ▪ Management could review a large sample of the entries made to the general ledger and trace back to the source documentation to ensure that unauthorized entries have not been performed.
Segregation of duties	▪ Although management has adequately segregated duties for accounting and finance personnel from a business process perspective, the access rights within the accounting information system have not been adequately assigned to the users. Users have more access within the system than necessary to perform their job responsibilities, and some of the access rights conflict with one another. In addition, management has not implemented an annual review process to analyze the access rights assigned to users to ensure that segregation of duties is maintained and access rights are appropriately assigned based on job responsibilities.	▪ For the financial cycle that has been impacted by the segregation of duties concern, transactions within that cycle may not be authorized or appropriate. ▪ Management could review transactions within the cycle and compare back to source documentation to determine if inappropriate transactions exist. Management could enforce system access rights to align with the business process practices.
User management	▪ Management does not have a defined process to manage new hires, transfers, or terminations. This has resulted in access being inappropriately granted to new users; access not being appropriately modified for transferred users; and/or access not being removed in a timely manner. In one case, it was noted that a user transferred departments and the previous access was not removed, thus creating a risk that unauthorized entries could be performed with the unnecessary access.	▪ When users have inappropriate access within the system, the financial cycle aligned with the inappropriate access right should be further examined to ensure that no unauthorized transactions have occurred. ▪ Management or auditors should consider increasing the sample size of substantive testing if management or auditors cannot determine if unauthorized activity occurred.

(continued)

TABLE 13.1   (*continued*)

IT Audit Area	Illustrative IT Audit Deficiency	Potential Financial Audit Impact
Password management	▪ Password management is ineffective. Passwords are not configured with a minimum length or required change interval. Specifically, password length is set at 1 character and passwords are not required to change.	▪ Inadequate password management could result in unauthorized usage of a user's account. ▪ Management should enforce strong password configuration controls. In absence of effective passwords, management should review the failed login attempt logs to see if any unauthorized attempts to access accounts have occurred. If management or the auditors cannot get comfortable with user accounts due to the password settings, the financial cycles could be reviewed with larger sample sizes.
Administrative users	▪ Administrative and power users associated with the financial application were not limited to authorized personnel.	▪ Multiple personnel had access to all transactions within the system. ▪ Management should review the users to determine if any transactions occurred that were not appropriate or authorized. If inappropriate or unauthorized transactions occurred, management should review the associated financial cycle transactions and make the appropriate adjusting entries.
Change management documentation and approvals	▪ Changes were not documented or approved.	▪ Potentially inappropriate transactions posted through system. ▪ Management should determine what financial cycles the changes affected and substantively test the transactions at a higher sample size to ensure the appropriateness of the cycle transactions.
Change management testing	▪ Changes are not tested in a test environment, testing is not performed, or testing is not signed off by end users.	▪ Changes may corrupt the data processing of accounting transactions. ▪ Management should review transactions affected by the change and determine if transactions are processed correctly.

TABLE 13.1 (*continued*)

IT Audit Area	Illustrative IT Audit Deficiency	Potential Financial Audit Impact
Segregation of duties for promote to production	▪ The programmer made changes and promoted the changes into production. There was no segregation of duties between programming and operations.	▪ This means that inappropriate or unauthorized code may have been introduced into production. This is similar to fraud schemes where fractions of pennies were skimmed off accounts by an unauthorized system code that was inserted into production. ▪ Management should do a complete review of all changes implemented into production and increase the sample size of substantive financial testing.
Postchange review	▪ Management does not perform a review of all changes after they have been implemented into production.	▪ This process is not necessary unless other change management controls are not working properly. This control is meant to help catch any unauthorized changes implemented into production. ▪ If this control is not in place, management should rely on the other change management controls, if effective, or perform additional financial substantive tests.
Backups	▪ Backups are not performed on a daily basis and/or backup tapes are not taken offsite.	▪ Backups should be performed daily to prevent the risk of loss and the backup tapes should be kept offsite in a secure location. If this control is not effective, management can still rely on the financials, but needs to understand that data could be lost in the event of a system failure.
Contingency and disaster recovery planning	▪ Management does not have a disaster recovery plan developed.	▪ While this does not directly affect the reliability of the financial statements, in the event of a disaster or significant system outage, data could be lost or misprocessed.

(*continued*)

TABLE 13.1 *(continued)*

IT Audit Area	Illustrative IT Audit Deficiency	Potential Financial Audit Impact
Data center	▪ Within the data center, the environmental controls and physical security controls were not adequate. No fire suppression system existed. Programmers had access to the data center and the terminal for the production system.	▪ While the environmental controls do not directly affect the financial statements, inadequate fire suppression could prevent the safeguarding of the production system. The inadequate physical access to the data center could enable the programmer to access the live production system.
		▪ Management should ensure that the financial cycles associated with the production system have appropriate transactions to ensure that the programmer did not alter the production system.
IT entity level	▪ Management does not have well-documented IT policies, strategies, or organizational structure to adequately manage the IT environment.	▪ While this does not directly affect the financial statements, inadequate processes could lead to an IT organization that is prone to error, which could cause production issues.
Application controls	▪ Configuration settings are not set up correctly, which prevents accurate processing of data.	▪ Management should review all application controls and do a test of one to ensure that the controls are working appropriately.
Spreadsheet management	▪ Spreadsheets are not well-controlled to prevent unauthorized access or changes that may result in inaccurate calculations.	▪ Management should review all spreadsheets to ensure that the spreadsheet controls are working as intended.
Report writers	▪ Reports are not designed or managed to prevent unauthorized access or changes that may result in erroneous reporting.	▪ Management should perform sample calculations, footing, and cross-footing of reports and trace select numbers back to source documents.
SSAE 16(SOC 1)	▪ The statement of controls (SOC) report for the payroll processor was not adequately reviewed and the user control considerations were not considered to determine which controls management was responsible for versus the third-party service provider. This resulted in the identification of missing controls that were not being performed internally or at the third-party service provider.	▪ This affects the payroll process and the missed controls affected the reliability of the payroll reports. Therefore, management needs to perform additional substantive review of the payroll information to validate the payroll calculations.

TABLE 13.2 Illustrative Case Studies of IT Audit Deficiencies

Company	IT Audit Area	Illustrative IT Audit Deficiency Reported in Financial Statements
Rockwell Medical Technologies, Inc.	▪ Segregation of duties and application access	▪ As discussed in the Company's Annual Report on Form-10-K for the year ended December 31, 2008, there were two material weaknesses in internal control over financial reporting identified by management relating to (i) inadequate segregation of duties pertaining to access to information technology applications used in our business operations and (ii) inventory. ▪ During 2008, we implemented a new inventory control and enterprise resource planning information system. The two weaknesses we identified pertain to the changes we made in 2008 related to this new information technology platform and operating environment. We determined that we do not have adequate segregation of duties pertaining to access to information technology applications used in our business operations.
Mechanical Technology, Inc.	▪ IT resources and turnover	▪ As of December 31, 2008, management determined the turnover of its accounting and Information Technology staff and resulting lack of resources is a material weakness.
Porta Systems CP	▪ Change management	▪ Based on this assessment and those criteria, our management concluded that the Company did not maintain effective internal control over financial reporting as of December 31, 2007 as a result of a material weakness relating to Information Technology, as described below. ▪ Management identified the following significant deficiencies that when aggregated may give rise to a material weakness. Management identified certain control procedures that were not sufficiently documented relating to a) program change management in the Company's PROCOMM system, b) lack of integrated modules with the general ledger and c) excessive manual adjustments to the inventory module are required. ▪ Management is continuing to investigate new integrated ERP systems that will include complete general ledger and reporting which will eliminate the need for manual updates and significantly reduce the need for journal entries in the financial reporting process. Our inability to finance this major capital expenditure has significantly limited the ERP systems available for us to evaluate.

(continued)

TABLE 13.2 (*continued*)

Company	IT Audit Area	Illustrative IT Audit Deficiency Reported in Financial Statements
Patriot Scientific	▪ Logical security, change management, and operations	▪ In connection with our assessment of internal control over financial reporting, we identified the following material weakness in our internal control over financial reporting: As of May 31, 2008, a material weakness existed relating to SSDI's information technology . . . including ineffective controls relating to following: ▪ There is no IT security policy, ▪ There is no change management policy, ▪ There is no evidence of changes that have been performed, ▪ There is no physical security over servers, firewall, router, and switches, ▪ There is no documentation of the granting of user access rights process, ▪ There is no documentation of the user access termination process, ▪ The firewall configuration does not reflect SSDI's current usage, ▪ Remote access is not well controlled, ▪ Two of five systems did not have recent antivirus signature files, ▪ The antivirus software is not installed on the server, ▪ All named users, plus the CIO using the administrator account, have full access to all areas of QuickBooks, ▪ All authenticated users are allowed full access to the files in the Finance directory, ▪ The domain administrator list is not limited to the minimum appropriate personnel, ▪ Passwords are only required to be five characters, which is deemed insufficient for good security, ▪ There is no evidence of the CIO's weekly backup review occurring, and management is not being notified of failures, ▪ There are no stored backup tapes off-site or in a media safe, and ▪ There are no regularly run test restorations.
Endeavor Acquisition Corp.	▪ Logical Security, Change Management, and End-User Computing	▪ The Company has also identified information technology control weaknesses in the areas of information security, end-user computing, systems program development and change controls. . . . The Company has adopted an Information Technology framework. . . . ▪ The Company's world-wide financial information systems were not integrated and contained many manual processes that may prevent the Company from meeting regulatory filing requirements on a timely and accurate basis. The Company has also identified information technology control weaknesses in the areas of information security, end-user computing, systems program development and change controls.

TABLE 13.2 (*continued*)

Company	IT Audit Area	Illustrative IT Audit Deficiency Reported in Financial Statements
		▪ Inadequate Financial Information Systems: The Company has identified systems and applications that impact financial reporting and is taking actions to safeguard financial reporting information assets as well as to help ensure the integrity of financial information used in the preparation of financial reports. The Company has adopted an Information Technology framework, is documenting key information technology controls and is addressing control weaknesses that could potentially impact financial reporting.
		▪ In addition, the Company has implemented a number of new policies, procedures, and controls in the areas of information security, change management, operations and end-user computing. The Company is in the process of implementing an integrated ERP system for its U.S. operations. It has reviewed its personnel and information systems for foreign operations and has added professional staff resources for review and control over financial reporting by the foreign operations.
		▪ The Company has placed substantial mitigating controls around its heretofore manual consolidation process, and is in the process of implementing a high-level replacement system for those manual processes to further improve controls and to reduce the time required to produce its financial statements and regulatory filings. In addition, the Company has identified and implemented additional review controls over financial reporting to validate information derived from its information systems and ultimately reported in our financial statements. As the Company continues to upgrade various systems, controls and procedures, it is continuing to make substantial progress and is continuing its efforts toward remediation of this material weakness.
Power 3 Medical Products Inc.	▪ Logical security	▪ . . . security over information technology; and (iv) lack of evidence to document compliance with the operation of internal accounting controls in accordance with our policies and procedures . . . These control deficiencies could result in a material misstatement.
		▪ The material weaknesses identified during the preparation of this report were . . . (iii) inadequate security over information technology; and (iv) lack of evidence to document compliance with the operation of internal accounting controls in accordance with our policies and procedures. These control deficiencies could result in a material misstatem ent of significant accounts or disclosures that would result in a material misstatement to our interim or annual financial statements that would not be prevented or detected Accordingly, management has determined that these control deficiencies constitute material weaknesses.

(*continued*)

TABLE 13.2 (*continued*)

Company	IT Audit Area	Illustrative IT Audit Deficiency Reported in Financial Statements
Tower Tech Holdings Inc.	■ IT environment	■ . . . acquisition through our fiscal year end, we have identified several items that represent material weaknesses or significant deficiencies in the internal control over financial reporting at Badger. . . . These material weaknesses are related to internal financial expertise, accounting policies and procedures, information technology environment and segregation of duties. . . . The Company has begun remediation efforts to mitigate the effects of these deficiencies.
Natures Sunshine Products Inc.	■ Access control, change management, and spreadsheets	■ Information Technology Systems . . . reporting related to certain information technology applications and general computer controls which are considered to have an impact on financial reporting and which resulted in a more than reasonable. . . .
		■ Information Technology Systems
		■ Description of Material Weakness as of December 31, 2008
		■ The Company did not maintain effective internal control over financial reporting related to certain information technology applications and general computer controls which are considered to have an impact on financial reporting and which resulted in a more than reasonable possibility that material misstatements in our financial statements would not be prevented or detected. Specifically, we lacked effective controls in the following areas:
		■ Access Control—the Company did not maintain effectively designed controls to prevent unauthorized access to certain programs and data, and provide for periodic review and monitoring of access including reviews of security logs and analysis of segregation of duties conflicts.
		■ Change Management—the Company did not maintain effectively designed controls to ensure that all information technology program and data changes were authorized, developer access to the production environment was limited, and that all program and data changes were adequately tested for accuracy and appropriate implementation.
		■ Spreadsheets—the Company did not maintain effectively designed controls to ensure that critical spreadsheets were identified, access to these spreadsheets was restricted to appropriate personnel, changes to data or formulas were authorized and appropriate, or that the spreadsheets were adequately reviewed by someone other than the preparer.

TABLE 13.3   Illustrative Compensatory Controls

Illustrative Compensatory Control	Description
Substantive IT audit procedures	Where possible, management could perform additional IT substantive audit procedures to minimize or mitigate the risk of IT exceptions. For example, if a user had inappropriate access to post adjusting journal entries, then management could review all posted journal entries for appropriateness. Another example would be reviewing all terminated user accounts to ensure that the account has not been used since the termination date.
Audit trails	Management could review audit trails to determine what access users have attempted to use, or what transaction activity occurred for the user account. This could be useful in detective situations where management needs to determine what activity occurred.
Risk acceptance documentation	For situations where mitigating controls are not available, management could consider documenting the risk acceptance. If this is done, management or the auditor should perform additional financial substantive testing.
Supervision	Management should implement additional supervision or workflow approvals for IT areas with known deficiencies to ensure that appropriate monitoring is in place.
Additional financial cycle transaction testing	Management or the auditor could perform additional testing of transactions if IT controls cannot be identified.

- **Examine random transactions:** A manager could review a small sample of supporting documents daily for a few select transactions. The sample could be generated with a listing of all transactions during the day. Transactions reviewed could be noted on the report and initialed by the manager as evidence.
- **Outsource activities when possible:** Using a third-party provider, such as a payroll service or lockbox bank account, can reduce the number of conflicting activities performed by one employee.
- **Use nonaccounting personnel when possible:** Transactions can be initiated or processed by employees who do not have a traditional accounting function. For example, a receptionist can open and log incoming customer checks, an office manager can manage petty cash, and an operational department head such as the vice president of research and development or operations manager can act as an additional check signer.
- **Take periodic counts of assets and compare them with accounting records:** When there is limited segregation of duties over transactions involving inventory, equipment, or other tangible assets, periodic counts and the comparison to the inventory records ensures assets recorded in the books are on hand.
- **Review analytics:** Although less effective, the review of budget and trend analyses of costs can be another compensating control. While this does not provide a detailed review, it can be a way to identify problem areas where further investigation is needed.

While application controls and their relationship to financial auditing issues constitute the primary focus of this book, consideration of fraud arises in the conduct of the financial audit and needs to be considered from an IT perspective. Julie Harrer, in *Internal Control Strategies: A Mid- to Small Business Guide* (Wiley 2008), discusses the difficulty that SMEs experience putting in place traditional segregation-of-duties controls. The following paraphrases some of her suggestions and briefly comments on relevant IT auditing procedures that can provide evidence that the control has been put in place.

Internal Controls and Fraud

- Ensure your system will not allow the same person to enter and post journal entries. Even if you have a manual requirement for a second approver on all journal entries, restrict your system so the independent postings are not a possibility.
- Do not allow executives system access to post journal entries. In most companies, the chief financial officer has no business recording journal entries.
- Make sure the disclosure and/or audit committee is aware of all related parties and the type of transactions they are involved in with the company.
- Make sure the audit committee reviews the methodology of all reserves or other management estimates at least annually and any time there is a change.
- Have the controller send the financial package to the audit committee directly. This procedure may limit the opportunity for management override by executives after the accounting department has compiled the financial data.
- Ensure that incentives are not linked solely to earnings or revenue growth. Mix in other indicators, such as low employee turnover, community service, compliance, or ethics programs.

Although management may utilize compensatory controls to minimize or mitigate risks, these controls should be used minimally, and the primary controls should be implemented to operate effectively. Management's overreliance on compensatory controls could lead to a breakdown in the overall control environment, thus bringing additional risk into the organization.

 SUMMARY

Deficiencies exist in every company. Companies are not perfect, but they try to minimize their risks. When companies identify deficiencies in their processes, the deficiencies need to be evaluated to determine their importance and impact on the organization. Companies *do not* have to eliminate all deficiencies. This would be costly and impractical. Companies need to manage their risks with the limited resources at hand.

References

107th Congress. 2002. Sarbanes-Oxley Act of 2002. www.pcaobus.org.

ACL. 2013. ACL Services Ltd. www.acl.com.

AICPA. 2013. AU Section 329. www.aicpa.org/Research/Standards.

Apple 1. 2013. www.apple-history.com.

Arens, A., and J. Loebbecke. 1980. *Auditing, an Integrated Approach*. Englewood Cliffs, NJ: Prentice Hall.

Association of Certified Fraud Examiners. 2012. *The 2012 Report to the Nations*. www.acfe.com/rttn.aspx.

Benford, F. 1938. "The Law of Anomalous Numbers." *Proceedings of the American Philosophy Society* 78:551–572.

Biafore, B. 2010. *QuickBooks 2011: The Missing Manual*. Sebastopol, CA: O'Reilly Media.

Brunsdon, T., Romney, M., and Steinbart, P. 2009. *Introduction to Microsoft Dynamics GP 10.0 Focus on Internal Controls*. Upper Saddle River, NJ: Prentice Hall.

CaseWare. 2013. IDEA Data Analysis Software. www.caseware.com.

Collins, C. 2011. "A Quick Guide to QuickBooks." *Journal of Accountancy*. www.journalofaccountancy.com/Issues/2011/Dec/20114555.

COSO. 1992. *1992 Internal Control—Integrated Framework*. Treadway Commission. www.coso.org.

COSO. 2007. *Internal Control over Financial Reporting: Guidance for Smaller Public Companies*. www.coso.org.

COSO. 2013a. *History of COSO*. www.coso.org.

COSO. 2013b. *2013 Internal Control—Integrated Framework*. www.coso.org.

Creeth, R. 1985. "Micro-Computer Spreadsheets: Their Uses and Abuses." *Journal of Accountancy* 159(6): 90–93.

Davies, N., and C. Ikin. 1987. "Auditing Spreadsheets." *Australian Account* 54–56.

Deloitte & Touche LLP. 2009. "Spreadsheet Management: Not What You Figured." www.deloitte.com/assets/Dcom-UnitedStates/Local%20Assets/Documents/AERS/us_aers_Spreadsheet_eBrochure_070710.pdf.

Ditlea, S. 1987. "Spreadsheets Can Be Hazardous to Your Health." *Personal Computing* 11(1): 60–69.

FASB 2010. Conceptual Framework. Statement of Financial Accounting Concepts No. 8. www.fasb.org.

Fogarty, J., L. Graham, and D. Schubert. 2007. "Assessing and Responding to Risks in a Financial Statement Audit: Part II. Guidance for Audit Standards for Nonissuers That Took Effect on or After December 15, 2006." *Journal of Accountancy*. www.journalofaccountancy.com/Issues/2007/Jan/AssessingAndRespondingToRisksInAFinancialStatementAuditPartIi.

Fowler, G., and B. Worthen. 2011. "Hackers Shift Attacks to Small Firms." *Wall Street Journal.* http://online.wsj.com.

Freeman, D. 1996. "How to Make Spreadsheets Error-Proof." *Journal of Accountancy* 181(5): 75–77.

Galletta, D., K. Hartzel, S. Johnson, J. Joseph, S. Rustag. 1997. "Spreadsheet Presentation and Error Detection: An Experimental Study." *Journal of Management Information Systems* 13(3): 45–63.

GAO. 2006. *Report to the Committee on Small Business and Entrepreneurship.* www.gao.gov.

Ge, W., and S. McVacy. 2005. "The Disclosure of Material Weaknesses in Internal Control after the Sarbanes/Oxley Act." *Accounting Horizons.* http://aaajournals.org/doi/abs/10.2308/acch.2005.19.3.137.

Godfrey, K. 1995. "Computing Error at Fidelity's Magellan Fund." *Risk Digest* 16(72).

Hall, J. 2011. *Accounting Information Systems.* Independence, KY: South-Western Publications.

Ham, J., D. Losell, and W. Smieliauskas. 1985. "An Empirical Study of Error Characteristics in Accounting Populations. *Accounting Review* (July):387–406.

Hayen, R., and R. Peters. 1989. "How to Ensure Spreadsheet Integrity." *Management Accounting* 70(10): 30–33.

Helms, G. 2012. "IT Risks and Controls in Traditional and Emerging Environments." AICPA Learning. http://aicpalearning.org.

Herrer, J. 2008. *Internal Control Strategies: A Mid-To Small Business Guide.* Hoboken, NJ: John Wiley & Sons.

Ho., S., and A. Oddo. 2007. "Lessons Learned from Section 404 of the Sarbanes-Oxley Act: A Conversation with Compliance Officers. www.nysscpa.org/cpajournal/2007/607/essentials/p28.htm.

Huxley, S. 2013. Why Benford's Law Works and How to Do Digit Analysis on Spreadsheets." www.usfca.edu/fac-staff/huxleys/Benford.html.

InformationActive. 2013. ActiveData for Excel. www.informationactive.com.

Institute for Internal Auditors. *Guide to the Assessment of IT Risk (GAIT)*, USA, 2007. www.theiia.org.

Intuit. n.d. Castle Rock Construction (QuickBooks Dataset). QuickBooks Software Sample Company.

ISACA. 2007. COBIT 4.1. IT Governance Institute. ISACA. www.isaca.org.

ISACA. 2012a. "History of ISACA." www.isaca.org/About-ISACA/History/Pages/default.aspx.

ISACA. 2012b. "COBIT 5.0." COBIT. ISACA. www.isaca.org/COBIT/Pages/default.aspx.

ISACA. 2012c. "COBI 4.1: Framework for IT Governance and Control." www.isaca.org/knowledge-center/COBIT/pages/overview.aspx.

ISACA. 2013. ITAF: A Professional Practices Framework for IT Assurance. www.isaca.org/bookstore/extras/Pages/ITAF-A-Professional-Practices-Framework-for-IT-Assurance-(e-book).aspx.

IT Governance Institute. 2005. "IT Alignment: Who Is in Charge?" www.governanceinstitute.com.

IT Governance Institute. 2012. The Governance Institute home page. www.governanceinstitute.com.

IT Governance Institute. 2013. "About ITGI." www.itgi.org/template_ITGI923a .html?Section=About_ITGI&Template=/ContentManagement/HTMLDisplay .cfm&ContentID=57434.

Kamnikar, J., E. Kamnikar, and A. Burrowes. 2012. "One Size Does Not Fit All." *Journal of Accountancy*. www.journalofaccountancy.com/Issues/2012/Jan/20114757.

Kelso, K. 2011. "Building Blocks of a Successful Financial Close Process. *Journal of Accountancy*. www.journalofaccountancy.com/Issues/2011/Dec/20114327.

Klamm, B., and M. Watson. 2009. "SOX 404 Reported Internal Control Weaknesses: A Test of COSO Framework Components and Information Technology." *Journal of Information Systems* 23(2):1–23.

Li, C., G. Peters, V. Richardson, and M. Watson. 2012. "The Consequences of Information Technology Control Weaknesses on Management Information Systems: The Case of Sarbanes–Oxley Internal Control Reports." *MIS Quarterly* 36(1):179–203. http://misq .org/the-consequences-of-information-technology-control-weaknesses-on- management-information-systems-the-case-of-sarbanes-oxley-internal-control- reports.html.

Metz, R. 2011. "Apple Co-Founder Wozniak Says He'll Miss Jobs." *USA Today*. www .usatoday.com.

Nigrini, M. 2011. *Mark Nigrin's Forensic Analytics: Methods and Techniques for Forensic Accounting Investigations*. Hoboken, NJ: John Wiley & Sons.

Palmas, E. 2011. "IT General and Application Controls: The Model of Internalization." *ISACA Journal* vol. 5. www.isaca.org/Journal/Past-Issues/2011/Volume-5/Pages/ IT-General-and-Application-Controls-The-Model-of-Internalization.aspx.

Panko, R. 1999. "Applying Code Inspection to Spreadsheet Testing." *Journal of Management Information Systems* 16(2): 159–176.

Panko, R. 2005. Spreadsheet Research (SSR). University of Hawaii, Honolulu. www .cba.hawaii.edu/panko/ssr/.

PCAOB. 2012. "Observations from 2010 Inspections of Domestic Annually Inspected Firms Regarding Deficiencies in Audits of Internal Control over Financial Reporting." http://pcaobus.org/Inspections/Documents/12102012_Release_2012_06.pdf.

PCAOB. 2013a. "Auditing Standard No. 5." http://pcaobus.org/Standards/Auditing/ Pages/Auditing_Standard_5.aspx.

PCAOB. 2013b. "AU Section 329." http://pcaobus.org/Standards/Auditing/Pages/AU329 .aspx.

Poe, T. 2009. *Spreadsheet Controls in the Real World. A Practical Approach under SOX 404*. Hudson Consulting Services.

PricewaterhouseCoopers. 2004a. "Sarbanes-Oxley Act: Section 404." www.pwc.fr/fr/ pwc_pdf/pwc_soa_guide.pdfwww.pwc.com.

PricewaterhouseCoopers. 2004b. "The Use of Spreadsheets: Considerations for Section 404 of the Sarbanes-Oxley Act." www.clusterseven.com/external-research/2010/5/3/ pwc-the-use-of-spreadsheets-considerations-for-section-404-o.html.

Raimondi, M. 2011. "Internal Controls for Small Businesses Using QuickBooks." Tax 11 Conference. www.mncpa.org/taxconference/materials.

Ramos, M. 2004. *How to Comply with Sarbanes-Oxley Section 404*. Hoboken, NJ: John Wiley & Sons.

Ramos, M. 2009. "Risk-Based Audit Best Practices." *Journal of Accountancy.* www.journalofaccountancy.com/Issues/2009/Dec/20091789.

Ratcliffe, T., and C. Landes. 2009. "Understanding Internal Control and Internal Control Services." *Journal of Accountancy.* AICPA. www.journalofaccountancy.com/Issues/2009/Sep/White%20Paper%20Understanding%20Internal%20Control%20and%20Internal%20Control%20Services.

Reithel, B., D. Nichols, and R. Robinson. 1996. "Spreadsheet Reliability Perceptions: An Investigation of the Effects of Size, Format, and Errors." *Journal of Computer Information Systems* 36(3): 54–62.

Rockart, J., M. Earl, and J. Ross. 1996. "The New IT Organization: Eight Imperatives." Center for Information Systems Research. Sloan School of Management. Massachusetts Institute of Technology. http://dspace.mit.edu/bitstream/handle/1721.1/2623/SWP-3902-40987801-CISR-292.pdf.

Romney, M., and P. Steinbart. 2009. *Accounting Information Systems*, 11th ed. Englewood Cliffs, NJ: Prentice Hall.

Romney, M., and P. Steinbart. 2011. *Accounting Information Systems*, 12th ed. Englewood Cliffs, NJ: Prentice Hall.

SEC. 2007a. "SEC Approves PCAOB Auditing Standard No. 5 Regarding Audits of Internal Control Over Financial Reporting; Adopts Definition of 'Significant Deficiency.'" www.sec.gov/news/press/2007/2007-144.htm.

SEC. 2007b. "Commission Guidance Regarding Management's Report on Internal Control Over Financial Reporting Under Section 13(a) or 15(d) of the Securities Exchange Act of 1934." www.sec.gov/rules/interp/2007/33-8810.pdf.

Shaw, M. 2004. "Avoiding Costly Errors in Your Spreadsheets. *Contractor's Management Report* 11: 2–4.

Shein, M., and R. Lanza. 2009. "Fraud Detection with ActiveData for Excel eBook." Information Active Inc. www.informationactive.com.

Shimamoto, D. 2011. "IT Governance for Small Business and CPA Firms." AICPA Practitioners Symposium and AICPA TECH +Information Technology Conference, June 2011. www.aicpaconferencematerials.com/techpractitioners/?select=session&sessionID=283.

Simkin, M. 1987. "Micros in Accounting: How to Validate Spreadsheets." *Journal of Accountancy* 130–138.

Singleton, T. 2011. "IT Risks—Present and Future." *ISACA Journal* vol. 4. www.isaca.org/Journal/Past-Issues/2011/Volume-4/Pages/IT-Risks-Present-and-Future.aspx.

Singleton, T. 2013. "Auditing the IT Auditors." *ISACA Journal* vol. 3. www.isaca.org/Journal/Past-Issues/2013/Volume-3/Pages/Auditing-the-IT-Auditors.aspx.

Turner, L., and A. Weickgenannt. 2008. *Accounting Information Systems: Controls and Processes.* Hoboken, NJ: John Wiley & Sons.

Vander Wal, K., J. Lainhart, and P. Tessin. 2012. "A COBIT 5 Overview." ISACA. www.isaca.org.

Vasa Museum. 2012. "From Wreck to State of the Art." www.vasamuseet.se/en.

Weill, P., and J. Ross. 2004. *IT Governance.* Boston, MA: Harvard Business School Press.

Whitehouse, T. 2012. "Internal Control Audit Failures Too High, PCAOB Says." *Compliance Week*. www.complianceweek.com/internal-control-audit-failures-too-high-pcaob-says/article/271992.

Whittaker, D. 1999. "Spreadsheet Errors and Techniques for Finding Them." *Management Accounting* 77: 50–51.

Wright, A., and R. Ashton. 1989. "Identifying Audit Adjustments with Attention-Directing Procedures." *Accounting Review* (October): 710–728.

About the Authors

Jason Wood, CPA, CITP, CISA, CIA, CFF, MBA, is the president of WoodCPAPlus PC, a certified public accounting firm that focuses on information technology auditing, consulting, and training. Mr. Wood has over 17 years of international business experience in information technology auditing helping middle-market and global Fortune 500 companies. He is an alumnus of the Big Four accounting firms and teaches advanced courses in accounting information systems and auditing at leading Rochester, New York, area colleges.

William C. Brown, PhD, CPA, CISA, CITP, is chair and assistant professor in accounting and business law for both graduate and undergraduate programs at Minnesota State University, Mankato. Dr. Brown has served as corporate financial officer in several high-growth small and medium-sized enterprises, including several Security and Exchange Commission registrants. He has also served as chief information officer in a large information technology organization following a merger and accelerating growth. Dr. Brown teaches financial accounting and accounting information systems.

Harry Howe, PhD, is professor of accounting and director of the graduate and undergraduate accounting programs at State University of New York–Geneseo. Dr. Howe has coauthored two volumes in the BNA Practice and Policy Series and published numerous articles in scholarly and practitioner journals. His primary teaching areas are financial accounting and accounting information series.

Index

Page numbers followed by an *f* or a *t* refer to figures and tables, respectively.

payroll burdens and, 159, 162, 244, 248

report access and, 373

Sarbanes-Oxley and, 14, 15, 20, 251, 257, 282, 291, 292, 357*f*

sensitive data and password protection and, 44, 345, 346*f*

Social Security data and, 345

spreadsheet management and, 337, 344, 355, 357*f*

Compliance reporting, in general ledger, 59, 67

Computer-assisted audit techniques (CAATs), 75

Computer logs, 26*t*

Computer Operations and Access to Programs and Data (Delivery and Support) section of COBIT 4.1, 280

control objectives of, 317–329

cross-referencing COBIT to PCAOB and COSO for, 295, 296*t*–301*t*, 302*t*

overlay of COSO framework against, 281*t*

Computer systems

auditor's check of configuration settings in, 4

availability of, 8

disaster recovery planning (DRP) for, 24, 28*t*, 391*t*

emergency power supply for, 28*t*

maintenance of, 19

power supplies for, 28*t*

preventive controls for physical environment and security of, 25, 28*t*

risk mitigation by controls outside, 112, 117

segregation of duties and logical security access within, 112, 115

uninterruptible power supply for, 28*t*

Concurrency issues

authentication mechanisms and, 323

data availability and, 5

Confidentiality of data, 5, 5*f*, 7, 7*t*

Confidentiality, integrity, and availability (CIA) of data, 5–8, 5*f*, 7*t*

Configuration settings

auditor's review of, 4

authorized access using, 26*t*

firewalls and, 324

inventory cycle and, 3, 147, 150

IT resources and, 324, 325–326

logic inspection and, 365

passwords and, 38–39, 44–47, 45*f*, 46*f*, 47*f*, 48*f*, 359

payroll cycle and, 167, 178, 193

revenue cycle and, 87, 87*f*, 88, 92

rights and obligations assertion and, 3

Configuration tables, 26*t*

Conflicts of interest, 262

Conservatism of financial reports, 270

Consistency of financial reports, 270

Contingency planning, 319, 391*t*

Continuity planning, 23, 25, 28*t*, 290, 318, 319, 320, 391*t*

Control activities

Computer Operations category and, 295, 299*t*–300*t*

COSO framework for, 254, 262, 280

cross-referencing COBIT to PCAOB and COSO for, 295, 296*t*–301*t*, 302*t*

internal controls and, 262–267, 265*f*

Monitor and Evaluation category and, 295, 301*t*

overlay of COSO framework to COBIT 4.1 for, 280–282, 281*t*–282*t*

Plan and Organize category and, 295, 296*t*–297*t*

Program Development and Change category and, 295, 298*t*

range of activities included in, 268

Sarbanes-Oxley weakness and, 283*t*

Control environment

board's role in, 12, 20

business continuity planning and, 28*t*

business processes and, 266, 280

company-level controls and, 279

Computer Operations category and, 295, 299*t*–300*t*

control procedures in, 19

COSO framework for, 254, 262, 280

cross-referencing COBIT to PCAOB and COSO for, 295, 296*t*–301*t*, 302*t*

framework for evaluating risks and, 16–18

internal controls and, 262–267, 265*f*

management's role in, 12–13, 15, 261

material weakness in, 16

Monitor and Evaluation category and, 295, 301*t*

need for systematic and repeatable support for, 20

ongoing evaluations of, 14, 15

overlay of COSO framework to COBIT 4.1 for, 280–282, 281*t*–282*t*

in payroll cycle, 159, 160, 176, 178, 248

periodic assessment of, 12

Plan and Organize category and, 295, 296*t*–297*t*

Program Development and Change category and, 295, 298*t*

resource limitations and, 15

risk-based auditing approach to, 18

Sarbanes-Oxley weakness and, 283*t*

significant deficiency in, 16

system review of, 19

tests of controls in, 19

types of errors and fraud in, 18–19

Control Objectives for Information and Related Technology (COBIT), 30. *See also* COBIT *headings*

Controls, 21–36

applications with. *See* Application controls

checks and, 11

completeness assertion on, 3

confidentiality, integrity, and availability (CIA) of data and, 5–7, 5*f*, 8

COSO process on, 30–33, 32*f*

as critical success factor, 13

Printed and bound by CPI Group (UK) Ltd, Croydon, CR0 4YY

16/04/2025

14658460-0006